# Hand Me My Travelin' Shoes

# Hand Me My Travelin' Shoes

In Search of
## Blind
## Willie
## McTell

Michael Gray

CHICAGO
REVIEW
PRESS

Library of Congress Cataloging-in-Publication Data

Gray, Michael, 1946-
Hand me my travelin' shoes : in search of Blind Willie McTell / Michael Gray.
    p. cm.
  Includes bibliographical references and index.
  ISBN 978-1-55652-975-7 (hardcover)
  1. McTell, Blind Willie. 2. Blues musicians—United States—Biography.
3. Blind musicians—United States—Biography. I. Title. II. Title: Hand me my
traveling shoes.

  ML420.M34187G73 2009
  782.421643092—dc22
  [B]

                                                                    2009022329

Interior design: Hewer Text UK Ltd, Edinburgh
Cover design: Jonathan Hahn
Cover photo: © Michael Ochs Archives/Getty Images

First published by Bloomsbury Publishing, London

U.S. edition published in 2009 by
Chicago Review Press, Incorporated
814 North Franklin Street
Chicago, Illinois 60610
ISBN 978-1-55652-975-7
Printed in the United States of America
5 4 3 2 1

to Donna and Kenny Sclater and family,
who gave me my Georgia home

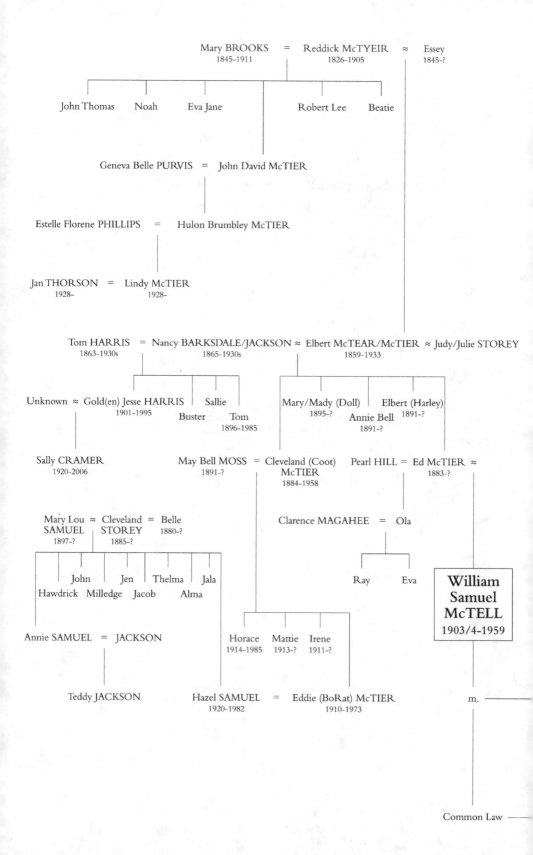

# FAMILY TREE OF BLIND WILLIE McTELL

## devised by Sarah Beattie, 2008

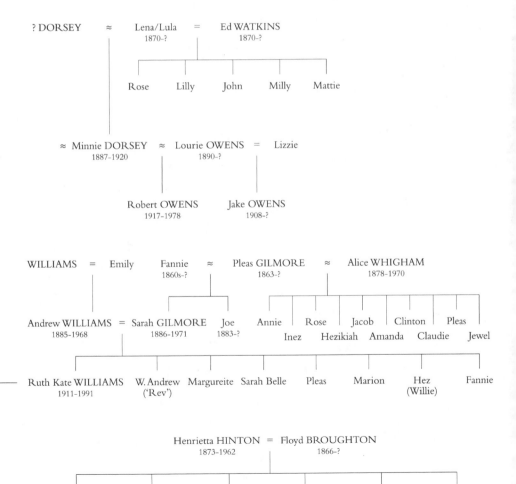

# CONTENTS

# PREFACE

FOR THE very tiny percentage of people in Europe and North America who have heard of Blind Willie McTell, he may be interesting, even important, as a great pre-war blues musician, but this book is written mostly for those who have never heard of him, and have no special interest in that particular kind of old music, or in the quirks and concerns and hobbyist rituals of those collectors and experts who have.

I wanted to write about him because he was a remarkable man who lived through amazing times in a still under-attended part of the American South, which was itself shaped by bizarre and extraordinary history.

So many books about the South are either travel writing that takes little notice of the music—the magisterial V.S. Naipaul's *A Turn In The South* does not mention the blues: not once, in its hundreds of pages—or else near-specialist biographies of musicians, usually from Mississippi, which hardly say more about place and landscape than by giving a few obligatory references to shotgun shacks and levees.

Certainly, Willie Samuel McTell was the most important Georgia bluesman to be recorded. He was a songster of wide repertoire and as fine a 12-string guitarist as ever lived. The dexterity of his playing was extraordinary, and his voice was an unusually smooth tenor, while the interplay between voice and guitar was also a demonstration of McTell's intelligence and wit. It was perhaps the fusion of all these elements that led Bob Dylan to write, in a 1983 tribute song, that "no one can sing the blues like Blind Willie McTell."

But McTell explodes every archetype about blues musicians. He is no roaring primitive, no Robert Johnsonesque devil-dealing womaniser. He didn't lose his sight in a jook-joint brawl, or hopping a freight train. He didn't escape into music from behind a mule plow in the Delta. He didn't die violently or young. Instead, blind from birth but never behaving as if blindness handicapped him, this resourceful, articulate man became an adept professional musician who traveled widely and talked his way into an array of recording sessions.

He never achieved a hit record, but he became one of the most widely known and well-loved figures in Georgia. Working clubs and parking lots, playing to blacks and whites, tobacco workers and college kids, Blind Willie McTell, human jukebox and local hero, enjoyed a modest career and an independent life.

He died in obscurity in 1959—the very year his song 'Statesboro Blues' became a "discovery" of the new folk and blues revival movement. It would become a million-selling hit for The Allman Brothers Band (also from Georgia) in the 1970s.

No inferior shellac crackle dooms Blind Willie McTell to the ranks of the almost unlistenable. His pre-war recordings, like his diction, are clear as a bell. His life, though, is enigmatic. Few documents exist about him from his own time, and those that do, such as his marriage and death certificates, contain false or misleading information. His very surname dissolves and re-forms as it is scrutinised.

He called to me as a beguiling character in a mysterious setting. What little was known about him drew me in to the backwoods of rural Georgia.

The call of the South is strong in my ears anyway, though I'm aware—especially having researched this book—of its murderous, bloodstained history. But Elvis Presley's voice singing "Oh I wish I was in the land of cotton" is one of the fragments of song I most often find in the back of my head. Ray Charles has only to utter the word "Georgia." Even Hoagy Carmichael singing knowingly and satirically of "oleander." Alan Lomax's description of the Delta in *The Land Where The Blues Began*. Anything, really. The very name Charleston, South Carolina.

While researching Willie McTell's life, trying to follow in his footsteps, it became clear that the near-total absence of any paper trail this man had left was part of the truth behind the where and when of his life. This is why, in what follows, the story of getting the story is itself part of that story.

This book is addressed to anyone curious about how things change and don't change, or about a strange part of the world, or how the past shapes the present. For anyone trying to understand the United States today, I offer, with an outsider's eye, an account of how it might still connect to the world of Blind Willie McTell—a charismatic man from that surreal place, the recent past.

Michael Gray, March 2007.

# INTRODUCTION

A TLANTA, GEORGIA—summer, 1956. Ed Rhodes, a white guy in his twenties who runs a couple of record stores in the city, is behind the counter of the one on 13<sup>th</sup> and Peachtree when an artist friend of his looks in with news he's a little shy about. He says he knows Ed takes an interest in black music, and he thinks he's found something a bit special, and will he come with him to check it out?

Ed thinks his friend just wants to show off his new car, but he's not averse to riding around in that and it's the end of the working day, so they drive along Ponce de Leon Avenue till they reach the Blue Lantern Club and then go through to the back parking lot, where it's very dark—"sort of like a lovers' lane," Ed recalls. Young white couples are parked up in their parents' enormous shark-finned Chevvies and Fords, and the only person walking around is this old black man carrying a big guitar. He looks about sixty, and a bit overweight. Ed watches him move slowly across from one car to another, a convertible. There's a brief conversation between him and the boy behind the wheel. A few coins change hands and the black guy starts playing the guitar, aiming the music at the couple in the big bench seat.

Ed still can't see properly in the darkness, but he can hear that it's a 12-string—it has that full, big sound—and the dexterity and poise of the playing comes as a shock. And then the old man starts singing. He's singing 'My Blue Heaven', a huge hit for Fats Domino that year, and the voice is a little croaky at times, yet mostly clear and unexpectedly light. It shines like something polished; it's adept and intelligent, sly and self-aware. This old street-singer, this busker playing for tips, this human jukebox to the heedless James Dean generation: could it be that this is one of the great blues artists of the pre-war years, a survivor from the days of Blind Lemon Jefferson, Robert Johnson and Lead Belly?

It was a tantalising, bizarre, perhaps even chilling prospect. Ed Rhodes didn't know who this musician might be, but he knew that the 12-string playing was as good as on any Lead Belly record he'd ever heard. He felt enormous excitement mixed with self-doubt. Was he right? He felt *almost* certain that here was a performer who, even in old age and poor shape, and having to play the pop requests of the day for giggling, privileged adolescents, still evidenced rare quality.

Ed Rhodes came back when he could over the next few weeks, and eventually introduced himself and asked the old man if he would make a tape for him. The answer was no. He said he wasn't interested in doing any recording—he'd done plenty of recording and had always come to grief. His name was Willie Samuel McTell—Blind Willie McTell. He had made records for several major labels in the 1920s and even in the 30s, when the Depression had decimated record sales. Ed Rhodes was incredulous, then thrilled. Blind Willie McTell was the greatest blues singer Georgia had ever produced.

Then, one weekend, Ed and his friend returned to the Blue Lantern and found the singer "pretty drunk." As they watched, he fell over and stayed down. They put him in the back of Ed's station wagon and some people inside the club told them where they thought the old man lived. The city was divided up into white districts and black sections, but the blacks had their own names for these sections, which made it hard to find a place. ("A guy tell you he lived in Mechanicsville—you didn't know where Mechanicsville was.") But Rhodes was told the old man lived underneath the Dixie Dancehall, and he knew where that was.

It was very late that Saturday night when they got him back there, and it wasn't easy to move McTell out of the vehicle. The dancehall was built into the side of a hill, and there were people milling about outside. When they saw these two white guys unloading a body from the back of a station wagon, they started shouting and closing in. Helen Edwards, the woman who lived with the singer in his later years, came out and told the crowd that things were OK, and they carried him down into the cellar where he lived.

When McTell woke next day, the first thing he felt around for was his guitar. Then he checked his pockets for his money. He was amazed. He had never passed out before without being robbed. This time he woke up at home, and not only did he still have his guitar and the money he'd made in tips, but he had some extra money too, which Ed Rhodes had slipped into his pocket.

A few days later, Rhodes' mother was looking after his 13th Street and Peachtree record store when the door opened and in walked an elderly black man, a guitar slung over his shoulder, asking to see the owner. He was rather breathless, unsteady, and Mrs Rhodes found him frightening. He and the guitar seemed to fill the room and, since he never wore dark glasses, his blindness was something you confronted in his eyes. In those segregated times, his sudden close proximity was unsettling.

Ed's phone rang. His mother sounded agitated, relieved to have got hold of him. She told him this, er, gentleman was up at the store waiting to see him. Would he come right away?

Rhodes hurried over there to find McTell. "And he had walked—he had walked all the way up there from where he lived, maybe six or seven or eight miles! For a blind person to walk that far, just to thank me for taking him home! Well, we became more friendly after that."

September 1956. McTell and Rhodes are in the store with a couple of Rhodes' friends when McTell suddenly says, "You know, if you want to, you can turn on the machine and we'll see how it sounds. But you gotta play it back for me." Rhodes wastes no time. His big old tape machine is right behind McTell in the back of the store, he sets it running and McTell begins to play the 12-string. He drinks from a bottle of corn whiskey and he sings songs and talks about them, answers questions about his life and times, and, when the tape is finished, he listens back to it eagerly.

As Ed Rhodes tells it, when the playback is over, Willie says, "I don't want this ever published while I'm alive, 'cause if I *did* ever get any money for it, I would just drink myself to death." Ed drives him home. They never meet again.

At the same time, 375 miles away in Memphis, Tennessee, another enthusiast, a Pittsburgh-born thirty-year-old called Samuel Barclay Charters, is traveling around with his first wife, Mary Lange, and recording old blues singers a bit more systematically.

Anyone else with a keen interest in music who finds themselves in Memphis in 1956 is in the thrall of rock'n'roll. Memphis is *the* place to be in 1956. It is the home of the wondrous Sun Studios, where Sam Phillips has just been producing Elvis Presley's revolutionary first records in one small, dark room that is also now capturing on tape the early golden exuberance of Jerry Lee Lewis, Carl Perkins, Roy Orbison, and more. In the same room Phillips has also been commissioning pioneering modern electric blues records since 1951, when he had glued the little white baffle tiles up on the walls and ceiling himself to make the room a studio. Howlin' Wolf had started here, right then and there. Phillips said later, "When I heard him, I said, 'This is for me. This is where the soul of man never dies.'"

But that's not how Samuel B. Charters feels. He's not in Memphis for this stuff at all. He doesn't even notice it. Decades later, when I interview him, I say, "You were in Memphis in 1956?! What a wonderful time to be there!" and he replies, "It really was, yeah. They were all there"—and the people he means are old, pre-war blues singers and street musicians from Memphis jug bands: the very people that everyone else in Memphis has forgotten.

These are the people he finds and records: "Gus Cannon and Will Shade and everybody with the jug bands." Gus Cannon and friends, under various names but mostly as Cannon's Jug Stompers, had done a slew of recordings between 1927 and 1930, and never been back in a studio since. Will Shade had led the rival outfit, the Memphis Jug Band, and they had recorded prolifically between 1927 and 1934.

When Charters finds them, and records them again for the first time in over twenty years, it makes him realise something simple and powerful— "that these people weren't from another planet, they were part of our life and some of them were still alive."

Three years later, in 1959, Sam and Mary are divorced and in March Sam marries his second wife, Ann Danberg, whom he's met in music classes at the University of California years earlier, and who will later write the first biography of Jack Kerouac and edit his letters. Sam and Ann Charters live in a basement apartment in Brooklyn, but that fall they've driven all the way across the States to stay with Ann's parents in California before embarking on a year-long trip to Europe.

That November, the New York publisher Rinehart publishes Sam Charters' book, which is called *The Country Blues*—and it proves to be one of those rare books that actually makes something happen out in the world. Effectively, it kicks off the blues revival that becomes a shaping force within the whole burgeoning scene that encompasses the New Left, the Civil Rights Movement, the Greenwich Village folk phenomenon, the rise of Bob Dylan, and more.

The blues that Charters draws to people's attention, and which he invents the phrase "country blues" to describe, is neither the vaudeville-jazz sort they've heard by Bessie Smith, nor the electric post-war blues they've heard by Muddy Waters and Sonny Boy Williamson and Howlin' Wolf. It is pre-war, mostly down-home, southern and un-amplified, and as richly diverse as life under the sea.

On the LP that he issues alongside the book, Charters' compilation of a few of these old records includes an elegant but restless, exhilarating track made in 1928, 'Statesboro Blues', written and recorded by Blind Willie McTell. (Statesboro, Georgia, is the quirky town Willie grew up in, forty-nine miles north-west of Savannah.) The LP is, in effect, a bootleg, since the companies that really own the rights and the masters to these recordings have no interest whatever in releasing them officially, while at the same time their procedures for allowing others to lease them make it prohibitive for any blues enthusiast to compile such an album legiti-mately. Charters deals with this matter head-on in his sleevenotes to this "bootleg" LP.

He has acquired the mint-condition 78rpm record of Willie's 'Sta-tesboro Blues' that is copied onto his LP from a cache of ancient but never-played Victor records found somewhere in New York State by another key figure on the scene at the time, Len Kunstadt, who edits the tiny, amateur-looking magazine *Record Research* (which Charters writes for) and acts as the manager of one of the known surviving grandes dames of the pre-war blues, the redoubtable Victoria Spivey, who now lives in Brooklyn and is just about to re-emerge from semi-retirement. Len will also prove to be her last husband.

The 78s that Len Kunstadt finds are, of course, regarded as riches among the interested few, but their monetary value is derisory, and will be slow to rise. Paul Garon, writer and blues-specialist Chicago bookstore owner, recalls the prices when, back when the 1950s were just giving way to the '60s, some Robert Johnson 78s were put up for auction by another enthusiast, Chris Strachwitz: "I stretched my budget enormously and bid $2.50 each. I lost. When I saw Chris later that year, I bemoaned losing the RJs (he was auctioning three of them), and he said, 'Oh, you lost by a mile. They went for $7.50 each!' " In December 2004 a Robert Johnson 78rpm of 'Come On In My Kitchen', coupled with 'They're Red Hot', recorded in late 1936 and issued on the Vocalion label soon afterwards, in only fair condition, sold on eBay for $4,495.

When his book comes out on 5 November 1959, Charters is working for Minke's Closet Shop in Beverly Hills, putting up wall cupboards for the Hollywood actress Cyd Charisse. In his lunch hour he stands around in a little Beverly Hills bookstore, holding a copy of his own book so that people might see the photograph on the back and realise that he's the man who's written it.

Charters' book doesn't impress everybody. He pips to the post the rather more precise and thorough blues scholar and British architect Paul Oliver, whose book *Blues Fell This Morning* would arrive in 1960, as would American jazz writer Frederic Ramsey's *Been Here And Gone*, a richly photo-laden account of travels through the 1950s South in search "of what might still remain of an original, authentic African-American musical tradition".

There is much carping too, from some of those who feel they already know about all this music but haven't troubled to write books about it. They feel that, despite all the fieldwork Charters has done, in Alabama, New Orleans, Memphis, and even the Bahamas, he doesn't have a proper folklorist's interest in "the tradition," but rather has the sort of flighty interest in "originality" and "creativity" that is just what you might expect from a literary person with an inclination towards Beat poetry.

Charters' critics also complain that there are far richer seams of pre-war blues than those he looks at and that he gives too much attention to lightweight hokum at the expense of heavier, superior material born in the Mississippi Delta.

Actually, this remains the main divide in the world of blues appreciation—among the enthusiasts who start up small record companies, the fieldworkers and scholars who persuade the subject into academic legitimacy, and the writers on small magazines. Most of the white post-war champions of this black pre-war music are predisposed to find heaviest best. Dark, smouldering, Mississippi blues good; lighter, cheerful, south-eastern blues much less good.

When we come to ask how and when, after his death, Blind Willie McTell becomes famous, we find that the answer is slowly and moderately. And part of the reason is precisely because he isn't Mississippi, he isn't raw and dark.

In any case, Sam Charters' *The Country Blues* spreads the news of this music to a larger number of people. It also prompts many a young urban white to take a trip down to the Deep South in search of the old rural blacks whose records from decades earlier are just beginning to be issued for the first time on 33rpm vinyl by like-minded young enthusiasts—records that reveal to them this other, more magical music universe.

Some successes are scored. The frail, eerie recordings of Skip James from 1931 are all people have to go on, but he is found, alive, back where he'd started from, in a tiny town in Mississippi. He will appear like a ghost on stage at the Newport Folk Festival in 1964, having never recorded in the intervening thirty-three years. Mississippi John Hurt, a kind and gentle man, whose last foray into a recording studio was in 1928, is descended upon similarly and plucked back into the world of public performance—a world where that public has changed out of all recognition.

Son House, another once-towering figure, is rediscovered—not in a shack in a field in Mississippi, but in a rough part of Rochester, New York—and he too finds himself up on stage for the first time in decades, playing to young white audiences in the coffee-houses of Greenwich Village, Boston, Philadelphia and Washington, DC.

Blind Willie McTell is one of those sought out—but too late. Nobody knows it yet, but he is already dead. He dies eleven weeks and a day before the release of his 'Statesboro Blues' on the Sam Charters LP. He is buried with the wrong name on his tombstone in the grounds of the little clapboard Jones Grove Baptist Church in Happy Valley, the community he'd been born in, nine miles out of Thomson, the tiny center of McDuffie County, Georgia.

February 1960. Sam and Ann Charters set off from California for their big trip to Europe. Most of their time is spent in Edinburgh, but at the end of the year they are in Israel, and it is here, in a pile of mail waiting for him in the American Express office in Tel Aviv, that Sam receives a letter from a young musician and R&B enthusiast in Atlanta, a man named Jan Cox, asking if he knows that Blind Willie McTell has been recorded as recently as 1956, and that there is an hour's worth of tape in the possession of record-store owner Ed Rhodes. This is certainly news to Charters and, for the rest of his time in Israel, he is impatient to return to the States and get hold of this tape.

When, finally, Charters and Rhodes meet in New York City, some time in the freezing early months of 1961, they spend a day together and Charters gets to hear the tape of Blind Willie McTell's last session.

Its very existence seems miraculous to Charters—and he learns from Rhodes that this is doubly so because, a couple of years after he made the tape, he sold the recording equipment and threw all his tapes into a discarded barrel in the attic of his store. When, later, he looked for them again, the only one not ruined was Willie's.

They listen to the recording together three or four times, hunched over an old Pentron tape machine in a small apartment on West 72$^{nd}$ Street that belongs to Ann's cousin. Charters recalls it later:

> It was an unforgettable moment. Because, at that point, even though we knew a little bit about the recordings, the blues was still this world that we were exploring—and, as I listened, I realised that there were things of McTell's that I'd never heard and that I didn't know that he performed. I was hearing a whole different dimension of it.
>
> What I was hearing was well-recorded, and having the kind of glimpse into the person that McTell had been—and this is what I'd

been searching for. When I found people, I wanted to know who they were, not just what they'd done, and, with this, Ed Rhodes was giving me McTell as a human being. And for Ed himself it was something much more than the opportunity to make money. He was excited by it and he recognised the uniqueness of the experience, just sitting there in this very small room, on a New York noisy outside afternoon. And the two of us were walking into the world of Willie McTell. Incredible.

At the end, after the spell was broken, Rhodes handed over the tape and Charters walked him towards Columbus Circle, where Rhodes was giving himself the treat of playing chess at a club before he flew back to Atlanta. They parted company, and though they spoke many times on the phone over the ensuing couple of months, they, too, would never meet again.

*Blind Willie McTell: Last Session*, an LP, was issued in the US in the fall of 1961 by a company based in Bergenfield, New Jersey, then a town of 27,000 people, sixteen miles from New York City. It was an edited-down version of the recording, though the record sleeve didn't say so.

It's one of the many ironies in the story of how Willie has been processed since his death that this, the first LP of his work to see release, represents the last work to have been recorded. Instead of the shimmering radiance of youth coming first, vinyl gave us the coarser, more faltering artist of middle age. It was like seeing him through the wrong end of a telescope.

It took another five years before the next full album of McTell's work—and again it was a session made on portable machinery, issued in incomplete form without admitting it, and from a period long after the days of his youth.

This time it was *Blind Willie McTell: 1940*, a combination of awkward interview and wide-ranging song performances, recorded for the Library of Congress in a hotel room in Atlanta that 5th of November by the famous septuagenarian folklorist John A. Lomax and his rather younger second wife, Ruby T., who had spotted McTell on the street the day before. As was Mr Lomax's habit in the course of a lifetime's indefatigable fieldwork, he tended to push for songs that interested him rather than document what interested the artist.

Yet here, in the age of *Blonde On Blonde* and LSD, of soul music and civil rights success, here, at last, we heard, from over a quarter of a century earlier, the upshot of this meeting between the fiercesome great white ballad hunter and the anxious, diplomatic, mercurial black musician.

The photograph on the album's front cover was the one of the young Willie McTell that people now regard as the "classic shot" of him—a portrait taken in the late 1920s in the Kelly Studio, a professional photographer's studio in Atlanta—a shot that shows him as handsome, smooth-skinned and dapper, and holding that big 12-string guitar.

This picture only exists because it was rescued from a garbage pile at the offices of a small arts magazine in Manhattan in the early 1960s.

The trashpile was in the basement of 168, East 91$^{st}$ Street, a brownstone building bought by one of J. Paul Getty II's ex-wives, Ann Light, who came from Tennessee but interested herself in the Manhattan arts scene. She bought the building to give it to an avant-garde lay-Catholic magazine called *Jubilee* when the lease had expired on its office on Park Avenue South.

This privileged bohemian enterprise had been launched in May 1953 by the writer Edward Rice, who was godfather to the poet and ex-Hollywood screenwriter Robert Lax (a convert from Judaism to Catholicism) and to the trappist monk and mystic Thomas Merton. Run by these writers, poets and shamans, the magazine secured both rich Catholic patrons and contributors who were Beat poets and art photographers. Jack Kerouac wrote for it and it ran lavish photospreads.

*Jubilee* also attracted volunteer workers, and one of these was a young New Yorker named John Reynolds, who had subscribed to the magazine while in the navy in Japan, and, when he got back home, saw an advert appealing for people to help with their Wednesday evening mailings. He volunteered.

One night he was helping to clear out the basement in the newly acquired building. A box on top of a trash can attracted his attention. The first item he found inside the box—and the only one he kept—was the photograph of Blind Willie McTell.

No one alive now knows how it came to be there. The magazine's editors collected photos of jazz and other musicians, had an arty sort of an interest in Lead Belly, and wanted jazz journalist Nat Hentoff to write a piece about him—and, as it happens, John Reynolds is a big Lead Belly fan who became friends with the singer's family—but it's unlikely that any of the *Jubilee* people had ever heard of Blind Willie McTell.

Reynolds took the photograph home, held on to it for a long time, but, in 1965, gave it to Larry Cohn, a one-time law-enforcement officer who was by now a member of the self-styled New York Blues Mafia and an independent producer who happened to be working on putting out Blind Willie's Library of Congress recording.

John Reynolds reports, "I don't recall how long I had the McTell photo before giving it to Larry Cohn . . . an article on Lead Belly written by Larry served as my introduction to him. He invited me to several get-togethers of kindred spirits [the Blues Mafia] and one night I brought him the photo of McTell."

It's a great picture. It shows so much. McTell himself, of course, well dressed and well-groomed, with that perfect scalloped pencil moustache that you just know he trims himself—a triple signal of the blind man's pride: in his appearance, his dexterity, and the triumph over his handicap that all of this makes clear.

The stylish serge cap with the peak is a highly individual item that might just be playfully subverting the three-piece suit, white shirt, tie and tie-pin, and gold watch-chain. The fully buttoned waistcoat is effortlessly lined up just so, with the guitar placed across it, absolutely balanced without recourse to the shoulder strap. The guitar is an enormous acoustic 12-string, as big as it could possibly be, with a stencilled motif around the soundhole but generally looking plain.

All this says that he could be at ease with both formality and informality, with city style and with himself. Sharp-pressed edges on the suit, the turn-ups, the big solid ring on the right hand, the slim fingers. The long leather shoes not quite so nifty, a bit scuffed, on the long slim feet. The self-aware reverie, eyes closed, that hint of a secret smile on the nervy fine features.

And then there's the rest of the scene. This is a professional photographer's studio, but it's a black one in a segregated age. These are cheap props. He's sitting up, back to the wall, on a crude wooden chair. Behind him is a faded mural of some classical Ancient Greek miasma on a cloth backdrop. It often happened that these were bought second-hand when more affluent, white studios in the same city refurbished.

Not till 1968 did we get a whole album of Willie McTell's work from the same period as that photograph: an album of some of the tremendous recordings he'd made for big American companies such as Victor and Columbia, between 1927 and 1933. And even then, the telling fact is that those labels weren't interested in this golden material—the album itself, *Blind Willie McTell: The Early Years*, was issued on Belzona, a tiny, you might say amateur, label named knowingly after an insignificant town in Mississippi that was pronounced Belzona though spelt Belzoni. Apart from *Blind Willie McTell: The Early Years*, this label released only four other LPs before disappearing to reconstitute itself as another label aimed only at dedicated pre-war blues enthusiasts, this time called Yazoo (after a small Mississippi river). These labels were the passionate hobby of a young man named Nick Perls, son of a rich art-dealing family in New York. Perls had been able to buy large numbers of old blues 78s, and was, therefore, able to turn them into bootleg LPs. He was twenty-six years old when he put the McTell collection together. He died of AIDS in 1987, shortly after selling the company.

It took until the 1980s for a major American record label to release an album of pre-war McTell material that *it* had recorded in the first place.

But McTell had also been acquiring an afterlife in wider spheres.

In 1968, a young English folk guitarist made his first album for a small folkie label called Transatlantic Records, which was owned by one of the British music biz's favorite rascals, Nat Joseph, and kept going by the profits from three early releases by the sex therapist Dr Eustace Chesser under the pseudonym Dr Keith Cammeron. The folk guitarist's LP was called *Eight Frames a Second* (the rate at which films are played to achieve "slow motion"), and it was by twenty-three-year-old Ralph May—except that, in tribute to his own little-known musical hero, he had re-named himself Ralph *McTell*.

How had this young man from Croydon, in the English Home Counties, discovered Blind Willie?

"I was one of the lucky ones," he says, "who heard that album with 'Statesboro Blues' on it. Much earlier than that, I fell for the work of Woody Guthrie and so on, as heard on an LP by Ramblin' Jack Elliott. It was all quite intoxicating for me: a music that made sense when I was living through the confusion of being a teenager. And then there's that mysterious process where like-minded people find each other. People came from all over to the Whitgift Arms in Croydon, to drink cheap cider and discover this music. And in London, too, I knew people who were into blues and Beat poetry. There was a lot of that scene: a lovely mix of jazz, folk, blues and Beat poetry. A time of finding that sense of freedom through art and travel and music that I'm still very sentimental about.

"We sat for hours at a time over coffees listening to all this stuff—Blind Boy Fuller and old jug bands and everything. And all this music, and I include people like Woody Guthrie in this, it doesn't conform to acceptable forms and disciplines. They played chords that aren't in the chord books, and they played 13 bars, or 11 bars, in a 12-bar blues. And all this gave it a simple purity, I felt. It was all magical to me.

"And then my brother bought this LP, this would have been in 1962, and it included Blind Willie McTell's 'Statesboro Blues'. So then I had to have a 12-string guitar. And I got one. I bought it at Pan Music in Wardour Street for £45. It was a Harmony Sovereign jumbo 12-string, and it was a beast. The action was crippling. But, for me, listening to it with my head just above it, it was like listening to a whole orchestra. There are limitations to a 12-string, but it was great."

And why did McTell stand out?

"Well, first off, I knew he tuned his guitar unlike anyone else. McTell played tuned a whole tone down, in D—he played in D shapes—and it gave it such a majestic, intoxicating sound. 'Statesboro Blues', well the song is just an excuse to play—to play those runs and things. At first I didn't even listen to the words. It was all about the playing of the piece, and that big sound, and then the singing—singing in this beautiful tonality. It's unique. He's gorgeous.

"And then when I did listen to the words there's this optimism about him. Even when he's singing about sad things. And, with 'Statesboro Blues', he's got these blues and everybody's got 'em, but he's leaving them behind. I've always preferred the happier, lighter kind of blues, and he's just so dazzling. And his gift for lyric writing and storytelling is unique, in my opinion, even though I know a lot of people do those sort of storytelling introductions. After 'Statesboro Blues', a friend gave me the LP of that *Last Session*, and I loved it—all that enthusiasm about the songs, and the stories behind them. And I used to study that photo of him, you know, when he's older, and look at his shirt and so on, and that crap guitar—how did he do all that on a $20 guitar? Amazing."

How was it that the young Ralph May went further than that, and changed his own name to McTell's?

"I bumped into Wizz Jones, who was one of the real shapers of the British scene, and Wizz asked if I'd like to team up with him and come to Cornwall and do these pub gigs he'd got down there. So we did, and this went well and, in the end, we took over this really primitive place called the Folk Cottage at Mitchell, in mid-Cornwall, just off the A30. People would come thirty and forty miles to this place, where you had to piss in a bucket in a field sort of thing.

"Anyway, so Wizz was going to get this poster made, saying 'WIZZ JONES and RALPH MAY', and I said, 'Oh, no, I don't think that sounds very good.' It sounded too plain to me. I felt it needed a two-syllable surname, and the first person I thought of was Fuller, from Blind Boy Fuller, but 'Ralph Fuller' sounded plain as well. So then I said, 'What about McTell?' and Wizz said, 'Well, sure. Call yourself whatever you like!' So I went with McTell.

"And then, when I came to making my first album, I tried to get it back to Ralph May, but the record company said, 'Oh, no, you've got to keep McTell!' So I did. And I don't regret it. And I've never come across anyone else with that name. In America I've looked it up in phone books and never found it."

When Ralph released his second album, he had to include a song of his that he'd been surprised to find drew novel, wild enthusiasm from folk-club audiences—a song called 'Streets of London'. It made him far more famous than Blind Willie had ever been, but, in doing so, it bandied the name McTell about hugely. ('Streets of London' was rather more noticeable on the album than another track, 'Boodle Am Shake', which offered a conscious shake-up of Willie's own 'Beedle Um Bum'.)

In New York City in 1965, a twenty-five-year-old of Caribbean descent who called himself Taj Mahal had moved west from Massachusetts, worked with others in the group the Rising Sons, and finally made an album, *Taj Mahal* (it wasn't released until 1967), which looked afresh at old country blues—a lone furrow to be plowing in the psychedelic period. He included a revival of Blind Willie's 'Statesboro Blues'.

Soon after, two young blond-haired brothers from Macon (rhymes with bacon) in Georgia, Duane and Gregg Allman, gave up on a group called Allman Joys and formed another, Hourglass, in Alabama. When they signed with Liberty Records, they were flown to Los Angeles—and there they heard Taj Mahal and his band playing 'Statesboro Blues' and duly began to include it in their own sets. When the bottom fell out of Hourglass and they formed The Allman Brothers instead, they rebuilt their own guitar-fireworks version of Blind Willie's 1928 composition.

They were recorded performing it in a run of concerts at the Fillmore East in New York in March 1971, and, after the release of the excitingly titled *Live At The Fillmore East* that July, the song was a hot favorite, and the band became the best and biggest-selling Southern band across the hip and mega-selling world of 1970s rock music. The Allman Brothers were big on the scale that Frank Zappa was big, or Led Zeppelin, or the Grateful Dead. They were lords of the universe, and everywhere they went 'Statesboro Blues' rang out.

It's there on their greatest-hits LP of 1975, *The Road Goes on Forever*. But, by then, the road had already failed to go on forever for two key members of the band, lead guitarist Duane Allman (fatal motorbike crash, late 1971) and fellow band member Berry Oakley (ditto, late 1972). The survivors played 'Statesboro Blues' at Duane Allman's funeral at Rose Hill Cemetery, Macon. Both men lie buried in the Carnation Ridge section of this expansive nineteenth-century cemetery park.

It would have surprised Willie McTell to find himself drawn into another part of the 1970s social fabric, the Women's Movement. Yet there was the American poet Hettie Jones, in 1974, taking a phrase from another of Willie's early songs, the lovely 1927 blues 'Mama, 'Tain't Long Fo' Day', for the title of her book *Big Star Fallin' Mama: Five Women in Black Music*. She quotes three verses of the song in the frontispiece and identifies him as their author.

Hettie Jones, who was forty that year, was at least as interested in "black issues" and the bohemian life as in "women's issues," but in the mid-1970s many people experienced them as all of a piece. She'd been married to Amiri Baraka when he was LeRoi Jones (and when, in 1963, he'd published *Blues People*, the first modern book about the blues by a black person). Hettie had co-founded and co-edited a progressive Beat-is-best magazine with him, named *Yugen*, which published work by Philip Whalen, Jack Kerouac, Allen Ginsberg, Uncle Bill Burroughs and all, and a small poetry press, Totem, whose contributors included Gregory Corso, Gary Snyder and Ed Dorn. Years later, she would publish a memoir of these times and of her marriage, the nicely titled *How I Became Hettie Jones*.

So, as it happened, this was Willie's second posthumous brush with the world of hip New York bohemia and its small magazines. It also proved to be the first use of his work within a book written by a black American, and the first time a phrase from one of his songs had provided the title for a book.

In 1991 Bob Dylan released for the first time the marvellous song he had written and recorded in 1983 *entitled* 'Blind Willie McTell', and which he has since played in concert many times. Each stanza of this beautiful and complex creation ends with "And I know no one [nobody] can sing the blues / Like Blind Willie McTell."

And by the time Bob Dylan was paying this tribute, more or less every track that Blind Willie McTell had recorded had been released on CD: and without counting minor back-up jobs, this was well over a hundred tracks. They had never been so easy to acquire. McTell would have been amazed.

# ONE

T HE AMERICAN STATE of Georgia divides itself into a huge number of counties, more than any state but Texas. They've been splitting off from each other like amoebas for two hundred years, and now there are 159 of them. (Florida has sixty-seven, Arizona fifteen.)

One of Georgia's smallest and poorest is Warren County, two-thirds of the way east on the 141-mile trip from Atlanta to Augusta. It's a rural county, and very pretty. Driving within the speed limit on Interstate 20, you'll pass through it in under thirteen minutes.

I didn't, though. The best way to slip back in time, back into the Georgia that Blind Willie McTell knew, is to take the old roads through farmland of rolling brown hills and small, sad towns.

You more or less have to leave Atlanta on the interstate, but twenty-nine miles out you can escape at Covington, the main town in Newton County, and move onto Highway 278. Under its old name, Highway 12, this was the main road before the interstate was built, and it runs all the way east to Augusta, where the Savannah River divides Georgia from South Carolina. Highway 12 follows the route made by all the little roads that linked up the towns between the two cities before the highway was built in the 1920s. A line the same shape runs across the state map for 1895, marking out the route of the Georgia Railroad Company before the roads were there.

Leaving Covington, the old highway runs east through miniscule Brick Store, where Willie's second wife, Helen, grew up, and on towards the grand old town of Madison. Somewhere along the road a white plastic church sign, lit from inside and topped by colored lightbulbs flashing on and off, urges DON'T WAIT FOR SIX STRONG MEN TO CARRY YOU INTO CHURCH!

Madison was voted nicest small town in America in 2000. It doesn't say by whom. Naturally it is all antique shops and Ye Old Colonial Restaurant, a doll shop and Ruffled Rooster knick-knacks. You can't move for Heritage plaques, yet half the sumptuous, exhausted-looking "historic homes" are up for sale. Baptist and Methodist churches compete for pomposity and size.

There's no alcohol on Sundays in this part of the country, though in some towns they relent if you're eating a restaurant meal—and Madison is unique for many miles around in having a proper restaurant. The Amici Italian Café serves real food and wine and, after a week or two in the gastronomic desert of rural Georgia, it begins to seem reasonable to drive back there from fifty miles away for something decent to eat.

After Madison, the road takes you over the hushed expanse of Lake Oconee and through the middle of the Oconee National Forest. This is rich farmland—it could almost be Gloucestershire. Out the other side comes Greensboro, Union Point, and then Crawfordville, one of those towns that's waiting to die.

Built in 1910, with a huge redbrick courthouse as florid and forbidding as a Dickens orphanage, old Crawfordville is tiny—one short street flanked with shops, like a town in a cowboy film. Bill's Grocery: building for sale. Candy Store: empty. Milliner's: empty. Café: closed. The Crawfordville Supperette: closed. Part of the grocery store is open, and so is an extraordinary machine-crammed place where fifty people ought to be making overhauls and nurses' uniforms but where just one woman is walking around. And then there's the Southern Magnolia Restaurant, Home of the Magnolia Onion (a big onion opened up like a flower and deep fried).

Back on the road, the railroad line runs alongside for many, many miles. There are only freight trains now, and these are rare and sometimes a mere three trucks long. You cross from Taliaferro County into Warren County just north of a speck on the map called Barnett. Two miles later you pass underneath the interstate and, after eleven more miles south-west, you reach the small county seat of Warrenton.

This is no distance at all from Happy Valley, the sprawl of land in adjacent McDuffie County where Willie McTell was born and is buried, in pineywoods country south of the small town of Thomson. His body was brought to Warrenton by train the day after he died down in Milledgeville, and he was embalmed here on a late August day in 1959.

In August heat, little downtown Warrenton is an oblong of dazzling white emptiness centered on the county courthouse—full afternoon sun bouncing off white buildings and near-white concrete sidewalks, off shiny cars and pick-up trucks, off the white columns and plinths on brick buildings, off the white and green frontage of Miss Jane's Restaurant, off plate-glass shopfront windows with battered aluminum frames, off the white water-tower high up on white metal stalks, and off the white soldier on top of the white Confederate monument.

The old brown Knox Theater squats dying across the way, its dirty brick façade fading to dusty invisibility. On the corner of Main and Norwood is the Petro Gas Station and Store (No Restrooms), the one place downtown where black guys hang out. Down Norwood you cross the railroad tracks to reach the black part of town. It's literally the other side of the tracks.

The Chamber of Commerce, trying to promote tourism, says that Warrenton has "that down-home feeling, that everybody-knows-everybody feeling when you're walking through town. Coming here, it's like stepping back in time."

So is eating here. Avoid the fast food of mall and strip, eat instead in any small town in this part of Georgia and you get, cumulatively, a sense of how unchanged the diet is since McTell's day. To follow in his footsteps is to eat his food: food that is lumbering and uninspired. Meatloaf, spaghetti, breaded chicken, grits, rice, meat sauce, tomato sauce, liver, gravy, corn dogs, bread, and biscuits. Everything's big and brown and heavy, except when it's big and lurid red and heavy. Willie was eating barbecue under a tree when he had his second and lethal stroke.

You can help yourself to all of this for lunch at Miss Jane's—you'll find it laid out in its open, stainless-steel coffinettes—but you can't have a salad, not even at the height of summer. They're kindly and sorry about it, though they're not so polite in the Gents, in which a lavatory-seat-shaped sign above the bowl reads "Stand Closer, It's Shorter Than You Think."

Just 6,336 people live in this county now, a quarter of them below the poverty line. The racial mix is 60/40 black to white.

This was one of Willie McTell's stomping grounds. He knew Warrenton like the back of his guitar and he spent plenty of time in Warren County. He had friends and relatives here. His cousin, Gold Harris, lived here, on County Line Road, where one side of the road is in Warren and one isn't. Other relatives attended Mount Aldred Church, and lie buried there now. His singer-guitarist friend Buddy Moss spent part of the late 1930s locked in Warrenton's brand-new jail.

But Willie's story holds a much older Warren County connection, reaching all the way down from the late eighteenth century.

At American Independence in 1776, the new nation had appropriated little more than the east coast of the continent, and was only just groping west. Georgia ran all the way over to the Mississippi River, but west of Georgia were the vast French, then Spanish, territories of Louisiana (soon to be French again), which stretched from the Mississippi all the way to the Rockies and north-south from Canada to the Gulf of Mexico.

On Georgia's southern border was Florida, so you had to watch your back, too. "Georgia," as Tom Henderson Wells wrote, "was a frontier area, subject to depredations from Florida" (whose ownership was fought over by native Americans, the French, the Spanish, the British, and the States—this last a body that Florida wouldn't join till the third decade of the nineteenth century). Even Savannah, then Georgia's biggest city, was re-taken by the British two years after Independence—as if to emphasise that 1776 was the middle of the American Revolution and not the end of it.

So Georgia was a frontier state when Warren County came into existence, which was on a Thursday, six days before Christmas in 1793. It made itself from modest bits of Burke, Columbia, Richmond, and Wilkes Counties, and named itself after a Harvard graduate, political agitator, doctor, and freemason from the Royal Province of Massachusetts, one Joseph Warren, who had volunteered to fight the king's men and got himself killed at the Battle of Bunker Hill in 1775, six days after turning thirty-four.

Warren County was far more populous when it was new than it is now, and its boundaries bigger. (Several parcels of land split off in turn to make more new counties over the decades that followed.) This had been the land of the Lower Creeks and Chickasaws, who had combined farming and fishing. In the spring they'd planted maize, hunted animals and fished in fresh water. In the winter months they'd migrated south to the warmer coast and caught clams, oysters and crabs.

In the Warren County of 1800, the Native Americans were long gone. Now there were 8,300-odd people, and a quarter of them were slaves owned by the others. The total number of "free persons of color" was just nineteen, and they were a great deal less free than white people. In 1815 the state decreed that they could be tried for crimes under the same laws as slaves; in 1819 it decreed that once a year they must register with the clerk of their county's inferior court, on penalty of being sold back into slavery; and in 1833 it became just as illegal to teach a "free person of color" to read or write in Georgia as to teach a slave these skills.

A few rich whites owned a lot of slaves, but most white people were not rich and therefore owned just a few slaves—commonly two or three. You could be a poor white tenant farmer—a cracker—and still have a couple of slaves, just as, in the early twentieth century, you could be an underpaid middle-class clerk and still have a domestic servant, and just as you can be a working-class man of any color and still have a working-class woman to fetch and carry for you.

On the other hand, here in the nineteenth-century South, the fetchers and carriers really were *slaves*: they were your personal property, they had no rights as people and were counted alongside your cattle, farm machinery and tools as items to be taxed, bought, sold and bequeathed in your will. If you wanted to, you could separate slave children from their parents, or from their brothers or sisters, and send them off else-where.

As slave states went, Georgia's totals were never huge, but in the ten years after 1790 the number doubled to almost 60,000. The greatest concentrations were in the counties that included Augusta and Savannah.

They came through Augusta from South Carolina and into the port of Savannah by ship. The Savannah River was a crucial link between the two. Slaves were literally sold down the river. And up it.

White people were also flowing through Augusta, albeit willingly, on their way from the Carolinas into Georgia.

One of these migrants was a man named Kendall McTyeire. Or Kendal or Kindal McTyare or McTier. Or McTyrie, McTyire, McTyre, McTear, McTyere, or any number of further enterprising variants. People just didn't care, in those days any more than in Shakespeare's, how they spelled their own names, let alone other people's.

We'll call him Kendall McTyeire, and note in passing that his middle name was Lee. Everyone seems agreed on the spelling of that one.

He was born in South Carolina but, by early 1819, a young man in his twenties, he'd moved into Georgia, settled in Warren County, and married above himself. Elizabeth Bass was the daughter of a landowner and slaveholder, Reddick Bass, and his wife Obedience, whose maiden name was Persons and whose family lived nearby. We don't know how many slaves Mr Bass held, but we know that he paid taxes on just one adult slave in 1791, two the next year, and thirteen by 1805. Kendall's own father, John McTyeire, held none.

Kendall and Elizabeth's first child was a girl, Narcissa, born in 1825. Next came a son, born on a Sunday, 16 April 1826. When he was born, John Quincy Adams was President of the United States—the sixth president, and the last to represent the Democratic-Republican Party. In Georgia, the state capital was no longer Savannah but the town of Milledgeville, just forty miles south-west of Warrenton. Milledgeville had been built to be state capital, with streets one hundred feet wide, to accommodate horses, buggies, and ox carts. They've never had to widen the streets since.

Kendall and Elizabeth named their son Reddick, after his grandfather. He is a main character in our story.

His names, too, would come to be spelled in many different ways. His first name comes up as Rederick, Riddick, Redrick, and more. When he puts his signature on a document in later life he writes it *Reddick McTyeir*, so that's what we'll use here—though he might have spelled both names differently if he'd signed that same piece of paper another day.

22

In the farming community he's born into, his father is a solid citizen—he sits on juries, he's appointed one of five commissioners who "divide the negroes belonging to the estate of McCoy, David, deceased," and, when Reddick is three years old, his daddy is on the jury in the murder trial of a black man named Cato.

Despite these civic duties, the family is not well off. The farm seems to have struggled from the start, and to have kept going with difficulty through the years of Reddick's childhood, with Kendall selling off slaves in ones or twos to keep things going. In the 1820 census, "Kindall McTear" has three male slaves aged between fourteen and twenty-six, and one female aged under fourteen. He sells one of these the following year at a sheriff's sale on the courthouse steps in Warrenton.

By this time there are just over 4,000 slaves altogether in Warren County and nearly 150,000 in Georgia. (In 1820 also, King George III dies in England and, in theory, the slave trade is abolished in Spain and Portugal. The year after, Spain loses Mexico, which now becomes an independent nation.)

Early in 1829, grandfather Reddick Bass dies, leaving his wife Obedience nearly three hundred acres of land and four slaves for her lifetime. Kendall is a co-executor of his father-in-law's will, and has to fight off various claims against the estate.

At some point in his adolescence, Reddick's mother Elizabeth dies too. We don't know when or why, but we know it must be after 1836, because that year she gives birth to Reddick's fourth and final sibling, brother Solomon. Reddick is ten then, and already has two younger sisters, Teresa (born 21 April 1830) and Synthian (13 August 1833), as well as his older sister Narcissa. When their mother dies, Narcissa looks after the younger children.

(Actually, it just might be that, before any of these children, Kendall and Elizabeth have a child named Larkin. Certainly there *is* a Larkin, born around 1823; the doubt is whether he is really their child. If he is, why doesn't he feature in his father's will? Why doesn't he inherit anything, as the oldest son? There is still a dispute about Larkin's status among the family's amateur genealogists.)

Either way, in the early summer of 1844, when Reddick is eighteen, his father remarries. This second wife is a widow, a Mrs Rebecca Culpepper, *née* Duckworth. Perhaps the marriage of these two middle-aged people improves the McTyeire family finances. Three years later they buy some land previously owned by Rebecca's first husband (why it didn't belong to her already we don't know) and, by 1850, Kendall has built up his tally of slaves to ten. Meanwhile all his daughters have married.

Out in the wider world, these are times of exceptional foment, even by the rambunctious standards of the nineteenth century. In 1845 the first iron ship crosses the Atlantic, and Texas becomes a state. In 1847 thousands of small investors are ruined when the first Railway Boom collapses. In 1848 the Republic of Venice is proclaimed in St Mark's Square, John Stuart Mill publishes *On Liberty* and Karl Marx and Friedrich Engels publish *The Communist Manifesto*. Revolutions erupt in France, Italy, Austria, Hungary, and Germany. In 1851 Herman Melville publishes *Moby-Dick* and Harriet Beecher Stowe starts to publish *Uncle Tom's Cabin* as a magazine serial. In book form, it becomes the best-selling novel of the century and helps turn public opinion against slavery. Today its hero's name has become a byphrase for contemptible kowtowing to a racial oppressor, but back then it was intended, and received, as an incendiary anti-slavery work. It is particularly strong on the suffering caused by the callous splitting up and dispersal of black families by their white owners.

Reddick, now twenty-seven, buys some land from his father in December 1853—and, four days after Christmas, his father makes him a gift of a slave child. Kendall has clearly not been moved by the arguments in *Uncle Tom's Cabin*. This slave child is eight years old. Her name is Essey and, separated from her family, about whom we know nothing at all, she goes to live on Reddick's farm.

The phrasing used in the legal document that gives her to Reddick— phrasing you come across again and again at this time—is uncannily, discomfitingly similar to the marriage vows: "To have to hold to keep . . ." But then, the phrasing of these white people's wills is pretty grandiose, too. Here goes William Zeigler of Crawford County, Georgia, in 1855: "Item 1$^{st}$ My soul I submit to God . . ."—how very good of him, God must have thought—"Item 2$^{nd}$ I give devise and bequeath unto my beloved Nephew . . . the following described family of Negroes to wit—Sampson and his Wife Hannah & their children Julia Tom & Nathan & their Increase forever . . ." Forever!

You can even use a slave as a mortgage. The first mortgage ever recorded in Reddick's part of Georgia is given by a Mrs Jerusha Kent, who borrows \$337.50 from three men in January 1858, promises to repay the loan on Christmas Day, and gives as the mortgage to secure the debt a "certain negro girl, named Mahalah, of dark complexion, about 18 years of age, of about ordinary height."

In November 1854, Kendall tries to get his eighty-seven-year-old mother-in-law, Obedience Bass, declared insane; the Lunecy [sic] Commission finds her perfectly sane. He tries again in 1855, but this time she saves him the trouble by dying. How Reddick feels about his father's attempts to have his grandmother locked up, we can't know.

Five years later, in the summer of 1860, Reddick reports to the census taker that there are now three people living under his roof: they are Reddick himself, now aged thirty-four, Essey the slave girl, now fourteen, and a nine-month-old "mulatto" baby named Elbert.

"Mulatto" was a technical term—the simplest in a list of terms that had once been as ludicrous as they were obscene in their determination to measure just exactly what proportion of a person might be white and what black. These terms dated back to the seventeenth century, when slaves could intermarry with indentured servants and so there was much gradation to be kept track of. To be considered white, you had to be less than 1/32$^{nd}$ black, so it was no good being a Quadroon (1/4$^{th}$), an Octoroon (1/8$^{th}$), a Mustifee (1/16$^{th}$), or even a Mustifino (1/32$^{nd}$). This is also where the word "Sambo" comes from: it was the term for the child of a Mulatto and a black person.

By the time Reddick McTyeir was born, these classifications had been whittled down and simplified.

"Mulatto" wasn't complicated at all. It meant that baby Elbert was officially recognised as half white and half black. He was Reddick and Essey's son . . . and, in time, Willie McTell's grandfather.

# TWO

Reddick remained a bachelor and a small-time farmer. He owned a hundred acres of land, a third of it in production. He had two horses, two oxen, two milk cows, one other unspecified "cattle," and six pigs. He grew Indian corn, wheat, sweet potatoes, peas, beans, and a small amount of cotton. He also made and sold a little butter. His "real estate" was valued at $400 and his "personal estate" was reckoned to be worth $2,200. That would have included the value of his slaves.

He got on with his neighbors—a farmer much the same age as himself, James Denton; a farm laborer in his late forties called Jacob Mathis, who had a wife and three teenage daughters; and a family named Kitchens. (A lot of local people were named Kitchens.) Lawrence Kitchens would remain a lifelong friend.

In December 1857, Reddick's land had been part of the territory removed from Warren County and given to a new creation, Glascock County, named after a soldier, lawyer, and politician from Augusta.

If Reddick had business in the county seat—to call on the sheriff or fill in a form at the courthouse—it was now the tiny town of Gibson he had to ride into, instead of Warrenton. Otherwise, the county boundary change made no difference to Reddick. His younger brother Solomon's land, and their father's, which were no distance away, stayed within Warren County.

A more significant reallocation, of Reddick's land and everybody else's, happened on Friday, 19 January 1861. Georgia seceded from the United States of America.

Reddick was just days away from turning thirty-five years old when, on another Friday in the spring of that year, 12 April, the guns of Charleston, three hundred miles away, fired on Fort Sumter and began the American Civil War—or, as they call it in the South, the War Between the States.

When Reddick heard the news, he rode into Gibson and signed up as a soldier, a volunteer. Perhaps it was his thirty-fifth birthday present to himself, after sitting at home on the porch, conscious of hitting the halfway point in his life, and mulling it over. Wasn't the war his only chance to see the wider world, to do something more than scrape along, a small-time farmer tied to corn and pigs, to making do and mending?

Or maybe he was outraged by Yankee provocation, so that the news of the attack on the hated Fort Sumter thrilled him and he burned to do his bit to protect the Southern way of life. He was a bit long in the tooth to be an enthusiastic volunteer for the glories of battle, but he wasn't alone in that.

Nobody knew. How could they? The sheer fact that it had come to war at all had been such a surprise. And, after that, both sides assumed it would be over in a flash. No one could possibly know that they were embroiling themselves in what would be the biggest war in the western world in the hundred years after the fall of Napoleon. Looking back now, we know that it cost more American lives than the two World Wars, Korea, and Vietnam combined, and introduced the special horrors of "modern" warfare: the trenches, prisoner-of-war camps, the targeting of civilians, aerial observation, propaganda, ironclad ships, the Gatling gun, and, eventually, the first American conscription.

Reddick enlisted as a private in the Glascock Independent Guards, along with his friend Lawrence Kitchens, eleven other men named Kitchens—it was the commonest surname in the company—and nearly two hundred other volunteers.

And so it was that, on 4 July 1861, a Thursday, Reddick marched back into Gibson as one of the soldiers in uniform assembling to put on a show for the citizenry as the razzamatazz of war caught the public imagination.

It was flag day. An editor from the *Augusta Chronicle & Sentinel*, Mr Hancock, came to watch. Arriving at ten o'clock that morning he was "forced to wonder, at beholding such a concourse of people assembled." He reckoned the crowd to be twenty-five hundred. (Today in Gibson you'd be forced to wonder if you beheld a crowd of twenty-five.)

The excitement in Glascock County reflected the momentousness of events in the country. The attack on Fort Sumter in April had prompted four more states to secede from the Union, and Richmond, Virginia, had been declared the Confederate capital.

Not everyone in the South was an enthusiast for secession. In Virginia, opposition was so strong in the western counties that, in June, the idea of a separate state of West Virginia was born. (Two years later, in mid-war, West Virginia would be admitted to the Union.) And though Delaware, Kentucky, Maryland, and Missouri were slavery states, they refused to join the Confederacy. Even in Georgia, the further north you went, towards the foothills of the Appalachians, the less support it enjoyed. Yet it turned out in the end that in Georgia 244,812 men fought for the Confederacy; 195 fought for the Union.

In the North, public pressure for action precipitated an ill-prepared attack on the South, so that, within weeks of the flag-day parade in Gibson, other Southern soldiers were seeing action and success. The Confederacy won the first battle of Bull Run, Virginia. But, even as this was being celebrated, the federal navy was beginning to be effective in its blockade of the Confederate coast.

In August the Glascock Independent Guards became Company B of the 22$^{nd}$ Regiment Georgia Volunteer Infantry, a regiment formally organised on 31 August under Colonel Robert Harris Jones, a lugubrious-looking man with a pudgy, unstrained face and a shiny beard and moustache.

On Tuesday, 3 September, the Glascock men were officially mustered and the whole regiment was ordered immediately to a tented camp twenty-five miles north-west of Atlanta, Camp McDonald, just outside what's now Kennesaw. Here they trained and drilled for two long months. Then, via Augusta, they crossed the river into South Carolina. Reddick had never left Georgia in his life before.

They were not yet marching off to war. Winter was arriving and they were simply moving north for more training on the outskirts of Richmond, Virginia, in position for when war would resume in the spring. Here Reddick served as a guard, and lived in a tent, despite the onset of winter. The men of the 22$^{nd}$ were billeted alongside the 16$^{th}$ Georgia Regiment, whose soldiers had already been so sickly that in October only half of them could turn up for parade.

After less than two weeks here, Reddick and his fellow soldiers were sent a short distance south and spent the rest of the winter in camps close to Portsmouth, Virginia, the oldest naval shipyard in the United States, which had been captured by the Confederates in the first days of the war. Three of Reddick's fellow soldiers died of illnesses in Richmond before the year was out.

The winter was mild, with only flurries of brief sleet in January. When snow fell, it never outlasted the day. The men were housed in cabins they had built themselves, and generally had enough to eat. The main enemy was mumps, which was widespread.

When the spring of 1862 arrived, so did action. Reddick fought in many battles. Some of them were inconclusive skirmishes, but others were prolonged nightmares of importunate slaughter that left huge tracts of field and forest strewn with the swollen corpses of men and horses, congealed in mud and blood.

Reddick's early battles were at South Mills, North Carolina; Seven Pines (aka Fair Oaks); the Seven Days Battles (from a first indecisive engagement at Oak Grove, aka King's School House, to the last, at Malvern Hill, on the first day of July 1862); Falling Creek, Virginia; and Second Bull Run. Some of the regiment then fought at Harpers Ferry,

Virginia (now in West Virginia), and Fredericksburg, that 13 December: the most terrible, pointless battle of the war so far. But Reddick's company doesn't seem to have been among the fighters here, for not a single man from Glascock is recorded as having been wounded, let alone killed, in this day of slaughter, in which the North lost over 12,000 men and the South saw 5,000 killed or wounded.

Fredericksburg demoralised the North and heartened the South, but proved almost the last significant Confederate victory; and those who witnessed it knew it was largely a victory by default. People on both sides now sensed for the first time that the war had become a hopeless struggle with no end ever in sight.

The 22$^{nd}$ Georgia Regiment camped in Virginia that winter and suffered tough privations. Many men now had no tents, little clothing, and no shoes, and could only make themselves rawhide moccasins.

In January 1863, Abraham Lincoln issued his Emancipation Proclamation, declaring that almost every slave was free, and, on the 25$^{th}$ of the month, Joseph Hooker replaced General Burnside as commander of the North's Army of the Potomac. Reddick's regiment fought minor battles late that February. There was a severe snowstorm on the night of the 22$^{nd}$, a Sunday, and it was colder than any weather the men from Georgia had ever known; but, at the beginning of March, they were moved to a camp at Guiney's Station (Guinea Station), Virginia, where they found wooden bunks and more comfortable quarters.

Reddick's unit saw no action till the beginning of May. His whole regiment was with Lee as they won the battle on which Stephen Crane would base his *Red Badge of Courage*—the battle of Chancellorville. Lee's victory here allowed his troops to press north right into Pennsylvania. (Stonewall Jackson never reached it. Riding at night, he was accidentally shot by his own troops and his left arm had to be amputated. Lee wrote: "He has lost his left arm; but I have lost my right arm." On 10 May, soon after three o'clock in the afternoon, Jackson died of pneumonia back at camp at Guiney's Station. He was thirty-nine years old.)

Reddick was with General Lee that June, too, when they marched on up to Gettysburg, an insignificant little town in Pennsylvania.

There Reddick took part in the biggest battle of the Civil War—a battle that began by accident and raged through the first three days of July, 1863.

Lee's Army of Northern Virginia totalled 75,000 men; the Union Army of the Potomac, now under General George G. Meade, was 97,000 strong. They met by chance when a Confederate brigade, foraging for supplies, caught sight of a forward column of Meade's cavalry.

The fighting that erupted was one of more than 2,000 land battles of the war yet in its three days more men fought and more men died than in any other in North America before or since. As in so many other cases, it achieved no major war aim for either side.

On the third day, under General George E. Pickett, 15,000 Confederate troops marched for a mile across open ground in a massed infantry assault on the Union line, pounded by artillery and rifle fire as they came. They reached the Union line but failed to break it. In under an hour there were 10,000 Confederate casualties.

Gettysburg, a town of only 2,400 inhabitants, was left with 51,000 dead and wounded people. Over 172,000 men, 634 cannon and 569 tons of ammunition had been deployed. Five thousand dead horses lay among the human bodies and the wreckage.

Reddick survived these horrors physically unscathed. Twenty of his fellow foot soldiers from Company B were killed or wounded and/or captured.

Lee's retreat began on the afternoon of 4 July, his army depleted, demoralised, and exhausted. Hampered by drenching rain and horrendous mud, they found the rivers so swollen that they could not cross the Potomac until the 13th of the month, at Williamsport.

After crossing, Lee's troops withdrew up the Shenandoah Valley. As they retreated south, carrying wounded men who were dying every day, their wagons stuck again and again in the mud—and they came under attack from Union cavalry units. General Meade, too, had crossed the Potomac and chased Lee's troops into Virginia.

At dawn on Thursday, 23 July, Unionist soldiers were ordered to cut off the retreating Confederate columns at Manassas Gap. From Company B, three men died in this attack. Altogether fifty men from Glascock

County had been killed or wounded, or were missing or captured. Now, in the day's fray, Reddick went missing too.

At dusk, the Union attacks were abandoned. Within twenty-four hours what remained of Lee's army would be safely beyond pursuit. But Reddick had been captured at Manassas Gap that day.

Reddick was taken to Point Lookout prison camp, Maryland—a series of buildings arranged like a wagon wheel right on the tip of the barren peninsula where the Potomac River joins Chesapeake Bay.

Point Lookout had been ordered in haste after the battle of Gettysburg, and it was still unfinished when Reddick arrived. It was designed to hold 10,000 men, but for most of its existence it held between 12,600 and 20,000. It was the Union's largest prison camp.

A nice touch was that the prison guards included men from the 24th, 26th, 28th, 36th, 41st, 181st, and 190th US Colored Infantry, from four units of the US Massachusetts Negro Cavalry, two US North Carolina Negro regiments, three US Maryland Negro regiments, two US Maryland Colored Regiments, the 4th US Infantry Negro Regiment, and the 72nd US Volunteers Negro Regiment. The number of known black prisoners was eleven.

Drainage was poor, and the men were subject to extreme heat in summer and extreme cold in winter. Food, clothing, accommodation, fuel, and medical care were all inadequate. Almost 3,000 prisoners died there in under two years. Water surrounded three sides of the camp. You couldn't hope to escape. If you tried, you were suspended from a pole by the thumbs until you lost consciousness.

Reddick was sent to Point Lookout so early on that he might even have been one of the first consignment of 136 prisoners. A further 1,700 arrived in August, and almost 6,000 more in the next two months.

In a report written that November, the camp authorities were ordering tents to house many of the men, even though winter was already coming in hard and there was a shortage of blankets as well as of clothing and firewood. One of Reddick's compadres from Glascock County died in the camp that month, from unspecified causes.

Smallpox, scurvy, and diarrhea were already significantly present. The hospital wards inside the camp were tents too, each a long row of about thirty beds. An inmate named Luther Hopkins described how as soon as a patient died he was "taken to the dead-house, the sheets changed and another brought in." When he was admitted to one of these wards, "the bed that I was on had been occupied by a smallpox patient, and I was put on it a few minutes after the patient was taken out." One of the smallpox patients was from Reddick's own company, and, like him, had come to Point Lookout after capture at Manassas Gap. He died in his smallpox bed two days before Christmas.

Whether Reddick got sick, we don't know. If he did, he recovered. We do know that for Christmas dinner, after a breakfast of a piece of bread and a cup of coffee, he got a small slice of meat, a cup of soup, and five crackers.

New Year's Eve was a rainy day, the first daytime of 1864 pleasant—but that evening, a Friday, the cold grew so intense that next morning a number of prisoners were found frozen to death. Others were so hungry that they began to catch rats to cook and eat.

Within days part of the water in the bay froze solid, the prisoners ran out of wood for fuel and, on 7 January, it started snowing. Two days later another of Reddick's fellow inmates from Glascock County was moved to the camp's hospital, and six days later he too died of smallpox.

That month, each prisoner was asked to choose from one of these options: to be sent south and exchanged as a prisoner of war, to take the oath of allegiance and enlist in the Union army or navy, to take the oath and be sent north and assigned to public works, or to take the oath and be sent home, should home happen to be inside Union army lines.

Reddick chose to be sent south and exchanged. Not everyone got the option they chose, but Reddick did, though it took many weeks' waiting in the camp before he learned his fate. Early in the war there had been an agreed procedure for exchanges, but this had broken down back in 1862 because the South couldn't countenance the North's demand that black captives be included in the process. By the spring of 1864, limited exchanges had resumed. Reddick was an early beneficiary.

On Thursday, 3 March, he was escorted from the prison camp and, three days later, he was placed in the hands of the Union officer in charge of exchanges, one John E. Mulford, Major and Assistant Agent for Exchange at City Point, Virginia. This small town was nothing, at the time. Three months later it would become Union General Ulysses S. Grant's headquarters. Mulford swapped his prisoners with those of his Confederate counterpart, Acting Adjutant General W.H. Hatch.

Reddick was one of 800 enlisted men exchanged there and then. He had endured Point Lookout for over seven months. A week after leaving, he had rejoined his regiment. He was issued with new clothing on 10 March.

His regiment was now at Camp Rescue in Caroline County, Virginia, alongside the Richmond and Fredericksburg railroad line, not far at all from Guiney's Station, about thirteen miles south of Fredericksburg. Soon they would be back in the mayhem and mud of battle.

Ulysses S. Grant had been appointed by Abraham Lincoln the previous November, and, as the spring of 1864 approached, the showdown between Grant's forces and Robert E. Lee's began. The Unionists called this the Overland Campaign.

Huge battles ensued, and Reddick's regiment fought in many: in May alone they pitched into the two-day Battle of The Wilderness, the fourteen-day Battle of Spotsylvania Court House, and the four-day Battle of North Anna. The first three days of June pushed them into the start of the protracted Battle of Cold Harbor, and then, from June right through to April 1865, came the terrible siege of Petersburg.

Grant's offensive began in the Wilderness, in Spotsylvania County, Virginia, on Monday, 5 May. Fighting was fierce but inconclusive as both sides attempted to gain position inside the thick woodland. All day they slogged it out, till darkness halted the fighting, and both sides brought reinforcements forward. At dawn next day, the Unionists attacked again, driving back Confederate troops. More men were thrown in and, at noon, a ferocious Confederate counter-attack began, only to collapse when the Southern Lieutenant-General James Longstreet was wounded by his own men. Late in the day, one more Union attack was repulsed. Almost 163,000 men had been fighting, the Unionists outnumbering their enemy by ten to six. Casualties, in roughly the same proportions, totalled almost 30,000, including two Union generals and three Confederate generals killed. The battle was a draw.

Grant refused to retreat. On 7 May, he advanced towards the Spotsylvania Court House crossroads. The next day he was stalled—and two weeks of fighting began.

This time over 150,000 men were involved and 30,000 of them became casualties. They were two-to-one Unionists to Confederates, survivors and casualties alike. Two more Union generals were killed, two Confederate generals captured, and two others mortally wounded. Again, nobody won.

The writer William Least Heat-Moon gives a vivid description of the futile, wanton carnage at Spotsylvania, in his great book *Blue Highways*, published 120 years later:

> The fighting here in the wet spring of 1864 was so close that cannoneers, standing ankle deep in mud, fired at point-blank range; soldiers, slogging it out in a smoky rainstorm, fought muzzle to muzzle, stabbing with bayonets . . . clubbing each other into the mire from dawn to midnight, and trampling fallen men out of sight into the muck. The intense rifle fire cut in half oak trees two feet in diameter. One soldier, Horace Porter, wrote: "We had not only shot down an army, but also a forest."
>
> On that single day, May 12, nearly thirteen thousand men died fighting over one square mile of ground abandoned by both sides several days later.

Again, at the end of it, Grant would not retreat. On Saturday, 21 May, he simply disengaged and continued his advance on Richmond. General Lee tried again and again to halt this inexorable advance. North Anna was one such attempt, Cold Harbor another.

Even here, knocked back by a rare Confederate victory, Grant was not deflected. Reddick's regiment seems to have been taken from the fray after 3 June, when a mass slaughter of Unionist forces was in mid-flow. For others, though, fighting went on until the night of the 12th. Then

Grant changed strategy. He abandoned his assault on the well-defended approaches to Richmond and, using a 2,200-foot-long pontoon bridge at Windmill Point, hurried his army south across the James River to attack Petersburg instead.

Petersburg had already been attacked by smaller Union forces on 9 June, and the result had been a modest Confederate success. Now the big guns arrived. This small, strategically important Virginia town came under siege as Grant and Lee once again hurled the whole Army of the Potomac and the entire Army of Northern Virginia against each other, in the terrible series of battles that, in time, would push the war shuddering to its close.

At 4.45am on 30 July, Reddick and his company were asleep, positioned to defend Petersburg, when the Unionists exploded a mine underneath them—literally blowing a hole in the Confederate defenses, and leaving a vast crater in the ground. The miners of the 48th Pennsylvania regiment had spent a month tunneling under the Confederate lines to achieve this. Within eight hours, they saw their efforts fail. Northern units charged in, confusion followed, the Confederates recovered and counterattacked. The break in their lines was mended and the Union army was repulsed, with severe casualties, especially among a crack division of black troops.

This should have been Grant's chance to end the siege. Instead, eight more appalling months of trench warfare followed, as he and Lee resumed their bloody struggle.

This time, Reddick's luck on the battlefield ran out. When the mine exploded, his jaw took a hit. Others from his company were killed, though, and Reddick lived. On the last day of July he was admitted to the Receiving & Wayside Hospital at Richmond, and, on 1 August, he was transferred to Jackson Hospital in the city. His timing was lucky. Jackson Hospital had opened only a year earlier, but, like the other five main hospitals in the city, it had been overcrowded with injured soldiers for most of its time. Three days before Reddick's admission, all six city hospitals were ordered to give each patient more space.

He was examined in one of the hospital's forty-nine buildings, and his injury diagnosed. "VSR Jaw m B," say his notes. He stayed in the hospital a week while his jaw was treated, and then he was given forty days furlough—home leave.

There's no record of whether he managed to get home. He hadn't been paid all year, he was hundreds of miles from Georgia, and he'd been given this respite only because he was still wounded and unfit to fight. Did he go home at all? If so, how long did he give himself before setting off again? All we know is that, still a private, still a foot soldier, and now thirty-eight years old, he was back with his regiment that November— and back near Petersburg.

Before the year was out, Reddick had been paid, but only up to the beginning of March. He was still owed ten months' back pay. In January 1865 he was paid up to the end of the previous October. He was paid nothing more after that. The regiment's camp now moved up around Chester Station, Chesterfield County, about halfway between Petersburg and Richmond.

In all the years of combat, only three men from Company B had deserted, and only one of these had simply slipped away; the other two had switched sides, swearing allegiance to the United States army and then plunging back into the fray.

In early February, Reddick's regiment fought its last battle. On Thursday the 5th, they were at Hatcher's Run, Dinwiddie County, Virginia. Three days of fighting between comparatively small numbers of troops, led by minor commanders on both sides, resulted in the Union forces gaining a little ground and extending the area besieged around Petersburg.

Two months later, almost to the day, it was over. Richmond fell on 3 April. Lee led his Army of Northern Virginia west in retreat, pursued by Grant's Army of the Potomac. On the 7th, Grant initiated a series of letters between the two men, exploring the possibility of Confederate surrender.

The two generals met in the town of Appomattox Court House, on the afternoon of the 9th, in the large, white-painted, red-carpeted first-floor parlor of local resident Wilmer McLean's house. They sat ten feet apart, facing each other, and talked of other matters for nearly half an hour before Lee broached the mutually embarrassing subject of the surrender.

Grant said that his terms were as outlined in their correspondence. All Confederate military equipment was to be relinquished, but officers and men would be free to go home. Lee asked Grant to put these terms in writing. Grant did so at once, and handed them across the room. Lee put on his glasses and, when he'd finished reading, asked if the terms allowed his men to keep their horses. He said that in the Confederate army, men owned their own mounts and might need them as farm animals back in civilian life. Grant wouldn't change the terms as written but said he would order his officers to allow any Confederate claiming a horse or a mule to keep it.

There was a formal signing and an exchange of copies of the surrender terms and of Lee's acceptance. By three o'clock it was all over. Grant and Lee rode off.

Back in the upstairs parlor there was an avid scramble for souvenirs. One general got the chair Grant had been sitting in, another Lee's chair, a third his marble-topped table, and a fourth the wooden table on which Grant had written out the terms of surrender. This later passed to General Custer. There was even some competition for the rag doll left in the room by Wilmer McLean's small daughter, Lula.

In contrast, it had been precisely the courtesy, tact, and dignity of Generals Grant and Lee that had made it possible for both sides to accept this outcome—and this despite the assassination of Abraham Lincoln just days later. (Shot by John Wilkes Booth at Ford's Theater, Washington, on 14 April, he died early the next morning.)

Surrender followed swiftly on all other fronts.

Reddick was among the few to be there with Robert E. Lee when the end came. From his regiment, just nine officers and 196 other men could say the same. He was one of the first men in America to hear that the war was over.

He had survived much of its recurrent, murderous nightmare. He had seen a gruesome, gory, sustained parade of horrors. He had endured many battles, months of prison-camp life, long nights of freezing weather, illness, and hunger, injury in the field, and the dangers of fever-ridden hospital wards. And, at the last, surrender.

If by miraculous fortune he still had a horse, he rode it home. If not, he walked. Appomattox to Glascock County was 400 miles, through devastated countryside, lawless terrain and swollen rivers, finding sparse supplies, abandoned homesteads, and displaced people like himself, along trails of the ragged dispossessed.

Reddick never wrote any of this down. Perhaps he never spoke of it. Maybe he just carried it in his head, conscious of the abyss it put between him and the pre-war past.

He made it home sometime in the summer of 1865. And he wasn't quite alone there, on his side of that abyss. His friend Lawrence Kitchens had survived too, and been with Reddick at Appomattox. Younger brother Solomon, who had enlisted in a different company of the same regiment, had also survived, though with a slightly different fate. Just days before Appomattox, and very nearby, Solomon seems to have been one of six thousand Confederate troops taken prisoner at Lynchburg, Virginia. Four days after terms were agreed by Grant and Lee, he was released and allowed to go home.

The mysterious Larkin McTyeire survived too, but he had been long gone from his home patch of Georgia. He'd married more than fifteen years before the war, moving to Florida in the mid-1850s and signing up there during the war. Afterwards, he and his family moved back to Georgia—but to Americus in Sumter County, way over in the southwest, about at the halfway mark if you draw a line due south from Atlanta to Tallahassee.

In December 1865, Congress ratified Lincoln's Declaration as the 13th Amendment after twenty-seven of the thirty-six states had ratified it in the course of the year. The last of these to do so, on 6 December, had been Georgia.

Back home on the farm, Reddick was coming up for forty years old. His son Elbert was now a boy of six. And no longer a slave. Reddick took him under his roof.

Elbert would become Blind Willie McTell's paternal grandfather. And Willie's white great-grandfather would still be alive, a few miles down the road, when Willie himself was born.

# THREE

T HE FIRST TIME I went to Thomson, Georgia, to look for Willie
McTell was in late October, 1998. I went by bus from Atlanta,
something Willie had himself done many times in an earlier era. There's a
widely held, mistaken view that only the poor, incompetent, and scuzzy
take buses—but you can disabuse yourself of this notion from the safety of
your sofa simply by reading Irma Kurtz's radiant, humane book *The Great
American Bus Ride*, published in 1993.

The efficiency of the whole system; the warmth and wit of the drivers;
their solicitude in making sure everyone alights where they mean to; the
variety of age, class and style of the passengers: these long-haul buses are
uplifting—even literally so. That sense of being high off the road, as if
hover-powered, is part of what wraps the tingle and warmth of benign
adventure around you as you take your seat.

Downtown Atlanta was looking terrific: big-city, skyscraper architecture with flair—with an emphasis more on slimness than sheer size—and
so light and clean. As we leave on the South Eastern Stage company bus,

the driver intones a splendid list of the places en route. These include Thomson and Augusta, Georgia, and Sumter and Florence, South Carolina; it terminates at Fayetteville, which he pronounces Fateville.

"You sure you wanna go to Thomson?" he asks me playfully. "I think it just closed down and moved."

We drive out along DeKalb, alongside the railroad tracks through modest, leafy clapboard suburbs and past one of those untruthful, upbeat signs that claim you're in a Drug-Free School Zone. The bus is nearly full and I sit near the back alongside a determinedly unchatty young black dude in a baseball cap. We nod at each other. Southern politeness demands nothing less.

First stop is Decatur (rhymes with alligator). Hallowe'en is coming up but there are no pumpkins and skeletons out on these decaying porches. We get onto the Interstate going east. My new companion sleeps in the sunshine.

Heading for Monroe, we're back on a small road, through tall, deep woodland with the odd brick bungalow set in a clearing it has made for itself. One such building says it's the In The Grove Café. The dancing yellows, browns, and greens of the trees, so bright through the windscreen at the front of the bus, are muted through the side windows. Now there are little wooden houses too, and two glistening dark brown horses in a paddock with jumps, and we're back to pumpkin porches.

I've been reading Rebecca Wells' novel about the South of the early twentieth century, *Divine Secrets of the Ya-Ya Sisterhood*, in which she regrets the passing away of the "porch time" that was part of normal life down here in the 1940s. I don't believe it has passed away down in these small Georgia places.

We glimpse a Full Gospel Holiness Church and there's a sudden, brief swathe of grassy farmland on one side of the road. The trees reassert themselves. Every so often there's a self-proclaimed Flea Market. We're on Highway 78 East. A hideous mall signals the nearness of Monroe. There's a Drive Thru Pharmacy & Food Mart, and then we're downtown, which is one set of traffic lights and a small, pretty main street.

Back on the highway the fields grow more frequent and the land less hilly, though it still rolls, slow and luxuriant. We're heading for Athens now—a town that Willie often came to, to play music and to visit friends, including Sister Fleeta Mitchell, whom he'd first met when she was a little girl at the Academy for the Blind in Macon. We cross the Apalachee River and we're thirteen miles away. Turkey vultures circle in clear sky. The "units for sale" in an upscale new housing development look down their well-groomed noses at the scruffy old trailer park all too close by in the woods.

In populous Athens it's 84° Fahrenheit. This town has 30,000 students and 30,000 other people. The bus station is halfway out of town, set back from a busy, shabby street. You can't see much of the city except its detritus from here. When we head out it's through East Athens, past the road to the airport, heading for the landfill.

Inside five minutes the highway has become a one-lane-each-way road again, the stripe of paint down the middle a rich, eggy yellow. We're back in the countryside, with rolling pastures, trees turning autumnal, Baptist churches, farm barns and white clapboard houses: a lovely landscape and an enviable climate.

We head south-east on Highway 78 and soon enter Oglethorpe County, where Willie's cousin Gold Harris' wife Margaret was born. As we race through Lexington, I just have time to gasp at the redbrick high-Victorian Gothic courthouse. Even its name is written in gothic faux-handwriting, like something from a Mötley Crüe album cover. It's gone. We pass Critters Crossing and drive over Buffalo Creek. There are cattle now, and a sign reads "For Sale: Horses Ponies Mules." Mules!

We're out on high rolling plains one minute and down in woody glens the next. There are bales of hay, kudzu, pines, logging trucks, creeks, lakes and a light smattering of traffic.

The earth is red. James Baldwin writes that when he first visited Georgia, in the 1950s, he "could not suppress the thought that this earth had acquired its color from the blood that had dripped down from these trees. My mind was filled with the image of a black man, younger than I, perhaps, or my own age, hanging from a tree, while white men watched him and cut his sex from him with a knife . . ."

We enter Celeste Community, where there are apples and Hot Boiled Peanuts for sale at the roadside. Then we hurry through the neat and pretty little town of Washington, which has a shady square and some fine big old houses.

Back onto 78 East and now we're just twenty-two miles from Thomson. I'm excited—I'm coming, at last, into Blind Willie McTell's home terrain, his first and last territory. A sign points ahead to Wrens (where his first wife, Kate, lived) and right to Warrenton, and now we're entering McDuffie County, in which he was born ninety-five years earlier.

"Boiled Peanuts." "Honey." We're running through heavily wooded hills and past a wildlife management office. The driver is roaring along now. "Hot Dogs." "Sorghum." There are houses and little churches in clearings in the trees. Big Creek, dark and deserted, looks like a large lake to me. A farm, breeding Tennessee Walking Horses, precedes the sign that says "Welcome To Thomson, McDuffie County. Country Living, City Style." Yeah, right.

The bus doesn't stop downtown but out on the highway, just off the interstate, in strip city. The driver asks me again, "You sure you wanna go to Thomson?" and as we pull up in the middle of this nowhere, he adds, "Nobody goes to Thomson. People *leave* Thomson."

I step off the bus. Inside the store, whose every other patron comes and goes by car, I ask about taxis into town. I wait by the counter facing a gigantic, luridly pink bottle of Hannah's Pickled Pigs Feet. I can't resist telling the old lady hidden behind it what the bus driver has said about the town. She bends forward, lowers her voice, and asks, in a well-meaning sort of a whisper, "Was he a white man or . . .?"

Frank the cab driver arrives in an audaciously dilapidated yellow cab, with an unexplained friend in the front seat, and takes me downtown to the rundown Knox Terrace Motel, which, at $36 a night, is far too expensive. The pleasant young Asian woman who receives this observation from me points out that, if I don't like the price, I can always stay somewhere out on strip city instead of downtown.

The room is tiny, smells of roachzap and loneliness, and seems to crumble around me as I survey it.

I ask Frank about car rental and he says he'll phone me later when he's got hold of his friend the car-rental guy. When he does, it's to tell me:

"He says, if you live here, or you rented a car here before, you can rent one. But if you don't live here and you ain't rented a car here before, you can't rent one"—long, long pause—"without a major credit card."

When people say there's nothing in Thomson, they're very nearly right.

There's a quiet grid of leafy streets, and a main street that has no proper shops. When you first find it, just the other side of the rail junction from the Knox Terrace Motel, you think there are shops, but it turns out that there's a hairdressing parlor, a dying womenswear store, where the clothes in the rotten wood-framed windows have been bleached to forlorn and anemic colours by long years in the sun, and a seriously cheap and shoddy supermarket tucked in a corner of the parking lot. All the other shopfronts are dentists' clinics and attorneys' offices pretending to be shops. There's no bakery, no greengrocer, no teashop, no coffeeshop, no butcher's, no newsagent, no drugstore—nothing remotely like that at all.

There is, however, still a small cinema, which, this being Hallowe'en, is showing a trilogy of gore movies. A young man is delighted to show me, when I tell him why I'm in Thomson, the staircase that used to be "blacks only" when McTell was alive. He tells me, too, that it was by no means unusual for blind customers to go to the movies. I look around appreciatively.

Thomson is also completely flat. The only rise is in the surface of the road that carries you across the railroad line right alongside the old brick building that used to be the station: the Thomson Depot. This was built about 1860 and kept on working as a station and telegraph office till 1981. It's nicely preserved, painted two tasteful shades of gray, and now houses the Chamber of Commerce, the Convention and Visitors Bureau, the Tourism Office, and a community center.

Down the side of the main platform, which you see when you cross the single-track trainline from the direction of the Knox Terrace Motel, or driving in from Warrenton or from Wrens, there's a well-maintained sign that reads THOMSON, and then, to one side, it says ATLANTA 134 MILES, and the other way it says AUGUSTA 37 MILES.

The whole of Thomson once centered around the railway. The town is named after the young railroad engineer from Philadelphia who was assigned the surveying and building of the line between Atlanta and Augusta for the Georgia Railroad, the longest line ever built in the US by one company up to that time.

Before Thomson was named after him, it was known as Hickory Level, Frog Pond, and The Slashes, and it was just a village in Columbia County. McDuffie County was carved out of a bit of Columbia County and a bit of Warren County on Tuesday, 18 October 1870.

The station used to be heaving with people, and so did the wide streets outside. Now there's no one: just a few cars parked in a chevron pattern on the far side of the depot building, and, in front of it, alongside the tracks, the minuscule "park" where, in 1911, an association of Civil War veterans erected a memorial statue to "the Wives, Sisters and Mothers of the Sixties."

You come into Thomson now and read this inscription on the side of this small, creamy monument, and, without benefit of any town history at all, you just know that they mean the 1860s, not the 1960s. Undying obsession with the confederacy is everywhere in the South; it's in that warm, soft Southern breeze. The veterans camp was disbanded back in 1922 because "there were few veterans left and those being quite feeble." Their soul goes marching on. But now, on the wall overlooking the depot and the monument, there's the more recent civic effort of a mural depicting some of Thomson's other features—a horse and rider; Thomson High School's AAA State Championship football team, the Bulldogs; the Ray Guy Raiders, 1973–1986; a camellia blossom (because Thomson calls itself the Official Camellia City of the South); the depot and the railroad line (which you might think unnecessary: this mural overlooks the real ones); and a waist-upwards portrait of Blind Willie McTell.

As depicted, he's a thin, pinched man wearing what could be a hunting jacket and helmet or might be a nightwatchman's uniform, he's closing his eyes and holding up a guitar without using his hands, and he looks about as much like Willie as Bill Cosby. But he's there, and if he wasn't blind and closing his eyes, he'd be looking down upon the memorial to the women of the sixties. The Confederate veterans would be appalled.

I decide against the car rental and wait for another cab to take me out to visit Willie's grave, at the Jones Grove Baptist Church at 1062 Happy Valley Road SW. It's about ten miles out of town. The road we travel on, the Wrens Highway, seems narrow and darkly fringed. The pine trees dramatise the way the lonely road stretches thinner and thinner to a distant horizon: it looks as if you can see it for ten miles or more up ahead. This is an illusion. The land bucks and dips like an infinitely stretched country version of a San Francisco hill. I think of Willie walking this road between Thomson and Happy Valley, as he sometimes did—he had a choice of routes—and I can hardly get a grip on the stamina and inner strength he must have had.

At the homely crossroads where Happy Valley Road meets Highway 17, small and ancient signposts for competing churches lean exhaustedly against the fence across the road from the crumbling wooden building and gas station that is the Happy Valley Store. We take a right and ride along past farmland, where sheep and mules share a field, before the trees take over again, accompanying the road for a couple of miles, until suddenly, in a clearing on the left, there's the little white church sitting raised above the grass set back a little way from the road, which curves away out of sight to the left. A mile and a quarter further along it and you'd be in Warren County. All the land around here, I'm told, belongs to an Alex Hobbs.

Between the church and the road lies a little cluster of gravestones. Looking from the graves across the road, a little way off on a slight rise is a line of bungalows set back behind narrow strips of driveway. The smallest one, in very poor condition, up on bricks, is more or less opposite the church. Five small children are playing out in the yard and, as I walk around the front of the church, a tiny yellow dog comes skittering out from between a child's legs and across the road, yapping and throwing itself at me like a deranged guinea pig.

I humor it back across the road to the bungalow, where a stage yokel aged about twenty-one sits on the steps in front of his open door. I can see

46

a dark small room inside, with dirty gray drawn curtains, and, on a sofa stretching the length of the room, the prone figure of another man lying with his head propped up, watching TV.

The stage yokel is stunted, pasty, quiet, polite, and slow-minded: trailer trash to the point of caricature. Instead of watching television, he is watching the world go by, and at one pick-up truck per three minutes, it is probably going by at a pace that suits him. Yet two of the children—blonde slim girls with tangled hair and bare feet, dirty dresses and pretty faces—are bright, sparky, and outgoing. When I explain why I'm walking round the church grounds taking photographs, one child says, "I know where his grave is! I can show you!" She is persuaded to stay put when several others clamor to join the party, and I re-cross the road alone.

The church is open, and a service is in progress, which I don't wish to interrupt but am thrilled to hear, and I loiter in the foyer listening to gospel music with chills up my spine.

The church is no longer clapboard, but has been rebuilt in concrete, and Willie's original, accidentally pseudonymous gravestone is gone. His cousin Eddie "Bo-Rat" McTier had commissioned it and it arrived bearing Eddie's name in place of Willie's. It must have been a little creepy for Eddie to see it, but they went ahead and used it anyway. It was a pleasing, simple stone, with unpretentious lettering, that read EDDIE McTIER 1898—AUG 19 1959 AT REST. This has been taken away by the Atlanta filmmaker and writer David Fulmer, and replaced by the fulsome new one he paid for. You stand there and you can't help but feel robbed of the atmosphere the place has not been allowed to retain.

On a later visit, I went to a service at the church, and talked to the pastor and the deacon. I thought I was going to be late, but when I went in, it was to find that the rather bored and gloomy Sunday-school session that precedes the grown-up service was still murmuring along.

The interior is red and white: white walls, with red plastic over the several sets of rectangular windows, letting red light in down each side of a long, wide room. There's a muted red carpet, and a wide central walkway flanked by nine wide, red-upholstered benches on each side framed in wood veneer. Each bench could hold six people comfortably, or eight to ten squashed together. Up at the front, facing the congregation, is an assemblage of wooden tables and chairs in honey-colored oak, and two rows of wooden benches facing these sideways on. Behind all this runs a little white-painted fence, making a sort of stall all across the front end, with old white wooden pews beyond it for the choir, and with a piano at one side and a drum kit at the other. Above this choir stall, an extravagance of white curtaining forms a pelmet across the room.

When I walked in and sat at the back, there was a woman sitting with three small children on one of the benches near the front—children barely able to see over the top of the bench ahead of them. They seemed to have been left to talk among themselves while the pastor, the Rev. Robert J. Mixon, was clearing up some kind of theological misunderstanding with a voluble, cuboid, very dark-skinned man in a voluminous smart brown suit, who proved to be the deacon. In contrast, Rev. Mixon was tall, thin, sallow, and balding, with understanding, wearied eyes.

It was early November, but the air was humid and subdued. A woman came round the near-empty church with a collection plate. I put in a dollar. The service resumed briefly for a closing prayer, and a morose young man came forward and declared: "We thank you, Lord, for the six dollars."

As things seemed to have fallen apart, I went up and introduced myself to the pastor, who summoned the deacon. The deacon looked well-to-do and more than a little self-important, and I thought of all those blues songs from the 1920s, which probably took their lyrics from much earlier down-home songs—blues about greedy deacons who come around and eat your food and hit on your wife while you're out laboring hard in the fields. (The pioneering old Memphis singer Frank Stokes, 1887–1955, is very good at these splendid anti-clerical rants.)

I kept these thoughts to myself. I explained that I wanted to learn about Willie's relationship with the church, and even where in the room he'd sat when he came to sing and play. The pastor somehow faded himself away as if it were nothing to do with him, and the deacon gave me a leery look and started into his own version of the not uncommon rap about how I was going to be making money from this and, therefore, so should the church—and I gave him the usual futile rap back about how, if I was

48

in it for the money, I'd have chosen a different line of work, adding that I was trying to write an honorable book that dealt with McTell not only as a blues singer, but also as a religious man with an interesting relationship to the church.

They said they'd talk to me at the end of the service, and was I going to stay for that? I said, well, was I welcome to attend?

"You are always welcome in the house of God."

"Oh, OK then."

I don't think an outsider to Southern culture should assume that whites would be welcome in black churches, or blacks in white. The very fact that the churches are separate comes as a surprise, at first, to foreigners. That separateness seems a very visible illustration of how much segregation still perpetuates itself, forty years after it was meant to be dismantled. It's the same now as when Martin Luther King Jr lamented that "the most segregated hour of Christian America is eleven o'clock on Sunday morning."

Everywhere you go in Georgia there is a superabundance of Baptist churches, and one reason for this is that, in every community, you need one for the black worshippers and another for the white. When they split into factions, you need twice as many new ones for the same reason. There is also, of course, a ready supply of all the other versions of Protestantism. In Statesboro, the almost-octagenarian Naomi Johnson told me with some emphasis: "The Baptists ain't no more segregated than the Methodists or the others."

The history of this segregation of worship in the South is, of course, that black Americans were unwelcome and discriminated against in the early church. Not *right* at the beginning, perhaps. And that beginning goes back to before the docking of the *Mayflower*. But, as early as the eighteenth century, African-American Methodists in Philadelphia and New York broke with their white counterparts because of discrimination against them that included prohibiting black ministers from preaching to racially mixed congregations.

In the slavery era, Southern whites would bring their slaves to church—and slaves were forbidden to work on the sabbath—to make sure they got the Biblical message that slaves were duty-bound to obey their masters. Which didn't work, of course: the most potent Bible story for African Americans became the story of the escape from slavery in Egypt, as the great wealth of black spiritual and gospel music shows.

In any case, slave owners seemed as confused as their slaves were likely to be by these mixed messages about the soul. In Jenkins County, Georgia, which lies north of Statesboro, there is a lone slave grave erected by a Jones Johnson, to which you're likely to respond in a mixed way yourself. It reads: "To the memory of Kit, who I shot by accident while hunting. He died in faith. May his ashes rest in peace till the day when all shall meet, 12, 27, 1855."

When slavery gave way to legalised segregation, the racial divide was widely maintained in the churches of the South, and many black churches were founded to provide an alternative to the insult experienced in white ones. In Catholic churches too, blacks were given separate pews, separate places at the communion rail, and in the graveyard.

Similarly, in civic cemeteries all over the South, you'll find a large, well-maintained white section and a smaller, scruffier black section—even in towns where the white population is smaller than the black. You'll also find that the funeral-home business is racially separated—completely separated.

The core point is, though, that for most black Americans in the South today, having a separate church is a boon: it's a segregation voluntarily entered into. The kneel-ins at white churches in the years of the Civil Rights struggle were making a point, rather than a religious demand.

There is another factor, too. The black church can often seem to be upholding the same right-wing values, the same conservative positions, as the white church in the Bible belt, just as the Christian church in Africa does. Unlike the intellectual liberal urban churches of New England and their like-minded allies in Old England, the black church in the Southern states of the US is just as anti-gay marriage and anti-abortion as George W. Bush's Religious Right. Yet the black church keenly dissociates itself from the Republican Party's version of God and worship. At the headquarters of the Church of God in Christ in Memphis—an evangelical church that split off from the baptists in the early 1900s and was founded by the son of

50

slaves—presiding bishop G.E. Patterson says: "I've seen the tone of the religious right. It seemingly was born out of the fact that African Americans were making too many gains. Every law that has anything to do with leveling the playing field for blacks, they are against it."

There's also a strong divergence along racial lines in preferred styles of church service. It's telling that the black churches that are doing best today tend to be those whose style of worship is the most clamorous, demonstrative, and musically hot. In other words, the least like white styles of liturgical deportment. Black Americans probably don't like what the British comedian Jeremy Hardy calls "the unedifying spectacle of white people trying to clap in time."

For all these reasons, the separate black church is now what black worshippers want.

Nonetheless, here at Blind Willie McTell's old church in Happy Valley, I was made welcome. I walked to the back of the church to wait for the grown-ups' service to begin. A young woman at the entrance, one of the two designated ushering staff, handed me a blue leaflet giving service details and a pink printed sheet that welcomed visitors.

A few people straggled in. Three women, the middle one probably only about thirteen, spread themselves across the front bench of the choir stall. The lugubrious young man who'd totted up the proceeds of the Sunday-school collection stood behind them, looking very tall. At the same time as being the choir, they were sharing the job of looking after two very young children, one just old enough to run about a bit and have to be fetched back from the piano and the drums—usually by the young man—and the other, in a babygro, just old enough to go "la la la" in gaps in the proceedings, and to stretch out her arms touchingly to be picked up by her mother from time to time.

The deacon and an assistant deacon (also in a brown suit) stood by the honey-colored tables and the minister took up his place with a high-backed chair behind him, and things got under way.

First the deacon stood behind the table and shimmied slowly from side to side, his hands stuck out sideways but his arms kept down at his sides, and began an unaccompanied chanting song, with long, eccentrically

51

extended lines that moved from low down to a few higher notes and down again, marking out the rhythm with parallel shivering movements of his body. Others joined in behind him with humming and handclaps. I don't know what song it was. Then, while he carried on with another chanted kind of song, kept quiet and low, the assistant deacon alongside him got down on one knee and intoned a long, spoken prayer as counterpoint. They both achieved the same low volume, and I couldn't hear what was being said. It was no less effective for that.

Then the pastor stood up behind them and said a few words and announced the choir, and they sang several songs—rarely in unison. It was mostly chant and response, the way that preacher's daughter Aretha Franklin does it in secular song. A short woman on one side took the lead and sang confidently and well. She turned out to be the assistant pastor, Sister Shonta Y. Smith. The singing from the congregation was timid and lacklustre, but there were only seventeen people in the room, including the small children who couldn't see over the pew in front of them, the children up in the choir stall, and me.

For the hour and a half of the service, prayer and sermonising were interspersed with song, but far more regularly the speechifying from the deacon was supported by interjections from the assistant pastor up front and from the ladies on the doors behind.

"That's right!" "Sure 'nough!" "He do! Yes He do!"

When the pastor started sermonising, he was supported not only by these stalwarts, but by the deacon too, who had moved to a pew that faced the pulpit area.

"That's right, Rev.!" "Tell it, Rev.!" "Sure 'nough!" "Say it, Rev., say it!"

This was so odd yet so familiar to me from the copycat oratorical devices employed in soul music and rock'n'roll ("Are you ready?" "Yeah!!" "I said, are you ready?!" "Yeah!!!" "Awright!"). By halfway through the service, it had come to seem as normal and natural as the genteel silences of a Church of England congregation.

The main portion of the service began only now. It consisted of the pastor's own leading of prayers, and (to me) the most extraordinary sermon. This had two strong, distinctive features. The dominant one was that he spoke millimeters from a very poor quality microphone, so that only when he thrust his head back a couple of feet with an emphatic jerk did he cease to be horribly, indecipherably distorted. No microphone was needed in that room.

The other feature was the effective, impressive way that his sermon shifted imperceptibly from spoken mode to sung: a most compelling shift, achieved first by tacking a long, sustained "mmmmmmm" onto the end of each of a long series of rhythmically repetitive sentences that were reflective and ruminative in character. By this process, which was surely of ancient and African origin, the Rev. Mixon's initially quiet, mild words became an intense, dramatic meditation. The long, slow, insistent build of it was masterly and its drama was sustained over a lengthy period. It was quite an experience.

Towards the end, there was much praying for the sick of the community—for specific, named individuals (including Sally Cramer, the elderly daughter of Willie's friend and cousin Gold Harris, whom I was going to interview later that day)—and for those unable to be there that day and those who were housebound: "the sick and shut-in members."

At long last it was over and a number of people shook my hand and said hi, and after that we went outside and I was able to chat to the pastor, the deacon, a lady on her way back to her white Mercedes, and an elderly woman who looked equal parts fragile and rigid.

We walked over to stand amongst the gravestones—they pointed out Gold Harris' for me—and became much more friendly and forthcoming. Rev. Mixon was quiet by nature, but also remained so because he had only arrived here in 1991, whereas the others had lived here all their lives.

The deacon told me his name was Jasper L. Burnett and he made sure I wrote his name down and told me firmly that he was also chairman of the Deacon Board. I asked him if he were related to the Margaret Burnett who had formally married Gold Harris when both were very senior citizens in the 1980s, and he said, "Yeah, sure, we're all kin." I think this was meant in a genealogical, rather than a theological, sense, but he couldn't quite say what his relationship to Margaret was, saying instead that he had always called Gold Harris "Uncle Gold." I said but everybody called him Uncle Gold, didn't they, and he laughed and said yes. He said, too, that Gold and Margaret had been married anyway, long before. They clearly regarded the 1980s ceremony as just that: a ceremony.

As the level of co-operation grew warmer and as they started to enjoy the reminiscing, the lady with the white Mercedes told me she was Flory Mae McNair, maiden name Moss; that her husband's name was Harvey McNair, and that his aunt Annie Jackson was sister to Hazel McTier (the deceased wife of Willie's also deceased cousin, Eddie "Bo-Rat" McTier). I learned later, from talking to the said Annie Jackson, that *her* mother's maiden name was Moss too.

They couldn't tell me who was in the graves with indecipherable lettering just to the left of Willie's, but they could tell me that there were no church records that would tell me that.

They told me that, in January 1992, shortly after the Rev. Mixon arrived, they'd pulled down the clapboard and the tin roof and rebuilt the church. But, they said proudly, they made sure they didn't pull down the big old tree in the clearing, where people used to tether their mules, and they showed me which one it was and I took its picture.

"Of course," I said, "it's a pity the church isn't clapboard anymore because it was, you know, prettier."

They laughed.

"Well, it may have been prettier, but it was all tore up," said the deacon.

"Specially the floor," said Flory Mae. "It was bad."

"So it was prettier but it was falling down?"

"Yes," said the Rev. "It was falling down."

Actually—and I want to say characteristically—they're wrong about the date of the rebuild. Duncan Hume's photographs of the church are from November 1992, and it's still clapped-out clapboard then, just about holding together under its three-stepped tin roof. Its small, wonky, wooden tower totters upward from tin rusted the same rich brown as the autumn leaves below, and sports a jaunty tin hat.

This must have been its last go-round. They'd already thrown out an exhausted piano, which Hume photographed decaying grotesquely outside the church, its open keyboard collecting more brown leaves and its thin strips of wood veneer curling and peeling away from the contorted frame like skin off a desiccating corpse.

We stood by the graves looking over towards the church, with the road running past on our left. Behind us, in a left-fork sort of direction, you could be looking towards the patch of land on Sand Hill Road where all these McTiers had lived. The deacon suddenly said, "Well, see, I remember Willie."

"Oh yes," said Flory Mae.

I was surprised. Neither of them looked old enough.

"You remember Willie himself?"

"Oh yeah," said Jasper. "See, we was little children and we was scared of him, 'cause he was a blind man. He'd walk anywhere, all around, by himself—"

"Even at night!" said Flory Mae. I wondered if night made any difference to Willie. People's comments tended to vary on whether he could discern light.

"Yeah, we was frightened by him, just 'cause he was blind and an old man," said Jasper. "He'd be sitting by hisself in that room over there," meaning over at one at one of his relatives' houses off Sand Hill Road, "and we'd peep at him and then dart back!"

"He'd be sat there, sometimes with his guitar, sometimes not. Plus he wouldn't say a whole lot."

This, of course, was the Willie of his last days. They didn't remember his funeral, though. As children, they hadn't gone.

The deacon reiterated, as we were getting ready to go our separate ways, that, if I made a lot of money, I was to remember to give some to their church. There was a woman he wanted to tell me about, as a good example of this charity in action.

"This lady—I can't remember her name. Her daddy knew McTell real well."

"Oh, d'you mean Curley Weaver's daughter, Cora Mae Bryant?"

"Yes! That's it, Cora Mae. She comes back 'bout once a year and she *always* makes a donation. We gave her the bench. You know, the bench that Willie used to sit on and play guitar and sing when he used to come and play on Revival Days."

"Oh!" I said. "Now I see! I went to talk to her and she showed me this little pale gray bench that she said Willie used to sit on, but I didn't realise it came from this church! Ah, now I understand!" And I felt much better about the bench, which I'd seen marooned in the middle of Cora Mae Bryant's careeningly surreal "museum", in a tiny side room of her small house in Oxford, Georgia—one small, solid item, half-hidden under swirls of ephemera labeled unreliably where labeled at all, in a room you pay to be allowed to peer into. Now I felt better about my visit there: satisfied as to the bench's authenticity, and the veracity of Cora Mae's claim. Reluctantly, I felt a fibrillation of gratitude to this very hostile old woman for having shown it to me.

Ms Bryant lives in a small white shack on a suburban street in Oxford, which these days merges into Covington, her father Curley Weaver's home town. He was one of Willie's greatest fellow-guitarist friends, and certainly the one with whom Willie teamed up best in recording studios, before and after World War II. Cora Mae's house has a pretty front yard of rich red earth flanked by two big oak trees and a lovely catalpa.

I had tried to phone in advance of calling on her, but had failed to get an answer and turned up on spec, as I had on many a doorstep before without meeting anything but kindness after those moments of initial suspicion, when you're explaining yourself outside somebody's screen door while they stay on the inside where you can't look them in the eyes.

Almost always, I found that being English was to my advantage. White Georgians relaxed because I wasn't a Yankee; African Americans relaxed because I wasn't a white Georgian.

Not Cora Mae. I knock on her door. A disembodied voice: "Yeah?"
I explain.
The same bored voice shouts "Mama!"
Mama comes to the door: another old lady in a blatant black wig. She's seventy-five, tall, comely, with perfectly smooth-skinned upper arms. She's wearing a sleeveless black dress and glasses. She has a very booming, dark voice and an unfriendly face. I'm allowed to come in and sit down on the narrow strip of verandah immediately inside the screen door.

She bridles as soon as I tell her what I want, which is an interview about her father's life with Willie. I find the detail of her sentences hard to grasp but the gist very clear: "I've been ripped off by you people—and that's you white people." Which no doubt she has, but who hasn't? Undisguised hostility is still highly unusual in these parts.

She asks me if I've heard of various people whose names she slurs. I say no, and she expresses contempt. She asks if I've heard of various others, and I have. She expresses disbelief and contemptuous unimpressedness. She launches into a rather poor parody of hillbilly singing to prove that white music is worthless and tells me that we white people have no history, we know nothing, and that having mistreated her people forever, now we come along wanting their music and their knowledge too. We're not going to get it from her. The Georgia Music Hall of Fame, she spits out, wants stuff from her; they're not going to get it and neither am I.

And I'd better not go out to the graveyard at Almon to take photos of Curley Weaver's grave, either. If I'm seen out there without a black person with me, someone'll call the police. I've no right to be there: it's just for black people. "You stay away. I'm going to keep my information. I've built my own museum in my house."

It's a room about twelve foot square, darkened except for little leakages of light from outside and lights on inside in the middle of the blazing afternoon, and tiny yellow Christmas lights on black plastic-coated wires looped around the far wall. Behind them, folds of yellow cloth hang down the wall from ceiling to knee height.

Stuck to the walls and the hangings of cloth are random photographs of very minor celebs embracing Cora Mae, photocopies of old photos and newspaper cuttings and, hanging from the ceiling, several large blow-up photocopies of parts of pages from the sleevenotes to the LP *Atlanta Blues 1933*, issued in 1979, including the lovely photograph reproduced within those notes of Curley Weaver as a baby on his serenely dignified mother's knee, which Cora Mae lent in the 1970s to the white folklorist Peter B. Lowry, whom she now says "will have to answer to God for what he's done," though she doesn't say what that is and Lowry himself has no idea.

Superficially there's a parallel with the case of Willie's gravestone here—for Peter B. Lowry replaced Curley Weaver's original marker. He didn't remove an original gravestone, though: he had one installed where there was none before. And he's adamant that this was done with Cora Mae's blessing. "She was pleased at the time," he tells me, "because before that there was just one of those little metal funeral-home things with a piece of paper in it."

One of her photocopy blow-ups is of a photograph of this grave, a photograph taken by the white folklorist, cultural anthropologist and photographer Cheryl Thurber (then Cheryl Evans), reproduced from the same LP's sleevenotes. I mention that I recognise the photo. Cora Mae denies that Cheryl Evans took the photo and says she's never heard of her.

She wants $10 to let me look at her "museum," and $20 for a copy of a blues CD she has made (on which she's supported by two young white guitarists). She tells me she has the bench that Willie McTell used to sit on. Where from? "Don't ask me where from!" She was given it after he died. Why was it given to her? "Why?! Because I deserved it! I deserved it all!" The money from McTell's records, Curley Weaver's records, Buddy Moss' records: it should have all been hers . . .

What about his partner Helen's family?

"Pah! I knew Helen. They can make her look black all they want but her mother was *white!*"

So, did you go to Willie's funeral? I ask.

"No."

In the end she sells me the CD and the museum entry for $20 combined, and there's still no question of an interview. She walks me through a slender curtained doorway and shows me, in the clutter of this inner sanctum, a dove-gray painted church pew, just long enough for two people to sit on. It's the first time I've seen an object touched by Blind Willie himself. She hurries me out of this room, saying I might have a hidden tape-recorder.

Outside in the yard as I'm leaving I say hello to her tiny dog, which grins at me. "Don't take no photos of *my* house," she says in farewell.

Back at Jones Grove Baptist Church, I showed the deacon and the pastor a photograph of Willie's original gravestone, because they said they couldn't remember it. They were pleased to see it, and fond of it immediately. I told them about David Fulmer having replaced it with the big new one when he'd been making his documentary film *Blind Willie's Blues* in the 1990s, and how he'd told me that no one had seemed to want the old one at the time, and he didn't want to think that it might get dumped, so he'd taken it away in his rented van and put it in his own front yard.

The deacon and Rev. Mixon wanted to phone up Fulmer on the spot and demand the old gravestone back. I asked if they would mind waiting till I'd finished my research first, and they readily agreed.

We parted warmly, with them urging me to visit the church again next time. They drove away. I stood again for a few minutes at the foot of Willie's grave, and then I drove away too.

# FOUR

I'M IN THE Howard Johnson's on the strip that runs out of Thomson, straight and flat and north, and takes you to the Interstate (turn right for Augusta, left for Atlanta). In the lobby a notice reads "For night services please ring Zol and Use Loby phone. Thanking you by manager." Many of today's motel managers are from the Indian subcontinent.

From my room I can see a field, a bungalow, a rich line of tall green trees and many different bushes; I can see the Holiday Inn Express, the Econolodge, the Best Western, the Western Sizzlin', Denny's, Waffle House, Wendy's, McDonald's, Burger King, and Long John Silver's. It's always the same view from these hotels on the strip. If you can't see a McDonald's from your window, you can always see an ad for one on a billboard shining malevolently at you through the orange night.

In so much of the US, once you're out of the cities, this really is what people eat. These places call themselves family restaurants, and families really do go and have sit-down meals in them. Meals without alcohol. Here you are in this vast acreage of plastic banquettes and paper cups and fried food and smiling servers paid virtually nothing but their tips, and out of the window across the parking lot there are other near-identical eateries everywhere you look—and no one seems to care that the food is so gross or that you can't be a grown-up and have a drink.

The very idea of dinner as a real meal, naturally accompanied by glasses of wine—this fundamental pleasure, this daily benefit of civilisation— seems utterly absent from North American consciousness outside the big cities, as if they've had a social and culinary lobotomy and haven't noticed.

The fast-food chains need people to be marooned in this swollen infancy, so that what the punter thinks of as keenness of appetite never develops into an interest in food, but remains an atavistic craving to stuff the face. The punter, of course, is the real fodder here.

In Willie McTell's day at least the chicken would have been free range.

Another visit. I'd reached Thomson, by car again this time, late on the last evening of January, 2004. It was Saturday night. There was no one on the downtown streets except a plump, doleful black youth in a knitted pudding-basin hat, loitering in the entrance area of the cinema, right alongside the NO LOITERING notice. (US officialdom is obsessed with loitering, and is forever telling you not to. Bus stations sometimes welcome you with this warning: "Absolutely No Loitering, Profanity, Panhandling . . .")

In my room at the White Columns Inn I found I'd been left a quirky package of goodies by the lady from the Thomson Convention and Visitors Bureau: magazines and a T-shirt, postcards and notelets, a mug with chocolates and sweets inside, a packet of Nutter Butter biscuits, a packet of Oreos, cans of fizzy drinks, plus—and I was grateful for this—a small can of Michelob Light, a small and unattractive bulwark against the teetotalism of Thomson on the sabbath. You have to drive thirty-seven miles to Augusta to buy a beer on Sundays.

The 1st of February was a sharp, cold, windy morning. The guest-use computer wasn't working. They phoned the Holiday Inn Express across the street and asked if I could use theirs. Yes I could. I drove across. (Getting from one side of the highway to the other on foot is absurd. I know this from experience.) In the Holiday Inn lobby a preposterously showbiz black church sermon blazed away on a huge flat screen. I fought their computer for an hour and then went to the Waffle House for a coffee. It must have been the only Waffle House in the entire South with no black person either side of the counter.

I wanted to see if I could find the Mount Pleasant Road route, the back road route, from downtown Thomson to Happy Valley—that nine-and-a-half-mile road Willie sometimes walked between town and his cousins' houses. In daylight it's a very pretty road. In the night, what a long, dark road it seems, and that's when you're gliding along on tarmac in a twenty-first-century automobile. On and on it runs, winding through the cold pines. How much more long and lonely it must have been for Willie. Again, I had to wonder whether, visually, daylight made any difference to him.

Suddenly, as I drove, thirty feet or so up ahead on my left a deer materialised like a wraith at the roadside. She was the near-invisible color of dead pine needles and she was bending her long neck down to eat at the verge. Her raised eyes caught in the headlights. She held their gaze for a long moment and then she pulled her neck up as she turned around to face the woods and, with ineffable grace, she leapt, as if over a fence, back into her natural domain.

These woods that are the deer's refuge are so eerie and unsettling for us. Walk a hundred yards down one of these dirt roads, even in daylight, and you start to feel you've lost your shell. "I ain't goin' down that dirt road by myself," as an old blues song has it.

After the defeat of the South and the end of slavery, we enter the time of Reconstruction. This is shortlived, and almost no white Southerner has a good word to say for it.

In Georgia it began with the passing of two post-abolition laws in 1865: an Act to define "persons of color" (defined now as anyone of $1/8^{th}$ "negro" or "African" blood) and offer a declaration of their rights—this Act repealed "all laws in relation to slaves and free persons of color which militate against this Act"—and another that prescribed and regulated "the relationship of husband and wife between free persons of color." Those living together as husband and wife were deemed legally married (if both consented), while those living with multiple partners were required to pick one.

The war itself had caused little direct damage in this part of Georgia, except for the toll it had taken on the lives of the young men who had gone off to fight, and on their families. Major General William T. Sherman's burning of Atlanta and his subsequent March to the Sea were the sole direct assaults on Georgia soil.

His route on the March was east-south-east from Atlanta to Savannah, through the towns of Covington, Madison, Eatonton (destined later to be the birthplace of Joel Chandler Harris—the man who gave us Uncle

Remus, Brer Rabbit and the Tar Baby—and, less famously, birthplace of a singer called Peg Leg Howell), Milledgeville (the state capital), Macon, Gordon, Sandersville, Louisville, Millen, and Ogeechee. This route took Sherman's troops nowhere near Thomson—nowhere, in fact, near Warren, Glascock, or McDuffie Counties.

Where they did march, crops and bridges were often burned not by Union troops, but by resisting Confederates, who towards the end planted landmines in the roads. "This was not war, but murder," Sherman wrote later. His response was to put his Confederate prisoners at the front of the columns of marchers. News of this went ahead of them, and the laying of landmines stopped. Southern histories tend to demonise the march, claiming that Sherman devastated everywhere in his path, but when you visit these places you find that their own tourist literature boasts of how by their bravery and cunning, and by the sheer beauty of their particular township, they managed to stop Sherman burning anything much.

The indirect devastation caused by the war was another matter. The economy of the South was paralysed, Confederate money worthless, the plantation system in collapse, and the new free-labor market unsettled. Livestock was almost 50 per cent down on pre-war levels. Many white landowners became what they termed "land poor"—which didn't mean that they no longer owned land, but that they owned far more than they were capable of cultivating or of paying the taxes on.

The liberation of Georgia's 400,000 slaves had begun in wartime, and Sherman's troops had liberated more along the route of the March to the Sea—rather against his wishes: he regarded these thousands of freed camp-followers as a hindrance and a burdensome expense, which, militarily speaking, they were.

Liberation accelerated after the South's surrender. Many ex-slaves felt marooned, with nowhere to go and little idea what lay ahead. Laura Smalley spoke for many when she was interviewed in 1941 about the end of her family's slavery days: "Mama and them didn't know where to go, you see, after freedom broke. Just turned, just like you turn something out, you know. Didn't know where to go. That's just where they stayed."

The *Georgia Encyclopedia* entry on Emancipation, written in 2003, says that black Georgians often began to test their freedom in small ways: "They took a few hours off work, or they wore their finest clothes, to promenade through city streets." Others took bolder steps, with very large numbers streaming away from the countryside into the cities—mostly to Savannah and Atlanta, but also into smaller towns, instead of remaining in rural areas.

Those who stayed behind "hoped to separate themselves completely from their old masters by becoming landowners themselves. That independence was nearly achieved by a few, primarily those who settled on the coastal reserve set aside for their exclusive use by Sherman." But most freed blacks failed to take possession of land of their own and many were compelled to work for the same people they had worked for as slaves. These former slaveowners tried to keep things the same—even including the use of overseers armed with whips. "In the lexicon of the day, liberated slaves would live and 'work as heretofore.'" But they refused. They no longer "apprenticed" their children unpaid to Georgia planters; they exercised a new legal right to prosecute employers who used the whip; they shortened the working week; they got paid. They began to organise their own education and worship.

At any rate, those ex-slaves who had envisaged a future freed from the dictates of the annual harvest, free of hard agricultural labor, and of gross inequalities at every turn, found that such visions were not shared by the Freedmen's Bureau agents, whose vision was only to see slaves become employees and their former owners become employers. This was seen as the route to restoring the economic prosperity of the South. There was no Plan B.

In this situation, "Georgians—black and white—hammered out a compromised freedom. For better or worse, most freedpeople henceforth sought their living through paid labor, usually on white-owned plantations."

Virginia H. Wilhoit's *History of Warren County, Georgia 1793–1974* was written and first published in the 1930s, and you might feel that still nastier than the views expressed then is the fact that the text was so minimally updated when the book was reissued in the 1970s. Without any amendment of these telling 1930s views, the book sits there still, in the public library at Warrenton, where the county's black citizens can still encounter, not as the history of the history, but as history itself, material like this, which is how the book's Chapter 10, titled "Negroes," begins:

The Negroes of Warren County are a peace-loving, quiet, respectful race. They are industrious and thrifty. Many of them have acquired homes and lands, and only the aged and infirm ask or expect aid from their white friends.

On very rare occasions do troubles arise, and then the Negroes, as well as the whites, are willing and eager for justice to be meted.

There has always been a very close tie between the whites and blacks of Warren County. It began in slavery time when the masters and mistresses loved and cared for their slaves. When the Emancipation Proclamation was declared, many of the slaves were fearful of leaving the protective care of "Ol' Marster". Some remained faithful and loyal and refused to take advantage of the opportunity to strike out for themselves.

Two pages later comes this elaboration:

The masters were generally kind and considerate of the slaves' comfort and welfare. There were some owners who were tyrannical and mean to their slaves, as they were mean to their families and other people. Generally, masters were indulgent, and loved and took great pride in the health and happiness of their slaves.

And "Slaves were not necessarily unhappy . . . The economic worries of providing food, clothing, housing, fuel, and comfort for the enormous investment in labor were the responsibility of the slave owner."

It wasn't only in artless local histories that these views were being expressed, as I found when I visited the Georgia Historical Society's marvellously fusty library in Savannah. It's on a street that starts out quite menacingly shabby at one end, but grows more and more leafily colonial and calm, and the building looks to have been a sizeable private house. There is nothing to tell you it's the library: you just have to know the address.

Inside, beyond a vestibule and behind double front doors, you step into a vast, musty brown room two storeys high, with a spindly wrought-iron balcony running all the way around the upper storey of shelving—the whole place acting out as dustily and decrepitly as possible its rôle as your typical antebellum mansion library. Everything is brown, old, and hushed. Even the woodwork creaks in whispers. The room's old air tingles with book spores and weevil dust.

I was the first visitor of the day, so I was able to receive, when I sought guidance, a good deal of supercilious steering about from a very thin, very white young woman with a strong opinion of herself and a relish for the many arcane quirks of the place and the power they permit her over the novice.

The library's manuscript collection has slave bills of sale, slave manifests, photographs of slave huts, data on fugitive slaves, care of slaves, correspondence about slaves, and much else.

Among their enormous collection of books, I found a copy of *Plantation Slavery in Georgia*, by Ralph Betts Flanders, published by the University of North Carolina in 1933. This contains much valuable material, but it is also revealing in other ways. Flanders has to feel defensive about offering a book on this subject at all, noting that "It is the current opinion that the field of American Negro slavery has been exhausted by historians, and that specialised studies are unnecessary." He is protesting, rightly, at the preposterousness of this "current opinion," but his own opinions, revealing the respectable 1930s academic's unapologetic position, encompass this: "It can hardly be denied that Negroes have a comparatively low standard of morals . . ."

Of course, this wasn't every 1930s academic's view, and the same decade also gave us John Dollard's lovely landmark study *Caste and Class in a Southern Town*, which is always rigorous, alert, and warm-spirited. Here, from 1937, is what *he* had to say about the switch from slavery to Reconstruction at the end of the Civil War:

The folk sense of the South, habituated to the subordination of the Negro, reacted to reconstruction by intensified pressure for his subordination . . . the defeated South turned its spent and fruitless hostility for the North to the Negroes who were in part the cause of the conflict. Southerners could not avenge themselves directly against the North, but could and did take action against the Negroes for whom the North had fought.

Dollard argues that "slavery was a method of subordinating Negroes which, once established, did not require continuous, active white pressure for its maintenance, but tended to fall into routine . . . The caste system, on the other hand, is a less secure method of subordinating Negroes, and, at least while it is being imposed, requires quite active aggression against them. From this standpoint it appears that the relative infrequency of lynchings under slavery was evidence of the fixity of the subordinate rôle of the Negro."

But, as you'd expect from someone writing in terms of "caste," Dollard also weighs up the changes within white society:

The aristocratic domination of southern politics was destroyed by the Civil War, and during reconstruction the poorer white people were increasingly admitted to political participation and power; otherwise they might have combined with similarly disadvantaged Negroes. In this sense the white South did indeed become more "solid", in that more white men achieved a formal stake in the operation of the political system. Whites were needed at first to outweigh Negro votes . . . To some extent the traditional rivalry of these poorer white people with Negroes became conventionalized as the total white attitude.

But, when he scrutinises the Southern town, he finds that "the poorer whites show less than the predicted resentment of Negroes and the middle-class whites much more."

With all this in mind, let's go back to that little patch of land where Warren County, Glascock County, and McDuffie County come together: that home patch of the McTiers around Happy Valley.

★   ★   ★

It's the 1870s, and McDuffie County is still new. It's named after a dreadful old presbyterian lawyer and politican from the region, George McDuffie, born in what was then part of Columbia County in 1790. This is part of a speech he delivered to the South Carolina legislature in 1835:

> No human institution, in my opinion, is more obviously in keeping with the will of God than slavery. No one of His laws is written in plainer letters than the law which says this is the happiest condition for the African.
>
> That the African was meant to be a slave is clear. It is marked on his face, stamped on his skin, and proved by the intellectual inferiority and natural helplessness of this race. They have none of the qualities that fit them to be free men. They are totally unsuited both for freedom and for self-government of any kind. They are, in all respects, physically, morally, and politically inferior.
>
> From an excess of labor, poverty, and trouble our slaves are free. They usually work from two to four hours a day less than workers in other countries. They usually eat as much wholesome food in one day as an English worker or Irish peasant eats in two. And as for the future, slaves are envied even by their masters. Nowhere on earth is there a class of people so perfectly free from care and anxiety.

Ah. We seem to be back here again. But at least this is a hundred years earlier than the uncomfortably similar views being published with cheerful lack of abashment in the South of the 1930s.

Nevertheless, this was the hero after whom McDuffie County was named, and whose name is therefore perpetuated on the respectful lips of African Americans in this part of Georgia even today. This is the name of the county that Willie McTell was born in, just up the road from where his white great-grandfather was living—a great-grandfather who must surely have had slightly different views on matters of race.

Reddick McTyeir married local girl Mary Brooks, on Sunday, 14 November 1869, nine days short of her twenty-sixth birthday. Reddick was forty-three. Mary came to live in his house, sharing it with his son

Elbert. Within a year, Elbert had a white half-sister, Beatie. Mary and Reddick would have five more children, including a set of twins.

There is no further trace of Elbert's mother, the slave girl Essey. If she were still alive, she would have been coming up to twenty-five years old, and free, but she's not mentioned in the 1870 census.

We know almost nothing of Reddick and Essey's relationship. It might have been full of love, conversation, kindness, tragic depth of feeling. It might not. The sole thing we know is that he had had all the power—the power of ownership.

When McDuffie County comes into existence, Larkin McTyeire is living on the other side of the state, at Americus, in Sumter County. The others are all a stone's throw from McDuffie, in Glascock County, and the black McTyres will drift that little bit further, right into McDuffie, soon enough.

Reddick is there in Glascock, living with his young wife Mary and eleven-year-old Elbert. Two houses away, Reddick's father Kendall and second wife Rebecca are still alive, at seventy-eight and sixty-five respectively. He's still farming; she's still a "Domestic." These are not rich people.

At the house in between son and father, the household entirely consists of black McTyres: namely Govoner, aged twenty-seven, a farm laborer; Sallie, aged twenty-three, a laborer; and two daughters, aged eleven and one, Emma and Dellia. Emma is already working as a "Domestic". (These spellings tend to demonstrate, as so often, that the census enumerators were almost as illiterate as the interviewees.) Govoner—or Governor, as he's called elsewhere—would have been a slave until the age of twenty-two. The only member of his family not born in slavery is Dellia.

We can be sure that Governor had been a slave of the white McTyeires. He had almost certainly belonged to Kendall, and almost certainly not to Reddick. (In the 1860 Georgia Agricultural Census Reddick's slave holdings were Essey, Elbert, and a boy stated to be ten years old; Governor would have been around seventeen at the time.) What we don't know is whether Governor was also related to Elbert's mother Essey, and, therefore, in due course, to Blind Willie McTell.

69

On the other side of Reddick's farmstead, the next house is occupied by his war-veteran brother Solomon, now thirty-four, and wife Milley, aged thirty-two. They have three children: a one-year-old boy named after his uncle, Reddick L; Mary, aged eight; and Savanah, aged eleven. This white eleven-year-old is not a "Domestic."

Reddick's sister, Synthian, who married silversmith and watchmaker George Guimarin when she was fifteen, has not fared so well. There's no information on their first child, Jonathan, but their second, Clara, dies of "convulsions" at age six in 1859. The same year, their son Boze is born; he dies a year later, of "inflamations of the bowels." Less than four months after this, Synthian's husband George dies of consumption at the age of thirty-six. She will outlive him by more than fifty years.

Meanwhile, in the last days of the 1860s, ex-Union General Ulysses S. Grant has become the 18th President of the United States, and Milledgeville has lost its rôle as Georgia's state capital, replaced by Atlanta, long the commercial heart of the state, yet so recently the victim of Sherman's fiery siege. And, in the tiny town of Goodman, on the so-called Big Black River, in the absolute middle of Mississippi, John Avery Lomax is born. He will grow up to become a towering figure in the world of folklore fieldwork, and, in time, as a redoubtably energetic, fierce old man, he will corner Blind Willie McTell in an Atlanta hotel room and record him for the Library of Congress.

Britain introduced compulsory civil registration of births, marriages, and deaths on 1 July 1837. Some counties in Georgia didn't get around to such arrangements until a hundred years later. State law didn't require the registration of births until 1919. Federal law didn't require the registration of deaths until 1938.

There's no birth certificate for Willie McTell, or even his much younger brother, let alone for either of his parents. There are very few official documents.

As for the censuses, their inaccuracies are legion—those that are available to us at all. The ones that ought to be available for scrutiny and yield information about individuals are those from early in the nineteenth century through till the census for 1930. The personal data they contain is released only when it is seventy years old, to protect people's privacy, so the 1930 is the most recent you can trawl through.

Catastrophically, practically none of the 1890 census exists. It's generally said to have been destroyed by fire in 1921: a fire for which they never found the cause. The reality is more complicated, and worse. With earlier censuses, duplicate copies were kept at county courthouses (which had often gone up in flames themselves in an earlier era when they were wooden buildings full of tobacco smokers) but, with the 1890 census, the original and only copy of each schedule was sent to Washington, DC, where no adequate storage facilities were provided. Within six years— before final publication of even the general statistics—all the special schedules for crime, mortality, pauperism and benevolence, and for people who were deaf, dumb, blind, or insane, were badly damaged by fire. What was left of them was then destroyed by order of the Department of the Interior in March 1896.

The general population schedules survived—in orderly piles on pine shelving in an unlocked room in the basement of the Commerce Building. There they stayed till Monday, 10 January 1921, when dense smoke was seen pouring from the room. Firemen put out the blaze by flooding the place with water. Then they opened the windows to let out the smoke and everyone went home for the night.

Next day the census records, some sitting in ankle-deep water, were guessed to be 25 per cent destroyed, with half the rest damaged by fire, smoke, and water. Some from other census years were damaged too. They decided they couldn't do anything before insurance companies had poked about and reported, so the whole lot was left sitting there in soggy ruin. This mess was then moved into "temporary storage." Thirteen years later it was deliberately destroyed—the day before President Hoover laid the cornerstone of the first proper National Archives Building.

As today's National Archives & Records Administration says itelf, of all the census schedules "perhaps none might have been more critical to studies of immigration, industrialisation, westward migration, and characteristics of the general population" than the one taken in June 1890— the one destroyed. As they note, "This is a genuine tragedy of records" and "eternally anguishing to researchers."

It would certainly have been invaluable for looking into the family of Blind Willie McTell—but it's gone. Georgia's sole surviving 1890 record is for Muscogee County, a tiny triangle of land on the Alabama border.

The whole sorry story of the 1890 census, of how amateurishly the others were looked after, and of the incompetence and semi-illiteracy of the enumerators who did the house-to-house calling and logging—all this shows how little care was taken over anybody's documentation in the United States in Willie McTell's lifetime.

When it came to taking care over the details of Southern blacks, the situation was inevitably much, much worse. This means that tracing Willie's ancestors, discovering documents, pinning down detail and nailing fact is always hard and often impossible. These brick walls are themselves an eloquent part of the story when you try to track the footsteps of a black man who lived in Georgia in these times—a man who, in Willie's case, never complained about race or disability, a man who shone and thrived and rose above many an adverse circumstance, but who lived, just the same, in an oral culture and under this white regime.

# FIVE

I N  T H E  C L I M A T E of the times, no one gave a damn about document-
ing black people's particulars accurately, if they bothered at all.
Everybody you speak to in Georgia today agrees that this is how it was.

You could hardly deny it. Look how much more the lives of poor
whites who fought in the Civil War in the 1860s have been logged than
the lives of black Georgians in, say, the 1920s. We know far more about
Willie's white great-grandfather than we can ever know about his father
or mother.

When, in January 1934, Willie and Ruthy Kate Williams crossed the
river from Augusta into North Augusta, which is in South Carolina, and
traveled a few miles further to the courthouse at Aiken to swear their
affidavits to obtain a license to marry, they knew they could give the
Aiken County probate judge any information they liked. As Cheryl
Thurber has observed:

> You know, you deal with *so* much difficulty with any kind of black-
> related official records in the South in that time period. The clerks

would have been white. They didn't care! If the people said, "We're twenty-six," fine. They were not worried about accuracy in black records. And the same would have been true in terms of the censuses as well, and on *any* kinds of things. So you're dealing with whatever people want to say.

And, if they're telling the truth, it's not necessarily believed. On Tuesday, 5 June 1917, Willie's uncle, Cleveland "Coot" McTier, walked into Thomson and stood in line to register with the Draft Board. Every male adult was required to do this under the newly introduced Selective Service Act, though many didn't bother—including, typically, Willie's father, Ed, a gambler and drifter Willie is never known to have mentioned. Ed's brother, Coot, was given a physical examination and asked a number of questions. One was whether he had dependents. He replied that he had four dependent children, which was true. The registrar wrote it down but added a note on the back: "I doubt answer to question no. 9."

You may think this comment alone shows something about attitudes towards black people by white officialdom, but it might say more about class attitudes than race prejudice. Isn't it likely that the same official felt a similar skepticism about the answers given him by poor whites?

Lincoln County (next to McDuffie to the north) holds some very good records, by Georgia standards. They include a listing of *Black Marriages . . . 1866–1939*. In other words, they started logging these within months of the end of slavery. But, in the library in Lincolnton, there is a volume of census indexes for each decade from 1850 to 1880—and not only did the compilers not bother to include any black people, but they don't even *say* this until the last volume. It's titled *1880 Lincoln County Georgia Census Index White Population*, the only time these last two words come into it. And this is work done in the 1990s.

But when it comes to the lives of black Georgians, the lack of documentation runs deeper than any of this. First, this was an oral culture, so that personal paperwork is as sparse as the official sort. If you write a biography of someone middle class and white, you'll probably be able to draw on diaries, letters, journals, postcards—a plethora of personal detail set down by your subject and by his or her friends and relations. There is no equivalent of this in the black communities in Happy Valley or Statesboro in Willie's lifetime.

Just as crucially, in these black communities themselves, there is still a near-complete lack of expectation that paperwork should exist, that records should be kept, that the past should be archived or guarded. There is a striking general indifference to any preserving of records.

Time and again as you walk around graveyards, in town and countryside alike, you can tell whether the souls at rest were once encased in white or black flesh by the general level of upkeep around the place. In a black cemetery there will be a far higher proportion of unmarked graves, broken gravestones, and mounds bearing only illegible markers.

I visited black funeral homes in Atlanta, Warrenton, Thomson, and Statesboro—and only in Atlanta did anyone running these businesses keep any old paperwork at all. Even here, the logging of where Willie's long-time partner, Helen, had been buried was puzzling and vague, and contradicted what it said on her death certificate.

In Warrenton, at the funeral home where Willie's body was embalmed, they no longer know where the older records would be. The same is true at the funeral home in Thomson used by many of Willie's Happy Valley relatives. It's in the poor part of town, on Martin Luther King Jr Street (which used to be Pine Street), where the newer tiny homes are cinder block and the old ones like this are rotting wood once painted white. Inside its brown office there are stiff rolltop desks, a photograph of John F. Kennedy, a framed browned clipping from the *Augusta Chronicle* about Willie McTell's wife, Kate (the owner's late husband had helped the journalist to find Kate in Wrens), and a framed color print of the Last Supper, but no archive paperwork beyond what happened to have come to rest and grown old within the rolltop desks.

In Statesboro, where Willie spent the greater part of his childhood, and where I was looking for his brother Robert's grave, I called at the funeral home on a decrepit part of Van Buren Street, stood in a room swirling with the smell of cats, and asked if they kept records of which cemetery plots held the people they had buried there twenty-five years earlier. The woman in charge gave an involuntary laugh—the very notion of such record-keeping seemed absurd to her. I might as well have asked to see their collection of doubloons.

Local white indifference has compounded the problem. In Statesboro, not only while Willie was growing up, but throughout his lifetime, the newspapers ran no obituary column at all. The consequence was that black people never died, according to the papers, except in violent incidents or lurid accidents worthy of news coverage. The deaths of white people would be reported and positioned in the paper according to the individual's social importance; the deaths of black people were as unacknowledged as most features of their lives. As Statesboro historian Delma E. Presley puts it:

> According to the newspapers of Statesboro, few if any unremarkable black people actually died before the 1970s. In the first part of the century, one reads of an occasional "esteemed negress" or "loyal worker" who passes on. In the 1950s, on occasion, a known teacher or preacher dies. But in early December 1970, when the *Bulloch Herald* paper changed its name to the *Statesboro Herald* and went daily, Monday to Friday (instead of weekly on Thursdays), the editor introduced a new section called "Obituaries." Within a few weeks, they began including deaths of black citizens in this new section.

In the 1970s, the Metropolitan Association for the Blind in Atlanta— previously the Association for the (Colored) Blind—still held a tiny amount of information on Willie, but it was fragmentary and inaccurate. He had been, apparently, a tenor in their Glee Club in about 1950. Did they have records of this? Could there even be a photograph of this Glee Club, with Willie sitting there plain as day in the front row?

In 2003 I went to find out. The institution has gone through several name and address changes since Willie's time, not least when it was merged with Community Services for the Blind in 1972. It is currently called the Center for the Visually Impaired, a title arrived at in the comparatively early days of political correctness in 1987.

The receptionist in the new building's gray-carpeted, hot, glassy lobby was a huge blind black woman. I explained my quest and she phoned someone else, saying, "I have a walk-in." I was directed to wait in an area of insistently designer furniture and modern art. After a time, a pudgy and rather dense young black guy came to speak to me in hushed tones.

He told me that they "probably" don't have any archives "on site" because they've moved buildings several times and that, anyway, people in the old days knew no better than to throw stuff away—but that, even if they did have any old documents, they certainly wouldn't tell me. They wouldn't tell me whether Mr McTell had ever been helped by them, let alone anything else, because of patient confidentiality. "This man would have to have signed a form to indicate that you were blessed with his permission." He was unmoved by the snag that Mr McTell had died some forty-four years beforehand.

That the archives of the old Association for the (Colored) Blind had gone missing was no surprise. It's part of the same story: of that deeply ingrained lack of expectation that records should be looked after.

So looking for Willie and his families in the written records was always going to be difficult. While I was in Georgia, looking through dusty old red leather-bound books in county courthouses, trying to read unreadable microfiche copies of census records in small-town libraries and waiting behind the counters in health departments while people disappeared to search for non-existent certificates, my wife Sarah was doing twelve-hour stretches and more at the computer, trying to squeeze every morsel of information she could from census return images and transcriptions before I had to return home.

But although there was plenty we never found, what we did find proved very exciting. It contradicted so much of what we thought we knew before, from the research on McTell that had been conducted in the 1970s.

As with any family history research, we started with what we knew— or what we thought we knew. We knew that Willie's father was Ed McTear (or McTier), who seems to have vanished without trace. This fugitive, elusive figure didn't hang around long in Willie's life, but we knew that his family always accepted Willie as one of them, and that their home patch was Happy Valley, outside Thomson, in McDuffie County.

Willie himself says he was born near Thomson, "about nine miles and a half from the little town. 'Between the two creeks,' they call it: Little Brier and Big Brier." This makes for a very small area indeed, at its largest no more than five miles long and three miles deep.

We knew that Willie had an uncle—a younger brother of his father— called Cleveland "Coot" McTier, who remained in the area all his life. We knew that Cleveland had a son called Eddie, Willie's cousin—usually called Bo-Rat—who married a Hazel Samuel[s], and that this couple had taken Willie in and looked after him in the last months of his life.

We took it from there and, since Cleveland was the mysterious Ed's brother, and promised not to be mysterious at all, we tried to trace people backwards from him.

I began in Atlanta. I walked from my scruffy hotel near the old Fox Theater twelve bleak and desolate blocks to the Atlanta-Fulton Library, the main library for the city and for Fulton County, meeting one request for money every block, from the obsequious raggedy poor and black. It started raining in big warm drops.

In 1970 an old warhorse architect of the Bauhaus Movement, sixty-eight-year-old Marcel Lajos Breuer, was asked to design a new Atlanta library, to replace the one that had opened, as it happened, in the year of his birth in Hungary, 1902. He had been, in the 1920s and 30s, an inspired designer of those classic ultra-modern chairs, and slid from furniture to houses to high-profile public buildings.

For the new Atlanta-Fulton Library, Breuer and his associate, Hamilton Smith, planned a building that would have a "monumental" look from the outside, even if far taller buildings would grow to loom above it—as they were likely to, granted its downtown location at the corner of Forsyth Street and Carnegie Way, on what is now called Margaret Mitchell Square. Inside the new building they wanted maximum use of natural light.

The result, opened to the public in May 1980, is an elephantine overhang of concrete layers galumphing above the sidewalks, disguising a stubby office block, each of its six large square floors looking exactly like the open-plan offices of any modern newspaper or insurance company, where timid white featureless pillars of no great height consort with flimsy polystyrene ceiling tiles, hard lighting, and a peculiar faint blueness in the slightly blurred air. On the five floors that are above ground, vast man-made-fiber blinds in wan colors hang in front of the windows as the staff attempt to avoid the cruel excesses of all that hot natural light. Marcel Breuer died in New York fourteen months after his building opened.

Up on the fifth floor, I sat at a computer in the Georgia Local and Family History Department, where the excellent William A. Montgomery gave me quiet, intelligent guidance about sources and then left me in peace. It doesn't surprise me at all to read that the author of *Gone With The Wind* felt the same gratitude to the reference department staff seventy years ago when she was researching, for that book, details like whether women spoke of "scent" or "perfume" in the Civil War period.

Of course in Margaret Mitchell's day it was a whites-only library, and it remained so for customers until the year of Willie McTell's death, 1959, when by direct action black professor Irene Dobbs Jackson shamed the system into change. For staff it took until 1973 to achieve full integration. But at least all this is stated honestly right there on the library's own website and in its literature. We couldn't expect that the library of previous times would be out there alone, floating in a different galaxy. And today, rather more modestly, it is out on a limb, quietly pioneering erudition while a world of belligerent greed and vulgarity howls outside its doors.

Library staff see all the corner-cutting and encroaching bureaucracy, but what I see is that, discounting small obduracies in small branches, the library system in America stands for all the civilised values that George W. Bush and the boyz-in-the-hood equally would destroy at a stroke if they could. In the library you're treated with courtesy, no one discriminates against you because you're not American, or from Georgia. The resources are immense and the philosophy behind it is to allow you to use it as fully as you wish to. There's no red tape for the foreign user, no hindrance, only unfailing help.

On top of which, Georgia libraries have not yet gone the way of English ones—it may be different still in Scotland—where they seem hell-bent on sweeping books away to make room for more and more computer games, DVDs, sub-teen pop CDs, and all the other para-phernalia of dumbing down, in the mistaken belief that if you get more people in through the doors that's good, regardless of what you provide when they get there. Here in Atlanta, the library still subscribes to thirty-six international newspapers, including papers from China and Iran.

Up in his fifth floor eyrie, the shelving that holds Mr Montgomery's collections of old Atlanta City Directories was closed for strengthening and upgrading, so that many chances to track Willie's life and movements in the city were temporarily closed to me, but, for tracing his family roots, there was much to work through.

Their subscription to Ancestry Plus allowed me to search through the Georgia Deaths Index, scanning it for the promise of familiar names. Mostly it gave you, for each person, their name, death date, race, gender, age, county of death, county of residence, death certificate number, and filing date.

I found Willie's neighbour in Atlanta in the 1950s, Emmitt Gates, and learned that he had survived to the age of eighty. From his date of death, 7 December 1983, I hoped I could find an obituary notice that would tell me the names of his surviving relatives, and that among them I could find his son, whom Willie had taught a little guitar. Time would tell.

I found Hazel McTear, who had nursed Willie at the end; she had died in 1982. I found her husband, Willie's cousin Eddie (Bo-Rat). I found Horace McTear, Eddie's younger brother. I found Willie's half-brother, Robert, who died in 1978.

When folklorists and blues enthusiasts had made fleeting visits in the mid-1970s to look into Willie's background and the Georgia blues scene in general, all of these people had been alive except Eddie, and he had died not long beforehad, in 1973.

And then I found Helen, Willie's much under-attended-to second "wife", who had lived with him for many years in Atlanta, and who had died there in 1958.

Almost immediately after this, I found Willie's mother, Minnie.

"BINGO!", I wrote in my notes. It more than made up for all the days of finding nothing, and hitting brick walls, and feeling that sitting in libraries was a foolish waste of precious, limited Georgia time.

We already knew that Minnie had died in 1920, or at least we believed it, because Willie himself had said so, but after so many false leads and such long invisibility, here she was on the Georgia Deaths Index. And still using the surname McTear till the end, down south in Bulloch County, many, many years after she and Ed had gone their separate ways.

Seeing the words on the screen, "Minnie McTear, date of death 21 Dec 1920"—it was a great moment, and it confirmed that, as so often, Willie's statement had been the truth.

Search as I might, I couldn't find Ed, Willie's father. Finally, I found Cleveland instead. This was almost as good. His death certificate would yield crucial information: it would state the names of his mother and father—the names, in other words, of Willie's grandparents.

I walked back those twelve blocks much less bowed down by their dusty concrete brutalism. Next morning, after a night of thunder and lightning, I traveled across the city and out into the suburbs to the Vital Records Office, to buy copies of five death certificates.

The building is a bus ride beyond the far reaches of the city's metro system. The bus waits outside Oglethorpe station and, when I asked the driver to let me know when we reached the corner of Skyland Drive and Skyland Terrace, he said pleasantly, "I know where you goin'." Ten minutes later I stepped off the bus in a small estate of public housing—at least, it resembled an English housing estate—with rusty leaves on wide grass frontages and pine cones on the road. The driver said, "I hope you find what you want."

One of the vital records being preserved here is what a 1950s elementary school looked like. That's what the Vital Records building once was, and it's in a time warp. What I saw of the interior is perfectly preserved, and outside you can see it as the architect's drawing would have represented it in the first place.

Naïvely, I thought I'd be virtually alone—only one other person got off the bus when I did, and it was early in the day—but, when I reached the right door and opened it, the room was seething with people, in many cases parents looking after their restless children while waiting to receive copies of their birth certificates. Almost everyone wanted birth certificates.

It was well organised. There was a counter with three glass booths, the first labeled START HERE and the last one PAY HERE. A microphone on a stalk sat behind the glass in the middle. I filled in the forms, paid $50, and then waited half an hour. I'd been told it would be longer. When my name was called, they had all five of the certificates I'd requested.

I collected them without looking beyond the names to check that they were the right people. I was determined, despite the temptation to read greedily through all five of them on the spot, in that sweaty room full of the bring-me-your-poor-your-dispossessed, that I would save them all till I got back to my hotel room.

Back at the hotel. So much information! I read through it all, over and over, taking it in, failing to take some of it in till the second or third or fourth time of staring at it.

Minnie, Robert, and Helen all come later. One of the others I'd decided to ask for proved to be from outside the clan, in spite of being an infant from Warren County whose father bore the irresistible name of Homer McTell—not Mc*Tier* but Mc*Tell*. The details were touching but irrelevant for my purposes.

Cleveland's certificate was the key one right now. It told me that his father, Willie's grandpa, was "L. McTier." The hand-written first version had been crossed out and the typo "L. NcTier" typed in. Cleveland's mother was named as Nancy.

If I could find further paperwork on "L." and Nancy, we'd be making further progress. I didn't have enough information, or time, to pursue them in Atlanta, via the excursion to Skyline Drive. I had to wait until I could return to Thomson to pursue Willie's family back in time.

Pointing the car towards Thomson from Warrenton, I feel that irrational affection for somewhere I'm revisiting, just because I've been before. I pass through feeling a gratifying familiarity with its more obvious land-marks.

In many counties the births and deaths records have been taken away from the county's probate court and given over to the local Health Department, where the staff tend to be busier and less interested in old documents and genealogical research, where you can't look through things yourself but must rely on a health clerk to do it out of your sight and you can't tell if they're doing this competently or not, and where waiting for all this to happen means hanging around amongst the ill and injured. It's not an improvement, for the researcher.

At the Health Department office in Thomson, I pressed my way through its fetid air to find that, in McDuffie, the Probate Court still retains all the records.

At the court I was lucky to find a surprisingly large cache of records and also to find Valerie Burley, Probate Judge Albert E. (Eugene) Wells' excellent clerk, who not only knows exactly what records they have, and keeps them in good order, but also combines good sense and resourcefulness with great local knowledge, not least about black Happy Valley, where she lives herself.

I had no trouble finding the death certificate for Cleveland's father, Willie's grandfather, now that I knew his name. On this certificate he's named as "El McTear." He dies in January 1933, and the informant gives his age as "about 73".

The usual lack of scruple prevails here. According to his certificate he's not a widower but a "Widow," and he's buried at "Mt Olie Church" at Thomson. It isn't a typo for Mt Olive, there isn't such a church here; Ms Burley is confident that it means Mt Aldred, and that's not in Thomson or McDuffie, but, straddling the county line, is officially in Warren County. The spaces on the certificate for father's name, father's birthplace, mother's name, and mother's birthplace are all marked "Don't Know" and "D.K." They haven't even bothered to fill in, at the top, the registration number of the certificate, nor the address of the deceased.

Then I found Willie's aunt, Annie Bell McTear, Ed and Coot's sister: another child of El and Nancy. She had applied for a "delayed birth certificate" when she was sixty and living in New York City in 1953. She, too, had to name her parents, and there they are again—El is there as Albert, and his wife Nancy's maiden name is given as Barksdale. I also found a death certificate for El's later wife Judy/Julie/Julia, who died before he did, in 1930. On her certificate he's back to being named "L." McTear.

Later that day, back at home in England, bent over the computer for hours at a stretch, and propelled forward by the news of El's death certificate, sent through by e-mail that morning, my wife had made our first *huge* breakthrough: she'd realised that not only was El the same person as L., but that Elbert / Albert was the same person too—that he was not only Ed's and Cleveland's father, and, therefore, Willie's grand-father, but that he was also the "mulatto" named Elbert way back there on the 1870 Census, the boy who'd lived in the same house as Reddick McTyeir!

He's "L. NcTier" on his son Cleveland's death certificate in 1958; he's Albert on his daughter Annie Bell McTear's application for a Delayed Certificate of Birth in 1953; he's El McTear on his own death certificate in 1933; he's "L. McTear" on his wife's death certificate in 1930; he's "All MacTer" on the 1910 census; he's "Ell Metier" on the Mormons' transcription of the 1880 census (though not on the census page itself); and he's Elbert in the 1870 census, back when he's an eleven-year-old boy—and this means that he's the unnamed nine-month-old slave belonging to Reddick, along with fourteen-year-old Essey, back on the 1860 census.

We had at last made the connection between the white McTiers and the black ones!

Of course, the strong likelihood, all along, was that the black in-habitants of the McDuffie-Warren-Glascock region whose surname was McTier would have acquired that name, and would have put up with it for want of anything better, from having just freed themselves from being owned by white people with that name in the same neck of the woods. Now we had a stronger connection still, a case history, a moment of personal conjunction between black and white. We could track Elbert all the way back to his birth.

Like his father, Elbert would have two families. His future first wife, Nancy Barksdale, had been born at the very end of the Civil War, in September 1865. Her father, an R. Barksdale, was born in Georgia in 1813; her mother, Jane, twenty-three years younger, was born in Virginia in January 1836 and would survive until the 1920s. This couple, Nancy's parents, would become, just like Reddick and Essey, Blind Willie McTell's great-grandparents.

By 1880, Elbert had moved out of his father Reddick's house and Nancy was living with him as his wife in the Happy Valley area of McDuffie County. He was twenty-two and she was fifteen. They had five children together, beginning with Ed, who was born in August 1883, when Nancy was a month off eighteen. Next came Cleveland, and then Elbert Junior, in March 1888 and April 1890 respectively. Annie Bell was born in May 1891, and Mary, sometimes written down as Mady and mostly known as Doll, in August 1895.

Here in Happy Valley on the 1900 census are the characters in our story: Doll is only four years old, yet Elbert has already moved out of the family home—and a lodger called Tom Harris has moved in with Nancy and the children; Nancy, now aged thirty-four, is Head of Household, and listed as a farmer; son Ed is now sixteen; Cleveland, Elbert Junior (Elbert H., on this document, that "H" standing for Harley, we believe), and Annie B(ell) are still children. All but Annie and Doll are already farm laborers. The household is augmented by Nancy's mother Jane and by a sibling of Nancy's, her much older brother, Pomp Jackson, also a farm laborer, who is forty-eight. Then there is also the lodger, Tom Harris, thirty-seven—and now there is another little child in the house, another child of Nancy's. His name is Thomas, and he is stated to have been born in November 1896 and to be three years old.

We know that four-year-old Mady, or Doll, is Elbert's child, and we can be pretty sure that three-year-old Thomas is Tom Harris' child. It follows that El and Nancy must have drifted apart and Nancy taken up with the lodger sometime between November 1894 and February 1896. He, too, is a farm laborer. He and Nancy will have three further children together.

Elbert, meanwhile, has a new partner named Judy (or Judie) Story, though their family structure is less clear. On the 1910 census they appear to have a four-year-old daughter with an indecipherable name; ten years later, aged fourteen, she has become their granddaughter, and her surname is Story, not McTier.

At any rate, by 1910, Elbert and Judy, and Elbert's former wife Nancy, with new husband Tom, and all their children, form two adjacent households: they are living next door to each other, presumably amicably, on what's written as "Bryer Head Road," in Happy Valley.

Of the children of Nancy and Tom, the ones that matter in the Willie McTell story are the first two, Thomas and G. Jesse Harris. The latter is Golden Harris—Gold Harris, for short, or "Uncle Gold," as we have heard—who became a lifelong friend of Willie's, as well as being his cousin, and who, at the end, brought Willie's body back home on a train from the mental asylum at Milledgeville, to be embalmed in Warrenton and buried back in Happy Valley.

My wife Sarah had also worked backwards to find key parts of this story, starting with Cleveland. By working back from 1930, via the 1920 census, on which he is identified only as "Kute," a misspelling of Coot (and is living with his wife, Mary/May Bell, in nearby Dearing), and then by going through every census page in the whole region, she had finally found, in the 1900, the first mention of Willie's father, Ed. And found that, by 1910, when Nancy is logged as Tom Harris' wife, and Elbert is next door with Judy, Ed has left the family home and disappeared, never to be found on record again.

Working backwards again, Sarah had gone through the 1880 census for Mount Auburn and found El and Nancy listed as Metier. They hadn't shown up on any online search of the census indexes. But because Nancy's mother appears on the later censuses, it was possible to find her parents and brother—R., Jane and Magor Barksdale—on the 1880 also.

McTiers, Barksdales, Storys, Harrises, Mosses, Samuels . . . To work late into the night, time and again, in a concentrated period, poring over these ill-written, ill-reproduced pages that can never be taken at face value but must be rubbed up against each other and compared, their variant misspellings reconciled, and their wayward inaccuracies weighed in the balance, Sarah found herself becoming more and more involved with all these people she had never met.

As she read the same names in their shifting patterns and representational disguises, re-encountering them at decade-long intervals, the communities at Happy Valley and elsewhere began to teem with people she "recognised." Names of families became as familiar as those of old schoolfriends. In the state of heightened emotion induced by these long-past-midnight scrutinies, these twelve-hour weekend shifts at the screen, she felt she was beginning to know something of their lives:

I felt I could "see" their wooden houses, with slatted covered porches, out in the piney woods. When I "found" characters in this drama, in black and white on the screen, in my head it was like a reunion, or a returning prodigal. When connexions were made, it was exhilarating. When the link between Reddick and Willie was finally clinched, through Elbert and Ed, I was elated! It was thrilling.

My thoughts went back to Jan McTier, the white farmer's wife whose voluminous and dedicated research into the white McTiers had given me so much information on their side of the divide that wasn't, as it turned out, quite such a divide after all.

I had first phoned Jan McTier from Thomson on a broiling August day in 2001. She's a McTier only by marriage, yet she's undertaken this vast genealogical dig, and she helps organise annual reunions of the Kendall McTier Family Association. She was happy to talk.

Before I told her the subject of my own investigation, I asked her if she'd ever researched the black McTiers.

"No," she said, in a soft but lively voice. "I never did. I wish I had. You ever heard of Blind Willie McTell? I wish I had researched these connections, because he'd be the only famous member of the family!"

Indeed—though actually it's not true that Willie is the only slightly famous one. Kendall's nephew was Holland Nimmons McTyeire, 1824–1899, a cousin and contemporary of Reddick (and a man who never owned any slaves), and he's slightly famous too. He became Bishop McTyeire, a nationally prominent figure in the Methodist church, and he played a key part in establishing the African Methodist Episcopal Church, ensuring that it started out with assets of over a million dollars: a huge sum in the Reconstruction period. Later he persuaded Commodore Vanderbilt to endow a small college in Nashville, Tennessee. Holland McTyeire became its President and, in 1873, the college became Vanderbilt

University. Bishop McTyeire is buried there, under magnolia trees he planted himself.

After the phone conversation with Jan McTier, I drove the short distance out of Thomson to visit her and her husband Lindy. He is the son of the wondrously named Hulon Brumbley McTier and Hulon's wife, Estelle Florene Phillips—and Hulon Brumbley McTier was one of Reddick's grandchildren, a child of Reddick's son John David, born in 1875, and the first of his two wives, Geneva Belle Purvis.

To visit Jan and Lindy, you drive out of Thomson along the old Highway 10 towards Augusta, passing the chic, white Thomson McDuffie water tower on the right. Its big splayed feet are hidden behind a one-storey bar with tiny red and blue neon beer ads glowing from the top right-hand corner of the big, dark plate-glass window, as if a shameful, best-not-be-seen attitude to drinking applies around here. Yet, right outside it, on the roadside grass, touting for business and implying a promise of jollity, a large, steel-frame message board accommodating four rows of changeable letter signs shouts TURKEY SHOOT SAT AT 2 KARAOKE FRI.

Out of town, the highway wiggles south-east for a while alongside the old railroad line that passes through Boneville on its way to Dearing—by which time you're close to the Columbia County line, inside which snooze the minuscule townships of Sawdust and Harlem: the Harlem that became, on 18 January 1892, the birthplace of Oliver Hardy, and the Harlem that five years later gave its name to the 'Harlem Rag,' the first published instrumental rag by an African-American composer (Thomas Million Turpin, 1873–1922).

Still just inside McDuffie, a mile past Dearing—a town with an almost alpine look and, most unusually, a café in the center that could be somewhere cheap by the roadside in Italy—I turned off to the right at the McTiers' mailbox, down a peaceful old lumpy track to an unremarkable house with vinyl siding and a lovely grassy yard. A row of open-fronted sheds with small old-fashioned tractors lined up across the yard facing the house, and ahead of all this was a picture-book pond, tranquil and old, circled by shady trees. Meaty black cattle lay peaceably beneath them.

This was the beguiling, *Wild In The Country* kind of farm. Outside the house, gray haired, small but spry, and with smiling pale gray eyes, Jan McTier waited to greet me.

"Are you the gentleman who phoned?"

"Yes I am."

"Well, come on in."

We went into a long room, an annexe running all the way down the side of the house that overlooks the pond, and sat over enormous beakers of iced water, talking of family history research and the patchy nature of the documentation available.

"It's my husband Lindy's family that's from this area," Jan said, sitting back in a gray dress with black buttons, looking at me shrewdly with her gray eyes, "and when I first moved here I was amazed that none of the family knew that they had an ancestor who had been a Confederate soldier. So I started from that—with Reddick. And then, through research, found the brothers and sisters and so on. It's like a full-time job. One thing leads to another.

"But there are seventeen spellings of McTier in the Warren County courthouse records alone. Names weren't important, spellings were not important, dates were not important. They should have known we'd come along and need all this!

"We'll never even be able to get a real birth certificate for my husband's mother, whereas me being of Scandinavian origin, those records go back to the 1500s.

"The way my husband started trying to find McTiers was, he went through the Augusta phone book and called every McTier in it, and told them what he was trying to do. And I got very interested in the earlier city directories for Augusta. They tell what people's occupations were, and whether they were roomers, or what. And Warrenton was a thriving town at one point. But cotton moved out. Cotton had been the biggest crop. My husband and his generation on back, they all had to pick cotton as kids. Till they left home. That's why they left home!—to quit the cotton business. As a child in the 1930s, Lindy was still picking cotton. And that generation, they traveled by horse and wagon, which is incredible to me."

They lived on a small farm in the Warren County panhandle—eighty-six acres, fifty in cultivation, with mules, cows, hogs, and chickens. They rented it from Reddick's son John (Grandpa John, to Lindy). But Lindy's father died at thirty-four, of typhoid fever, when Lindy was eight years old, and, before long, the farm was too much for his mother, and Grandpa John felt he had to ask them to move, to stop the farm's ruination. They moved around after that, but never far off.

They would have worked just as hard and been almost as poor if his father had lived. Everyone was "dirt poor." Some may have owned land, and the poor houses or shacks they lived in, but many lost their land and almost no one had money.

"There was no cash around," Jan tells me. "People bartered for everything. This was the time of the Great Depression. Everyone worked hard to just survive, including the children."

Not only was there cotton to pick, but, at thirteen, Lindy was working in Aaron Rabun's saw mill, holding down an adult's laboring job. If you got there by sunup, they'd give you breakfast.

"Anyway, now we have family reunions, every September since 1990, and we put it in newspapers all over the state of Georgia. We've had calls from black McTiers and white McTiers, and we've said, everybody's welcome, but so far we've not had any black McTiers at the reunions. I sell copies of the book that I've put together, but, as you'll know, if you write family history, the day after it's printed you find out something new."

Lindy arrived home from visiting the dentist (with a temporary crown looking altogether more like a proper one than the horrible look-at-me plastic ones they offer you in Britain, of course). He was silver-haired, soft-skinned, quiet and wiry, and wearing overalls. I pictured the boyhood version of him, wearing overalls then too, riding a horse-drawn wagon and picking cotton in Warren County, like his ancestors before him.

I took my leave of them, and, as I climbed into my rented car, they stood at their farmhouse door watching me depart. They looked like a friendly, comfortable flipside of the couple in Grant Wood's *American Gothic*.

Now, at the other end of these research trips and of my wife's travails through the censuses, Jan McTier knows for sure something she must always have suspected. In her family history book, alongside the information that Reddick's slave holdings in 1860 include a fourteen-year-old girl and a near one-year-old boy, Jan puts the comment "history is history, whether we choose to report it or not." And the history of the family includes the fact that Reddick McTyeir was the great-grandfather of Jan's husband, Lindy David McTier, and of William Samuel McTell— a white man who picked cotton through his childhood and a black man who never did.

# SIX

Paul Reed and Will Cato, who Murdered and Burned
entire Hodges family of five, July 28, 1904, near
Statesboro, Georgia.

W E HAD TRACKED the life of Willie's grandfather Elbert. We'd
confirmed his name, his birth year, and the date of his death.
We'd found the adult Elbert's two families, and so identified Willie's
grandmother, Nancy. We'd found Elbert's children, and so filled in the
family history of Willie's elusive father, Ed.

What had we discovered, beyond her death certificate, about Willie's
mother Minnie? It seemed frustratingly little new information at first, but
it helped lead us to major new facts about Willie himself. We found that
her maiden name was not, as long thought, Minnie Watkins, but Minnie
Dorsey, that she and Ed were never married, and that Willie was born
several years later than previously believed.

This young girl, no more than fifteen when she gave birth to Blind
Willie, took him out of Happy Valley to Jefferson County, then moved
again, settling further south in Statesboro, and was dead at thirty-three.

As the twentieth century began, Ed was a sixteen-year-old unskilled
laborer, eldest son of a mulatto former slave. He'd been born in Happy
Valley in or about August 1883, and was still living at home, now with his

grandmother, mother, brothers and sisters, "lodger" Tom Harris, and little Thomas Junior. He was doing farmwork and his future prospects were nothing but more farm laboring.

A dozen families away (a page and a half down the census) lived a girl called Minnie Dorsey.

She was born in October 1887 and now, in 1900, she was a twelve-year-old, living with her stepfather, Ed Watkins, and his wife, Lena, or Lula—in all likelihood Minnie's mother—along with Ed's children, all much younger than Minnie and including a new-born daughter, Milly, plus another stepchild called Eddie Burnett, aged ten, and a twelve-year-old lodger called Alonzo Harris. (Another lodger called Harris . . .)

Because Minnie's surname is Dorsey, and the other stepchild in the house has the surname Burnett, it's not possible to know from this census whether Dorsey is Minnie's mother's maiden name or the surname of Minnie's absent father. But one thing *is* clear: Willie is not yet born. (And if, as so often stated, he had been born in 1898, especially if his putative birthdate had been that May, Minnie would have been ten years old at the time.)

By the time of the 1910 census, not only has Ed left home, reputedly by now a drifter and gambler, but neither Minnie nor the Watkins family are any longer in Happy Valley. By going through the Jefferson County censuses page by page, Sarah finally found them at Spread—a name used interchangeably with Stapleton, though people just as often mean a specific patch around this tiny town. It is barely more than ten miles south of Happy Valley.

Ed Watkins is there with wife Lula and their children—and three doors down the road is Minnie, now head of her own household and calling herself McTier. And with her is a son: "McTier, William S."

This is the first time we see him enumerated. It's also the only time in his whole life that we see his first name given as William rather than Willie. He is stated to be six years old. So he was born when Theodore Roosevelt was President, in 1903 or 1904.

To be exact, the census date that year was 15 April, which meant that all the data collected was supposed to log the family's details as of that date, even if the actual date of the enumerator's visit was months later. It's impossible to say whether the census takers adhered to this rule or not, but, on the assumption that they did, then if Minnie was being accurate, Willie must have been born between 16 April 1903 and 15 April 1904.

If we give any credence to the specific date held temporarily on file by the Metropolitan Atlanta Association for the Blind back in the 1970s, namely 5 May, then we might argue that the strongest contender for a specific birthdate for William Samuel McTell is 5 May 1903.

If there were any doubt that this is the right Minnie and son, it is removed by the fact that here on the 1910 census, she and Willie are sharing their household with one of Ed's sisters, Mady, aka Doll McTier. Ed himself, of course, is not there.

There is a column on the 1910 census form headed *Whether Blind (Both Eyes)*. For Willie the column is left blank. The question of whether he was blind from birth or whether his blindness developed in early child-hood has never been answered reliably. Are we any further forward now? If anything, we're further back, because now we can't be sure whether he was blind even by the age of six. We must fall back on the balance of probability from other people's testimony, and that seems to argue that he himself always said that he was blind from birth.

In the McDuffie County Probate Court office in Thomson, I had found the old *Colored Marriage Books*, and, inside them, the marriages of Willie's uncle Cleveland to Mary Bell Moss, and of their son Eddie McTear to Hazel Samuel. There was no other Ed, Eddie, Edward, or E. McTear/McTier listing, nor any credible variant name. There was no marriage, nor any application for one, for any black female Watkins in the entire hundred-year stretch from 1871 onwards, and no marriage for any Minnie Dorsey.

At any rate, Minnie had been fifteen and a half when Willie was born. When he was conceived, Ed had only just turned nineteen, and Minnie was fourteen. How likely was it that they had ever even lived together?

What had life been like in this period, for African Americans in the South in general, and for people of all colors in McDuffie, Warren, and Glascock Counties in particular? What had been going on, for our families and others, here in this small patch of north-east Georgia between the time of Reconstruction and the birth of William Samuel McTier?

Illness was rife, and the killers included cholera, dysentery, malaria, measles, meningitis, and pneumonia. Poverty was greater than before the Civil War. Everyone but the rare big landowner was suffering from the ills of the post-slavery agricultural collapse. Reddick McTyeir and his wife Mary's patch of Glascock County was typical of the decline. In 1880 their acreage under cultivation was down from thirty-five acres to fifteen, the farm's cash value down from $400 to $350, and the value of their livestock had plummeted from $170 to $25. On every smallholding, things had deteriorated. The neglect during the war years, the economic downturn since, the uncertainties of the post-slavery labor market: all these had taken their toll.

But while disease and rural poverty affected everyone, politics and social divides made black Georgians' lives shockingly worse than white, despite the good intentions of the post-war reform movement. In 1867, black men in the South were enfranchised by the Military Reconstruction Act, and were able to vote in the federal elections of 1868. As we've seen, they voted Republican. So did large numbers of poor Southern whites. In 1870 the 14$^{th}$ and 15$^{th}$ Amendments guaranteed the right to vote and freedom from discrimination—the 15$^{th}$ specifically prohibited the denial of franchise on the basis of race. The number of Southern black state and federal legislators reached around 320 in 1872—a number never to be exceeded in the next 120 years.

The backlash was ferocious. Actually, it isn't quite accurate to describe the formation of hate groups like the Ku Klux Klan, the Knights of the White Camellia, and the Columbians as part of the backlash against black emancipation—they were formed *before* the 1867 act or the 1868 elections. The KKK came into being in 1865 itself: the minute the South lost the war. The purpose of these groups was to kill and intimidate not only blacks who attempted to vote, but blacks in general, to terrorise them out of becoming "uppity." A number of groups organised together in 1867 as "The Invisible Empire of the South." Technically, the KKK disbanded in 1869 and the Knights of the White Camellia in 1870.

President Grant sent in federal troops to guarantee black enfranchisement, but within a shockingly short period—as early as 1873—the Republican party was losing its enthusiasm for protecting black rights. The crucial moment came during the 1876 Presidential election. Democratic contender Samuel Jones Tilden won the popular vote, but after disputes over returns in Louisiana, South Carolina, and especially Florida (does this sound familiar?), a deal was done between the parties and the election was conceded to the Republican, Rutherford Birchard Hayes, in exchange for the promise that he would withdraw the 3,000 federal troops still stationed in the South.

That was the end of Reconstruction and the beginning of white supremacy and black suppression. The number of Southern black legislators nose-dived to under seventy by 1878. Two years later white Democratic political control of the South was total.

Black enfranchisement was dismantled in every Southern state, by means of new state constitutions, poll taxes, literacy tests, and arbitrary "citizenship" tests. These devices also managed to disenfranchise a huge number of poor white men—no woman in America enjoyed the vote until 1920—but it was black disenfranchisement that was backed up by overt, concerted violence.

In Georgia, the specifics were these. Nearly 100,000 black males registered to vote between 1867 and 1877. They elected thirty-two African Americans to the state legislature. Two months later, white legislators expelled them. They were reinstated in 1870, but then, after the Tilden-Hayes deal, a series of state laws was introduced, designed to dismantle black voting rights.

These included a swingeing poll tax in 1877. By the end of the century, the Georgia Democratic Party had started to prevent *any* blacks from voting in state primaries, and in 1908, the last of the Southern states to do it, Georgia passed a state constitutional amendment that effectively ended African-American enfranchisement.

Violence dissuaded black people from exercising what limited rights they enjoyed. Thousands of men and women were lynched throughout the South, the perpetrators so confidently above the law that the process became known as "lynch law."

★　★　★

In Georgia, between 1882 and the 1960s, almost 500 black people were lynched and immeasurable numbers tortured. Georgia's lynch-victim totals were second only to those of Mississippi. Far less lynching happened in former big slave states like Virginia, because up there industrialisation quickly replaced the plantations.

As early as 1899, the political intent of all this murder and violence was being spelled out by the anti-lynching campaigner Ida B. Wells-Barnett, 1862–1931, who wrote: "The real purpose of these savage demonstrations is to teach the Negro that in the South he has no rights that the law will enforce."

The terrors of the lynch-law decades were an ever-present part of what put blacks so in thrall to white behavior. In 1945, Oliver C. Cox, writing an article in the *Journal of Negro Education* called 'Lynching and the Status Quo', explained that whenever a lynching happened, other African Americans in the area would be hunted down and flogged or attacked, and sometimes the only refuge would be inside a more decent white person's house.

Such a contingency could only intensify the circumspect character of the way that black people had to behave towards white. "Negroes would put on a broad smile and act like they are satisfied with this miserable lot and that they hold no malice for what the white man was doing," as the inelegant summary of this article has it in the Atlanta library's bibliography of material on lynchings.

The last group lynching in the US was probably that of two black couples in Walton County, Georgia—very close to where Willie's wife Helen grew up—on 25 July 1946. The last lynching of a single individual was not until 1981—the lateness of that date in itself an indication of how strong was the race-hate psyche of the South.

On Sunday afternoon, 23 April 1899, in Newnan, Coweta County, Georgia, a man named Sam Holt, aka Sam Hose, was tortured and burned to death. This murder was seized upon by Ida Wells-Barnett and even investigated by the *Atlanta Constitution*. It was the atrocity that provoked the great W.E.B. DuBois to turn from writing and research to activism.

In the same town at the same time, twenty-year-old Millard H. McWhorten was struggling to become only the second black person in Coweta County to qualify to practice medicine. He would do a lot for the city in which he had to live in fear, and today, posthumously, he has a federal housing complex named after him—which is, actually, a kind of discrimination in itself. If Coweta County had wanted to honor a white citizen similarly, they'd have named a decent building after him, not an undistinguished example of the kind of social housing everyone else in town despises.

But lynching was going on all over the state, all the time. A man in Baker County was lynched in error in 1921: it was a case of "mistaken identity." A man in Bleckley County two years earlier was hanged for "boasting about race riot." Another, in Brooks County two years before that, was lynched for writing an "insolent letter" to a woman. And those are just some among the forty lynchings in counties with names beginning with B.

They lynched a man in Columbia County in 1910 because he was the father of a murderer, and another three years later for "disorderly conduct." In Dodge County in July 1909, a man was lynched because he "Frightened [a] woman." In Walton County in June 1911, a man named Joe Watts was lynched for acting "suspiciously."

In Wilkes County on 27 November 1888, two men were lynched for "insurrection"; in Early County in 1896, the vividly named Sidney Grist was hanged for what was baldly stated as "political activity"; in Laurens County in 1919, an Eli Cooper was lynched for "incendiarism"; in Montgomery County in 1930, another man with a memorable name, S.S. Mincey, was lynched for, er, "race hatred".

Nor was it only men who found themselves slain by white vigilantes. In Tattnall County in 1907, two women identified only as the daughter and the wife of Sim Padgett were also lynched for the crime of "race hatred" (as was his son, while Sim was killed the same day for "aiding [a] criminal"). Another woman, Meta Hicks, was killed for being "the wife of a murderer" in Mitchell County in 1911. Mary Turner was lynched in Lowndes County, on 19 May 1918, for making "unwise remarks."

All these lynch victims were black, though Georgia's history also includes the case of an unnamed white in Dawson County, lynched in 1890 for being "an informer," and another, the white Henry Worley, lynched in Gilmer County in 1894 for the crime of "testifying."

These murders were by no means all spur-of-the-moment events. They were often planned and deliberately staged as public spectacle, watched by large crowds, with adults bringing their children in tow, as if to a picnic. The hanging and torture of the victim was frequently photographed, and you could buy, as souvenirs, amateurish picture postcards of black—and often blackened—corpses hanging from trees: 'Strange Fruit', as Billie Holiday first sang in a New York club in 1938 and recorded the following year; "they're selling postcards of the hanging," as Bob Dylan first sang in a New York studio in 1965, in 'Desolation Row'.

These spectacles also suggest that the perpetrators felt some kind of guiltless entitlement to behave in this way; but, in turning a lynching into a public entertainment, they were only following a barbarous practise the forces of law and order had introduced. Public hangings of condemned murderers were still being held in Georgia in the 1890s.

In Statesboro, a black man, Drew Holloway, was hanged in public on East Main Street at about two o'clock in the afternoon on Friday, 19 December 1879, for the murder of another black man, Benson Brown. People came into town from all over the county all morning to see it, and, to augment the saloons, people set up stands on the streets, selling whiskey and fruit. Ten years later, one Alonzo Evans was hanged in public in the same town, under the supervision of Sheriff S.J. Williams. Almost seventy years later, this was remembered by the elderly newspaper columnist Maude Brannen Edge: "People came from everywhere, bringing their children, spent the day, and had a picnic . . . What tales our public square could tell!"

This entertainment seems to have developed out of Big Court Week, by which people meant the annual sitting of the county's Superior Court, first held in May 1797, which, in the nineteenth century, grew into an annual festival of disorder, with the small village of Statesboro invaded by men from all over the countryside, roaring in for a licensed wild time:

A hanging, a lynching, a whipping were always drawing cards, and the mobs came to town, especially in Big Court Week! Every horse trader in the state made his appearance with his drove of horses. South Main was the race track and the gambling was worse than Reno's . . . The only difference between this town and the Wild West: no dance halls, no fancy women.

But lynching was a public phenomenon of special character, and it was about more than either mob entertainment *or* politics. It betrayed a desperate urge to suppress blacks at every level in the aftermath of their release from slavery. So degrading and panicked a response to the African–American presence obviously betrays a deeper agitation than opposition to enfranchisement alone could provoke.

John Dollard suspected, back in the 1930s, that sex was at the heart of it, and he reminds us, usefully, of the gulf between the psychic reality of post-Civil War race relations and the official white position.

The official stance was that the two races did not mingle, that black people were so intrinsically inferior to whites that physical contact between them was anathema—which is why individuals like our Elbert, people who were visibly of mixed race, were always denied "legitimate status," in Dollard's phrase. The reality was that "many, if not most, Southern boys begin their sexual experience with Negro girls."

Wasn't this likely to have been true for Reddick, way back in the first half of the nineteenth century? It remains true for many white Georgian men still alive today. Bob Hammond, the middle-aged, white curator of the Burke County Museum in Waynesboro, told me there was "so much hypocrisy about this." He said: "There was twenty-four years between my oldest brother and me, and it was quite usual when you were growing up on a farm that, if you had a bit of money, your first sexual experience would more than likely be with blacks."

As Dollard puts it: "One might ask why, in view of the many derogatory attitudes whites have towards Negroes, Negro women are still attractive sexually." His answer includes saying that "Sexual behavior is almost always more complex than it appears and deep taboos and anxieties are in most cases associated with it; but certainly the factor of straight sexual desire must play a role. After all, monogamy involves much renunciation . . ."

He adds that "It may be again that Negro women are valued because they provide a zone of freedom in an otherwise tight cultural situation as respects sexuality; with them the white man can have a transitory irresponsible relationship, whereas otherwise sexuality is loaded with cares, threats and duties. In relations with Negro women the psychic strain may be much less."

This connects with the widespread notion that African Americans were generally less *uptight*, to use a word that hadn't been coined at the time, so they were seen to have more relaxed attitudes to sex than white people. Alan Lomax, the son of the folklorist Willie McTell would encounter in 1940, wrote this about black culture as reflected in the children's songs and games and the adults' song performances he had witnessed and collected in the 1940s—and wrote it in the 1990s, unhindered by any notions of political correctness:

A note of unconflicted happy eroticism rings out . . . all the little double- and triple-entendre rhymes of the ring games, of black minstrelsy, of ragtime jazz, the blues and rock—have gradually chiselled away at the starchy standards of nineteenth-century propriety . . . Nowadays the language of song employs the explicit argot of the streets. In all this, the driving force has been the sexually more permissive African cultural tradition, in which fertility rather than continence is a central value.

At the same time, the structures of Southern society pressed black women into making a sexual accommodation with white men *and* prevented black men from being able to express—or even hint at—their anger in white company. Black anger could only be multiplied at being so doomed to this humiliation.

We might say that this absolute prevention of all possibility of protest is what underlies the endemic black-on-black violence in the society in which Willie McTell grew up. Violence often ruled the home. Men killed each other with knifes and guns, revenge was physical, and there was no idea among the black working class that women should not be beaten up in anger. The jook joints and black clubs, late at night, were truly dangerous places. People got killed. When the blues emerged as a recognisable genre in the 1920s, the theme of murderous violence was a prominent part of its lyrics.

McTell himself was, mostly, as genial and kind as people get, yet one of his records, 'A–Z Blues', still shocks even seasoned blues aficionados with the gleeful sadism of its words, as it tells in anatomical detail how the singer is going to carve his initials onto the face and body of his woman. It was not autobiography, but it was a narrative born of its time and place.

The absolute power of the white man, the arbitrary unfairness of every unwritten rule you must obey your whole life long, the ever-present knowledge that you may be killed or driven from your home if you challenge him in the slightest way, that he can act without restraint—this explains, too, the delight with which African Americans heard the news of the sinking of the *Titanic* in April 1912.

It was like a message of deliverance from God! It was whitey's come-uppance. Pride had come before a fall. The Man was not all-powerful after all. The unsinkable ship had sunk! All over the United States, black singers rushed this iconic event into songs of covert celebration, and, well over a decade later, they were still relishing the symbolic power of the story when some of them were finally able to record.

Dollard also cuts to the heart of the tension between the official line about sex between white women and black men, and the white Southern man's anxiety over the possibility of reprisal for his own exploitation of black women:

We have seen white men guarding the border line of their caste, belligerent and suspicious, repelling every overture of a Negro man across the caste line. We might also ask how the white women feel who are defended in this manner. The official attitude is that sexual attraction to Negro men simply does not exist.

The reality, of course, was different.

Dollard sums up by observing this:

It seems clear that any move towards social equality is seen on its deepest level as really a move towards sexual equality, that is, towards full sexual reciprocity between the castes. Social equality would mean that the white men would have to abandon their exclusive claims to women of the white caste and admit reciprocal rights to Negro men.

Some Southerners had seen their nightmares loom close when they'd fought in World War I and seen, in France, black men sitting with white women—even dancing with them. Lynch-law was born out of panic at such prospects, and murderous mob violence was a flailing around trying to assuage the turmoil of guilt.

It may be, too, that the lynchings and torture such emotion calls into being become more palatable to their practitioners if robed in religion. Eric Millin offered an interesting Ph.D. thesis in 2002 in which he argued "that the religious rhetoric of white Georgians created an environment in which violence against African Americans was not just an option, but a sacred duty."

Millin notes that, in 1904, "a mob in Statesboro, Georgia, lynched two black men who had been repeatedly described as 'black devils' and 'demons.' A year later, Thomas Dixon accompanied his play *The Clansman* to Atlanta. His stage production and his best-selling novels celebrated racial violence as a component of progressive religion." (It was Thomas Dixon's work that inspired the Ku Klux Klan in its twentieth century form.) In 1905 and 1906, Hoke Smith "ran a religiously charged gubernatorial campaign that included black disenfranchisement among his central objectives. 'Holy Hoke,' as some called him, promised to secure white supremacy with violence, if need be." He got elected.

There were many lynchings in the counties where the characters in our story lived and died.

In Jefferson County, where Minnie and Willie were living in 1910, two men were lynched, one in 1908 and one in 1911. The other side of McDuffie, immediately north, in Lincoln County, there were six lynchings in twenty years, starting in November 1889.

In McDuffie, in the early hours of Sunday, 3 June 1888, a man named

Allen Sturgis was lynched for the crime of burglary, and another, Charles Harris, for "murderous assault," on 6 May 1907.

The Allen Sturgis case was reported in the *Augusta Chronicle* under the headline "FROM AN OLD OAK LIMB—ALLEN STURGIS A VICTIM OF THOMSON LYNCHERS—A Mob Take Him From the Jail and Hang Him on the Outskirts of the Town—His Mother Refuses to Care for the Body of her Dead Son."

Sturgis was reported to be the leader of a band of burglars who specialised in sneaking into houses where "young ladies" were known to reside. "In every instance, their attempts were made on the rooms occupied by the young ladies." The next subheading is "HAD GONE TOO FAR". Sturgis, "an unmitigated scoundrel" about twenty-one years old, who had already served two terms on a chain gang, was caught and jailed. Quietly, and without waking the night watchman, about thirty people broke him out of jail, took him out onto the Wrightsboro Road, and, at about one o'clock in the morning, strung him up. The newspaper commented: "While the more conservative of our citizens prefer seeing the law take its course, yet the entire community is a unit that Sturgis got no more than he deserved. Even the colored people of the community approve of the step taken."

Another account, in the same issue of the paper, said that "The tree looked like it had been grown for the special purpose to which it was put." Describing the response next day, the account read:

> "When was the body discovered?" "Long before sunrise. By 6 o'clock the town was agog with excitement . . . by 10 o'clock, the town was crowded with people. The scene of the lynching was visited by great streams of people who came and went all day."
>
> "Were there many negroes in town?" "Yes, the woods were full of them . . ."

That last sentence says everything.

On Tuesday, 7 May 1907, east of Thomson in the little town of Dearing, a farm hand called Charlie Harris was said to have shot "and fatally wounded" a prominent local farmer, Pearson Hayden. "A posse was immediately organised," the *Augusta Chronicle* reported, and Harris was captured. "He was starting towards Thomson, but never got through a deep swamp which had to be crossed." He was lynched that same night by about forty masked men, who riddled his body with bullets before going round to his house, "severely" whipping his family, and giving them "a brief time in which to get out of McDuffie County." Charlie was a month short of thirty years old, and, if the family whipped and driven out of the county by the mob were the same people as on the 1900 census, they were his much older wife, Mandy, by now aged fifty-four, and Mandy's son, Tom Hamilton, aged thirteen. Naturally, no one was arrested.

When Harris was lynched, Willie and his mother were probably in McDuffie; certainly Elbert, Nancy, Coot, Ed, and the rest were there.

In Glascock County, home turf of Reddick Mc Tyeir and Essey, there was only one recorded lynching, that of a Joshua Ruff, in 1897—and this was an unusual case, as a headline in the *Times-Journal* of Eastman, Dodge County, suggests: "Negro Is Lynched by Negroes." The story, dateline "Gibson, Ga., Nov. 16", read in full: "Josh Ruff, a Negro desperado, was shot to death by a mob of his own race near here. He had been robbing the blacks of the community, and the latter, growing tired of such treatment, took the law into their hands." In context, it's a story that almost reads as light relief.

In Warren County there were no recorded lynchings until 1911, when Charlie Jones and John Veazey were killed on 25 February, as punishment for "murder," but eight years later, on Saturday, 2 May 1919, local black farmer Benny Richards (aka Benny Brown), was driven from his hiding place in a swamp by a self-appointed posse who poured gasoline onto its shallow waters and set it alight to drive him out. He had reportedly murdered his ex-wife with a gun and shot her sister and four white men. He was immediately hanged and his body shot through with bullets at the edge of the swamp before being taken down and brought into Warrenton, where it was burned in front of "a crowd of 300 who took off a day's holiday in order to be in at the 'killing'," the *East Tennessee News* reported.

This was one of five similarly gruesome events of that year featured in contemporary accounts in a pamphlet first published by the National Association for the Advancement of Colored People in 1919. After the

Benny Richards case, their Secretary, John R. Shillady, wrote to the Governor of Georgia, the Hon. Hugh M. Dorsey, urging him to demand legal action against the lynchers and pointing out that, since the murder had happened in daylight, it should be possible to identify them. Assuming that his correspondent was black (which, as it happens, he wasn't), the governor didn't reply.

In Candler County, adjacent to Bulloch and centered on the town of Metter, which Willie would come to know well, there was a lynching the same year Willie's younger brother was born, 1917. In nearby Jenkins County, three black men were hanged by a white mob on 13 April 1919, for "complicity in murder." In Screven County, seat of little Sylvania, also adjacent to Bulloch, they lynched men in 1886, 1910, and 1925.

In Bulloch County—where Statesboro is the county seat, where Minnie and Willie settled around 1911, and where Willie then grew up—there were seven recorded lynchings, beginning with that of a Jake Brasswell in 1886. The other six were all in the twentieth century, the last of them the lynching of one Henry Jackson in April 1911: just about exactly when Minnie and Willie were moving to Statesboro.

Perhaps what brings home hardest the sickness and horror of life in this period in Georgia is not the lurid detail in specific, protesting accounts, nor even the murderous, righteous partisanship of the local press when it is reporting a lynching close to home, but the scary matter-of-factness in contemporary newspaper accounts in the unsensational cases.

From the *McDuffie Weekly Journal* in 1900, for example, here are two news items in their entirety, the first from the issue of 23 March and the second two weeks later:

A Lynching In Alabama. Lee County, Alabama had a lynching Sunday when Charlie Humphries, a negro who had attempted to outrage a young white girl, was caught and shot by a number of white men.

Allan Brooks Lynched. Allan Brooks, the young negro who assaulted Mrs. F.W. Hart near Bloomingdale, Ga., was identified Tuesday afternoon and lynched. Brooks admitted his guilt.

The casual implication of this sparse prose is that such summary justice was justice enough, and certainly not worth worrying about. It's chilling to read, and the more so when the surrounding tone, focused on white people, is so gushing:

> Mrs. DeJarnette, of Albany Ga., is visiting her sister, Mrs. S.F. Morris. Mrs. DeJarnette spent several years of her girlhood in Thomson, and time has only added to the beauty and winsomeness that rendered her so attractive as Miss Nora White.

This was the white womanhood that so much violence was needed to preserve.

Except when black people were being lynched, the papers were not inclined to notice them. In news items reporting that people have been injured, for example, whites are always named and blacks never are.

But, of course, so few black people could read the *McDuffie Weekly Journal* in 1900.

The most sensational case took place in Statesboro itself, in 1904—either the year of, or the year after, Willie's birth. It exercised the whole town greatly, yielded lurid newspaper stories, and made the town notorious as far away as New York, where the case was picked over "so that we may understand just what the feelings and impulses of a lynching town really are," as the monthly magazine *McClure's* said, smacking its lips.

That 28 July, a Thursday night, a forty-six-year-old farmer, Henry R. Hodges, his twenty-six-year-old wife, Claudie, and their three children, eight-year-old daughter Kittie Corrine, two-year-old son Harmon, and six-month-old Talmadge, were murdered at their farmhouse, which lay way out of town to the west, in an area of scattered homesteads called the Sink Hole.

The Hodges were a salt-of-the-earth white family from early settler stock, and descendants of the murdered man's brother and sister still live in Bulloch County. Two local blacks, Paul Reid and Will Cato, were quickly arrested, as were their wives and eleven other African Americans, and locked up in the jail in Statesboro.

Within two days of the murder it was clear that a lynching might take place. The state governor ordered the Statesboro Volunteers out to guard the jail and, on 31 July, the prisoners were taken to Savannah by train under military escort. The two men's wives had been questioned in jail, Harriet Reid had "talked," and stories were rife. On 1 August, the *Augusta Chronicle* and the *Savannah Morning News* both hinted that the Hodges females might have been sexually assaulted before, or even after, they were killed.

The inquest was held at the beginning of August, while the prisoners were still in the Chatham County Jail in Savannah, where Reid was reported to have made a partial confession. He made many contradictory statements in the days that followed, once claiming that the murders were the work of a black organisation called the Before Day Club, whose purpose was the robbing and killing of whites. This story went nation-wide and Before Day Clubs were discovered in Clarke and Tattnall counties and the town of Pavo, all in Georgia, and even in Alabama and Virginia.

Harriet Reid was first on the stand at the inquest on 2 August. The local paper reported: "She's as black as the ace of spades, and said she was about 17 years old." It added that the witness, "while not believed to be possessed with an average amount of intelligence, told her story in a straightforward way." Ophelia Cato, the next witness, was "a bright mulatto negro of about twenty years old." Between them they relayed a vivid tale of what they said their men had recounted about the events on the night of the murders.

Soon after dark, the men had gone out to the Hodges' home to steal money. They reached the house, where Henry Hodges confronted Reid. Reid knocked him down and one of them slit his throat. Then they went into the house, where Cato killed Mrs Hodges. Then they found the two young boys asleep on a bed in the front room and killed both of them. "They were brained with an ax," the paper reported. Reid and Cato started to leave, but then remembered that the Hodges' daughter was still in the house, and turned back to hunt for her. They heard a scrambling noise behind a trunk and pulled Kittie out from her hiding place. Terrified, she asked the two men what they wanted. They said they wanted money. She offered them all the money she had, which was a nickel. They killed her by smashing a lamp into her skull. Then they ran back to Reid's home, got some matches and returned to the Hodges' house, where they piled up the bodies and bedding and set the place on fire.

The inquest jury deliberated for just thirty minutes before ordering the release of all the prisoners except Cato and Reid, who were to be tried for murder.

The headline in the *Statesboro News* of 5 August, ten days before the trial and eleven days before the lynching, was "REID AND CATOE THE GUILTY DEVILS WHO BUTCHERED AND BURNED THE HODGES FAMILY. Their Guilt Has Been Established Beyond a Doubt." An editorial in the paper demanded that, after their trial, they should be hanged in public. (When this history was revisited in a 1960s Statesboro newspaper's publication that looked back over the previous hundred years, the headline to this tale had become "County's great tragedy was in July, 1904.")

On 12 August, the *Statesboro News* printed the names of the prospective jurors, confirmed that the trial would start three days later, and carried an advertisement for picture postcards of the murdered family copyrighted to T.M. Bennett, owner of a local photographic studio. The Savannah and Statesboro Railroad announced a special round-trip fare for the price of a one-way ticket.

Both men were brought back to Statesboro for trial, which duly began on Monday, 15 August, which was as soon after the crime as the law allowed. The state tried the two prisoners separately, so that each wife could testify against the other's husband. At 7.15 that evening, after eight minutes' deliberation, the jury found Cato guilty. Judge Daley, a cadaverous man too small for the ornately carved backdrop to his judicial chair, adjourned the court till next morning, without pronouncing sentence.

Next morning, they raced through Reid's trial and, before noon, he too was swiftly found guilty. Both men were sentenced to hang on 9 September, and were returned to Statesboro jail.

The crowd would not wait, and the soldiers deployed from Savannah and Statesboro took no action to prevent the crowd building up or capturing the prisoners. The sheriff himself unlocked the cell door and pointed out Cato and Reid to the mob. One of the murdered man's brothers, a minister from Texas, was among the crowd and, in tears, begged the mob to let the law take its course. "We don't want religion, we want blood!", somebody shouted. Cato and Reid were seized.

The magazine *McClure's* published a reporter's eyewitness account of what happened next: "They rushed up the road, intending to take the negroes to the scene of the crime. But it was midday in August, with a broiling hot sun overhead and a dusty road underfoot. A mile from town the mob swerved into a turpentine forest, pausing first to let the negroes kneel and confess." It was a small irony that this should have been where they met their ends, for both men were turpentine farmhands.

A debate now took place as to whether the men should be hanged or burned. Cato is said to have begged to be hanged.

"Someone referred the question to the father-in-law of Hodges. He said Hodges' mother wished the men burned. That settled it . . . the negroes were bound to an old stump, fagots were heaped around them, and each was drenched in oil." The crowd stood back to let a photographer through.

"Citizens crowded up behind the stump and got their faces into the photograph. When the fagots were lighted the crowd yelled wildly. Cato, the less stolid of the two negroes, partly of white blood, screamed with agony; but Reid, a black, stolid savage, bore it like a block of wood."

No arrests were made and no one was charged with any offense, and, as Judge Daley had predicted, the mob's actions immediately led to more illegal violence in the town and the county.

Two young women had already been whipped in the days leading up to the lynching, for jostling white women on the street. On the morning after the lynching, their father was viciously beaten up, and that same day, *McClure's* reported, "two other young negroes, of the especially hated 'smart nigger' type, were caught and whipped—one for riding a bicycle on the sidewalk, the other, as several citizens told me, 'on general principles.'" An old man and his son, in their cabin some miles out of town, were shot at through the window and badly wounded.

The third man to die was Sebastine McBride. This "respectable negro" was visited in his home at Portal by a gang of five whites, who whipped his wife, who was nursing a three-day-old baby, "and then beat, kicked and shot Mr. McBride himself so horribly that he died the next day," 17 August. Portal is a small country town and area a few miles north-west of Statesboro. In later years, Willie McTell would visit his brother Robert on his farm there. Descendants of Robert's wife live there still.

The Methodist minister of the time, Whitley Langston, announced that he would dismiss church members who had participated unless they would confess their sinful deeds and ask for forgiveness in public, at church. There was sufficient interest in the case that the *New York Evening Post* noted the minister's stance with approval (and, indeed, *McClure's*, which had covered the case so closely, was a New York monthly). In the end, Langston expelled two members of his congregation known to have been lynchers. In protest at this, twenty-five members withdrew from the church.

The local paper thrashed back and forth on the whole subject. "If the Negroes really think the South imposes on them let them go North," it declared, though there was widespread concern at the potential loss of labor if blacks were indeed being driven from the area by violence and by the fear of it. It was harvest time, and crops would rot in the fields if an exodus continued. On 18 August a meeting of local citizens demanded an immediate end to the "riot."

On 23 August, the *Statesboro News* editorial page published conflicting comments. One read, defensively: "We trust that the yankees will remember that they burnt a negro at the stake in Delaware last year." The other, unsigned but written by the progressive owner-editor, James Alonzo ("Lonnie") Brannen, said this:

The war is over, and the mob dispersed, and all is quiet in the county of Bulloch. Madness has given way to reason, and violent passions are now subdued. The better nature has re-asserted itself and the demon of frenzy has given way to the refined senses of humanity. The enraged lion has been caged, and the man comes forth again. Human passion has spent its fury, and reason again enthroned . . . There are many valuable lessons to be learned from the awful crime and its awful culmination.

That same week, more of Mr Bennett's photo-postcards were advertised for sale in the *Statesboro News* under the header "PHOTOS OF THE STATESBORO HORRORS FOR SALE", this time including pictures of Reid and Cato being lynched.

As Charlton Moseley and Fred Brogdon wrote in the *Georgia Historical Quarterly*:

> There is little doubt that the lynching had a political connotation. A number of the men most involved in the prosecution and defense of Cato and Reid were candidates for office in the Fall elections, 1904. Among them were the sheriff, J.Z. Kendrick (unopposed), J.A. Brannen and H.B. Strange, both special prosecutors in the case, J.J.E. Anderson, a counsel for the defense, D.Q. Stanford, coroner, and Mayor G.S. Johnston. J.M. Terrell also ran for re-election as governor and although he was unopposed a number of Statesboro citizens wrote in . . . protest against Terrell for ordering the militia into Statesboro during the trial.

They add:

> Initially, Assistant District Attorney W.R. Leaken in Savannah urged an investigation and prosecution of the Bulloch County men involved in the lynching. Leaken received virtually no support from Federal District Judge Emory Speer or from Attorney General William H. Moody and his proceedings were quickly dropped.

These historians note, too, that nationally, even President Roosevelt was blamed by white supremacists for the lynching in Statesboro: "Professor Willard B. Gatewood has shown that . . . Roosevelt was blamed for 'a wide variety of problems in the South, ranging from the shortage of domestic servants to the burning of . . . Negroes at the stake in Statesboro, Georgia, in 1904.'" The President was blamed for provoking lynchings, riots, and racial disorders because, at a White House dinner in October 1901, he had dared to include on his guestlist the eminent black educator Booker T. Washington.

This was the time and place, the world, into which Willie McTell was born.

# SEVEN

IN THE SAME years that saw the McTiers and Minnie Dorsey and our host of related characters growing up or growing old, a special generation was being born, in Georgia and other states: the generation of men and women who would become immortal names in the world of the blues, the singers and musicians who would create this new music.

Late nineteenth-century Georgia alone produced many key players: the future Ma Rainey was born in Columbus, over on the state's western border in 1886; the future Peg Leg Howell at Eatonton in 1888; Lucille Hegamin in Macon in 1894; Ida Cox in Toccoa, up in the mountains in the far north-east, in 1896; and, three weeks later, Jesse Fuller at Jonesboro, south of Atlanta (and now a suburb of it). In 1899 Georgia Tom (later to re-create himself as Thomas A. Dorsey, a founding father of the new gospel music) came into the world at Villa Rica, a very small town a short way west of Atlanta.

We can add a couple of white figures to this list too: men who would make distinctive contributions to the musical life of Georgia. James Gideon (Gid) Tanner was born in 1885 in tiny Thomas Bridge (a place that no longer exists but must have been around Dacula, east of Atlanta); in 1894 Riley Puckett was born in Alpharetta, just north of what's now Greater Atlanta. They would come together in what their advertisements called the "Rip Roarin', Snortin', Burn 'Em Up String Band", Gid Tanner and His Skillet-Lickers. Riley Puckett would be their blind lead guitarist.

They would get on record before any down-home blues, and attract black listeners too. Puckett would also record an instrumental version of the traditional 'John Henry' under the title 'The Darkey's Wail', prefacing this by saying: "I'm gonna play for you this time a little piece which an old Southern darkey I heard play, comin' down Decatur Street the other day, 'cause his good girl done throwed him down." It's pleasant to imagine that the "darkey" was Willie, and that these two blind guitarists passed each other on the Atlanta street. McTell, of course, was not "old" but young when Puckett made his record in April 1927—six months before McTell's first session—but then Riley Puckett wouldn't have been able to see that.

(It has also been imagined that these two would have met up at the Georgia Academy for the Blind in Macon, and it's true that both men attended it—but Puckett was there from the age of seven until he was about twelve, which is to say 1901 to about 1906, whereas Willie didn't reach the Macon Academy until the early 1920s. Even if they had attended concurrently, they wouldn't have met: blacks and whites were in separate buildings, on different streets.)

Outside of Georgia, the same last years of the nineteenth century saw the birth of many more of the great pre-war blues performers: Mamie Smith, whose first record can be said to have "started" the blues, was born in Cincinnati in 1883, the same year Gus Cannon was born in Red Banks, Mississippi; Sara Martin, another of the early "classic" women blues singers was born in Kentucky in 1884; Cripple Clarence Lofton in

Tennessee in 1887; and, the following year, Frank Stokes (also in Tennessee) and Huddie William Leadbetter (Lead Belly) in Shiloh, Louisiana.

In 1890 Jelly Roll Morton was born in New Orleans, and, in 1891, Elizabeth Cotten in North Carolina and Charley Patton in Mississippi. The remaining years of the decade gave birth to an extraordinary roster of talent: Blind Blake, Mississippi John Hurt, Furry Lewis, Bo Carter, and Blind Lemon Jefferson; Will Shade, Bessie Smith, Frankie Half-Pint Jaxon, and Alberta Hunter; Robert Wilkins, Blind Gary Davis (Rev. Gary Davis), Ethel Waters, Rosa Henderson, and, on an unknown date, that fragile genius Tommy Johnson, near Crystal Springs, Mississippi. Then came Blind Willie Johnson, Lucille Bogan, Memphis Minnie—and to mention another important white man, Jimmie Rodgers—Big Bill Broonzy, Sippie Wallace (the same year, to take a wider musical glimpse, as Paul Robeson, George Gershwin, and Jimmy Yancey), Sam Chatman of the Mississippi Sheiks, Sleepy John Estes, Lonnie Johnson, Little Hat Jones, and Whistling Alex Moore.

Many of these people were pushing forty before they had the chance to record, so the repertoire they carried with them, which naturally stretches right back to the songs of their youth, if not their childhoods, offers us patchworks of nineteenth-century material, even when sewn into the new cloth of the blues. This tapestry of vaudeville, minstrel show, variety theater, jazz, country hokum, field holler, African chant, and transmuted Anglican hymnal—all this and more was the musical heritage of this generation, and the same applied to those born into the same culture in the earliest years of the twentieth century.

In its first decade, Georgia's births of future blues performers include these men and women: Charlie Lincoln, in 1900, in Lithonia, east of Atlanta, and his brother, Robert Hicks (Barbecue Bob), two and a half years later to the day, in one of two small Georgia towns called Walnut Grove; James Kokomo Arnold in 1901, south of Atlanta in Lovejoy; and Georgia White in 1903, in Sandersville, a significant-sized town west of Jefferson County, roughly halfway between Macon and Augusta.

Then comes Blind Willie himself, born between mid-April 1903 and mid-April 1904, with the date of greatest likelihood being, as we've seen,

5 May 1903. Then comes the future Tampa Red (born in Georgia too) and Big Maceo, and then Bumble Bee Slim is born at Brunswick, way over on the Atlantic Ocean coast, a few miles north of the Florida border and surrounded by some of the Georgia Sea Islands whose Gullah peoples have been the subject of much linguistic and folkloric study.

Curley Weaver comes next, born near Covington on 25 March 1906, and three years later the idiosyncratic Frank Edwards, born in Washington Georgia on 20 March 1909—a man who survives Blind Willie by over forty years, consents to be interviewed for this book a couple of months before he dies, and dies traveling home from a recording session in 2002, two days after his ninety-third birthday.

There's one Georgia white man who deserves a namecheck here too: Emmett Miller, a forgotten figure from the world of blackface minstrelsy, born in Macon in 1900. You couldn't really claim him for the blues, but he influenced the great Jimmie Rodgers and many more, and his recording of W.C. Handy's 'St Louis Blues', backed by eminent jazz musicians, can hold its head up. Willie McTell, whose interest in popular music and in minstrel shows was eclectic and unapologetic, must have listened to him.

Beyond the borders of Georgia, the first years of the new century yielded innumerable notable figures, from Pink Anderson, Texas Alexander, and Black Ace, through Arthur Big Boy Crudup, Henry Townsend, and Tommy McClennan, to Victoria Spivey, Peetie Wheatstraw, and Bukka White, but, more especially, this futher roll call of the greats: Son House, Skip James, Big Joe Williams, Mississippi Fred McDowell, Leroy Carr and Scrapper Blackwell, Roosevelt Sykes, and Blind Boy Fuller. (Not to mention one Louis Armstrong, born in 1901, in New Orleans.)

Closer to home, an era was ending. On Saturday, 19 August 1905, at the age of seventy-nine, Reddick died.

He was buried at Zoar United Methodist Church. Its postal address is Stapleton (which is in Jefferson County), but it's on Zoar Church Road, which is, appropriately for Reddick, just inside Glascock and only half a mile from Warren and a further mile from McDuffie.

From Happy Valley it may be no distance as the turkey buzzard flies, but it's deep in the piney woods. You either zigzag right-left or else left-right, depending which turn you've taken off the road running south from Little Brier Creek. Either way, you're following distinctive, beehive-shaped white wooden signs to the church, on curving, desolate roads that skirt the remorseless pines. The only change of scene comes when, suddenly, dirt roads gash out to the sides in lurid wounds of luminous red clay.

When you reach the church, its suburban banality is a shock. I felt like protesting: at the super-clean building, a large brick insistence on rectitude rather than design; at the bushes, perfect as plastic ones; at the silly little brick wall around the edges of the bland grounds; and at the unremitting regularity and cleanliness of the graves. (Georgia is the largest producer of memorial granite in the world.)

It's such a well-ordered, *white* church! It took me less than one minute from parking the car to finding Reddick's grave. He's in the middle of a row of three, all white marble, flanked by son Noah and by Mary—she died on Christmas Day, 1911. All their surname spellings have been pruned and tidied to McTier. His first name is carved as Redrick. Inscribed, too, is "Father let thy grace be given That we may meet in heaven."

Here, marked by soulless white marble, sterile-clean in the twenty-first century, lies a man who lived the poor-white version of the antebellum life, a man whose young black slave girl bore his child, who left both of them behind to fight in the Confederate army, a man who served with Robert E. Lee, was wounded, captured, and then exchanged for a Unionist prisoner of war and who, after that war, came home to marry a white wife and bring up a family of six more children on a farm: a man who survived until 1905, by which time, living close to hand, he had a black great-grandchild who would become Georgia's pre-eminent blues singer. Quite a life.

In the wider world, 1901 had brought the death of eighty-one-year-old Queen Victoria; Theodore Roosevelt was President because William McKinley had been assassinated by a twenty-eight-year-old anarchist

118

promptly executed by the new-fangled method of electrocution. The same year saw the first use of fingerprints in crime investigation. Two million American households had a telephone. Sir Ronald Ross had just discovered that malaria came from mosquitos, and, in 1903, Orville Wright achieved what tends to be recognised as the first powered flight (a distance of forty feet). 1907 saw the discovery of blood groups and the invention of the electric washing machine. In 1908, Henry Ford put Model Ts into production.

But the gulf between life in the cities and the countryside, between the Gothams of the industrial North and the rural backwaters of the South, yawned so wide that Roosevelt appointed a Commission on Country Life that same year, 1908. William Samuel McTier's childhood years were the years when modernity began. But down in rural Georgia, almost no one noticed.

By 1910, Willie was six years old. He and his mother were gone from Happy Valley and McDuffie County, and they were living in their own place, with Ed's sister Doll as a boarder, and with Minnie's mother and stepfather's family nearby, in Spread, Jefferson County—back in what had probably been the county of Minnie's birth.

Spread is the old name for Stapleton, a small town then and now. By 1899 it was one of the station stops on the Augusta Southern Railroad line, and, in August 1903, it was still named Spread when it was incorporated as a town. (Confusingly, back in 1899, there was *another* place called Stapleton, four miles to the south-west. That's now a blank patch labeled Stapleton Crossroads on the detailed county map. Halfway between lies Stapleton Mill Pond.)

Spread changed its name to Stapleton around 1916, but many people still use the old name, and so does the church just out of town where many of Willie's wife Kate's family are buried.

Spread Chapel African Methodist Episcopal Church is barely over a mile from town, but it's out in deep countryside. You follow Highway 296 until this narrow road hiccups over the old railroad crossing, and there you take a right onto a narrower road, where two churches snooze on the right, mere yards apart. Spread Chapel AME Church is the second, and sits in a shady glade of deciduous trees, their roots disturbing the straight lines of the marble and concrete beds of the dead behind the church.

Today its white clapboard turns out to be vinyl siding imitating white clapboard. In August, ferocious mosquitos buzz the visitor. Across the way, cotton fields spread out beyond the railroad line. The church was founded in 1905, when Willie was a toddler and Kate hadn't yet been born. Spread is four miles west of Wrens, where Kate and her mother would have adjacent houses in a quiet suburban street long after Willie's death. If you were driving to Spread from Wrens, you'd be on Highway 102, and if you carried on out the other side of Stapleton, you'd soon arrive at Gibson, the county seat of Glascock, where Reddick McTyeir paraded back in 1860. Spread is only about a mile from the Glascock County line.

At the 66 gas station, an old guy filling up his quaint, green 1970s sedan tells me I should speak to Mr James Lee Hobbs: "He knows all about this part of the world, and he'll just love to tell you about it, too. He's an old-timer," he says approvingly, and gives me directions to the house.

The quiet orderliness of Stapleton's streets is disrupted only by the anarchy of people driving around them on white golf carts, as if they were cars. There's a craze for it here. It gives suburbia a hint of the sinister—as if a desperate Patrick McGoohan might come panicking round the corner at any moment, pursued by a lumbering giant balloon.

I walk up the steps in the humming heat and cross the wonderfully wide old porch to the door of Mr Hobbs' big white house, its paint faded and flaking, and from the porch I look across the road at a nouveau Southfork of a place, where a fat pink woman finishes whizzing a strimmer and promptly sits astride a mower as if disciplining a rodeo steed by squashing it. Her vast garden accommodates pagodas, a hot tub, fountains, and a motorhome. Its best feature is a row of blood-red canna lilies, thick as a hedge and functioning as one, running forty feet along the edge of her property, facing the big old wooden house.

Mr James Lee Hobbs comes to the door in his vest and trousers and, as so often, the first minute or two of conversation takes place with some apparent reluctance: he keeps the screen door between us and I can barely make out more than his silhouette. But then he emerges, pale and freckled, the once-ginger hair on his chest now faded to off-white like the paint on his house. He invites me to sit on a rocker on the verandah. The sound of the mower dies across the way and the fitful sounds of mosquitos replace it. We sit in the warm evening air, gazing out towards the small crossroads that is downtown Stapleton, and he tells me how the place used to be.

"Somewhere about the 1850s, a family of saddlers came here from South Carolina and established their headquarters here, by three huge oak trees."

They *were* the Stapletons, and they built Stapleton and Denton Mercantile about 1907 or '08, just about the time Minnie and Willie were drifting down here. They went in for horse trading, and mules too.

"They used to have 500 people working there, people from seven counties. I can remember ten stores in this town. It was a real thriving community at one time. Lot of farming in this area. That was the main thing. We had two railroads. One was Savannah to Atlanta, the S & A, and the other one was Sandersville to Augusta, the Augusta Southern Railroad Company."

This last had started as a narrow-gauge line, the Augusta, Gibson & Sandersville Rail Road—another reminder that Gibson was less inconsequential then than now—and it renamed and reorganised itself in 1893 when it swapped to standard gauge.

"Where the depot was, goods would come in. Salesmen would hire horses and buggies from the livery stable and take their goods out around to the little country stores. There was a restaurant that did real well, and a hotel where the 66 gas station is now. And there was a theater. They used to bring ice in too. The old ice house is still there."

I ask Mr Hobbs if he's always lived in Stapleton.

"I was born here in this house," he answers, "in 1925."

It's hard to remember, sometimes, how far the era that seems like The Old Days stretched on into the twentieth century. Hard travel by horseback, covering only short distances a day, was nowhere near vanishing when young Willie McTell was toddling around these sandy streets holding on to his mother's hand. The same world kept on going right on into the 1930s.

James Lee Hobbs can recall it: "I can remember when the road to Thomson was a dirt road. And to Warrenton. And all the way from the county line on through to Wrens. Going to Augusta with a horse and buggy, you'd camp out overnight on the way. It was more than a day's ride." Stapleton to Augusta is less than fifty miles.

All the old photographs of these towns, right up to the 1920s, show main streets of mud and sand and furrows, churned up by the hooves of horses and mules, strewn with piles of dung and planks of broken wood from dilapidated wagons. Buggies and propped-up wagon wheels are parked under trees that flank the raised sidewalks—trees that haven't yet been axed to make way for parked cars.

In 1900 there had been only 4,000 cars in the United States; the total number on British roads had been 750. In 1913 an American Ford took fourteen hours to build. By 1925, a Model T rolled off the assembly line every ten seconds, and, four years later, there were twenty-six million motor vehicles on American roads.

The 1920s transformed the downtowns. Railroad Street, Thomson, in 1908 looks like it's in a cowboy movie. The middle of the street is a chaos of cartwheels and hitched, undernourished horses, and thin men in spurs and boots. The same place in 1915 seems almost deserted; the few pedestrians are still making cowboy-hat fashion statements while great swathes of cloth and tent poles from the canopy of Hayes & Colvin's department store are falling all over the deep-dirt road outside—and no one worries, because the wide roadway is empty. Seven years later there's a notice about parking tied to a post at the edge of the sidewalk, the road is paved, big black automobiles bestride it, and everyone's clothes look much cleaner.

Outside the towns, the paved roads still halted abruptly. The 1933 State Highway Department map of Georgia showed as "unimproved roads" all the highways radiating out from Stapleton—east to Wrens, west to Gibson, right on up from there to Warrenton, and north up into Thomson. Stapleton's railroads died in the Depression, in 1935 and '36, though one line still carries local freight.

So the Spread in which Minnie and Willie lived, for an unknown period between Willie's birth in Happy Valley in 1903–4 and some point after mid-April 1910, was full of the bustle of visiting salesmen, steam locomotives, a theater attended by well-dressed patrons, a downtown restaurant, a hotel, and a busy livery stables. At the same time, for Minnie, a young mother with a young, blind child in a community of unskilled farm laborers, life went on as it had immemorially, separated from modern city life as by an ocean.

Her terrain was a patch of cotton fields and dirt tracks, trees and shacks, with no electricity, wooden stoves for heat and cooking, and oil lamps for light, where the water had to be drawn from a well with a hand-pump, and the toilets were outdoor latrines and chamber pots. No streetlamps lit the way to the neighbors', and no radio sang inside.

Few people had musical instruments either, except in middle-class white households where the pianoforte lesson was a recently introduced weekly fixture, or where a violin or classical guitar might have prevailed.

Rural blacks in Jefferson County not only made their own music, they mostly made their own instruments. The guitar was uncommon and pricey before the mass distribution of the 1920s mail-order catalogs, which could use the steel tentacles of the Chicago rail network and the postal service to reach right into the darkness of the nation's farms. Sears Roebuck, up in Illinois, would bring the affordable guitar and radio to rural Georgia, but not yet. Not while Willie was a child.

Yet both his parents are said to have played guitar. They must have acquired them somehow—they must have been keen to play.

Minnie played a mean guitar, according to Kate McTell, who was interviewed in the 1970s, half a century after Minnie's death. Kate said, "Willie always told me that, and his aunt Mattie told me, too, that her sister Minnie played a guitar real good."

Kate said she also heard it from her own mother—she always said the two mothers had been childhood friends—and that Minnie had played the blues. She went on to say that some people even thought Minnie was Memphis Minnie, because Willie's mother, "they say, could really tear up a guitar, work with it."

Kate, though, was a compulsive liar—I'm sorry to say this, for the sake of her living relatives, but there's no avoiding it. She always wants to put herself in the center of the story, and, when she can't do that, she will elaborate the tale so that she appears to be giving out treasures of detail no one else could supply.

But elaboration often blows up a story till it bursts. Nobody in Happy Valley or Spread could have mixed up Minnie Dorsey with the famous Memphis Minnie. Willie's mother died in 1920, while Memphis Minnie made her first record in June 1929, in New York City, and before that she had been heard only on the streets of Memphis, 400 miles from northeast Georgia, from the early 1920s onwards.

In any case, before 1920, would anyone in rural Georgia have described anyone as playing the *blues*? Debate is ongoing about when the blues began, but the present consensus seems to be that the term did not become a label attached to genres of music, and familiar to the general public as such, until at least 1923.

So Minnie Dorsey might well have played guitar, but we only have Kate's highly contaminated word for it. And her word was contaminated in a very specific way: before she was ever interviewed, folklorist David Evans' parents gave her a copy of Paul Oliver's book *The Story of the Blues*, and gave her time to read it. When she was interviewed, and already primed to tell these alien visitors what they wanted to hear, her recollections miraculously hauled in everyone most lauded in its pages, from Blind Lemon Jefferson to Blind Blake. It was an object lesson in how not to interview.

Gold Harris, one of Willie's grandma Nancy's children by Tom Harris Senior, and a lifelong friend of Willie's, may not be wholly reliable as a witness, but he's far more trustworthy than Kate, and never misleading by design. He recalled that Willie's father, and his Uncle Harley, played the guitar too. There are no extravagant claims here about how well they played, or about them playing the blues when Willie was a child:

His daddy used to play guitar . . . Both of 'em had one, you know. They used to didn't do nothing but be playing. They was pretty good sports, gamble all the time. They'd just go different places gambling. And so he [Willie] just took it up from his daddy, fooling with a guitar.

Gold Harris' view reflects a common one—that "fooling with a guitar" is all of a piece with gambling and drifting: it belongs with not working for a living. It belongs with escaping from the back-breaking labor and certain penury of working on the land.

Gold knew what he was talking about; he was renowned in Warren County as a bootlegger, and a "pretty good sport" himself. Uncle Harley, logged as Elbert H. McTier on the 1900 census, one of Elbert and Nancy's younger sons, would later disappear as mysteriously as Ed.

Minnie and Willie must have moved down to Statesboro quite soon after the 1910 census was taken that April: almost certainly within a year, because Minnie found work with a local white family called the Ellises—and their son, Henry, who became an admiring, ardent friend of Willie's, said later that Minnie "was cooking for my family for a great number of years." As we know, she died in 1920. How many fewer years than ten can you reasonably mean with a phrase like that?

Statesboro had grown remarkably fast. Bulloch County had been formed from one of Georgia's original eight parishes, St Philip's, in February 1796, and it was named after the son of a Scottish immigrant minister. Archibald Bulloch was born in South Carolina but bought a plantation on the Savannah River. Politically active in opposing the British, he became the first provincial governor of Georgia, in January 1776, and was to have been one of the signatories to the Declaration of Independence, but thirteen months to the day after taking office, he died, aged forty-six, in mysterious circumstances, probably poisoned.

There was no Statesboro in his lifetime, just a terrain of settlers driving out the Creek Indians. *Statesborough* was created in 1803, but was calling itself Statesboro by the time foragers from Sherman's army came through the nearby countryside on horseback in 1864. An officer in blue rode up to one man's gate, demanded how far it was to Statesboro, and was told he was in the heart of it. He looked around at a small wooden courthouse, two boarding houses, and a couple of liquor stores.

His men burnt down the courthouse, shot some chickens, hogs, and cattle, and left. The Court of Ordinary clerk wrote in the minutes book: "the Yankees was here and have burned the courthouse and there will be no court held today."

125

Statesboro became the county seat and a chartered town in 1866, but it was just a tiny settlement south of the old River Road—the stage-coach road that ran south-east down from Milledgeville, the old state capital, to Savannah (the even older state capital), parallel to the Ogeechee River, which slopes down the map and forms the north-eastern county boundary between Bulloch and Screven and Effingham: the two counties that stand between Bulloch and South Carolina.

The railroad, too, ran parallel to the Ogeechee River, on its swampy northern bank, so that there were little settlements and railroad stops on both banks of the river just a few miles north of Statesboro—places like Blitch and Cooperville, rail stops like Ogeechee and Dover.

When the railroad came to Statesboro, it began with a spur up to Dover. It was only eleven miles, but, in the 1890s, it was an hour's run and cost $1. The conductor, Dedrick Curry, collected your fare, and, up in the locomotive, Lonnie Wilson fired the engine and the Engineer was E.E. Smith. You had to take their train up to Dover to get the proper train. Even in the late 1950s, as Willie McTell was reaching the end of his life, he was driven up by car from Statesboro to Dover to catch the train from there back to Atlanta.

In 1880 the population of Statesboro was still a mere twenty-five, with 8,027 elsewhere in the county. Exponential growth happened from here, as outsiders arrived, sometimes with a flair and initiative lacking in the local saloons and on the chicken farms. In 1890 Statesboro's population was 525 (Atlanta's was only 65,550); by 1900 it was 1,150; by 1910, more than doubling in a decade for the third time, it was 2,630, and it would be nearly 4,000 by 1920.

The old world that was giving way to the new included the kind of rough-and-ready unqualified doctor who would cheerfully have a go at an amputation unphased by lack of equipment or medicine. There was a Dr George Ross in town in the early days who once had an old black male patient with a sore leg. He had him lie down on a table under a tree in his yard and, without offering any anesthetic, took the man's leg off with a butcher's knife and a hand saw. The patient recovered.

The new courthouse, ferocious in raw red brick, was up by the end of

1894. North of it was Mrs Margaret Lee's hotel, where a month's room rent was $10. There were many boarding houses by then, and this one was soon torn down to make way for the Statesboro Buggy & Wagon Company—a business that included the funeral-home service which, in December 1920, would take the body of Minnie McTier to the "colored section" of the city's Eastside Cemetery.

Everything was booming and thrusting. There was a lumber industry, and enough pine trees for the turpentine industry too, where great rackety two-storey wooden barns housed the stills that processed the oleo-resins extruded from the trees. There were planing mills, grist mills, and saw mills, and railroad lines built specially to haul this profusion of produce to and fro. Eventually, even one-legged, bicycle-riding Mr H.S. Blitch would hop on this bandwagon and run a lumber company.

These industries pulled in black workers as well as white, from all over this part of Georgia. In 1901 there was a strike of white carpenters on a building site in Statesboro because a black worker had been brought in and they refused to work with him, but unskilled laborers worked alongside each other, more united by class than divided by race.

The prospect of owning their own patches of farmland pulled people in too. Naomi Johnson, who knew Blind Willie from early in the 1940s, says of the much earlier exodus of people from around Stapleton, including Minnie and Willie, mutual friends Dave and Julia Howard and many more, that they came because only by moving south could they hope to farm their own land.

"Up there," she told me, "they didn't have any land. That's how come so many of 'em floated down here. There was big landowners, and they didn't sell land. They had to live on that land and work for him. All that up there, 'twixt Augusta and Atlanta, was mostly big landowners. I mean, thousands and thousands of acres. And they just hired 'em to work there. They felt like it was slavery. They had to slip away in the night to come to Statesboro because the man didn't want them to leave, he was losing so many."

The Stapletons were the big landowners, Naomi says: that's why the town is called after them. "So when they come down in here, a lot of 'em, it was different. They could rent their land and be their own, you know."

Even the lumber trade had partly come down from Jefferson County. The Howard brothers brought a significant portable saw mill down from Wrens in about 1898.

Statesboro soon had more than lumber, farming, and railroads. By 1895 there was a soda-bottling plant, by 1899 mains water, by 1901 a telephone company, by 1903 the Bulloch Oil Company, and by 1905 a volunteer Fire Department and electric street lights. (The countryside had to wait till 1937 for mains electricity.)

Nor was it only the lumber business that ran its own trains. In the early 1900s, the Patapsco Guano Company regularly sent the Patapsco Special, loaded with cargoes of processed birdshit, between Baltimore and Statesboro's Central and Georgia Railroad depot at East Main and Savannah Avenue.

Downtown business started up: stores, insurance companies, news-papers, banks, doctors, even hotels. In 1899 the county decided it needed to build a "pauper farm" a couple of miles west of town. Churches were as competitive as other businesses—the First Methodist and the Bethel AME arrived in 1886, the First African Baptist three years later, the First Presbyterian and the Statesboro Primitive Baptist in 1891, the Brannen Chapel Methodist Church in 1892, the Thomas Grove Baptist Church in 1895, and a whole lot more by 1907.

Above all, there was cotton, and then tobacco.

Cotton had been grown in the county for a hundred years before Statesboro existed. (Forty acres of it had been destroyed by hailstones as big as pullets' eggs in a storm of sci-fi proportions back in 1819.) Cotton dominated everything in south Georgia as the twentieth century began, and Statesboro was a key trading center. Farmers brought it into town on their mule-drawn wagons, and stacked it up in the cotton warehouse on East Vine. It was brokered and went out again, to be shipped across the world. By 1908 Statesboro was the world's no.1 marketplace for selling a particular, highly desirable kind of cotton: Sea Island cotton. Statesboro was selling ten times as much of it as Savannah. Men grew rich and built mansions around the town.

The cotton here was less hard on the workers, too, and this brought more people in from other parts of Georgia. Naomi Johnson remembers picking it:

They had blackseed cotton up there, and it had just about enough lint to hold the seed, and it was just seeded, and it had a big boll, and it was harder to pick than this down here. You had to work to get it out and it was hard, ruin your fingers and everything. But down here it was this Sea Island cotton, and you could just pull it up and it was fluffy, and people just floated here.

This ended with the arrival of the boll weevil. It crawled across the border from Mexico in the 1890s and reached Northeast Georgia in 1920. Sea Island cotton was especially vulnerable to its attack, and the last year of decent production levels for Bulloch County was 1920. In 1921 the acreage under production remained roughly the same, but the number of bales it made plummeted. The years that followed were worse. By 1943 there was no cotton at all. Today it's around again, you see little cotton fields in the area, but the days when it was called King Cotton are nearly a century ago.

Luckily for Statesboro, tobacco took over. Its Bulloch County pioneers had to cure their tobacco in a home-built flue, pack it into a hogshead, and take it to the Carolinas to reach a market to sell it at. No one else took much notice till 1913, when farmers turned up to hear about tobacco-growing experiments by a man named Smith in Effingham County, who said he believed the Bulloch County soil was perfect for it and predicted that it could become a major crop of the future.

He was proved right before the end of the 1920s. And the recurrent pattern of annual tobacco production and tobacco selling—when it was harvested, when it reached the warehouses, when the wheeling and dealing were done and the salesmen were in town—all this would come to shape the pattern of the adult Willie McTell's travels.

But the town would shape his development long before that. Its particular character would be a formative influence on him right from when he arrived there with his mother, in 1910 or 1911, at seven or eight years old. He and the town would grow together.

# EIGHT

STATESBORO, 1911, was a far bigger, busier place than anywhere Willie had lived in his admittedly short life. All this bustle, all the accelerating pace of industry and trade, automobiles and buggies, cotton wagons and rival railroad lines—this was all around the alert, intelligent boy. The town, centered on its pugnacious courthouse flaunting a sixty-five-foot high tower, was laid out in blocks in the classic pattern of a grid of cross-streets, though a few of these were somewhat out of kilter and the railway lines looped around regardless.

It was a vibrant mix of whiskery nineteenth-century gusto and the thrust of an evolving modern world that was new to him and Minnie. He couldn't see it, but he could hear it, smell it, touch it, taste it, and feel it in the warm, dusty air.

If the young Willie could discern light through one eye, as several who knew him said he could, then he'd have felt the difference between walking under the streetlights of prospering Statesboro and standing in the absolute blackness of Spread or Happy Valley.

Here, tangibly, was the twentieth century! Here, alongside prosperity, was the excitement of the new, and a widespread belief in progress. This seems lost to us now, but back then every new invention proclaimed a leap forwards in the human condition. Each scientific advance abolished some back-breaking labor, speeded life along, and thrilled the spirit.

Even to live in a little shack by the Savannah and Statesboro Railway line, a few blocks south of the courthouse, down in the easterly scrubland between South Main and South Railroad, as Willie and his mother are said to have done when they first came to town: even this was to have your senses intoxicated by the smokey aromatic roar and blast of the ever-busier and more powerful steam locomotives passing. They must have thrilled the child with all their monstrous glory, and, whistling loud enough to blow the house down, shouted the dangerous promise of travel.

The power and drama and saving grace of the railroads are celebrated all through American popular music. It was at a station in Tutwiler, Mississippi, around 1903, that W.C. Handy first heard a blues holler—and the words were about the railroads: "I'm goin' where the Southern cross the Dog . . ." The railroads and the blues, in part the music of migration, would intertwine all through Willie's life.

There is one story about Willie and the dangers of the railroad that dates from this part of his life: his earliest Statesboro days. According to testimony recorded in the 1970s, older people in town then remembered when Willie and another boy had once been playing on the tracks when a train suddenly bore down upon them. Willie heard it, shouted to his friend and jumped clear just in time. His friend was slower and lost a leg.

If Statesboro was rapidly becoming a place of consequence when Willie and his mother arrived, it was of a size that both of them could handle. To browse through the scrapbook-sized town history still on sale in the library, *Statesboro: A Century of Progress 1866–1966*, is to see over and over the same names, the same families, running through every aspect of the town's life, from the shopkeepers to the sheriffs, from county court to country club, from the doctors and teachers to pharmacists and farmers.

It's not only the wealthiest, pushiest white families that recur in every list of who does what (though they certainly do). Look through the census returns for 1900 and then turn to those of thirty years later, and, in every walk of life, for blacks and whites, the same clusters of names bounce back again and again.

At the powerful end of things are Averitts, Brannens, Simmonses, Olliffs, Cones, Laniers (not pronounced in a French way, "*Lann*-yea"—as I'd assumed until I got laughed at—but "Luh-*near*"), Blitches, DeLoaches, Groovers, Franklins, Zetterowers, Hintons, and a handful more. At the farmhand, turpentine-worker, and domestics end are the Lewises and Hendrixes, the Joneses and Johnsons and Kettles.

The fact is, as Statesboro illustrates no more or less than any other provincial town in Europe or the United States, most people don't move. The world is full of the stories of the people who do move: those driven to join great sweeps of migration, those forced into the inexorable worldwide drift of the poor from countryside to city, and those individuals not driven or forced at all, but who leave Pleasantville for big-city careers. It's the latter who write the stories, and everyone sings the songs.

Ambitious people move, and desperate people move. A black wage in 1940s Chicago would be four times Mississippi's. A quarter of that state's black population would leave. (And trains, more than muddy highways, would be the means of that escape.) But, as everyone who looks into their own family history discovers, most people don't move. The best place to find out about Great-Auntie Jones, who grew up in Little Middling a hundred years ago, is to drive over there and ask around.

You may have to stifle the egocentric feeling of amazement that Little Middling still exists, and is getting along fine without benefit of you having given it a thought in forty years, but you'll find at least a handful of people still living there who remember not only Great-Auntie Jones, but a fiancé of hers who got killed in the war that you didn't know about at all.

Unless they're driven out, most people don't move. For people in Minnie and Willie's situation, it was a significant step to migrate even from McDuffie and Jefferson County to Statesboro. Spread to Statesboro is seventy miles. Regionally, it's a jump. Naomi Johnson calls McDuffie "up north," Statesboro is "south Georgia."

Willie's father, Ed, moved by becoming a "no-good gambler and drifter," but most McTiers stayed put in that small patch of land where you can swing a cat across the county lines of McDuffie, Warren, Glascock, and Jefferson. They were farmhands and unskilled laborers. If they didn't say goodbye to everything they'd known and migrate up to Atlanta or far further, they were stuck where they were. And in this they were typical of the vast majority of Georgia's black inhabitants.

When Willie McTell is a grown-up, what makes his life truly different is that he *travels*. Foreigners (like me) are often puzzled by Americans' geographical pedantry— the irritating way that, even if you name a city large enough that everyone has heard of it and knows roughly where it is, such as, say, Baltimore, Americans are compelled to interject "Baltimore, Maryland?" Less irksome but just as noticeable is everyone's stress upon their home county. It confesses the importance of that county as the defining limit of mobility for most people in the past.

When Charlie Harris was lynched in Dearing by those masked men who then went round to his house and beat up his family, they ordered them out of the *county*. On all sides, that was what mattered. The adult Willie stands out from all those cousins and aunts and uncles he visits in Happy Valley, and in Statesboro, because he comes and goes: he moves freely out of the county. Blindness might force him into music, but music sets him free to move around.

Today in the US, middle-class whites often give me information about which county such-and-such a place is in or where such-and-such an event occurred, and they drop in the county name from the sheer relish of esoteric knowledge. It's their affluence and modern mobility that makes it esoteric. Yet despite it, still, most people don't move.

So in Statesboro they're all still around today—the Averitt of the new Averitt Arts Center; the Strickland who heads the local history and genealogy section of the library; the young ex-City Marshall, Mr W.H. Ellis, whose great-grandmother, Mrs W.H. Ellis, employed Minnie; the Franklin who is innkeeper at one of the chain motels and used to do PR for the city, whose father ran the downtown drugstore for close on fifty years; and the relatives of Willie's half-brother, Robert Owens.

One warm March day in 2003, I walked along South Main Street from the courthouse square, having just read in some semi-literate City Hall PR handout that Minnie and Willie's little hut was the one still standing, out at the back of what's now the Statesboro Historic Inn—and, more improbably still, that this was the very building inside which Willie wrote his 'Statesboro Blues'. It's called the Hattie Hallaway (or Holloway) cabin, the only survivor of several that used to squat down here in the scrubby woods with the railroad line beyond. Preposterous, of course, but I went looking for it anyway.

Hattie H.'s cabin has been "restored," and is rented out to holidaymakers. I left its bijou fakery and went poking around in the trees beyond, looking for evidence of the other, long-collapsed little huts that might really have heard Willie's footsteps once upon a time.

John Armstrong was mending something in his garage nearby, and was happy to walk me through the wispy trees and bramble bushes. A thick dishevelment of barbed greenery clusters around the trunks of the gone-wild pecan trees, chasing up them about eight feet and then giving up, falling back on itself and letting the slender grey limbs of the trees escape upwards. I followed John, thorns snatching and twigs snapping around us, to the spot where one day, by chance, he'd found the barely discernible remains of an old fireplace in the litter of dead leaf mulch and undergrowth. There it was. It *might* have been Minnie and Willie's . . .

In Willie's time, the combination of booming prosperity, manageable size, and one more factor made it as near as possible the ideal town to grow up in, if you had to be poor and black and blind in Georgia.

That factor was the town's progressive character. A relative term, of course (don't mention the lynchings, or the absolute of segregation), but, compared to the rest of South Georgia, it was progressive—and this small mercy made a large difference to the forming of Willie McTell.

It was a town with early ambitions for betterment in education, health, and broadness of horizon, and these had begun with the outsider who became mayor in 1889, James Alonzo Brannen, who saw the need for a railroad, a bank, a telephone company, a utility company, and a college, and worked to achieve them. Though wealthy, he lived frugally, investing money in books, travel, and philanthropy. He donated land for the black church, the black school, and a park.

In surprising ways he swam against the dull drift of the day's opinion. He was not a church member, he challenged the advocates of the temperance movement, he invited Jews into town and helped them enter the business community, and his hero was Abraham Lincoln. Not your average 1900s Southern white male, yet his was a formative hand in the making of Statesboro.

The town also had one of the first women newspaper editors in Georgia, in the 1890s, decades before American women could vote, while the Jaeckel Hotel, opened in 1905 by a forty-six-year-old German immigrant called Gustave Jaeckel, was the most civilised hostelry this side of Savannah, and drew big-name visitors from Henry Ford to Glenn Ford. In 1908 the town opened both a hospital, the Statesboro Sanitarium, and a college.

Black education was, of course, a poor second to white, as everywhere, but in Statesboro it was offered surprisingly early, pushed for by black residents as early as 1902, delayed only by their inability to afford land. In 1907, though, the City Colored School was founded and inspired by a great man, a role model for African-American aspiration.

William James was thirty-five years old and stood six foot, six inches tall: in every sense a large presence in the black community and respected in the white. He had come to Statesboro from just outside Bartow, one stop west on the railroad line from Minnie's alleged possible birthplace of Wadley, in Jefferson County.

After two years, he added an industrial department to the school, and brought in an instructor from the Tuskegee Institute in Alabama, which was the country's leading school for African Americans and had appointed Booker T. Washington its principal at the age of twenty-six.

Just as Washington hired in distinguished outsiders, like the black scientist George Washington Carver, to raise up Tuskegee, so William James imported all the talent and assistance he could to his school in Statesboro. The black Atlanta editor B.J. Davis was invited to address the pupils and open their eyes to a wider, literate world; other speakers came in from Washington, DC, New Jersey, and New York State.

To pay for extra teachers, James secured money from the nationwide Slater Fund, established in the 1880s by an industrialist to help educate former slaves, and from the New Orleans branch of the Jeanes Fund, established by a rich, tiny Philadelphia Quaker named Anna Jeanes, who started her fund off with $1,000,000, but then died the same year, 1907. (Thirty years later the Jeanes Fund merged with the Slater Fund to found the Southern Education Foundation.)

A new building was achieved with help from the Rosenwald Foundation, set up by Julius Rosenwald, president of Sears, Roebuck & Company; and Tuskegee remained a constant source of help. Through this relationship, William James was able to bring George Washington Carver to Statesboro too.

Today we might question whether James' emphasis on self-improvement without politics was altogether good or progressive. Sometimes the respectable black guest speaker could patronise Statesboro's black children shockingly. In 1912 one eminent visitor was the Rev. C.T. Walker, who had spent five years as a New York City pastor and preached to John D. Rockefeller. The local paper reported that he told his Statesboro school audience they were "not handicapped on account of their color, but by their own personal conduct. He pointed out to them that individual conduct makes the reputation for the race, and that the reputation for lawlessness and worthlessness is not on account of color, but of conduct. He told them that when they, by right living and integrity, deserved recognition as citizens, they would find that color is not in their way." Beat that for poisonous Uncle Tommery.

Yet, through his own determination and breadth of vision, William James built an institution in Statesboro that offered a far better standard of black education than its pupils could have expected, and received at least some support and encouragement from the rest of the town. What practical alternative route to betterment for blacks in the rural South could James have offered? Revolution? Working-class people have always seen education as a means of rising above their circumstances, and they've been right.

James also inspired by personal example. Everyone knew what he stood for and the dignity he personified. Willie never went to school—blindness meant exclusion, back then, from what we now call mainstream education—but when we picture the grown-up Willie McTell, whether as a blind man picking his way along Georgia's red-clay dirt roads or as a street singer in the big city, and then ask why he routinely wore the best clothes he could, and always wore a tie and that snazzy hat, isn't the answer the powerful example of William James?

Everybody comments on Willie's clothes. Earl M. Lee, a ninety-one-year-old white Statesboro resident, was representative of everyone with memories of Willie when he told me in 2004: "I've lived here all my life. I remember him. He always wore a cap. A cloth cap with a short bill. And he wore a coat all year round. He was never ragged—always clean and presentable. He was always presentable. Blind Willie was respected."

As for that hat, with its stylish peak transforming a sort of chic cloth cap, you'll find it in the new-season fashion illustrations offered in the *Bulloch Times* for spring, 1916. It wouldn't be the only time a boy just reaching adolescence discovered an interest in looking cool and fixed on a particular fashion item that he'd retain a soft spot for all the rest of his days.

Nor would Willie ever seem to doubt the value of education. He would attend several blind schools, become literate enough to read Braille, take formal music lessons at the Georgia Academy for the Blind in Macon, use libraries, and more generally relish his own intelligence and his talent as a wordsmith as much as his musicianship.

Beyond William James, there were other education professionals in Statesboro who were progressive-minded people too, a little later on, and all through Willie's adulthood, as he returned again and again to Statesboro—the place he called "my real home"—the impress of these individuals could be felt upon the town's character and its relatively congenial personality.

One such inspiration was the only black physician in town, Dr Harvey Van Buren. He had moved to Georgia in 1911 from his hometown of Sumter, South Carolina, after gaining his medical degree at Howard University in Washington, DC, in 1907 and completing postgraduate studies at Boston College of Physicians and Surgeons in 1910. His first Georgia job was in Louisville, in the very south of Jefferson County, and he moved to Statesboro in 1915. Van Buren was so good that, during the flu epidemic of 1918, he was even allowed to treat white people.

He was better qualified than most doctors in the South, let alone black ones. He was certainly the best-qualified doctor in Statesboro when Willie was growing up there, and, in December 1918, at the age of thirty-four, he opened his own modern hospital, the Van Buren Sanitarium. (The vile Rev. C.T. Walker gave a speech at the opening ceremony here too.) The Sanitarium was on West Elm Street, the street Minnie and Willie would live on after leaving the shack by the S & S Railroad line, when Minnie was working for the W.H. Ellises.

How Minnie got her job with the Ellises nobody knows, but she proved herself competent to be the cook for the family in their home on Main Street, right downtown.

To go home from his drugstore, which was at nos.3 and 5 North Main and stood facing the courthouse at the absolute center of town, the tall, reserved, moustachioed William Hays Ellis simply turned left onto the sidewalk and strolled two blocks north along North Main to no.45, his detached, one-storey clapboarded house on the corner of West Elm.

It had been built around 1909, and was typical of its time and place. People didn't have architects as such: they just saw a house they liked and copied some of its features. Every house had a big porch: not a show of antebellum columns but always a porch.

The front door in the middle of the porch opened into a hall that ran right through the house, so that in summer you could open both front and back doors to create a draft that would ease the heat a little. In winter it wasn't such a good idea, but almost every house in town followed this pattern.

As Mr Ellis entered his front door, the bedrooms were to the left off the hall. On the right, the first room was a formal drawing room, called the parlor, seldom used, with typical furniture of the period: a cane-back sofa with removable cushions and two matching chairs, and a piano. Next came the family living room; then the dining room; and then the kitchen. A back porch ran along behind, and near it, opening on to Elm Street, was the garage that accommodated their black seven-passenger Buick, the last word in luxury. Autos of the day generally lacked refinements such as interior lights, but when you opened the Buick's rear doors a light came on, embedded in the back of the front seat.

The porch that ran across the front of the house also went down the south side, where there was a small conservatory, mostly for plants. The grounds didn't stretch widely either side of the house, but at the rear the Ellis' large oblong plot ran all the way down the first block of West Elm to North Walnut, parallel to North Main behind it. This was maintained as an immaculate expanse of lawn, with a gazebo. Mrs Ellis entertained a good deal, and it was customary for guests to bring their children along with them, rather than leave them with nannies. They would come along and be put in a designated playroom and served food there away from the grown-ups. In fine weather, she would give the children little parties in the gazebo while entertaining their parents in her home.

The kitchen, Minnie's workplace, was a room about twelve feet by fourteen, the floor covered in linoleum bought off a roll. One door led into the hall, one into the dining room, and a third out on to the back porch.

The city-owned power plant could provide homes with electricity only for lighting. Even then, the current for residential areas was cut off at eight o'clock in the morning so that enough could be supplied to the stores and businesses downtown. At six o'clock in the evening you could have lights on again in the house.

Minnie cooked on a large wood-burning range. It had a firebox built into it and on top four big cooking plates that you could lift up. The flames from the firebox came over, the oven was underneath, and the pipe that carried the smoke away went up through the back of the stove and through a boxed-in, two-door shelf above, called the warming closet, before arriving at the flue. Everything had to be cooked on this range, which stood against the back wall, facing the door to the dining room.

The kitchen had a wall-hanging sink, but few cupboards. The windows were on the right, the north side, facing Elm Street. Apart from the stove, the room was dominated by two wooden work tables: one where bread and cakes were made, the other for vegetables and meat. Here, like everywhere in the South, the noon meal was the main meal of the day, because that's when the servants were on hand. As in most houses, the kitchen was scrubbed down with lye soap, daily, after this meal. Mrs Ellis' kitchen table surfaces were almost white from the bleaching they received.

This was the room Minnie worked in almost every day till the end of her life. But Mrs Ellis was a gourmet cook, and did her own baking. She, too, would have spent long periods in this kitchen, at first teaching Minnie how she wanted things done, observing this girl from north Georgia, and then, growing in confidence about her honesty and capability, working alongside her, enjoying polite but never unguarded conversation.

Servants frequently couldn't read or write, and often came not only without credentials, but also without experience. Recruitment arrangements were casual on both sides, and learning on the job was expected. Minnie inspired enough confidence that Mr Ellis built a small, two-room wooden house or hut for her and Willie, in their grounds, at the corner where Elm and Walnut meet.

This was another factor in shaping Willie's perceptions of what was possible in his world: he and his mother were now living right downtown, and under white protection.

This was not the fate of most black citizens. Downtown was whitey-ville, and if you were black, you could work in it—in domestic service, or as a watchman, or laboring on the buildings that were forever coming down and going up—but, with few exceptions, you couldn't live there.

Like the Ellises, some other white residents housed domestic servants in huts built on their own land. Two or three homes had servants' quarters over the garage, but these were separated from the houses. No servants lived in. Nor could black people own central downtown property: not even those few middle-class blacks who could afford such a house. An invisible line kept them a certain distance down the street. Yet Willie was right there inside the line.

Mrs Ellis was Nellie McQueen Ellis, from Cumberland County, North Carolina, and she was born there on 18 October 1881—which made her exactly six years older than Minnie.

She was William Hays Ellis' second wife, and he was eleven years older than her. He'd been born in June 1870, so that by the time Minnie and Willie encountered him, he was a man in his forties, well connected and well established in the business life of Statesboro, and he and Nellie had been married some twelve years or so. They were a polished couple. He traveled as far as New York and Philadelphia on business trips, he admired objets d'art, and he would bring her many of them back from his trips.

As a younger man, he'd known tragedy. Within a year of his first marriage, to Annie E., their first baby died the day it was born, in August 1896, and was buried in Eastside Cemetery without receiving a name. They had two further children, a boy and a girl, and both survived, but Annie died at the age of twenty-nine, on 9 January 1906. Three years later, W.H. married Nellie McQueen.

Financially, too, the Ellises were a family whose fortune went down and down, as W.H.'s grandson Ed confirms. He's a pleasant, deep-voiced, tanned man and, when I met him, he was sporting a cream shirt of noticeably good quality. Ed runs the Ed Ellis Construction Company. He builds and his wife, Johnnie, does in-house décor. Not surprisingly, they've built their own large house in the leafy southern part of Statesboro.

There are a hundred homes here, in amongst the trees, linked by loops and circles of roadway lined with streetlamps. This Ellis house has a huge verandah on which vast white wicker armchairs and sofas gaze out upon a small, featureless lake. Ed has a small, glass-walled study that overlooks it too, opening off an open-plan kitchen-diner-sitting-room, in which, waiting for me on the dining table, was a dark scrapbook of old photos. Scrutinise it as I might, it yielded no picture of Minnie standing in her apron, dishcloth in hand, on the edges of a shot of Williams Hays and Nellie.

But there is a picture of W.H., sitting on a hard, canvas-backed rocker on a porch. It was taken shortly before his death in 1937. He's sixty-seven and looks eighty, but he's still fastidiously dressed.

There's also an atmospheric sepia photo of Mrs Ellis sitting out on the porch with their son Henry (Ed's father). Henry and Willie McTell were friends. In the picture, taken about 1930, Nellie is sitting on a plain hard chair beside a wicker planter on which a big kitchen pot seems filled with roses. She sits with her back to the clapboarded wall of the house, in a soft cotton short-sleeved dress that buttons all the way down to the hem: the kind of dress that's good enough for around the house. She's in her late forties, comfortably plump, with a wide ring on one finger of her right hand and well-groomed hair pinned back off a high forehead. She's wearing thin-framed spectacles and looking out beyond the porch, perhaps lost in her thoughts, perhaps a little displeased with Henry.

Henry also looks a little down in the mouth, and stares off in the same general direction. He's sprawling lengthways on a two-seater rocker set sideways on the porch, so that he, too, has his back to the house. He's in slacks, white shirt, and business tie, the shirt buttoned right to the neck, but the sleeves rolled up to the elbows. He's barely twenty-one, yet already much of the way through the process of going bald, and looks thirty. He's still living at home at this point. He looks as if he's just been quietly rebuked and mustn't reply as he might wish to.

Neither mother nor son seems aware of the camera. Perhaps, after all, there's no discord here but only the companionable glumness of a family worrying about money.

W.H. Ellis' grandfather, Benjamin Ellis, born in 1810, came from North Carolina, but, by the time of the 1860 census, he was a Bulloch County farmer, and by far the richest man on the same page of the enumeration. His personal estate was valued at $23,640; compare this with Reddick McTyeir's $400.

Benjamin's eldest son, Joshua Ellis, eventually inherited a large amount of the family's land and probably many slaves too. His son, William Hays Ellis, was too late for the slaves but inherited, in turn, his father Joshua's farmland. Yet, in twentieth-century Statesboro, W.H. and Nellie ran one of the town's modest drugstores, their business interests mostly failed and, in the end, despite the Buick, they were forced first to turn their home into a boarding house, and then to manage a less genteel one down the street.

"I've always heard that Joshua Ellis, who was W.H.Ellis' father, was a big farmer," Ed says. "So then my grandfather Ellis, he had very large farms, in Candler County, and he was one of the few farm landowners that built a school on his own for the black children. I've had people *tell* me that when the slaves were set free that the people that lived on his farms, when they were informed of this, said they didn't want to leave:

142

that they couldn't find any person they'd rather be with than Mr Ellis. But that would have been Joshua Ellis.

"I never knew either of them—my grandfather died before I was born. And through the Depression he lost his wealth, but I do remember seeing the old schoolhouse, that my daddy took me to when I was a child. I remember—it was an old wooden building. But it was a large building. This was in Candler County. Metter. Twenty miles from here. But I'm sure that's all probably gone. Joshua Ellis is buried in a cemetery over in the Metter area and, at that time, it was part of this county, Bulloch County. Bulloch and some other counties gave the land for Candler County."

What kind of farming had it been?

"Typical farming round here. Just corn and cotton and maybe tobacco, that sort of thing. Before the war. He lost all his wealth at the height of the Depression. He was also a large stockholder in the Bank of Statesboro, and back then the stockholders took any losses personally: there wasn't any FDIC. And as other people experienced the Depression, you know, it came back to the bank, and so he had a hard time there for a long time."

W.H. Ellis was more than a farmer and stockholder in the bank, and he knew some failures before the Depression. A couple of people with money set up an oil seed mill in the town, processing a ton of cotton seed an hour, day and night, in 1904, but it failed to make money and then it burned down. One of the investors who tried to rebuild it, and who never recovered his money, was Ellis. He and J.G. Blitch finally sold it to a Carolinas firm in 1915 (and three years later, after another fire, it closed down for good).

Mr Ellis had his fingers in many Statesboro pies, and not all of them got burned. He served the City Council as its Recorder from 1899 to 1908, a part-time job without an office to work from, which meant that he did the paperwork inside what was then the McLean Drug Company's store and had previously been a furniture store and, earlier still, the medical office of Dr A.W. Quattlebaum. Mr Ellis' Recorder's pay of $300 per year doubled in 1907, in recognition of the extra work now that the city had a water works and a power plant. In March 1908 he took over the drugstore business and named it the, er, W.H. Ellis Company. The building, and those adjacent, belonged to that far bigger fish, James Alonzo Brannen. He had first built the row of shops as little wooden stores on the site of one Charney Fletcher's rooming house, which had burnt down in 1886; but his own replacements burnt down themselves two years later, and he had them rebuilt in brick. The history of Statesboro's constant early rebuilding can be seen as a history of fires.

W.H. Ellis was also in at the beginning of the Statesboro Hotel Company, which set itself up in 1905 to join with Gustave Jaeckel in building his new hotel. Ellis was one of the company's directors, though before long he seems to have dropped out, perhaps when the stakes got high.

He was also a freemason (who wasn't, apparently?), keen enough to serve as secretary of the Ogeechee Lodge 213 Free & Accepted Masons from 1898 till 1905. Ten years later he began a stint as its treasurer, which he remained until the end of 1919.

By the time he stepped down from this committee work, his surviving children from his first marriage were almost grown: William Louis Ellis was coming up to eighteen and Mary Belle to fourteen. His only child with Nellie, Willie's friend Henry J. Ellis, born in 1909, was a ten-year-old boy.

He was six years younger than Willie McTell, yet the two played marbles together, as Ed remembers being told: "I didn't have a clue who Blind Willie was. But every now and then Daddy would talk about him and how *close* they were as little boys, playing together in the yard, and I remember saying 'Well Daddy, was he really blind?' and he said 'Well he could shoot marbles! And he could shoot basketball with me! So I wondered.' He said 'I think maybe he just had bad eyesight.' I don't know. But I can remember him saying that he could shoot marbles and he was real good at it!"

Ed adds: "I do know that he thought a lot of the man, I remember that just from how he referred to him: that they were very close, that Daddy considered him a very close friend."

How did that work, I asked, in the days of segregation?

"I really don't know. I would assume that, since his mother worked with my father's mother, that as children they were thrown together, so

144

to speak, and, being normal little boys, they played together and didn't look at segregation."

Henry died in 1992 but was still around in Statesboro when California-based academic David Evans came though town in the mid-1970s, interviewing people who'd known Willie. Henry told Evans: "We kids in the neighborhood—he was just one of us. He was always highly respected and admired by even the youngsters in this section of town, even though he was blind. Statesboro was much smaller in those days, and he was known throughout the entire community."

Henry says he's referring here to the period around 1918 to 1924, and adds: "He was a pretty good-sized boy when I was big enough to play with him. You might say he was a grown man." Evans doesn't seem to notice that these remarks would make no sense had Willie been born in 1898, as he believed, and therefore been twenty in 1918, when Henry was nine. But they fit well with Willie as a *youth* in these years—as fifteen in 1918, when Henry was nine, and coming up to twenty-one at the end of this period. No one would say "You might say he was a grown man" about someone already fully an adult, nor describe someone eleven years their senior as "a good-sized boy" or "just one of us . . . kids in the neighbor-hood." All through the interview, Henry is clearly describing an older *boy*. They play marbles together. There's a six-year gap between them.

It's always an odd business, to the outsider, how these racially integrated friendships existed in the South, alongside the venomously maintained divides of the adults. It happened all the time, though—and, as Ed Ellis suggests, children played together easily and without the burdens of formality and restraint that encrusted the grown-ups. Lindy McTier had black friends growing up in the panhandle in Warren County, even though there was absolute segregation in the schools. "We had good black neighbors and we often played together. This was true almost everywhere in the county."

And yet, how did these white boys with black friends, who then became teenagers making sexual explorations into black terrain, how did it work that these friends became non-friends—unpersons, virtually—and the sexplorations became clandestine, breaking all the segregation régime's official party lines and supposed taboos?

Do these friendships simply fade to vanishing point, regardless of the white individual's politics or warmth of personality, when adult rôles have to be assumed?

At what point, in this particular case, did the friendship of Henry J. Ellis and William S. McTell evaporate? They grew apart whether they wanted to or not, because of the race divide, the class divide, the gulf between their expectations.

Henry went plodding along on the sensible route to Statesboro respectability and oblivion, while Willie McTell wandered off down the road, into major recording studios and the annals of the Library of Congress, leaving us all an artistic legacy.

Their friendship didn't quite evaporate. Years later, on one of his revisits to Statesboro, Willie called on Henry—more likely at his office than his home—and presented Henry with one of his shellac-made 78-revolutions-per-minute records in an illustrated cover. The two old playmates must have stood there, both holding the oddity of a blues record in their hands, savoring a moment of mutual pride and possibly mutual embarrassment.

Ed Ellis remembers not the artefact but the music: "I can remember when we lived on Kennedy Street, Mother and Daddy, and I was a child. My sister's four years older, and she had a record player—and d'you know I can almost think I can remember that we had some blues stuff and we put our fingers in our ears! Because you know, we'd never *heard* anything like that! I just thought about that, that's amazing. But I'm not a music sort of guy."

Ed's son, the "new" W.H. Ellis, the one who was until recently a City Marshall, remembers the record itself, or at least, remembers that there was a picture on its sleeve. So it was still around the Ellis house when young W.H. was a child, two generations after Willie recorded it and gave it to his old friend Henry.

Where is it now? Gone. The family gave it to the library many years ago, no one there now remembers this, and nobody can find it. There's a locked cupboard in the Local History and Genealogy Dept. office, with half a shelf devoted to Willie McTell materials—all secondary. The 78 is not there.

After I'd left the Ed and Johnnie Ellis house, I paid a courtesy call on their son Will. He's a keen musician and he plays in a blues band doing gigs from time to time around Covington, Curley Weaver's old stomping ground. He has Jimi Hendrix as the desktop picture on his office computer and is thrilled at his own connection to the Willie McTell story.

He tells me about a piece of great good luck that befell him and the family. He was on eBay one day and, just on impulse, he put "Statesboro" into its search engine and there, up for sale, was the big old accounts book from the Ellis drugstore, which had disappeared decades beforehand. The seller lived in Sylvania, twenty-five miles up Highway 301 in Screven County, so Will e-mailed her, explained his interest, and got the book back for $15. Amazing.

The first time I went to Statesboro, in 2001, the double shopfront that used to be the drugstore was separated into a junk shop and a hairdressing salon. In the junk shop they still had the old cash register that had belonged to William Hays Ellis. I took its photograph. Willie must have heard its satisfying ping and whirr sometimes. You can't be fussy when you're following old footsteps.

Willie the Statesboro child didn't just play marbles. While his mother walked up through the Ellis' garden, past the gazebo to their kitchen, Willie stayed home and played out on North Walnut and West Elm, dirt roads both, with the neighborhood boys and girls. He could do more or less everything: ride a bicycle, spin a hoop, and wrestle. When he was feeling wicked, he could throw stones very accurately at passers-by, mules, and horses, and chew tobacco. "He was blind alright," a friend is quoted as saying, "he probably never saw himself. But there wasn't much he couldn't do."

He was also learning guitar, of course, and harmonica, and he'd have messed around with a jew's harp too—lots of Statesboro children played them. They'd been in town since 1887. There were keyboard instruments to listen to: organs in the churches, small organs and pianos in people's homes. By 1916 there were also phonographs coming into town. For $12 you could buy "the crowning achievement among musical instruments," the Vanophone, which weighed "only 12 pounds," played

10-inch and 12-inch "disc records" and had its own inbuilt speaker. You could buy it from the stationery department of the *Statesboro News*. Or you could fantasise about buying it. If you were a black laborer, $12 was three months' pay.

Willie had a guitar mentor in Statesboro quite apart from his mother: a man called Stapleton, who is said to have migrated down from the town of that name at more or less the same time as Minnie and Willie. He was remembered in the 1970s as Seph (short for Josephus), but no one of either of those names can be found on any of the censuses. A Joe Stapleton lived with his wife Eva on the same Statesboro Street as Dr Van Buren, near to Willie's house, and Joe was a generation older than Willie.

Willie also grew friendly with a family called Smith, who lived on the opposite corner of West Elm from the Ellises on North Main, and he used to go up there and listen to the youngest of their three daughters, Miss Annie, play the piano. She was the same age as Willie, and perhaps they had more than this and music in common. As he would lose his mother, so Annie Smith would lose her father. By 1930 her mother is a widow and Annie, now twenty-six, has stayed at home to look after her. The other daughters and her older brother have left.

There was another girl in the neighborhood who Willie turned to in particular, and what he had in common with her was blindness. She was one of seven brothers and sisters living with her parents in a little rented house on Walnut Street. The whole family was enumerated as Mulatto on the 1910 census, except for the head of household, George Watts, who was logged as a black farm laborer, age thirty-two. He and his wife, Bessie, had been married twelve years. After their two oldest children came twins, Ada and Ida, who were the same age as Willie. According to the census enumerator, only one twin was blind, and that was Ada—but, in January 1920, it was Ida, not her sister, who was attending the Colored Section of the Georgia Academy for the Blind, on Madison Street, in the big city of Macon.

This was exactly where Willie McTell would go two years later.

Before that, though, came the eventful last years of the 1910s. While the World War ended and men from Bulloch County were coming home,

Willie was starting to run away. From the age of about thirteen, he started joining little carnivals and circus side-shows for a month or two at a time, finding his feet as a musician and entertainer, and then coming back home to Statesboro, staying a while before leaving once again. It would be the pattern of the rest of his life.

# NINE

M INNIE MCTEAR WAS still a young woman when she was living and working in Statesboro, and neither Willie nor the Ellis household kitchen occupied all her attention. Somewhere she met a man named Lourie Owens (the spelling of "Lourie" is uncertain), and by late 1916 they were having an affair. He was a couple of years younger than her, his family had come from nearby Burke County, and he was an unskilled laborer. By the time of the 1910 census, the family had moved into Bulloch County and Lourie was a nineteen-year-old, doing odd jobs to support himself, his twenty-three-year-old "wife", Lizzie, and two-year-old son, Jake. Next door, his mother Adeline, by now a widow aged forty-five, was still bringing up three of Lourie's younger brothers. Whether Lourie and Lizzie were legally married we don't know, but they were still living together in Statesboro ten years later.

In other words, contrary to the 1970s account of Willie's life, his mother never remarried. Not only did Lourie Owens never marry Minnie—they never even lived together. He had Lizzie and a child at home; Minnie was his lover on the side. In 1916 she became pregnant by him, and she gave birth to their son Robert in July 1917: a half-brother to the teenage Willie.

Perhaps it was while Minnie was involved with Lourie Owens, and having the baby, that Willie began to run away from home, start his music career in carnival showbiz and then move into bootlegging. Many years later, on the recording he made for Ed Rhodes in the Atlanta record store, the middle-aged Willie talked about his adolescent years, and said this: "I run away and went everywhere: everywhere I could go without any money. I followed shows all around till I began to get grown." He says he was "in the shows" by 1917: specifically he mentions that he "was on Robertson's sideshow. He had an old plantation show at that time, you know. John Roberts' [sic] sideshow." He stumbles over the name, which is an unusual imprecision from the normally exact and reliable McTell, and no outfit on any scale can be found to have existed under either name. He seems, therefore, to have meant the John Robinson Circus Show, and that he was employed as a singer and musician in one of the sideshow tents that were part of this well-known and long-established traveling show—one of the larger outfits that toured the country by rail, drawing large crowds, especially from rural communities.

John Robinson had been born in Albany, New York, in 1802 and had died in Cincinnati in 1888. By that time it was a lucrative family business, and featured, in the circus itself, such exotic novelties as an elephant that stirred lemonade with its trunk. The tented town of its sideshows included minstrelsy, salesmen, dancers and singers, freaks, and general hokum entertainment. It was all of a piece with the minstrel troupes, black and white, that were touring the land in those days, and giving many of the early blues stars their first career experiences. Bessie Smith began with the Moses Stokes Minstrel Show, Ma Rainey with the Rabbit Foot Minstrels, and Georgia Tom worked in the circus as a water boy.

Willie McTell loved it all, and here learned some of the repertoire that he would retain and perform all through his life. He told Ed Rhodes: "we was all show boys, you know."

How a blind youth got himself taken on by the traveling shows we don't know—Bessie Smith had to audition for her minstrel show slot—but everything about him suggests that, even if he couldn't draw on an intro from anyone amongst his extended family—from, perhaps, those "sports" on his father's side—he was a resourceful young man with his wits about him, bright, personable, and with no shortage of self-confidence. He must have been, already, a competent performer of the popular songs of the day, and he would have been cheap to hire. Ed Rhodes asks if he was singing with the show's owner, and McTell replies, correcting him: "Yeah, I was singing *for* him. I was working for them that particular time." But he also comments: "I was doin' pretty good with 'em."

Nevertheless, he says he soon returned to Statesboro and turned to bootlegging alcohol for a living instead: "I come home later and started work, you know . . . I started to work for a man down in South Georgia. He had a way that I could make a ... a little easy change, you know? So I started to work for him." McTell says only "South Georgia," but this will have meant Statesboro. It was home. It was the place he knew his way around best, and locals call this "South Georgia" just as they call counties like McDuffie, Warren, and Jefferson "up north."

When Willie says he could make "a little easy change, you know?", Ed Rhodes asks, "You weren't a bootlegger, were you?" Willie replies, laughing, "Sure was. Sure was."

Rhodes asks whether he made the whiskey or hauled it, and Willie, of course, says that because his eyes "were bad," he certainly couldn't drive: "So I had to make it." Ed Rhodes asks whether it was good stuff, and McTell's reply is telling again. Here's a man who takes pride in himself and has standards: "Oh yeah! I'm not gonna make—I make pretty good booze. I still could make it, I imagine. If I tried. But I ain't—I ain't been to a still in quite a number of years. But I imagine I could still make it. I could instruct how to make it, if I didn't make it myself. I'd give good instructions. I could give you good instructions probably."

Bootlegging was a perennial occupation for the poor in rural North America, and it became hugely more important because of Prohibition. Nationally, the US brought in this ban on the legal sale of alcohol on 16 January 1920—but, in Georgia, there had been prohibition throughout Willie McTell's lifetime. Bulloch County, largely dry since July 1880, voted to resist allowing drink dispensaries in 1903, though dealers in Augusta and Savannah advertised their whiskey, rum, and gin every week in the Statesboro papers in the years around Willie's birth, and it was brought in jugs by the trainload. But, in 1915, the state toughened up its legislation, stopping not only these dealers but private clubs and surviving Civil War veterans too from selling alcohol of any kind. It was, as they say, total dryness statewide. (National repeal of prohibition became law, on 5 December 1933, but after that states—and counties—could still legislate individually. It took until 15 May 1935 for Georgia—and Bulloch County—to repeal the prohibition amendment.)

152

Prohibition made the bootleg business ubiquitous and classless. Bootleggers were everywhere, and those who made decent quality drink, using brass pipes and generally hygienic equipment, were often upstanding citizens, white and black. So were their customers. From the time that Willie McTell came to consciousness, bootlegging was a natural, accepted part of the communities he knew, and continued to be so throughout his life. In the 1930s, living in Atlanta with his wife, Kate, Willie would be selling bootleg whiskey as well as his musical skills. Before and after that decade, many people on his father's side of the family were engaged in it, out there on the conveniently murky borders of McDuffie and Warren County and on the farmland around Happy Valley. It was a home industry and a hobby—not, as in Chicago, a big business controlled by the Mob.

Even on a small scale, though, the penalty for getting caught was a very stiff fine, so it could be a dramatic and risky way of making a living, as Annie Lou Jackson and her son Teddy told me, looking back across many decades. Annie is the surviving sister of cousin Eddie's wife, Hazel McTear, and she and Teddy still remember how scary it felt when they were taken along on dark nights.

Teddy: "When I came up, my Uncle Bo-Rat and them, they were still making whiskey. They was still moonshinin' back then, when I was small. One night I remember he took me with him to go get some. I said, 'Ooh, where we goin', no lights on?!' He said, 'No, you turn the lights on, the bogie man'll get you.' I still didn't know what he was talkin' about until I got older and realised he was talkin' 'bout the police would catch us, down in the woods. Oh yeah, we went down, way across the fishpond dam and through the water and then you start loading it down in the car. Outside it was so dark I couldn't see him, and then, when he came back, I saw he had two jugs in his hand, and he threw 'em in the car and we come on back."

Annie: "My sister took me with her one night—I didn't want to go with her another night! I was scared all the way down there and back! She went and hid it way down in the field. And I didn't wanna go with her anymore. I was scared. They didn't act like they was scared."

Annie, born in 1925, added: "See, that's all the drink back then long there. That moonshine."

I asked who would have taught Bo-Rat how to do it in the first place, and Teddy replied: "That's all they knew in the country. Everybody told everybody. All her brothers, every one of them were moonshiners. Couple of 'em got caught and a couple of 'em didn't. It was just common thing for the country, specially down this way."

Annie added: "That's the only way you lived. If it hadn't have been for that there wouldn't have been no way for the folks to live. All them federal men and state's men would come in from time to time and then they'd go back again."

And what happened when you did get caught?

"Charge you even money . . . charge them a thousand dollars! One of my brothers I know had to pay a thousand dollars." Big money, then and now.

While the McTears and Jacksons were bootlegging in McDuffie, on the Warren County border, Gold Harris was, as Probate Judge Lucy Bryant told me, a bootlegger and a dignified person "respected by black and white." I suggested that, if he was well known as a bootlegger, he must have had plenty of customers. "Yes," she said, "and more white than black." And there was Willie himself, down in Bulloch County, perhaps learning the trade from one Harper Myrick (arrested 1919), or from Willie Moore, a highly regarded Statesboro individual (arrested 1921). In 1930s Atlanta, Willie's supplier would be his Uncle Coot.

Meanwhile, Willie's mother Minnie was back in Statesboro with a baby to look after. Perhaps she was now working only part-time in the Ellis kitchen. We cannot know whether Minnie stayed in the hut on the Ellis' land or whether she went out to family in the country to give birth. Perhaps she had help from her sisters, or half-sisters, allegedly now in Midville, which is across the border in Burke County. Interviewed in the 1970s, Robert Owens said that he'd been born in Midville—though he also admitted readily that he knew precious little about his origins, and wasn't even sure what year he'd been born. (His second wife, supplying information for his death certificate later in the 1970s, gave the county of his birth as Jenkins: another of those adjacent to Bulloch.) After the death of his mother, it was said to have been a sister of hers from Midville who came to collect the three-year-old Robert.

Was Willie in Statesboro when Robert was born, or was he working away with the sideshows or the whiskey stills? We don't know. How often was he around while Robert was a child? Not much, perhaps. Robert, interviewed in the 1970s, offered no childhood memories of Willie, even when pressed, except for a general recollection that Willie used to make him little wooden toys ("a little wagon" and "a merry-go-round, you know—see-saw boards"); and added "No, when I got, say probably seven or eight years old, he was in his twenties then, and he were right in his prime, making music. He wasn't around me too much then. He was just, you know, in and out."

Willie's account of what happened when the three-year-old Robert first lost his mother suggests the same; he makes it very plain that he spent no time hanging around to look after the child. He told Ed Rhodes: "My mother, she died and left me 1920 . . . and after then I got on my own. I could go everywhere I wanted then, without lettin' anybody know where I was. I didn't have nobody to write back to but a brother three years old, and he wasn't able to understand."

Willie was reliable, however, about the date of his mother's death. It was indeed 1920—and the death certificate obtained in Atlanta gave the exact date as 21 December, at 10.30pm. She died in Statesboro, probably at home, and the cause of death tells us that Minnie was pregnant again shortly beforehand.

Whether her lover was still Lourie Owens, or now another man, we can't know. She died, according to the doctor, who claimed to have seen her alive that day, from "puerperal sepsis"—a delayed infection of the uterus—"following a miscarriage."

This need not have been a prolonged process. Minnie may have miscarried only the day before she died. And she probably brought on the miscarriage deliberately, with or without help from a home abortionist. Did she want another baby, when she already had a three-year-old to look after, and no man, and a job to hold down? This is necessarily conjecture, of course—but the medical facts support it. She's more likely to have become infected from external intervention, trying to have an abortion, than from involuntary miscarriage.

The informant for the death certificate was W.H. Ellis—though "informant" is a flattering term for it. He gave her marital status as "widow" (which was highly unlikely, but probably the story she had told), her age as thirty-five (she was thirty-three), and her residence address as merely "Statesboro Ga." He answered "Don't know" for Name of Father, Birthplace of Father, Maiden Name of Mother, and Birthplace of Mother. And, having given her occupation as "Cooking", his answer to the follow-up question—"General nature of industry, business or establishment in which employed (or employer)"—was, again, merely "Cooking".

I couldn't help but feel that had Mrs Ellis been the informant, we might have gained rather more information—but eighty-one-year-old Jack Averitt, the Ellis family friend who had been able to describe for me the very room where Minnie spent her working life at the Ellis house, was confident I'd be wrong in that assumption: "I don't think in that period the servants told that much to their employers . . . It would not have been a lack of interest. It would have been quite possibly the lack of marriage . . . But Mrs Ellis wouldn't have known—if Mr Ellis did not know, Mrs Ellis would not have known."

She wouldn't have had conversations in the kitchen?

"Well, very likely, but the Ellises discussed things. I think if she had known that he was the informant, if she had known information she would have given it to him. And I can just hear him saying, 'Now Nellie? Do you know any of this?' "

If she had known any of the information that is blank on the death certificate she would have told her husband before he filled in the form?

"Yes, because she would have said, 'Now Will, do you know this?' or 'Do you have this information?' Because she would have been somewhat familiar with what he needed to know, and I think they would have discussed it. It's a very interesting thing even today . . . I have a maid that's been with us twenty-two years. She was trained by my wife and greatly admired and she comes five days a week, and, since my wife's death, I have been in conversation with her much more; but I can tell when she is evading. She's very honest, but her family thing . . . There's always been the question of, 'I wonder why they want that information?' . . . so I am sure that in the 1910s and 1920s, it would not have meant that there would not have been conversation between Mrs Ellis and her servants, but it would not have been a rapport conversation, and Mrs Ellis would not have said 'Now who is your mother?' It just wouldn't have been done."

By this account, then, Nellie Ellis would have known nothing about Minnie's family background or personal history (and nothing, especially, about her Bulloch County lovelife), even though the two worked alongside each other at those kitchen tables almost daily for a number of years.

But there is another question raised rather than answered by the death certificate. Was the date Minnie died really 21 December, or was it the day before? Doubt arises because the time of death is given as 10.30pm on that day—yet the date on which W.H. Ellis gives his informant's statement to the registrar, and signs his name to affirm that "the above is true to the best of my knowledge," and the registrar countersigns it, is also 21 December. Is it likely that within ninety minutes of Minnie's death late that evening, the registrar would have been available and Mr Ellis signing a statement in his presence? Would this be possible if Minnie had been taken to hospital, and died there, rather than at home?

It's unlikely—and for this reason. The doctor who attended her, and signed her death certificate, was a highly successful, white physician: one of Statesboro's most prominent citizens, whose home was right across the street from the Ellises. He would not have attended a patient at the segregated hospital for black patients. He would certainly have crossed the street at the behest of the local pharmacist, his neighbor.

Dr Quattlebaum, Dr Mooney, Dr Whiteside, and Dr Floyd all had houses in the block right across North Main Street from the Ellis house. It was Dr Frank Forest Floyd who attended Minnie. He was a month off forty-six years old, he had been in the city since 1908, and he was in charge of (and would come to own) the Statesboro Sanitarium, the town's whites-only hospital. His professional reputation was a fine one.

His personal reputation, however, had recently been "blemished."

Around 1918–19, while his wife, Agnes, the mother of his two children, was ill, he was seeing another woman, Ethel. He used to bring his wife food from her, till she confronted him and said outright: "Don't ever bring me food from that woman." After his wife died, he remarried with indecent haste. Ethel was only nine years older than Dr Floyd's son, Waldo.

Was F.F. Floyd the one chosen by the Ellises simply because he was known as a fine doctor? Or because the Ellises felt that Minnie's predicament, however little they knew of its detail, was shameful too?

When Jack Averitt's own wedding was to be held at his mother's house, she told him that he could invite anyone he wished except Dr Floyd. She said: "I cannot have that man in my house." But, says Averitt, "When Dr Floyd died he had the largest number of floral tributes ever seen in Statesboro."

Ethel outlived him by many years, and, interviewed in the mid-1970s, said that she remembered the adolescent Willie well—and that she had given him a guitar:

> He used to come to the house. I was then married . . . He was singing and playing then, trying. So I had a guitar up at the house 'cause I wanted to learn to play. And I didn't. And I gave it to him. So he had had an old guitar somebody had given him, but he was awful proud of it . . . When I found out I couldn't and he was trying and didn't have anything much to try on, I gave it to him . . . Then later on, of course, I'm sure he got another one, but that was the beginning of it. Then he was just a boy . . . well, I imagine he was in his teens.

This must place these memories as coming from very soon after her husband had signed Willie's mother's death certificate.

Minnie's burial was modest, yet there was a touch of elaboration to it—perhaps a surprising touch. On the death certificate, the space for "Undertaker" is taken up with the rubber stamp of the "Statesboro Buggy & Wagon Co." This was a long-established, monied local company with prominent buildings downtown, and its clients were usually white.

Three days before Christmas 1920, Minnie's body was carried in the company's black hearse, drawn by two black horses, perhaps with long-service employee Mr O.L. McLemore holding the reins. She rode in unaccustomed style, then, to the black section of Eastside Cemetery, also known as Thomas Grove.

"I think," says local black resident Mrs Herbaline Rich, eighty-six, "there was a member of Thomas Grove [Baptist] Church that was on the original deeds purchased for that cemetery and a lot of times it is referred to as Thomas Grove, but it has never belonged entirely to any one church. I never know why some of the members of Thomas Grove Church think that it's their cemetery, 'cause it's not. Now that's the truth. It has never been named Thomas Grove cemetery, it has always been called Eastside—but it is, like you say, back of the white Eastside. Thomas Grove Church is right there on Highway 80, coming from the mall towards town. It's almost on the corner—it's just a bend around from the cemetery."

The church had itself only been organised in 1895; Willie McTell would hold at least one gospel concert here in later life. (The one we know of took place in September 1946, but this was unlikely to have been his only such visit.)

Mrs Rich's grandfather and others purchased the plot of land: "There wasn't a cemetery in Statesboro proper for blacks. They got together and said they would purchase this land and make a cemetery for the blacks in Statesboro, without having to go to some of the country churches to bury. This was . . . I would say 1900. I know that, in my family history, my father's youngest daughter was the first person that was placed in that cemetery, and that had to be 1900."

It was these individual founding volunteers who looked after the place: "All of them have passed, and when I came home to live with my mother she was 'bout the only survivor in the next generation, and mother was taking care of it. And now it's my generation, and since then I've been trying to do the best that I can."

Was there never any record kept of who was buried there, or where?

"That was something that I regret so very, very much. It's because when they first purchased their cemetery, some of the senior citizens purchased plots for their families, and those that didn't purchase plots, they just bought a space little by little—and back in that time that I'm talkin' about, before my grandfather died, spaces were like ten dollars a space, or maybe five dollars a space, and 'whatever you can pay me now and pay the rest later,' and, from what I can understand, you had to keep a record of your space—you had to mark it off and identify it and keep it yourself, because no one had time, or they didn't take the time, to try to set up a record or hire somebody to keep records or anything.

"So you bought it with the understanding that you will keep the record and know where your people are . . . So, through the years, it never changed, and that was the way it came down, and when my mother was not as young as she had been, I started helping there, and I had thought about having someone who was in art to draw me a plan and let me identify some of the places. But I never did that. But that was always the buyer's responsibility, to keep up. They were old, and nobody educated. Just dedicated, you know."

I tell Mrs Rich that I think Minnie's employers would have paid for her burial, and that they had used the Statesboro Buggy & Wagon Co. as undertaker. She responds with a memory that sheds a surprising light on local practise: "I'd say that, during that time, the white undertakers would bury the black people. I know a white undertaker took care of my grandfather when I was little. I can't remember who, 'cause, like I say, I was only little, but I know that white people came and moved my grandfather out the house, and they stayed for the wake, you know. They came and took him away, and then they brought him back and placed him in the living room. He stayed in the living room until burial time, and they took care of everything."

Jack Averitt, too, remembers a story his father told him—and he remembers it for its novelty: "My father told me about a black who worked at the Buggy & Wagon Company and had worked there for a long time and was greatly admired, and one time he was talking about it, and said at his death, if they could carry him in that black hearse, with those two black horses, it would make him happy. And according to the legend, they did."

Minnie's burial was highly unusual but not unique, then, in being handled by white Statesboro. Her body was laid to rest in the black part of

Eastside Cemetery all the same, in a $5 or $10 plot identified only by a wooden marker.

If Willie attended his mother's burial, or was even in town at the time, he seems never to have mentioned it. At any rate, he was a seventeen-year-old, and now he felt free. The phrase he gave Ed Rhodes—"My mother, she died and left me"—was a commonly used expression in speech and in song, and didn't necessarily carry that apparent subtext of complaint: of feeling desertion as much as grief. Eight years later, in 'Statesboro Blues', Willie used this commonstock line again—and perhaps then the word he added on was to offer that rare thing in his work, a flash of autobiography, for what he sings is not just that she died and left him, but that "My mother died and left me reckless . . ."

In truth, though, he was not wild by nature, and his reckless days were numbered.

# TEN

I F MINNIE HAD gone ahead with the birth of her baby, it would have been Willie's third, not second, half-sibling: because long before Minnie had Robert, Willie's father is said to have taken up with a woman named Pearl Hill. This liaison must have been before he ever went with Minnie: the child Pearl supposedly gave Ed, a daughter named Ola Moss, was born around 1901—that is, two years earlier than Willie himself, and when Ed was only about seventeen.

Pearl seems to have disappeared as mysteriously as Ed, but Ola remained in the Happy Valley region, and two days before Christmas 1916, while still in her teens, she married Clarence McGahee, a farm laborer. Ola gave birth to a son named Ray in 1918, and a daughter, Eva, a year later. I have been unable to trace this nephew and niece of Willie's beyond the 1920s.

Willie called Clarence cousin and included him in the cluster of people he would visit whenever he was in that part of Georgia; but Ola had already disappeared from the McGahee household by 1930—when Clarence is living right next door to Willie's grandfather El, with son Ray and another woman—so we might surmise that Ola died in the 1920s.

This might be why Willie, who never knew her as a child, never mentions her as an adult either. At any rate, the person Willie counted on visiting when he came back to Happy Valley was not Clarence but Coot. Willie was the traveler, but Uncle Coot, who spent his whole life in McDuffie, was the dependable, solid member of his father's family: the one Willie could always rely on.

Yet in the first years of the 1920s Willie must have spent most of his time in Statesboro, not Happy Valley, or he would not have received the

162

help he did from a Statesboro benefactor, who sent him to the Georgia Academy for the Blind in Macon, and kept paying for him to be there from 1922 to 1925.

You might think, too, that Willie would more reasonably have achieved this help if he were seen around town, singing and playing music and generally being agreeable, than if he were off elsewhere running "reckless" and "wild, wild, wild."

Did Willie really have a "wild" period at all? Could he really, at age thirteen, have got that job with one of the USA's most prominent circus shows—or was he, as the testimony of people like Ethel Floyd perhaps suggests, a boy who stayed at home and was eagerly learning guitar? ("Then he was just a boy. Well, I imagine he was in his teens . . . He hadn't traveled anywhere then.") Willie told Library of Congress folklorist John A. Lomax in 1940: "I used to go to the country churches, all out to the country where I was partly raised from a youth up to around fifteen or sixteen years old."

Others are certain that the young Willie worked at the B.B. Morris grocery store, next door to the pool hall on West Main Street, just a few doors down from the courthouse crossroads. Shopkeeper Walt Strickland tells me that Jane DeLoach's father owned this grocery store (and, though the store is long gone, the firm still makes its locally famous barbecue sauce on the floor above), and that, in his late teens and early twenties, Willie had a job sweeping up outside the store. He would be sent off delivering lunch pails to customers too—another testament, of course, to how remarkably he rose above the disability of his blindness.

Who was his benefactor? He was a man named Simmons—but, perhaps typically, there is nothing to tell us which it was of three prominent local men by that name: Lannie, Rafe, or Brooks Simmons.

Lannie Simmons was a colorful character, a self-made man, the son of a dentist from nearby Brooklet and his third wife. He was born in May 1899, making him just four years older than Willie. He received little education and went into commerce, by 1922 already heading his own business selling a "choice line of staple and fancy groceries" and pushing that modern method, telephone ordering. He branched out into the sexier business of selling automobiles, originally in partnership with E.A.

Smith, and, by August 1927, was taking large, stylishly illustrated newspaper advertisements for Studebakers—including, reduced to a mere $1,495, the Commander, "the greatest post-war achievement of automotive engineering." He became a member of the 1st Methodist church and gave each new minister a car. He bought an aeroplane, and had a lot of fun, yet gave to many good causes. His great-niece, Alice Budack, told me: "He had a great zest for life, and a great appreciation of what had made his own life successful. He only had an 8th grade education. In us children, if he heard a cracker accent, he discouraged it—but he had an incredible ear for people's speech. If someone came into his showroom well dressed and speaking well, he would speak that way too, but if someone came in with hay in their hair and wearing overalls, he'd match their speech just as well. I asked him why, once. He said it was only polite to avoid seeming superior to other people."

Did he keep a log of his expenditure, I asked, hoping some old accounts book would log his school fee payments for Willie McTell. "I wouldn't think so," Ms Budack replied, "he wasn't that kind of person. He kept his money in his pocket and he'd peel it off if people needed it." When he died, on 16 November 1963, the IRS peeled off the rest.

Naomi Johnson, who had lived in Statesboro since the early 1930s, felt that Lannie was probably Willie's benefactor: "Well, I knew him, he was one of the big mens here. And he built the little shopping center, the first little shopping center there'd ever been in Statesboro. And he built it right where he used to sell cars . . . I liked him very much. He was just for everybody, don't care who it was, he was for everybody. Just for everybody . . . Kind man, and a working man to be a rich man. He was a rich man but he was working. Lot of water under the bridge."

No one in Lannie Simmons' family, though, claims any knowledge of his having been the one who paid for Willie's blind-school education, and it seems to me that a twenty-three-year-old with a newly opened grocery store, which was his situation in the year Willie was sent off to the Macon academy, would not yet have felt ready to start distributing largesse.

The second candidate is Rafe Simmons—christened Rayford, and at one time the wealthiest man in Bulloch County. He owned a general merchandise store, brokering cotton on the second storey and selling dry goods on the first. A property owner and entrepreneur, he financed several buildings and was involved in banking. He was a much older man—born in the 1850s, and set to work on his mother's farm by the age of sixteen before rising to local eminence. However, in 1915, he migrated to Florida, and though his move was only part-time at first, and doesn't in itself disqualify him from having retained an interest in Willie McTell's progress, the fact is that he died on 22 December 1924, the year before Willie left the Macon academy. Again, no one in his surviving family (and there are a number still in Statesboro) tries to claim any knowledge of his having helped Willie.

The third contender is Rafe's son, Brooks Simmons. Robert Owens told the Evanses in 1975 that the Simmonses who sent Willie to blind school "had a clothing store." Brooks Simmons was the one who ran a store selling mostly clothing, and it was on West Main Street in the early 1920s. He and his wife, Anna, were in their forties at the time, and had no children of their own. He was also a liberal on social and religious matters, and perhaps even an atheist. Occasionally he wrote letters to the editor of the local paper coruscating those clergymen who liked to declare that doubters were condemning themselves to hell. In the 1930 census, his Savannah Avenue property was said to be worth $25,000—truly an enormous sum at the time. The Depression hit him fast and hard, and, on 29 May 1931, he killed himself in Atlanta after the failure of a business venture there. He was fifty-two.

Brooks Simmons, then, gets my vote. He died over thirty years before Lannie Simmons, and so left plenty of time in which to be forgotten, but, to judge by his situation in life at the relevant moment, and his political sympathies, he seems the most likely, by some way, to have been McTell's benefactor. And, though caution is needed here, Willie's brother Robert seems to have believed so. Robert was only a five-year-old when Willie went off to Macon, and, in later years, was the first to say his memory was bad and that he mostly knew Willie from the 1930s onwards—so he might have mixed up the Simmonses in his mind years beforehand—but he may be absolutely right in his recollection that it was the Simmons who ran the clothes store. He says so very definitely, and he's the only person to be specific, in effect, about the source of the money given for Willie's education.

Statesboro resident Lillie Mae Brown, whose brother was a friend of Willie's, gave me a further possible candidate. Her impression was that Willie was helped at least in part by a lady "with an odd name," which she couldn't recall. This will have been Doty Litchenstein, whose husband was another successful local businessman (though not a clothier). The Litchensteins moved in the same circles as both the Ellises and the Brooks Simmonses.

At any rate, Willie was able to go, and he arrived, at the age of eighteen, at the long-established, pioneering, and thoroughly segregated Georgia Academy for the Blind in 1922. Amost certainly he traveled the 110 miles or so by train, going up to Dover on the branchline and there picking up one of the fast and frequent Central of Georgia Rail Road services on its main line from Savannah to Macon. He would have arrived downtown in that city at the Cherry Street Terminal Station, opened only six years previously (and now Georgia's grandest surviving terminus).

The academy's timetable was designed around the seemingly immutable rhythm of the seasons. The school year started in January, ran till June, and then resumed from September till December. Pupils were needed on farms in the summers (though the boll weevil's arrival caused a dramatic slump in cotton production across the state). When Willie arrived at the school he was one of about twenty-seven boys and nineteen girls, and the principal was a Mr Louis Hampton Williams. The black pupils' building was at 247 Madison Street, a wide avenue in the city center. The building was three storeys high, with girls on one side and boys on the other. They ate at ground level, had school above that, and slept on the top floor. There were no indoor toilets. The school took pupils from the age of six or seven; there seems to have been no upper limit. They had to sew, clean up, and iron their own clothes. There was no schooling on Mondays—that was washday—but there were lessons on Saturdays, and on Sundays compulsory chapel attendance at ten o'clock. The school was run by the Welfare, not the Education, Department.

The institution still exists, though it is, of course, integrated now, and no longer at Madison Street—and, miraculously, as of January 2007, a child who had been at the school with Blind Willie McTell is still alive, aged almost ninety-four. The details of the building, its layout and its timetabling, all come from Sister Fleeta Mitchell, and, in order to learn what I could of Willie back in 1920s Macon, I drove to Athens, Georgia, to call on her for the first time in April 2001, eighty years after she first arrived at the school.

I phoned locally based folklorist Art Rosenbaum, whom I'd not met but who had told me of her existence, on the off-chance of being able to speak to Sister Fleeta that same day. He gave me her number, told me he'd call her up first and let her know I'd be phoning, and gave me directions for reaching her house. When I rang her, this big, throaty voice answered and said I could come any time except twelve o'clock: that was prayers. I said I would see her in the early afternoon, and hung up anticipating finding her a large, hearty woman in a nun's outfit.

I drove out of Athens on the Danielsville Road, taking the left fork onto the Ila Road, watching out for Helican Springs Road on the left and finding Mission Drive shortly afterwards on the right. Her address is 107b Mission Drive, but it's almost the first house (and there aren't many) down a little unmade lane winding through woodland. In a clearing in the woods opposite the ramshackle True Witness Holiness Church, Sister Fleeta lives in the cinder-block extension on the left-hand side of the house of the proselytising religious enthusiast who stepped in to save Sister Fleeta from being put into a nursing home after the death of her husand, the Rev. Nathaniel Mitchell. It is, from the outside, an almost improbably dilapidated small bungalow and, on the inside, smothered in rugs and woolly things.

Sister Fleeta was not, of course, as I'd pictured her. She was small, with the softness of the very old, and she was wearing a brown flowery dress, brown stockings, and white trainers. She sat in an armchair, very quiet and still, head bowed, her fingers running across the Braille pages of a large, creamy looseleaf book, in a brown-carpeted room with walls part-covered in the sort of linoleum that's meant to look like wood. There was a double bed, two old dining-chairs, a gas fire on the wall with its pilot light burning low and blue, a cupboard, and a dresser. She was good-natured and jolly, a little shy, and an invaluable witness.

She was born Fleeta Mae Echols, in Laurens County, Georgia, on 27 February 1913, and had moved to Gordon, just twenty-five miles east of Macon, in Wilkinson County, and moved again to Rome, Georgia, by the time she was seven. She gave me the context of her arrival in the world with disarming bluntness: "I was blessed to know my great-grandmother. Her mother was sold by somebody. That's how come she got to be in Georgia."

Fleeta was not born blind, but says that one of her eyeballs burst when she was five or six years old, and that the other was removed in 1939. Her sister, Maisy, had been scalded to death at the age of five, before Fleeta was born, and their mother died when she was fifteen. It was after this that she "sought the Lord," and renounced secular song, even though it had been the source of her strength when she had first arrived at the Macon academy at the age of eight in October 1921. "When I first went," she told me, "I wasn't happy, because I missed home, but I started music and I got happy."

The school offered relatively poor black children a longer, better general education than their sighted contemporaries could normally expect, but the academy's music department was one of its special strengths. For Willie, as for Fleeta, music lessons were liberating, confidence-building, and fun. Marjorie Miller was succeeded by John Allen Williams, who taught them Braille notation, encouraged ensemble singing, nurtured a choir, gave individual instrument tuition, and acquainted them with a wide range of musical styles, mostly of a rather drawing-room kind, but embracing spirituals too—including, from published collections, many they didn't already know.

Willie learned to read music here, but, while it expanded his repertoire, it doesn't seem to have interfered with his own styles of playing (formal tuition is often felt either to contaminate the folk artist with specious surface-sophistication or inhibit the exploratory openness that is a virtue of the self-taught). In fact, it was a help in a simple, obvious way. Whenever he wanted to play guitar together with a pianist, he could call out what piano note he wanted to hear, and tune his guitar strings accordingly. In Statesboro, people registered it as yet another skill Willie had acquired. Willie Battie Smith told David Evans: ". . . When he got to be professional, you know, when he started to playing and was playing, it was kind of like air"—by which she meant that he was playing by ear — "But, after he went to Macon to blind school, he was playing by notes. It was different, you know. You can, you know, learn a different music there and know it." She specified that it was at Macon that he learnt to play 'Amazing Grace'.

"That man knew music," Fleeta told Art Rosenbaum of their tutor John Allen Williams. "He knew American and Spanish, Italian, any kind." She also told Art that Willie was "very smart" in school, and much smarter than her at maths: "He was a real mathematician. He could do it . . ."

Willie, Fleeta, and the others were also taught clay modeling and practical craftwork, like making clothes, brooms, baskets, and purses. Willie was good with his hands, and, in later life, he drew on his skill with clay to make Kate an ashtray in the shape of a human hand. This was odd, granted that she said she didn't smoke.

Fleeta remained at the school long after Willie had come and gone; she finally graduated in 1934. "I stayed in third grade for two years," she told me, "because I had to remember too much. An' I grieved, 'cause I didn't want to repeat no grade. Tonsillitis interfered with my memory." There was also, early on, a cook called Miss Emira who went out of her way to give Fleeta a hard time. "She was a good cook but a hateful lady. She hated me." You were at the mercy of such staff, of course. "People who misbehaved took a whipping." But the whole place "was real clean," the Principal was a reasonable person, and so was their teacher, Miss Essie Mae Hubbard Carlisle, though she once set Fleeta to learn a thirteen-verse poem in a morning: she was given the poem at nine o'clock and had to know it by 11.30. "But I did it, and Mr Williams gave me $5!" The matron was Alice, the principal's wife.

Miss Essie Mae, who turned thirty the year Fleeta arrived, allocated the parts in a school play production of Little Red Riding Hood, which Fleeta remembers Willie McTell acting in. She landed the title role, Willie was the woodcutter who stopped her being eaten, and a boy named Willie Wiggins got to be the wolf.

More generally, she remembers Willie McTell in those days as "full of life": "He was always teasing someone. My friend Mattie Davis, she was my play-mother and she really liked him, so she called him my play-father. He was a boy loved girls too, y'know. He treated me like a sister." He would also disappear on his travels from time to time: "He loved to go."

Sister Fleeta added that Willie's friends were white and black. "Me too. I had a lot of white friends."

There's also no doubting that, for Fleeta and Willie, the school's teaching of Braille, for maths and music, but especially for reading, was empowering (to use a word no one did use then) throughout their future lives.

Towards the end of Fleeta's reminiscences, another old lady arrived. We shook hands but she said nothing and sat down. Fleeta sold me a copy of the cassette Art Rosenbaum had produced many years earlier of her singing and playing piano, and her husband singing with her—a generous collection of nicely old-fashioned spirituals, gospel songs, and jubilees, with performance help from four others. She had met her future husband at the age of ten, when Nathaniel had arrived as a fellow pupil at the academy in 1923.

When I left Sister Fleeta's home, after a two-hour visit, I wished I'd pre-planned my questions better. I never asked her, for instance, what the school had smelled like, which I imagined a blind person might remember vividly. In August, I tried again.

This time I remembered to ask the question about smells, and, though she couldn't give me an answer, it was a pleasure to see her again, and she told me more about the friendship she retained with Willie years after they'd both left the academy. She gave me the phone numbers of two other elderly ladies, Rosa Johnson and Pinkie Wilder, but then realised that they had only arrived at the school after Willie had left. (Rosa is one of those on the cassette.)

Sister Fleeta's silent friend arrived again, just as I was leaving. Sister Fleeta suggested that I might care to give a donation to help save her church, St John's Holiness, since its building has been condemned. I handed her a note and she asked what amount it was, so that she could impress it with a Braille punch and file it correctly in her bedside dressing table. As she shut the drawer, she told me something several other people have said too, down the years: that Willie could tell one denomination from another just by feel. Later that month, in Macon, the academy superintendent, Dr Richard E. Hyer, would disabuse me of this idea, insisting that distinguishing bills by feel was a physical impossibility but a common myth, perpetrated by the blind for their own protection as much as to impress, and that they practiced the trick of creating this illusion essentially by keeping different-value bills in separate pockets and pocket-linings and using sleight of hand.

I took my leave of Sister Fleeta that second and last time, and, as I stood outside her door finding my car keys, I heard the two old ladies talking softly to each other. "I remember him from before, but I still have no idea who he is!" laughed one. "Me neither!" chuckled the other.


When I headed to Macon, it was from Atlanta. I escaped the Interstate near Stockbridge, and, as I headed the remaining fifty-five miles south-east, it grew pretty, with lots of old buildings of a quaint, shack-like nature out in the countryside before I ran the long gauntlet of the city's outer strip. I pulled into Macon across the Otis Redding Memorial Bridge.

In the early August evening, I parked on 3$^{rd}$ Street, walked round the block along Cherry Street to 2$^{nd}$, down 2$^{nd}$, along Walnut, and back up 3$^{rd}$. The bank sign on Walnut said it was 99° at 6.45pm. From an outside table in front of the Acapulco Mexican Restaurant—one of the few downtown places open beyond the business day—I could take in two different milieux. The opposite side of 3$^{rd}$ is classical eighteenth-century architecture built of small, delicate bricks and multi-paned sash windows. The other side of Cherry Street is an old two-storey boulevard, wide as anything, tree-lined down the center, with little hedges and borders, but stared at on both sides by 1950s buildings (just like Moi Avenue in Mombasa).

A tiny black boy, no more than three and a half, walked by in a Superman costume, with little red woolly ankle-socks but no shoes. Occasionally an obese white person waddled past the junction. One checked whether there were any abandoned coins in the newspaper-vending machines, another for anything of value in the litter bins. Fewer people were on these central downtown streets that evening than in the marketplace of my own small home town (pop. 3,000) on early-closing day. Wide-avenued, cosmopolitan Macon is one of the cities that has been slain by the strip, the freeways, McDonald's, and Wal-Mart.

There was never, perhaps, a Macon golden age, though one of her other famous sons, the great, mad Little Richard (Richard Penniman), remembers a greater level of interchange between black and white musicians than history might suggest. He says that when he was young he used to listen to a local country band with a touch of western swing, Uncle Ned & the Hayloft Jamboree—that he used to see them live and he loved them. When he was older, he said, they even gigged together, and no one felt scandalised by this interracial mix. Yet, as throughout the South, musical collaboration belied the segregation and virulent prejudice of daily life. Nor was this directed only at black citizens. On one of the original handwritten sheets of the 1920 US Census for Macon City, District 25, for each person enumerated as Jewish, the word Jewish has been crossed out and the word Yid written in.

Willie McTell would return to Macon many times in later life, but he left the Georgia Academy for the Blind in 1925. He appears to have gone straight on from here into other schools for the blind. John Lomax asked how long he stayed at the Macon school and Willie replied: "From nineteen and twenty-two up till 1925, when I returned to New York and went to a little independent blind school out there. And then I went with a friend of mine to Michigan, and studied over there, as of learnin' to read the Braille."

Nor was this the end of his pursuit of special education. Folklorist Peter B. Lowry discovered that Willie had once sung tenor in the Glee Club of a blind people's organisation in Atlanta—I assume in the 1950s: "I went to the Atlanta Association for the Blind, previously the Atlanta Association for the Colored Blind, to see if they had anything on Willie, and they had this single sheet of paper, which said that he had been in the Glee Club, and said that he could perceive light. But I had no photocopying facility and, when I went back the next week to copy it, they couldn't find the piece of paper. They could find the folder, but not the sheet of paper."

It was also Peter B. Lowry who "discovered" Willie's Atlanta 1950s neighbour, Emmitt Lee Gates—and David Evans reports Gates as saying that Willie also went "every year in the 1950s to a blind school in North Carolina, evidently to study rather than entertain."

Unfortunately, like the rumored earlier school somewhere "in Lincoln, Georgia," the details of all these post-Macon schools and Willie's attendances at them remain utterly elusive.

Like so many things in Willie McTell's life, even his blindness itself still holds mysteries. We know that when Willie makes his first documented appearance in the world, on the 1910 census, the enumerator does not note his blindness in the appropriate column on the sheet. As we know, the enumerators were flagrantly careless of what they wrote down, so that their data is often seriously unreliable, but it's a tantalising omission all the same. And Willie's brother Robert, telling his 1970s interviewers with a nicely understated skepticism that Mr Simmons had paid for a number of eye examinations, nevertheless suggests that, at the time, there must have seemed some grounds for hope: "This Simmons fellow, I don't know why he was that much interested in him, you know, but he sent him to . . . specialists. He was a very rich man, and he tried to give him his eyesight. I guess he was givin' it to him 'cause he was very rich."

We can't know the truth though—and the results of those eye examinations would still be confidential even if we knew enough about when they took place to be able to track down whatever now exists of the notes taken at the time. These examinations took place, reportedly, on one occasion at the eminent Johns Hopkins Hospital in Baltimore and several times at Grady Memorial Hospital, which was, handily enough, on Butler Street, in the same patch of North-East Atlanta where Willie mostly lived.

The only medical examinations Willie underwent that I have been able to see details of are those from the last week of his life, in the hospital in Milledgeville—and, by then, Willie's blindness was not the center of anyone's attention. They do yield one "new" relevant detail, though: the doctor who first examined him on admission noted that his "Eyeballs were very small . . ."

If it's odd that no one who knew him ever said the same, perhaps it's equally odd that, though I talked to many people who knew him, only one, Hazel McTear's sister, Annie, described his eyes at all. "He would move his eyes real funny all the time," she told me. "Sometimes he seemed to have more trouble with them than other times. Sometimes you couldn't see nothin' but the reddest-looking part down here. He'd be blinking 'em, you know. He would blink his eyes a lot. And when he threw his head back and laughed, his eyes would go all over the place."

I think the rarity of any such comment reflects the fact that people find it impolite, even aesthetically distasteful, to scrutinise any blind person's eyes or eye-sockets. It is often to spare other people's feelings that so many blind people wear dark glasses. Strikingly, Willie McTell never did.

Never did. This seems a very telling ingredient in his make-up. It suggests, if not quite an act of aggression, an aggressive stance: a demand that people take him as he was, without any prettying up or sparing of people's feelings. An insistence upon the truth of his blindness, presented just ahead of his proving how little it disabled him.

I'm glad of this challenging stance he takes on the matter. Sometimes you feel that every witness' account of Willie's unfailing good cheer, good humor, generosity of spirit and readily positive approach to everything and everybody, adds up to an almost impossibly uncomplicated person. He was surely too intelligent a man to be so one-dimensional, so constantly cheery—and, however resourceful he was, he lived in difficult times, and cannot always have found life so easy to manage. To glimpse, just once in a while, a sharper side to Willie McTell's character, isn't to disparage him but to refute, and gratefully, the notion that he had been such a simple soul as he's been painted. And when we come to look at Willie's life in Atlanta, we find that life in the city, and life with Kate, brings out more of that sharper side of Willie. (Even that surreal ashtray, shaped like a human hand, surely suggests a touch of malice in the image it conjures for anyone who stubs their cigarette out on it. He teased Kate about it too: "He used to sing that song about 'There's A Hand Writing On The Wall', and he'd hand it to me, and told me that was the hand writing on the wall.")

As with the refusal to wear dark glasses, choosing the professional name

Blind Willie McTell was also thrusting his disability at people in the very act of introducing himself. It's at odds with his personal pride, and the overriding confidence he had in his own capability—yet he chose the name for his recording début, and, when he needed a pseudonym two years later, so that he could moonlight on another label, he called himself Blind Sammie. Another four years on, and another label, and he chose to be Blind Willie. In 1940, for the Library of Congress, he could have reinvented himself again, or dropped the first word of his original pro name—instead, he reiterated that he was Blind Willie McTell.

Again, there's some complexity to his character here. He was a proud man but he was also a realist who felt no hesitation about maximising his take. He knew he had no choice but to sing for his supper. One brief part of Kate's testimony to the Evanses shows Willie's mixed feelings as they traveled, the pull and push of his pride and practicality:

> Sometimes we had money, and then sometimes we didn't. We'd just go sit in the stations all night . . . He never rode with strangers. He would never let anybody pick him up, you know. He said "No, we're just going right up the road here a little piece." . . . And then a lot of times at the railroad station we'd be sitting there playing and then the porter or the waitress would come around and carry us over in the white section and let him play and make a lot of money. And they'd tell them we was traveling, my husband was blind, you know, and that he was sending me to school . . . and we was trying to make up some money to get me back in nursing school.

So Willie would make Kate, and himself, walk many miles rather than accept a lift, yet he wasn't averse to begging if someone else did the importuning on his behalf.

At the same time, everyone is agreed upon Willie's lifelong transcendence of his handicap. Stories about this abound, and people's admiration is always part of what they wish to say. Accounts of how brilliantly he comprehended the world often drift into attributing to him magical powers (like being able to tell the difference between a dollar and a $10 bill by feel), and these are entertaining if not credible.

David Evans summarises Willie's prowess like this, drawing on testimony from some of those still alive in the mid-1970s but long dead now:

> He had excellent hearing and could understand the slightest whisper in the same room. People would call to him from across the street and he would recognize their voices and call back to them by name. He could be in a car and tell when it was passing a house. His hands were also very sensitive. He could thread a needle and sew buttons, and one friend [unspecified] has reported that he could tell the make, model, year and even the color of an automobile by feeling the front fender. Many people have reported that he could count his own money.

He quotes Kate McTell as saying:

> He said that he felt like he could see in his world just like we could see in our world. And he could tell you how long my hair was, what color I was, and if you walked up to him and spoke to him, he could tell you whether you were a black person or a white person. And he could tell how tall you were, or whether you were short, just by listening to your voice. And he could tell you whether you were a heavy set person or a thin person. He was marvelous!

Of course, some of these accomplishments seem easily enough achieved by anyone who simply closes their eyes and tries it. You can tell the approximate height of a person by paying attention to where the sound of their voice is coming from; and most people would say that you can very often tell down the telephone—that is, by voice alone—whether you're listening to a black person or a white person talking, just as you can when they're singing.

Kate rushes to repeat the claim about money, and, as so often, cannot resist pushing it further than anyone else: "He could tell money too, tens fives, ones—I don't know how he did it—and twenties, a nickel, dime, quarters, fifty cents." Again, you don't have to be exceptional to distinguish by feel between coins that are all different sizes.

Evans continues that "Willie McTell never needed anyone to guide him around. He was able to make his way about the streets solely with the aid of a cane, which he would tap against the ground or the curb. He also made a clicking sound with his tongue as he walked along, listening for the sound to echo off objects or people."

He quotes Willie's cousin Horace:

He was ear-sighted. That's what he was. He'd walk that road out there. If a dog coming, he know it 'fore he got to him or anything. He'd turn his head like that and "K-K-K-K" [an unfortunate way of putting this in print, perhaps] he make a little noise. And he could tell if he was gonna stumble over something. He was ear-sighted. When I'd be walking with him, I'd say, "Hold my hand," you know, like how you leading a blind person. He'd say "You don't have to hold my hand." A lot of times he'd have his head like that. You'd be talking. He wouldn't say a word. He'd turn his head around to the side like that. And he had such a good remembrance. Don't care how long it was, when it was over with, he could go right back over it and tell you everything you said. But now, just like you sitting over there, long as you sit still, he wouldn't know where you at. But if you just moved there a little bit, just shake yourself any way, now he'd know exactly where you were. He could shoot you too. Ha ha ha. He kept his old pistol. He didn't miss when he shot. If you move, he was gonna hit you. He wouldn't hit you. He wouldn't know where you was at. But if you just shook he would hit you good.

Again, there's a hint of gullibility in this account—a hint, perhaps, of Horace's relatively unsophisticated, country outlook. Of course Willie didn't need help from his cousin; he'd have been in poor straits the great majority of his time, when Horace wasn't around, if he had. And, of course, Horace could only claim that Willie's recall of conversation was complete if he thought his own was too.

All the same, the account of Willie's ability—and preparedness—to use his pistol, is corroborated by Gold Harris, whose anecdote Evans dates to before World War I (though this seems improbable: there is nothing in Gold's account to imply that the McTell in his story wasn't an adult).

177

"Dogs," Evans writes, "are usually the scourge of blind people, but they never gave Willie much trouble, even on country roads where they were allowed to run free. He kept a cane with a lead weight on the tip that he called his 'dog stick' and would hit any animals with it that gave him a hard time." Here's Gold Harris:

> You know, long, long years ago, along at that time, cars wouldn't be out there, y'know, like they is now. He'd get in the road and walk to Thomson. And somebody had a bad dog up there beside the road. And he had told me, say, "I'm gonna kill that dog if he come out there at me again." He had hit him with a stick, kept him off further there. He said, "If I run into him again, I'm gonna shoot him." And he went back along there again and he killed that dog. That dog came out there on him and he shot him and killed him . . .

McTell is not the only blind blues figure reported to have wielded a gun—Blind Joe Reynolds is said to have "leveled one of his .45s at a dog that nipped at his feet during one street concert," and, in the 1960s, the Rev. Gary Davis carried a pistol and, it's said, pulled it on a club owner who was trying to avoid paying him and fellow-performer Arlo Guthrie. Nor would McTell be the only blind singer to own a car (and at some point in the 1930s, he's said to have owned two, and to have given one to a girlfriend named Gertrude Parrish). Blind Lemon Jefferson and (again) the Rev. Gary Davis are both said to have *driven* cars on occasion.

On foot at least, Willie could steer himself around cities as independently as in the countryside, as Gold Harris remembers, talking about visiting Willie in the big city of Atlanta:

> I went up there and stayed around there with him, you know, a day or two. He was carrying me. Now he was blind. Ha ha. Let me tell you, he was carrying me to places I didn't know nothing about. He knowed when the streetcars was running. And I'd catch mighty near any streetcar. And he'd stand there and listen. And I'd say, "Come on, let's take this'n." "No, no, that's wrong. We don't catch that. We'd be

going across town." He knew we didn't catch that. I'd just stay there till he say, "Let's catch it." Ha ha ha. Yeah, he told me. I'd catch it.

The only time Willie might have felt out of his depth was in New York City. Both Kate and Robert say so, but this isn't the impression fellow-musician Buddy Moss gained when he and Curley Weaver and Willie were in New York for the recording sessions of September 1933. Peter B. Lowry and fellow folklorist Bruce Bastin interviewed Moss at his Atlanta home one Sunday in 1969, and reported later:

> Buddy talked for a long time about Blind Willie McTell, for whom he had a feeling almost of awe . . . about his phenomenal sense of direction. He related one story of McTell taking them clear across New York once and said that, after one subway ride, he could find his way back again. Apparently McTell was quite independent and needed no one to lead him . . . he'd just catch a bus and ride . . .

And Bastin added, in his book *Red River Blues*:

> Buddy Moss spoke with disbelief at McTell's ability to get around despite his blindness. When they were recording in 1933 in New York, McTell . . . blithely led Moss and Weaver through the city's subway system. Moss, one noted, did not hesitate to follow and accept his directions.

Bastin adds his own hunch that Willie's blindness, his consequent heightened sense of hearing, and "a stubborn independence, enabled him to undertake a lifestyle which would have been too adventurous for most sighted persons."

Perhaps this is true in a more specific way than Bastin knew—for there was another man, once far more famous in his time than McTell, but long forgotten, a Victorian naval lieutenant who suddenly went blind at the age of twenty-five, and whose very power to negotiate the world in spite of blindness set him traveling. James Holman's life was revisited in 2005 in *A Sense of the World: How a*

*Blind Man Became History's Greatest Traveller*, by Jason Roberts, and reviewer Jenny Diski noted this about him:

> . . . Holman had taught himself a kind of echo-location, using a regular walking-stick with a metal ferrule, which he tapped on the ground to gather incredibly detailed information about his surroundings. And he wrote . . . that this gave him "an almost irresistible inclination to visit different parts of his native country, in quest of knowledge and amusement."

Sister Fleeta Mitchell said of blind, stick-tapping, echo-locating Willie: "He love to go." Willie himself told Kate: "Baby, I was born to ramble. I'm gonna ramble until I die." And Willie would indeed travel widely—but he was no aimless hobo. He made the big city of Atlanta his home base, and there, in 1927, he began his recording career.

# ELEVEN

T HE ATLANTA WHICH Blind Willie McTell began to make his
home in 1927 was a tumult of contradictions. The great black
pioneering intellectual W.E.B. DuBois placed Atlanta as "South of the
North, yet north of the South," and wrote that "the seething whirl of the
city seemed a strange thing in a sleepy land." Even today, to fly towards
Atlanta is to see it rising from a clearing in the trees.

Its growth in the first two decades of the twentieth century was
phenomenal—the city population more than doubled from 90,000 to
200,000. The city's first automobile accident was in 1903, when a car
collided with a horse-drawn surrey and a trolley ("car wrecked, horse
fine"), but, by the early 1920s, there was such congestion in downtown
Atlanta that the civic authorities started to build a grid of new central
streets a storey above the old ones—making traders turn their businesses
upsidedown: storage went down into the new de facto basements and
showrooms moved up onto the new street level above. (The "city
beneath the streets" would become Underground Atlanta, which, as a
tourist attraction, prospered briefly in the 1970s and has now been
revived; as a mall it has the advantage of some fine old shopfront
architecture, well preserved by decades of subterranean neglect.)

The Atlanta of the 1920s teemed with people and corporate business
headquarters. Some were regional HQs for the South, others national.
Atlanta was the home of Coca-Cola (which had stopped marketing its
cocaine-based product as an "uplifting medicine" back in 1892 and now
rebranded itself as fun refreshment for the modern age). The first radio
station in the South, WSB, was launched on the roof of the *Journal*
building on Forsyth Street, Atlanta, in March 1922. A dial-telephone
service was introduced in July 1923. Sears Roebuck opened on Ponce de

Leon Avenue in August 1926, a month before the launch of airmail flights to and from the city. As in every urban center, people felt that they were living in an age of unprecedented change. "Progress," unquestioned, was happening all around; the adrenalin of modernity flowed through the city's heart.

The exponential growth of cars created a quickening of pace, and began that speeding-up of eating that would lead, in the end, to McDonald's. It was in the '20s that car-hops began to appear: keen youths in white jackets who would clamp trays of steaming lunch to their customers' car doors.

A network of railroads brought goods and produce in from across the south-east and sent them out again to other regions. Passengers now had modern railroad connections to Washington and New York and to Birmingham, Alabama, and New Orleans. The pride of Southern Railways was a direct service all along this vast route of 1,377 miles. Named the *New York and New Orleans Limited* since 1906, it was re-named the *Crescent Limited* in 1925.

As Amtrak's *Crescent*, this great train still runs today. Eleven coaches long, silver and huge, seventeen hours out of New York, the *Crescent* pulls into Atlanta soaked in its own romance. Its city stopping-point is out in the suburb of Buckhead now, where Willie McTell would sometimes play, and where at least one of fellow-Georgian 12-string guitarists the Hicks Brothers, was "discovered" by Columbia Records Scout Dan Hornsby at Tidwell's Barbecue (hence his subsequent professional name, Barbecue Bob).

People poured in from the countryside in unprecedented numbers, yet its bustle remained less than cosmopolitan. Look at the clusters of black population on the census pages for, say, Detroit: people have come from everywhere, and their parents were very often born somewhere entirely different again. Look at those clusters of people in Atlanta and they are almost all born in Georgia, of parents also born in Georgia—and even the few born elsewhere are mostly from an adjoining state: Florida, Tennessee, or one of the Carolinas.

More rural migrants went north than settled for Atlanta, while foreign immigrants nearly all stayed in the north. Close to a third of 1920s

Chicago's 2.7 million citizens had been born in a foreign country; in Atlanta, almost none. The Atlanta of the 1920s was booming yet provincial.

It was a city with its own black newspaper, the *Atlanta Independent*, founded in 1903, and by 1920 Atlanta included over a hundred black-owned businesses, from corner drugstores to the huge Atlanta Life Insurance Company—founded, in a miraculous rags-to-riches story, by former slave Alonzo Franklin Herndon—while Auburn Avenue, which ran right downtown, had recovered from the great fire of 1917, which, one windy day in May, roared up Boulevard and across Ponce de Leon, destroyed seventy-three square blocks, and made 10,000 people homeless. A few short years later, Auburn offered nightclubs, jazz venues, and restaurants like the 100-seater Ma Sutton's, one of the many black businesses owned by women.

Yet the city's black population was treated no more progressively, and no more consistently, than people out in the sticks. The segregated train carriages rattled in and out, and, on the Georgia Railway and Power Company street cars that clanked through, over the door of each was a sign that read "White people will seat from front of car towards the back and colored people from back towards front."

As Ray Stannard Baker, the thoughtful New York journalist who had covered the Statesboro Riot, commented:

As the sign indicated, there is no definite line of division between the white seats and the black seats, as in many other Southern cities. This very absence of a clear demarcation is significant of many relationships . . . The color line is drawn, but neither race knows just where it is. Indeed, it can hardly be definitely drawn in many relationships, because it is constantly changing. This uncertainty is a fertile source of friction and bitterness.

There's a great book about many aspects of Atlanta life, including its racial divisions, in the period when Willie McTell was there: *Living Atlanta: An Oral History of the City, 1914–1948*, assembled by a team of editors in the 1980s. As its subtitle suggests, it records the personal

183

testimonies and memories of ordinary Atlanta citizens. They paint a vivid collective portrait of the city's racial divides:

Black residents [the editors note] were legally excluded from voting . . . Black schoolchildren received only a fraction of the funds allocated to their white counterparts. Black doctors could not practise at Grady Hospital, the city's only charity institution. Until the 1920s, black Atlantans could not visit a single park in the city. [After that they could use only one: Washington Park, on the west side.] Throughout the period between the world wars, there were no black judges or jurors, no black police or fire fighters. Access to other jobs was also extremely restricted.

Nor could you eat in any downtown restaurant if you were black. And, as physician Homer Nash recalled, "In the buildings downtown . . . one elevator was for Negroes, freight and baggage. The others—all of them— were for white people."

Racial tensions had erupted in violence on Saturday, 22 September 1906, and involved a white mob sometimes claimed to have been 10,000 strong. Four days of rioting ended with the perhaps surprisingly small total of, at most, two dozen black deaths and six white. This "Atlanta Race Riot" had been triggered by a frenetic newspaper campaign about alleged assaults on white women by black men (the usual story), but the deeper tensions were between underpaid, unrepresented black workers in over-crowded housing and a white working class that also felt itself being squeezed, economically and spatially, and whose fears were played upon in Hoke Smith's successful campaign for the governorship: a campaign that urged "any means within our reach to remove the present danger of Negro domination," and promised the abolition of the few remaining black voting rights not already rescinded by the ruling Georgia Demo-cratic Party.

The immediate result of the riot was a mayoral promise of police reform and the creation of a Commission on Interracial Co-operation— but the real effect was a redoubling of the discrimination against the city's black population, carried out in the name of the principle of "separate but equal" laid down by the US Supreme Court back in 1896. This slogan was, of course, a joke. The briefest set of facts and figures about education in Atlanta alone shows us that: a survey of black schools in the city in 1923 found that there were only seats for 42 per cent of those enrolled, that the average length of daily tuition was two and a half hours, and that the student-teacher ratio was seventy-two to one.

The shameful irony here was that large numbers of black Georgians had been drawn to the city at the end of the nineteenth century because of its opportunities for education as well as for jobs, and this influx of cheap labor had done so much to help the city grow. Not only that, but many of the new black residents' segregated neighborhoods and communities had grown up close to the pioneering black institutions of higher education, including the north-east's 4th Ward, where Morris Brown College had been founded and where Willie McTell would mostly live.

These different city patches became more strictly divided into white and black terrains after the 1906 riot. From the 1850s until the riot, the area around Auburn Avenue had been mostly a white residential and business district with a large black minority. By 1930 it would be almost entirely black, apart from a few struggling white Jewish immigrants.

Meanwhile, the sensational story of the murder of thirteen-year-old Mary Phagan in April 1913 had brought the hardships of life for poor whites in Atlanta to public attention. (The case became more notorious with the mob lynching two years later of the accused man, Jewish scapegoat Leo Frank, the manager of a pencil factory.) Mary had left school to become a "linthead"—that is, to work in a textile mill—at the age of ten. Only in Georgia could children that age legally be worked eleven hours a day. Maids worked an overnight twelve-hour shift at the age of fourteen. There was no minimum wage. A quarter of the city's population had no plumbing, and 10,800 "earth closets" were serviced by just fifteen horse-drawn wagons. The mortality rate was 50 per cent above the national average. The cost of living was high and wages low.

The tragedy of Mary Phagan and Leo Frank became the subject of popular poetry and songs, as on the 1925 recordings 'Little Mary Phagan' and 'The Grave Of Little Mary Phagan' by those hugely successful figures of the day, Vernon Dalhart and Fiddlin' John Carson. So too did the less symbolically loaded tale of white Frank Dupree, who acquired a diamond ring for his girlfriend, Betty Andrews, in December 1921 by helping himself to one priced $2,500 in a jewelry store on Peachtree Street, shooting dead the Pinkerton store detective who tried to stop him. He wounded another man with shots to the head and chest after running down the street to the busy Five Points intersection and darted into the huge Kimball House Hotel, which took up a whole city block bounded by Decatur, Peachtree, Wall, and Pryor Streets not far from the City Police Headquarters. There Dupree evaded his pursuers and took a taxi 100 miles to Chattanooga, Tennessee. He was caught, brought back, and hanged in Atlanta on 1 September 1922—"The Last Man to Hang in Georgia," as *Master Detective* magazine inaccurately headlined their story seventy years later. ("Last" because, after that, official executions used the electric chair; but, as we know, there were many lynchings of black Georgians later than 1922.)

This mini-Chicago-style anti-hero's story of city murder, jewelry, robbery, lust, escape, and retribution spawned a series of blues, mostly titled 'Dupree Blues' or 'Betty and Dupree', put on record first by the obscure Kingfish Bill Tomlin in 1930 and then by an unceasing flow of artists, including Willie Walker and Georgia White in the 1930s, Josh White in both the 1940s and 1950s, Brownie McGhee and Chuck Willis (who made the US pop charts with it) in the 1950s, Muddy Waters in the 1960s, Piano Red in the 1970s . . . and still they come.

In neither case did Willie McTell lend his voice to these narratives— not for Mary Phagan nor for Betty and Dupree, though he would twice record the comparable storytelling song 'Delia' and would write and thrice record a personalised version of 'The Dyin' Crapshooter's Blues'— in which he told the tale of a friend of his, a gambler named Jesse Williams, who he says was shot by the police on Courtland Street, Atlanta, in 1929. There is no record of this incident—but that's no surprise. Black murder, the *Journal* told its reporters, was not news.

(Willie is also said to have written and performed a song about the murder of a Statesboro friend, one Son Moselle, in which he identified the guilty, but he never recorded this one, and I have failed to find anyone called Son Moselle or a name halfway similar in any census, police archive, or other document.)

Willie's friend Jesse Williams was not only a gambler but, according to Willie, he had been to jail fourteen times and hung around the prostitutes on Hill Street—"during," as Willie puts it nicely on his 1956 recording, "his women-lovin' days": all of which suggests that Willie's Atlanta city life was not entirely one of upright endeavor. Though he had put himself through years of education and self-improvement, and he would believe in their value always, his Atlanta life did not simply embody the noble struggle of the deserving poor.

He was gregarious, a congenial personality with a fond appreciation of the human weakness he encountered all around him, and he had a warm affection for, and plenty of confidence around, the undeserving poor: lively minded "sports", especially—men like his thoroughly unreliable father and Uncle Harley. He was, as nobody said back then, non-judgmental: if people were OK with him, he readily befriended them, and he was thrust among them easily enough as a street musician—another chancey occupation that wasn't like holding down a steady job.

We don't know exactly where he was living when he first moved into Atlanta, but the patch of the city he made his own was that mesh of streets postally labeled NE, yet which, at its closest, lay only a couple of blocks from downtown.

That downtown was not so big, either: essentially it was about six major blocks across and about ten north–south.

In the middle of the middle, Decatur Street, Marietta Street, Edge-wood Avenue, Whitehall Street, and Peachtree all came together at Five Points, which was itself the south-east corner of an inner grid of thirty smaller blocks filling up fast with big new hotels squeezed in amongst the Federal Building and the old Post Office, bank buildings, the Carnegie Library, and the offices of the Railway Express Company (which would later employ Martin Luther King Jr as a laborer, until, in 1946, after one provocation too many, he quit when a white foreman called him a "nigger").

More broadly, you could say that downtown was bounded in the north by Cain Street, which took in the old Governor's Mansion, a

187

gloriously Victorian-Gothic horror on the corner of Cain and Peachtree, in which seventeen governors of Georgia had lived before its demolition in 1923. It was replaced the following year by the Henry Grady Hotel, a thirteen-storey high-rise in stone and red brick with 550 rooms and an elegant glassed-in, green-roofed verandah all along its frontage above the main entrance. Kate McTell would do menial work here to boost Willie's income within a year of their marriage in 1934. (Henry Woodfin Grady was the progressive nineteenth-century editor of the *Atlanta Constitution* who had campaigned inspirationally to make the city the hub of "the New South" before dying of pneumonia at thirty-eight; the hospital Kate attended as a trainee nurse in the 1930s was named the Grady Memorial Hospital, and a statue to him has stood at the junction of Marietta and Forsyth Streets, two blocks from Five Points, since 1891.)

A permanent revolution of buildings was taking place, as the grand products of nineteenth-century vanity were bulldozed and replaced by new ones fit for the Roaring '20s. People talk almost in wonderment about Blind Willie's achievement in constructing a map of Atlanta in his mind—a very detailed map, embodying an exact knowledge of buildings, stop signs, traffic lights, tram routes and more—but the genius of his achievement lay in the fact that he also had to keep on keeping track of the ceaseless changes happening all over this map of his throughout the first years of his life and work there.

(In turn, the great new buildings of the 1920s would mostly be pulled down a few decades on. The Henry Grady Hotel was demolished in 1972 and the Westin Peachtree Plaza now stands in its place: a brutish, gigantic, blank concrete cube that looms above the sidewalk and from which rises a seventy-three-storey round silver tower built in 1976.)

To the south, downtown was marked by West Hunter Street, where the New County Court House stood on the corner of South Pryor. The west side of this central rectangle was bounded by the old W & A Freight Depot, where what had been Thompson Street became Spring Street, which in turn veers north-west to rejoin West Cain. The easterly downtown boundary was Ivy Street, which ran parallel to and just east of Peachtree.

As Ivy Street ran south it was intersected by Ellis, Houston, Auburn

Avenue, Edgewood Avenue, Decatur Street, and Alabama Street—and the first few of these were the very streets where Willie's neighborhood sprawled out from downtown. In time he would live on Ellis and on Houston—both of which ran right downtown—and he would record on Edgewood Avenue. Just above Cain Street was Harris Street, which McTell would mention on his 1931 track 'Georgia Rag'. Just east of Ivy and also intersecting Ellis and Houston lay Courtland Street; east of that was North Butler, where he would live across the road from the Gate City Negro School, and near the spot where twenty-year-old harmonica-player Eddie Mapp was found dead in the street with a severed main artery in November 1931. (It was, Bruce Bastin writes, "a rough section of town where bluesmen often gathered to play.") Parallel with Butler rang Bell Street, a danger zone Willie would come to sing about in his 'Bell Street Lightnin'' (1933) and 'Bell Street Blues' (1935).

As Houston ran on east, it wandered askew so that it ran into Ellis at a three-way junction with Hilliard Street. Willie would live here also, and one street back west of it, on Fort Street, and one street further east of it too, on Jackson. Up Fort or Hilliard or Jackson, you'd get to Highland Avenue; he and Kate would live up there too—and that was about as far from downtown as he would accept.

Many of these streets—those nearest to the center—have also been utterly changed by subsequent development. Parts of Jackson Street, Edgewood Avenue, and Auburn have been caught up in the fancification of the Martin Luther King Jr National Historic Site and Freedom Hall Complex, but others have long since seen all their old wooden houses, their shotgun houses, their huts and slums, demolished to make way for the vast spaghetti junctions of Interstates 75 and 85. Bell Street and Hill Street are fused main roads south of Edgewood; north of it, Bell and Butler, Fort and Hilliard mix blocks of rough social housing with abandoned shells of old corner stores and blocks of emptiness, the roads left to lie there like dead limbs.

In Willie's day, though, this grid of streets was bulging with people, more and more of them crowding in all the time, as migration from the countryside kept accelerating, matched by the pace of change downtown. This rapid growth had also necessitated sweeping changes in the numbering of buildings on downtown streets in 1926, so that, for at least three years afterwards, people might easily direct you to entirely the wrong block for more or less anything. Another part of the shifting tumult Willie had to keep in his head was the way that streets not only changed their buildings, their numbering, and their outward reaches, but even their names. Auburn Avenue, which runs east from Whitehall Street downtown, had first been called Wheat Street. The New Wheat Street of 1900 later became Old Wheat Street (where Willie's acquaintance Charlie Hicks once lived). Houston Street would become John Wesley Dobbs Avenue. There were, in the end, about fifteen different Peachtrees (thought to have originated less picturesquely as Pitch Tree, named after that common and mundane pine).

Willie's north-east neighborhoods were also nurturing men and women whose struggle for their rights would succeed only after his death. Martin Luther King Jr was born on Auburn Avenue within two years of Willie's arrival, while Rosa Parks was a young woman living on Cain Street and working as a cook in a private apartment.

Set against all this Progress and the thrust of the future, the forces of the Old South and extreme political conservatism were fiercesomely strong in Atlanta. During the same three months of 1926 in which the splendidly named Hattie Harwell Wilson High donated the land for the city to build an art museum, that city forbade the teaching of evolution in all its public schools.

On 25 November 1915, encouraged by the lynching of Leo Frank three months earlier, the Ku Klux Klan had re-ignited itself under the leadership of one William Simmons, burning a cross on top of Stone Mountain, a large and curious exposed granite rock fifteen miles east of the city which, only the previous year, had been the site people agitated to have turned into a kind of southern Mount Rushmore on which the faces of various Confederate heroes would be carved. This obdurate work began in 1923 and the following year the face of Robert E. Lee was unveiled. The state of Georgia, meanwhile, had given the New Knights of the Ku Klux Klan an official charter, and just three years before Willie McTell arrived in Atlanta, Klan member William Harris won the Democratic Party's gubernatorial primary.

The sight of these Klansmen is never more eerie than when they're photographed standing tall and thin in their ludicrous but spooky white costumes, faces hidden, handing out leaflets to prosaic-looking businessmen on Atlanta's busy, 1920s city streets.

The Klan would remain a presence in Atlanta, and all across Georgia, throughout Willie McTell's lifetime. In June 1941 the KKK held a national convention in the city, drawing in delegates from all but ten of the United States. In October 1958 the Klan dynamited Atlanta's Hebrew Benevolent Society, the city's oldest and largest Reform congregation, often called the Reform Jewish Temple, on Peachtree—a late reminder, perhaps, that, as in other cities, the Klan "targeted radicals, Jews, aliens, Roman Catholics, labor organisers, and suspected violators of Victorian moral standards, as well as members of the black community."

In 1960, months after Willie's death, splinter groups known collectively as the National Knights of the KKK met at the Henry Grady Hotel to form a national committee, galvanised by their feud with city auto worker Eldon Lee Edwards, whose US Klans movement had drawn 3,000 people from seven states back to Stone Mountain in September 1956—the very month Willie recorded his *Last Session*.

Ironically, the Henry Grady Hotel would become a bit-player in the struggle for civil rights for black Atlantans in 1963. That 13 March, five local university students, four black and one white, presented themselves at the check-in desk with confirmed reservations made by mail for that night. The white student was accepted, the others refused. They staged a lie-in, unpacking their suitcases in the lobby and settling into the sofas. They refused to leave, and two were arrested.

Aside from the menace of the Klan, there remained, throughout Willie's time in Atlanta, the ever-present humiliations and officially sanctioned racist constriction of black daily life. For some of his generation, this had been made harder to bear by its contrast to their experience overseas in World War I—a pattern repeated in World War II for the next generation. Morehouse College president Benjamin Mays told *Living Atlanta*: "The government had drafted Negroes from all over the United States . . . And those Negroes got more decent treatment in Europe, particularly in France, than they had ever had before." Therefore, when they got back, "these folks just weren't going to behave themselves."

There were riots all over the South, and in Chicago, in 1919; in response, that Commission on Interracial Co-operation was founded in Atlanta. To little effect, as we've seen. As Mays said: "The Commission did a lot of good. But they were trying to get better treatment for the Negro within the segregated pattern. They didn't try to break down segregation. That was a sacred cow in the South."

James Baldwin writes marvelously about this South in general, and about Atlanta in particular—including the divide between the middle-class black and working-class black experiences of the city:

Atlanta . . . *is* the South . . . in this respect, that it has a very bitter interracial history. This is written in the faces of the people and one feels it in the air . . . It was an old black man in Atlanta who looked into my eyes and directed me into my first segregated bus . . . I cannot describe the look which passed between us ... but it made me think, at once, of Shakespeare's "the oldest have borne most". It made me think of the blues . . . It was borne in on me, suddenly, just why these men had so often been grabbing freight trains as the evening sun went down . . . His eyes seemed to say that what I was feeling he had been feeling, at much higher pressure, all his life. But my eyes would never see the hell his eyes had seen. And this hell was, simply, that he had never in his life owned anything, not his wife, not his house, not his child, which could not, at any instant, be taken from him by the power of white people. This is what paternalism means . . .

Writing of Atlanta in the 1950s, he goes on:

Atlanta's well-to-do Negroes never take buses, for they all have cars. The section in which they live is quite far away from the poor Negro section. They own, or at least are paying for, their own homes. They drive to work and back, and have cocktails and dinner with each other. They see very little of the white world, but they are cut off from the black world, too . . . I am talking about their position as a class—*if* they are a class—and their role in a very complex and shaky social structure . . .

Now I talked to many Southern liberals who were doing their best to bring integration about in the South, but met scarcely a single Southerner who did not weep for tha passing of the old order. They were perfectly sincere, too . . . They pointed out how Negroes and whites in the South had loved each other, they recounted to me tales of devotion and heroism which the old order had produced, and which, now, would never come again. But the old black men I looked at down there ... they were not weeping. Men do not like to be protected, it emasculates them.

You have to wonder how all this would have struck Willie McTell. His independence at getting around—around the city, the state, and a good part of the whole country—was remarkable, but it was independence of a limited kind. It might be emasculating to live the segregated, patronisingly "protected" life of the Southern black man in these times, but, if you were a blind man, didn't you need protection? Didn't Willie accept that, in his situation, he *was* dependent on white patronage, in direct and practical ways?

There's no knowing how he felt deep in his heart about the racially fixed table at which he had to play, but he played the hand he'd been dealt, and seems to have played it readily, without complaint. He never joined any political or grass-roots campaign. He never theorised about race or emancipation in song or interview. Rather, he settled for the relative liberty he enjoyed, inclined by personality and quick-wittedness to live his life adroitly and with optimism.

That relative liberty was considerable by the standards of his own people. He was the sophisticat to those he went back to visit in Statesboro and Happy Valley. He wasn't trapped in one county his whole life, in the grind of daily labor. And, in Atlanta, he was able to survive without a day job—unlike even the most talented musicians around him, like Curley Weaver, soon to become a good friend, and that other Hicks brother,

Charlie Lincoln. Both played it safe and worked for a living as well as singing for their supper.

Popular music, secular and religious, was segregated too—there would be no black music except some spirituals on the radio in Atlanta until the 1940s—but musicians like Willie McTell could play for white audiences as well as black. Indeed, much of Willie's experience of individual white people consisted of them handing him money, just as white generosity had given him his time at the Georgia Academy for the Blind. He was better paid by white people than by black, though in song he recognised the latter's generosity too.

What he exposes with a smile is the meanness of the "yellow man," by which he means James Baldwin's "well-to-do Negroes," that shaky Atlanta black middle class. McTell sings: "Black man gives you a dollar / He won't think it nothing strange / Yellow man give you a dollar / He'll want ninety-five cents change."

There were certainly elements of the upwardly mobile, educated black middle class who were discomfited by street musicians like McTell, and by the sub-culture they seemed to represent: the milieu of slums, fights, rowdy parties, loose living, and the threat of being dragged back by it all. The blues, and the music of vaudeville and the minstrel shows, was regarded as embarrassing ignorance, and even the old spirituals were disowned as atavistic.

If McTell was among those who made a certain strata of black citizens uncomfortable, he thrived among those above and below them. With rural and urban working-class blacks he was popular and only too obviously a dazzling musician—by 1927 already a masterly guitarist and a distinctive, confident singer always able to offer songs ideal for the occasion, be it a barbecue or a church concert or a busk in the streets.

This was a world in which the musician and the audience were not set apart but were entwined. The musician did not regard himself as "an artist," nor his purpose as to express his individual loftiness of mind or personal woes. When the blues emerged, its creators knew they were there to reflect and assuage the troubles of all, not to offer the angst of autobiography or personal confession. Nor was there a set-list or pre-planned performance, but rather a recurrent self-enforcing to and fro,

194

with the musician modifying repertoire and mood to fit the audience and the moment.

In contrast, for interested whites Willie was engaging light entertainment—and crucially, because he was a musician and not a worker, and especially because he was a blind musician, he *didn't count.*

The upshot was that this gave him privileged access. When he sat out on the front porch of the Jaeckel Hotel in Statesboro, resting between numbers played for the tobacco salesmen, they might talk unguardedly as they never would in front of others. They forgot he was there—he didn't count. And, as we know from Kate, unlike his black contemporaries, Willie gained profitable access to white railway carriages. He wasn't any kind of threat.

The segregated world of professional music that Willie entered via Atlanta was different. Here, whites controlled the fledgling recording industry, but that industry had begun to make records by black performers for a black audience. Mamie Smith, whose first record, 'Crazy Blues', can be said to have "started" the blues, was recorded in New York City in August 1920. Its million-selling success spurred other record labels to record blues for the previously unaddressed black market. These releases would become known as "race" records.

The dynamic, pioneering entrepreneur who coined that term, and co-produced 'Crazy Blues', was a suave twenty-eight-year-old from Missouri, Ralph Sylvester Peer. With a penchant for elegant clothes and a look of F. Scott Fitzgerald about him, he would later significantly shape the twentieth-century music-publishing business. He got his start because his father ran a store selling furniture, gramophones, and records in a suburb of Kansas City called Independence. This was the thrusting entrepreneur who, seven years after his success with Mamie Smith, would be the first to record Blind Willie McTell.

Peer had started working for Columbia Records in Kansas City at eighteen, and jumped from there to the assistant recording director's job with the General Phonograph Company's OKeh label in New York in 1920.

A hardnosed Atlanta dealer named Polk C. Brockman lured him to Atlanta three years later, with the promise of "hillbilly" stars in the making. Hillbilly—not a label that pleased its practitioners—was music from the other side of the racial coin from the blues. It was the old-timey precursor of what would become country music, made by and sold to white, initially Southern, people. Like the blues, it was a genre just clawing its way onto record.

It was kicked off by the little-known Vaughan Quartet, recorded by a small company from Lawrenceburg, Tennessee, in 1921, followed by a more widely recognised début: fiddle duets from Henry C. Gilliland and Eck Robertson, made for the Victor Talking Machine Co. in New York in June 1922. Next to pitch in was Ralph S. Peer.

There were no recording studios in Atlanta when Peer came to town in June 1923, so he brought recording equipment with him. This was the first on-location recording, and the first time anyone based in New York had gone to record in the South. He hired an empty room, wheeled in his cumbersome "portable" machinery, and produced, among other things, two sides of solo violin and singing by the rambuctious forty-nine-year-old Fiddlin' John Carson: his evocatively titled 'The Little Old Log Cabin In The Lane' and 'The Old Hen Cackled And The Rooster's Going To Crow'. Peer thought this music "pluperfect awful," but he was happy with its enormous success, first in Atlanta itself and then all over the South, ending up with sales of close to six figures: a huge number. Carson continued to record, in New York and elsewhere, including in Atlanta every subsequent year through the 1920s, with successes like the previously mentioned 'Grave Of Little Mary Phagan' and, almost certainly still under Ralph Peer's supervision, tellingly obnoxious titles like 'Run Nigger Run' (1924) and 'Flat-Footed Nigger' (1925).

Innovating at every turn, it seemed, Peer also made the first Southern location recording by a blues artist, and at the same sessions. This was the otherwise undistinguished début of a Mississippi-born, Alabama-raised twenty-six-year-old singer called Lucille Bogan (now notorious for bluntly lascivious records like 'Shave 'Em Dry', which starts with "I got nipples on my titties big as the end of my thumb / I got something between my legs'll make a dead man come") and when Peer returned to Atlanta in 1924, he put the first male blues musician onto record in the

South. The obscure Ed Andrews doesn't seem to have hung around long enough to connect with any of the other musicians just starting to come into the city, but his guitar-and-vocal performances of 'Barrel House Blues' and 'Time Ain't Gonna Make Me Stay' proved another first for Atlanta, as for Peer.

When he left OKeh in 1926, Peer talked Victor Records into an imaginative, canny deal: he would act as talent scout and would record for them, all without salary, but he would take the publishing copyright on all new material he secured on record. He had in mind, no doubt, that pianist Perry Bradford had earned $53,000 in composer's royalties from 'Crazy Blues', and that the music publisher made at least as much as the composer.

Armed with this agreement, and provided by Victor with the latest word in electrical recording equipment, Peer set to work searching the South for further talent. He paid $50 a side plus royalties of around half a nickel. Naturally, he insisted that people record new compositions and not, as his hillbillies would try for if he let them, old favorites like 'Home Sweet Home'.

Just two months before he recorded Willie McTell, he set up his gear in the empty second-floor warehouse of the Taylor-Christian Hat Company on State Street in Bristol, Tennessee—the other side of the road was in Virginia—and there "discovered" not one but both of the founding giants of country music: Jimmie Rodgers and the Carter Family.

When Peer arrived in Atlanta that October, he didn't yet know that his Bristol sessions would prove fruitful—let alone that they would become legendary—but he was already used to the idea that he had a Midas touch, for white music and for black.

Victor had a business relationship with Atlanta resident Charles L. Elyea, who lived with his wife, Rose, in a very large house set in beautiful grounds at 3316 Peachtree Road, and whose expanding business, the Elyea Talking Machine Company, had its premises downtown at 51 Forsyth Street SW, a street dusty with building works and contractors' yards.

Willie McTell, now aged twenty-four, walked in here on Tuesday, 18 October 1927, met Ralph S. Peer and, standing on a wooden platform in an empty room, with blankets hung on the walls and a pulley placed high up nearby to drive the Western Electric recording turntable, he made his auspicious recording début with five shimmering performances.

First came 'Writin' Paper Blues', the opening pace of which is just slow enough to be deliberate and arresting. The vocal glints like a diamond, shining yet tough, and Willie's opening word is "I." As it moves through its six conventionally shaped verses, largely of formulaic phrases, the playful complexity of his assured guitar-work yields a relaxation of expression and the illusion of an increase in pace.

Despite the general conventionality of the assembled couplets, what's striking is that here, straight off the starting blocks, Willie brings into his lyric a feature we can recognise as typical of him—of his personal frame of mind as well as his work: a relish for scattering far-flung place names and themes of travel into his song. The second verse gives us "come back to Newport News," the third cites Memphis and Birmingham—and here "meet me in Birmingham" is rhymed with "sent you a telegram": a further sign that here is a person whose orbit is wide. The last verse has "I caught a freight train special, my mama caught a passenger behind."

The second number, 'Stole Rider Blues', takes off with the temptation of another railroad escape: "I'm gonna grab me a train and ride the lonesome rail," he sings, on a number similar in pace and mood, again composed largely by gathering commonstock phrases together. The last verse declares: "I'm leaving town . . ."

One of this song's couplets can be heard recurring with variations all the way from McTell in 1927 to the great Mississippi singer, guitarist, and pianist Skip James in 1931, and Robert Johnson in 1936, and it ends up re-worked by Bob Dylan thirty years after that. McTell sings "I stole my good gal from my bosom friend / That fool got lucky, stole her back again." Dylan's *Blonde On Blonde* song 'Pledging My Time' offers the freshly playful "He stole my baby: then he wanted to steal me," and then "Somebody got lucky but it was an accident."

It's hard to know, in pre-war cases, whether the earliest recorded instance of such a couplet suggests originality by that performer or merely that he or she just happens to have been first into the studio with a pair of lines sung on every street corner for a decade or two beforehand. It seems likely, in this case, that McTell picked up the lines—because he liked them—from a recording by Ida Cox, one of the so-called "classic blues singers" who were recorded prolifically after Mamie Smith's success. Ida Cox was from the tiny town of Toccoa, Georgia, and her 'Worried Mama Blues', recorded in Chicago in December 1923 (accompanied by Lovie Austin and her Blues Serenaders), included the lines McTell adapted: "I stole my man from my best friend / But she got lucky and stoled him back again."

It was by no means the only time that Willie would draw inspiration from these stately, jazz-combo-backed popular records that dripped with the stage melancholy of formal orchestral arrangements and old-world showbiz presentation—and which, though made only a handful of years beforehand, sounded an elderly world away from the simple directness of a performer like McTell: a man who had, as Bob Dylan said of other individuals, "a lone guitar and a point of view."

Willie's third track, that warm Atlanta Tuesday, was a masterpiece: 'Mama, 'Tain't Long Fo' Day' (as the recording sheet rendered it)—an exquisite performance of a numinous song displaying another side of his instrumental genius: at times a keening and choral *tour de force* of slide guitar—using a knife or the broken neck of a glass bottle to shimmer along the strings—and at other moments a pent-up surging of cleanly picked, insistent individual notes, pressing with ominous contained emotion, as if attuned to a sky full of foreboding rather than promise.

All this matches the lyric sublimely—and to hear this creation is to recognise another key feature of McTell's imaginative work: that this blind man writes songs of great visual immediacy. "Big star fallin', mama 'tain't long 'fore day / The big star fallin', mama 'tain't long 'fore day / Maybe the sunshine'll drive these blues away."

It is astonishing, hearing this performance, to think that it was achieved without benefit of multiple re-takes or technical manipulation, by a man who had never before been placed in half so testing, unfamiliar, or potentially fateful a situation.

Lastly came two attempts at the fine, if less magical, 'Mr. McTell Got The Blues'. The first try was felt to be below par, and left unissued until over a decade after Willie's death. The second, paired with 'Stole Rider

Blues', was issued on one of the two Victor 78rpm releases this session yielded. The fact that Willie gave himself a namecheck in the lyric and the title tells us he was determined to talk himself up and thrust his name in front of as wide a public as he could reach.

At a time when the average working wage in Atlanta was around $13 a week, Willie McTell stepped out onto Forsyth Street that day with a promise of royalties and his name on a major record label, and $200 in his pocket.

# TWELVE

WILLIE HOPED HIS first record would make him a big star rising: that it would launch him into that elusive blues stratosphere, with sales to match those of Bessie Smith, Georgia's own Ma Rainey, and the Texan singer-guitarist Blind Lemon Jefferson, who had shot to prominence only the year before, the first male blues singer to achieve a hit. Jefferson's second release, 'Got The Blues', combined thrilling guitar virtuosity with the striking opening line "The blues come to Texas, loping like a mule," and he would soon colonise "race records" for male singers with guitars rather than women with pianists and orchestral combos. Jefferson would also reach out over the airwaves, in time, and come to influence generations of white Appalachian mountain musicians who wouldn't have liked his face at their cabin doors, but who loved his music and his high-pitched voice. He didn't live to enjoy stardom long. He recorded nearly 100 sides in under four years and then died in Chicago at the age of thirty-six, six days before Christmas 1929. It used to be said that he froze to death on the street in a blizzard, but his producer, J. Mayo Williams, alleged later that he'd collapsed in the back seat of his automobile and that his chauffeur, instead of helping him, had run away.

Willie McTell couldn't freeze to death in Atlanta, but nor did he rise among the stars. He never had a hit record—but he continued to be able to record for major labels, and the sides he made kept on glistening with promise, so that everyone who heard him recognised his artistry and his name became known all over the South. For the first two or three years he must have felt that next time, next time, he'd have a hit.

Victor chose first to release 'Stole Rider Blues', with 'Mr. McTell Got

The Blues' on the B-side. It was issued right at the end of 1927, and there on the label, as someone must have told him, his billing was large: "Blind Willie McTell, Singing with guitar." His undisputed composer credit—"W. McTell"—was there too. Willie must have traveled back to his old haunts, a copy or two held proudly to his chest, to hand this exciting and tangible achievement to Uncle Coot and Gold Harris, to play to friends down in Statesboro, and maybe to show off to girlfriends in Macon and Savannah.

It sold respectably. Then came the beautiful 'Writing Paper Blues', with the even more beautiful 'Mama 'Tain't Long Fo' Day' on the back. This sold respectably too. Nothing more.

These records were aimed at the black audience—but who exactly was buying them? The pioneering blues scholar Gayle Dean Wardlow spent a lot of time interviewing H.C. Speir, a now-legendary white Mississippi figure who discovered and auditioned a lot of talent and steered a lot of the era's blues greats into recording sessions. It was from hearing about Speir's experience running a record store in Jackson, Mississippi that Wardlow concluded this:

In the 1920s, there was no black radio, there was no television. The only medium they had was the wind-up Victrola and the record . . . Ninety percent of Speir's customers were black. Of that 90%, probably 90% were women . . . Speir paid 45 cents for the record and retailed it for 75 cents. He said the major companies told him it took about 28 cents to make a record. So they made 17 cents off the record and he made 30 cents . . .

Seventy-five cents was a lot of money in the 1920s . . . the share-cropper didn't buy the records. The woman who worked for the white man as a cook or a maid in his home bought the records—she had money. People bought records when they got their cotton money in the fall. Or if they got their spring planting money, they'd go buy some records. But the women bought the records, not the men; the women owned the Victrolas, not the men. And if you had a Victrola, you had a lot of prestige in your community.

Wardlow explained:

Victor called its machine the Victrola, and Columbia called its machine the Graphonola. He [Speir] said you could get a machine for under $100 . . . [but] You could buy a suitcase model for $9.95 up to $14.95. All these were pre-electric wind-up machines. Now Victor came out with an electric motor in 1927, but the majority of blacks didn't have electricity.

At any rate, Willie McTell's sales were sufficient—it may be romantic to say that the fine quality of his work was a factor too—that he was asked to come back and try again almost exactly a year after his first session. And this time, bright and early on Wednesday, 17 October 1928, supervised by Ralph S. Peer again but in a different empty room, starting at nine o'clock in the morning and working for four hours, he laid down four more songs, including the one that is now far better known than he is, the wonderfully dexterous and savvy 'Statesboro Blues'.

Cascading guitar mastery was entwined with yearning yet playful lines sung with feeling, but also with irrepressible spirit. It was a wholly distinctive creation but it welcomed every listener in. He drew on common experience with a cheery tip of the hat to the way that city and rural folks alike lived on top of each other in jumbles of extended family—yet he also gave effervescent voice to the push and pull people felt between their new urban life and their country roots, and to the widespread desire to be somewhere else.

He would say himself of his methods of composition: "I jump 'em from other writers but I arrange 'em my way." And it's true that, here again, he drew on early records by the female "classic blues" singers. Most obviously he drew from the Texas-born Sippie Wallace, who had once been a snakedancer's maid. Her début track had been 'Up The Country Blues', made in Chicago in late 1923 and released as the B-side of 'Shorty George Blues'.

Its first verse runs: "Hey, hey, mama, run tell your papa / Go tell your sister, run tell your auntie / That I'm going up the country: do you want to go?", and its last verse has the repeated use of "[so-and-so]'s got 'em"—all of which McTell reworks into the teasing catalog of piled-up people suddenly introduced into the middle of 'Statesboro Blues': "Sister tell your brother, brother tell your auntie now / Auntie tell your uncle now, uncle tell my cousin now, cousin tell my friends: / Goin' up the country, mama don't you want to go?" Spinning a long yarn out from Sippie Wallace's song again, Willie's ends with "Papa, sister got 'em, auntie got 'em, brother got 'em, friends got 'em, I got 'em . . . / I looked over in the corner, grandma and grandpa had 'em too."

He also uses Bessie Smith's 'Reckless Blues', twisting her "My mama says I'm reckless, my daddy says I'm wild" from parental complaint to parental death for that line from 'Statesboro Blues' quoted a couple of chapters ago—"My mama died and left me reckless, my daddy died and left me wild wild wild"—and, while he's at it, he takes her rhyming line too, turning "I ain't good-lookin' but I'm somebody's angel child" to "No I'm not good-lookin' but I'm some sweet woman's angel child."

Finally, he also seems to have used an April 1927 recording by the Alabama-based Ivy Smith, whose 'Cincinnati Southern Blues' includes the couplet "She leaves Cincinnati at five o'clock / You oughta see that fireman gettin' his boiler hot." Willie transforms this into "Big 80 left Savannah, Lord and did not stop / You oughta saw that colored fireman when he got them boiler hot."

Yet Willie's song, let alone the recording he made of it, was far more than merely something "jumped from" other writers, even if he was mostly composing in a way that was standard at the time—namely by pulling together, adapting, and combining anew a series of lines or couplets from the great oral ocean of blues lyric poetry. 'Statesboro Blues' was, like so much of McTell's work, unmistakeably McTell.

The record's abrupt start signals its restlessness. It's as if he had begun before the machinery was ready and the first couple of notes of the tumbling opening phrase are missing. And, as so often, he gives us place names and travel: not just citing the town he grew up in, but, by singing that "Big 80 left Savannah," celebrating one of the fast mail and passenger trains that ran on the Atlantic Coast Line. The no. 80 ran from Tampa, Florida, zigzagged up through Savannah, Macon, and Augusta in Georgia, and on up through the Carolinas to Washington, DC.

In turn, the ever-improving trains were speeding up the communication of the blues—distributing records and accelerating the oral transmission of song from town to town and state to state—as well as providing a range of beguiling noises for musicians to imitate and a good deal of jargon to be turned into slang and metaphor in their songs. As with his earlier song's "telegram", Willie was serenading the width of the world, and the speed of its communications and movement. And, in doing so, he was also signaling his modernity: his fast grasp of the happening, contemporary world.

It's easy to hear too why 'Statesboro Blues' became so much loved after Willie's death, when it was issued on vinyl, taken up by the Folk Revival crowd, and then again another decade on by The Allman Brothers Band: this 1928 recording is so rock'n'roll. The lyrics are full of these tricksy, evocative expressions that baby-boomers like me recognise from Jerry Lee Lewis records and the like: not just all that "Sister got 'em . . . brother got 'em . . .", but the grand call of "hand me my travelin' shoes" too. As we've seen, these come from earlier records, and, in truth, they probably arrived onto those from older orally transmitted routines and the rhetorical devices of the spiritual and the preacher, but McTell propels them forward with such fresh exuberance, and in a song that also shivers with pain, so that he's firing a whole range of feeling very directly at the listener.

What Peter B. Lowry says of Willie's recording, which he first heard when Sam Charters released it on that crucial compilation album of 1959, *The Country Blues*, might be echoed by any number of others who were around at the time and just being grabbed by the pre-war blues. Lowry told me: "I thought that he had a wonderful voice, I thought his guitar playing was absolutely stunning, I thought the lyrics were great and I thought the song structure was somewhat atypical: it's not a standard AAB structure all the way through. And that one has stuck with me from the get-go. That's still one of my all-time top five singles in the soundtrack of my life."

'Statesboro Blues' was the third recording laid down that October day. First had been 'Three Women Blues'—"One is a Memphis yellow, the other is Savannah brown / One is Statesboro darkskin," as Willie sings, in a girl-in-every-port boast that names places again, and makes distinctions that seem very visually based.

Next came 'Dark Night Blues' (which mentions Atlanta, Macon, Statesboro, and "Ridin' the Beale Street [Memphis] Special, baby, and I'm leavin' this town") and after 'Statesboro Blues' came 'Love Talking Blues', duly issued by Victor mistitled 'Loving Talking Blues'. All four sides were released: 'Three Women Blues' coupled with 'Statesboro Blues' on 4 January 1929, and the other two paired later.

Again, respectable but unexciting sales resulted. Yet Willie's name was made known far and wide. The McKee Music Company of State Street, Charleston, West Virginia, was advertising him in a select list of "New Victor Records Just Received" in the *Charleston Daily Mail* in early March 1929, and plugging his gorgeous 'Love Changing Blues' coupled with 'Drive Away Blues' in the *Charleston Gazette* a year later.

'Drive Away Blues' and 'Love Changing Blues' were the only two sides released from Willie's third session for Victor, which came in November 1929, this time recorded in the palatial new Opera House attached to the Atlanta Women's Club, built as the Wimbish Mansion in 1906 near the junction of 14th Street and Peachtree: a hushed and chandeliered spread he could not otherwise have entered, except as a servant. The building and the institution still survive 100 years later, the Club's website perhaps describing both as "one of the last remnants of the old south". It would be just after leaving the Atlanta Women's Club in August 1949 that the author of *Gone With The Wind*, Margaret Mitchell, was hit crossing Peachtree by a speeding taxi whose driver was drunk.

When Willie was there, again supervised by Ralph Peer, he recorded three items for Victor on Tuesday, 26 November, in the two hours from 11.30am, and a further five items that Friday evening, in the course of a week of sessions that also featured the now hugely successful Carter Family. The six McTell songs that never saw release, on recordings not preserved and therefore lost forever, were 'Death Room Blues' and 'Weary-Hearted Blues' (titles he used again on 1933 recordings), 'Hard Working Mama', 'Blue Sea Blues', 'Mr. McTell's Sorrowful Moan' and 'South Georgia Bound Blues'—this last a tantalising title, hinting that we'd have gained another song in celebration of the area of his upbringing down in Bulloch County.

From the quality of Willie's work on the tracks Victor did release from Willie's three annual sessions for Ralph Peer, it's hard to imagine that there can have been much wrong with the sides he chose to scrap, and Willie must have been sorely disappointed to have so little emerge from these November 1929 studio days.

But by this time Willie was also paid to be a back-up musician for another act, Harris and Harris. It was the first time he had worked as a studio musician on someone else's records.

The curiously named Alfoncy and Bethenea Harris were a vocal duet who had traveled across from their home in Greensboro, Alabama, for a follow-up session to one they'd done for Victor in Memphis the previous January. This time they were given two sessions, and Willie McTell contributed to both.

On the Tuesday, starting at nine o'clock in the morning and finishing at 11.30 (when his own session promptly began), he backed them up on guitar along with a William Shorter playing banjo. They cut two numbers: 'Teasing Brown', with Alfoncy's pleasant singing voice and Bethenea's gratingly strident spoken retorts, and the never-issued 'Lucaloosa Blue Front Blues', which was apparently augmented by Alfoncy's clarinet—the only time we would have been able to hear such a thing alongside McTell's guitar, had the recording survived.

On the Wednesday, Willie was called back to help again, this time as the sole musician behind the vocal duet. They recorded three sides that were rejected, plus 'This Is Not The Stove To Brown Your Bread', which offered a ponderous, overly careful dialog underneath which Willie effortlessly outshone them with a quietly relaxed melodic motif. It's telling that when this track was issued, coupled with 'Teasing Brown' and billed as by Harris and Harris, it was advertised across the South—or at least in Texas—as being "Singing with Guitar with Blind Willie McTell." Alfoncy Harris (no sign of Bethenea this time) would manage one more session, in San Antonio, Texas, in October 1934, before vanishing from the public world.

After Willie's own second session two evenings later, on Friday, 29

November—the day that gave us his beautiful 'Love Changing Blues'—it would be a further two and a quarter years before he and Ralph Peer would meet up again in Atlanta for one last Victor recording day. But Willie wasn't sitting around waiting for Peer to call on his services. Even before his 1929 Victor session, he had begun to moonlight for one of that company's main rivals, Columbia Records.

The month before his forays into the Atlanta Women's Club's premises, he recorded for Columbia on two consecutive days in the city, under the supervision of another white industry heavyweight, Frank Walker, assisted that year by Harry Charles. (We know these personnel details from Willie McTell's own recollection when interviewed in the 1950s.) The sessions may have been in the same building on downtown Pryor Street used to record other south-eastern musicians in April 1928, near the library where Willie would later borrow Braille books.

Frank Walker, who'd been born in the small and unappealingly named town of Fly Summit, New York State, had assembled in the studio one of the great hillbilly fiddle bands of the 1920s, Gid Tanner and the Skillet Lickers. For McTell's session, a week after Walker turned forty, he came down into Atlanta from Johnson City, Tennessee, where he'd been recording fiddler Charlie Bowman and, as a separate act, Bowman's young teenage daughters. Two years before Ralph Peer's famous Bristol Sessions he had recorded Charlie Poole and the North Carolina Ramblers, producing their 100,000-seller 'Don't Let Your Deal Go Down Blues', and later in life he was head of MGM Records when they signed country music giant Hank Williams. But, in the 1920s, he had also brought Bessie Smith to Columbia, and was her producer, and one of the few white people she trusted.

Walker could hear musical resemblances across the race divide, and thought this easily explicable. "On the outskirts of a city like Atlanta," he told folksinger-folklorist Mike Seeger in 1960, "you had your colored section, and then you had your white: I'm sorry to use the word, you had what they used to call 'white trash.' They were right close to each other. They passed each other every day, and a little of the spiritualistic type of singing of the colored people worked over into the white hillbilly, and a little of the white hillbilly worked over into what the colored people did."

Willie McTell, who would certainly have agreed with Walker about this, worked with his new producer the last two days of October, 1929, a Wednesday and Thursday. On the first day he cut four sides, beginning with two freewheeling virtuoso performances.

On 'Atlanta Strut' he memorably describes "a little girl" as looking "like a lump of Lord have mercy!", while his guitar imitates an array of different sounds, from a rooster and a walk upstairs to a piano and a cornet, and he ends the track with a sly hillbilly touch of his own as he puts a strong hoedown melody to mischievous lines that mention Kennesaw Mountain—site of the two-week futile stand of the Confederate troops against General Sherman's army as it closed in on Atlanta and burnt most of it to the ground—and then blithely moves on to sing about the "Prettiest girl in Atlanta," who "come steppin' up to my door / Hugged me and she kissed me, called me 'Sugar Lump.'"

Frank Walker seems to have freed McTell from the pressure he was under at Victor to offer nothing but straightforward blues—which were by no means his sole or even primary area of musical interest. It was the record business that pressed his generation of songsters into the confines of this commercially hot genre in the 1920s, whereas, by personal taste and in live performances for local audiences, they enjoyed a very wide repertoire drawing on everything from nineteenth-century minstrel numbers to current pop hits, from old-timey country songs to reels and jigs and ragtime, and from vaudeville hokum to jazz to old-fashioned spirituals and the wildly popular new gospel songs.

It paid for McTell to have an adaptable repertoire, to be able to perform different sorts of material at different sorts of gigs, but it's clear from the way he talks about himself and his repertoire, on both the 1940 Library of Congress session and the 1956 *Last Session*, that he took pride in being a songster, was acutely aware of the historic sequencing of his material, and felt a deep affection for many kinds of song. For Columbia Willie McTell seems to have felt he had more musical elbow-room.

He maintained much the same mood as on 'Atlanta Strut' for the partly spoken narrative tale of 'Travelin' Blues', proving himself a master of the talking-blues form right from his beautifully timed, insouciant spoken opening: "I was travelin' through South Americus / Walked up to a lady's house [pause] / Called her Grandma [pause] / Didn't know 'er name [pause] / She give me someth'n' to eat—/Walked on down the road." (Americus is another Georgia town, way over west on the Alabama border.)

His artistry and quick intelligence combine here in a creation of great good humor and poise, deftly quoting snatches of older popular songs ('Poor Boy' and 'Red River Blues'), imitating train noises on the guitar, recounting a long dialog between the speaker, a hobo trying to bum a ride, and the railroad man refusing and tormenting him, and sewing together all these elements and more into a quirky, playful, sardonic whole.

Willie's two sessions also yielded two more lost, rejected recordings, 'Cigarette Blues' and 'Real Jazz Mama', plus the lightweight, formulaic 'Kind Mama' and the similar 'Come On Around To My House Mama', a song that gets credited to McTell but which Bruce Bastin, an expert on the blues of the south-eastern states, calls a 'Newton County favorite', suggesting that it was an old communal composition well known among that set of musicians who included the Hicks Brothers and Curley Weaver, all of whom McTell was getting to know well.

All three of these Georgia contemporaries had been in Atlanta longer than Willie, and had already recorded for Columbia by the time Willie came to the label. Barbecue Bob had recorded copiously for the company, with six days in the studio in 1927 alone, another five in 1928, and three more earlier in the year—and he came back again and recorded some more on the same day as Willie's début for the label. Robert's brother Charlie had also been recording for Columbia for the previous two years, and Curley's own début sides had been made for the company in October 1928, including his first recording of what was to become his best-known number, 'No No Blues'.

When Willie McTell joined these fellow musicians on Columbia, he was breaking his contract with Victor—as Columbia knew full well and connived at readily—so he had to suggest a pseudonym for his billing on the label. Drawing on his real middle name, he went for Blind Sammie. No composer credit was given on the labels at all when first 'Travelin' Blues' coupled with 'Come On Around To My House Mama' and then

'Atlanta Strut' and 'Kind Mama' were released, the first pairing just a couple of months after the recordings, but the second not until a further two years later.

With 'Travelin' Blues', Willie gained respectable sales, as usual. In fact, with two pressings of the record, totaling just over 4,200 copies, it may have been his most successful release—but, as always, he failed to have a hit record. He must have been disappointed, as so many times before, but he was always superb at being a realist, and he would have known by now that he was never going to reach that stratosphere.

Instead, Willie recognised that he was destined to enjoy the far more typical fate of those in his profession. That is, he could be a recording artist with a major label and at the same time be busking on the street, and playing to entertain small gatherings at house rent parties, fish fries, barbecues, and small clubs, in city and country alike. Back then, with few exceptions, having a record deal didn't change your life, and being a recording artist didn't lift you out of the workaday world of performing other people's hits for dimes on the street.

Georgia Tom Dorsey described the pluses and minuses of this life's pay-offs (though it was a world he left behind with immense success himself, both with one of the biggest blues hits of the late 1920s and as the copyright-registering composer and music-publisher of his innovative, hugely successful gospel catalog): "I'll put it like this: you got all the food you could eat, all the liquor you could drink, and a good-looking woman to fan you . . . [but] If you left the party with seventy-five cents or a dollar, you had a good night, and yet you done played about two or three hours."

It was a scuffling kind of a life, and, as it turned out, a life suddenly pummeled on all sides by unlooked-for outside forces.

The timing of Willie's 1929 session for Columbia was, in retrospect, remarkable. On Thursday, 24 October, the stock market panicked and thirteen million shares changed hands—on that one day. The following Tuesday, 29 October, the day before Willie's recording session began, the New York Stock Exchange crashed. Sixteen million shares were panic-sold that day, and, in the ensuing days, traders went berserk. Banks and businesses failed, prompting a surge of suicides, all over the USA.

The record industry was affected like all others. Sharp falls in the sales of players and records meant severe cutbacks in the number of sessions held, and, within a couple of years, a halt to the labels' forays with recording equipment to those cities in the South that were, like Atlanta, without studios or record company headquarters of their own.

Willie McTell would manage to hang on to recording opportunities with major labels remarkably well, with sessions in 1930 and '31 for Columbia, a last Victor session in 1932, sessions in New York for Vocalion (part of Brunswick) in 1933, and in Chicago for Decca in 1935. In fact, 1934 was the only year of the entire Depression he didn't manage to record. But with sales so poor, and money so tight, Willie's 1930s really were the years of scuffling on the street and on the move, going wherever he could pick up a few dollars.

It was a world Willie worked supremely well, granted that his blindness left him too vulnerable to cope with the truly rough places, as Cheryl Thurber suggested to me:

> He just does not seem to have been playing in those dangerous places.
> Now jooks and black clubs late at night really are dangerous places—
> people really do get killed. And there's a certain kind of stature in that as
> well: people will talk about, "Well I was playing and so many people
> died": that's a common kind of boast, and I don't get the impression
> that those were the kinds of places that Willie was attracted to, to
> playing at. And as a blind person he would probably feel uncomfor-
> table.

I said he does stress that he played in every conceivable kind of place, and he does include jook joints in his list, but Thurber felt that for Willie "that would probably be a more rural term. I don't think he did much playing in jook joints: and if he did it was early in the evening and not late at night."

Blind Lloyd, a South Georgia guitarist who played with McTell and survived to be interviewed by David Evans and Cheryl Thurber in

Savannah in 1976, was similarly circumspect: "When I was with him he didn't go to no night clubs then. I reckon he would have went if I'd have wanted to go with him, but I never did . . . I don't go in them night clubs. You take on a Friday night and Saturday night. I'll be laying in my bed, I can hear them little pop pistols. Bam bam bam."

Willie McTell knew his limitations, and he worked within them so shrewdly and adeptly that you might say the Depression years saw Willie in his prime. He wasn't stuck in one place, he could entertain moneyed white people—going down to Florida in the winter to play to rich tourists, following the tobacco season through Georgia and the Carolinas and singing for the dealers and salesmen, a route that took in Statesboro, which had become an important tobacco town, so that he always had friends and cousins to stay with—and they always wanted him to stay longer than he did.

All this, though, was set against a background of hard times. The people Willie stayed with on farms around Happy Valley, and their white neighbors, like Lindy McTier and his family: none of these people saw any money in the 1930s. It wasn't a cash economy at all. You maybe helped your neighbor fix his dilapidated wagon, and he gave you some eggs. You walked miles with nothing to get any small something.

It's been said—not least by Cheryl Thurber and David Evans—that these were the times when black and white were in the same boat together, and that just as Willie had often been given support, perhaps very generous support, from specific white people, especially in Statesboro, so now the hard times were hitting everybody equally. But I don't think you'd find many black Georgians from the 1930s who'd agree.

At the beginning of the Depression decade, more than four out of five black Americans still lived in the South—inside what C. Vann Woodward called an "anthropological museum of Southern folkways." This Jim Crow system was, if anything, tightened up by the harshness of the 1930s, not reduced. Most of the few jobs still available were not available to black Georgians—and this applied to the educated middle class as well as the rest. Not until 1934 did the first black professionally trained librarian get an appointment in a Georgia library. Annie L. McPheeters, who was from Rome, Georgia, gained a B.A. in English in 1929 and a B.Sc. in Library

Science in 1933 before she was able to force herself upon the system. After two years at the Auburn Branch of the Carnegie Library, she became the first black librarian in the Atlanta Public Library service in 1936.

This was not even "just" a case of segregation and the worst of education and the rest. It was a clear matter of life and death too. Black life expectancy was fifteen years shorter than white; black infant mortality was almost double.

A new black newspaper, the *Atlanta Daily World*, was launched in 1928 (and now, stolidly conservative, it is the oldest black daily still in circulation in the US), but its creation underlined how excluded black Atlantans were from the white media. "Black musicians," *Living Atlanta* reported, were also "largely excluded from the local airwaves. While gospel and jazz musicians did get some air play, throughout the period blues musicians seldom received radio exposure . . ." One of its editors talked to Buddy Moss, late on in his life, and he confirmed this: "There was very little scene for the black man," he said. "I never heard none—blacks coming on radio. I don't remember any back in the thirties, not blacks that was doing no radio."

For those who could still afford to travel, Atlanta held its end up pretty well to begin with. By the end of 1930, the city's new airport was handling more flights than any other except New York and Chicago; the new Union Station had opened on Forsyth Street, replacing the earlier one at the corner of Pryor and Wall; and the new Greyhound Bus Station Willie would come to know was an ultra-modern art deco confection with swooping rounded corners and a lavish entrance, as if to a grand movie theater. Other building development came to a halt. Most black workers were unemployed and stuck, unless they were among the hordes who now took to hoboing on the rails, living a largely wretched existence that bounced them about between gut-rot alcohol and aimlessness, punctuated by the frequent violence—often lethal—of the railroad company men.

Willie never made it onto an aeroplane (not even Lannie Simmons' aeroplane in Statesboro) but, as we know, he certainly traveled, and managed this in safety and relative comfort, a whole level above the hobos.

Armed with his remarkable talent and an optimistic disposition, he worked the scuffling life as well as anybody, becoming one of the most widely known and well-loved figures in Georgia.

Among fellow-musicians, many of whom felt much less free than he was to roam and take risks for their music, he was liked for his personality, admired for his playing, and appreciated for his generosity with that talent. Cheryl Thurber recalled this from meeting, in the 1970s, people who had known Willie well: "All emphasised what a nice person he was and how he was looking out for other people, both black and white. You know, if somebody wanted to learn how to play, or do something in terms of playing, he would show them. He was not a musician who would keep his secret techniques to himself. He was very open and he was very forthcoming. I mean it's not just being a nice person, but that sense that he really tried to help other people out, and would share what he knew, and tried to encourage people to extend themselves."

The point here, though, is not to stress Willie McTell's superiority to others, but rather to remember that in this long-gone milieu, where you could have a record out on a major label yet spend most of your musician's working life on the street, there were many other skilled players, some of them highly celebrated in their local communities, who never got onto record at all: people we know only from later interviews with other musicians who remembered them, or else people whose names we don't know at all.

There were plenty of talented blues musicians and songsters who didn't *want* to make records. At Jimmie Rodgers' birthplace, Meridian Mississippi, a woman on the railroad station concourse would sing out the trains' destinations. Charley Patton's producer wanted her to make records too. She refused. The culture, like the station, has changed since then.

Willie McTell knew, liked, and encouraged lots of these diffident or obdurate talents, and just as he didn't sit around Atlanta waiting for record executives to call on him in the long gaps between sessions, nor did he mind risking the loss of such opportunities by making frequent trips out of town and taking to the roads and rails.

Blind Lloyd was one of these representatively obscure musicians Willie traveled with, starting in 1928. Cheryl Thurber told me: "He was *really* an interesting person, and a frustrated person as well, because he had had a stroke and hadn't been able to play any more, and he hadn't been able to live the wild life that he would like to have been able to. He was a fun guy."

She added: "He seems to have played with Willie on and off over an extended period, and, when Willie was down in the Statesboro area, they would get together. They would play together. And he indicated that Willie was far more capable of going about, that it was Willie who was leading him about. That Willie was arranging playing things but also that it was Willie getting him from one location to the next, and that they were really playing *together* . . . people tried to push them into competition but, in fact, he viewed Willie as a superior musician and he felt it worked quite well in terms of him backing Willie up. He played with quite a few musicians . . . Willie tried to get him to record and he just wasn't interested . . . he wasn't as comfortable going outside of his area. He played with Willie in his patch of Southern Georgia but—Atlanta was too much for him."

Blind Lloyd himself told Evans and Thurber this: "He'd take me up there. He tried to get me to go up there and stay . . . but I said 'No, I ain't going up there to stay.' . . . I'd go up there and stay there about two or three weeks at a time with Doog." Yet he also said, of a time when he and Willie played together early on: "I was in my prime then. I felt like I could go all over the world and come back." And he traveled widely enough to have met up with Sister Rosetta Tharpe in Oklahoma.

He said of traveling and playing with Willie: "We've been all everywhere in Georgia, I believe: some parts that wasn't Georgia. Oh yes. See, me and him together, we played like we was twins . . . And he would find that I was staying in Sylvania, and he was staying in Statesboro . . . Sometimes me and him would go to Macon together, go to Darien, Georgia, together . . . He'd be backwards and forwards then . . . Doog tried to get me to go with him up there to make records. I wouldn't go . . . I told him, well I wasn't going up there for that: 'I'll let you all make 'em, and I'll help you wear 'em out.'"

The better-known musicians who'd gravitated to Atlanta were unusual in that several of them were 12-string guitarists, which elsewhere was very rare. It has led people to write of a local guitar style, but we can say with confidence that, if such a thing really existed, Willie McTell did not typify it.

As Bruce Bastin sees it:

> The twelve-string guitar style of the Hicks brothers—probably a Newton County style—had nothing in common with the more melodious style of Blind Willie McTell. Indeed, the oft-mentioned twelve-string guitar school in Atlanta was less a school of shared musical characteristics than a number of idiosyncratic musical styles loosely grouped within the broader pattern of the Piedmont Blues.

(The Piedmont is the sweeping plateau between the Atlantic Coastal Plain and the Appalachians, taking in the mid-east of Alabama, north Georgia, the western halves of the Carolinas, and then forming a corridor up through the middle of Virginia—and, to be geographically correct, continuing up through Pennsylvania and beyond, though, for our purposes, Virginia is taking it far enough—and the Piedmont blues was, generally speaking, a style recognisably lighter and sunnier than the Delta blues of Mississippi.)

Willie played with these musicians, but he didn't play like them, and even those who learned from one another didn't necessarily retain the tutor's style. The younger key figure who would record with McTell and Curley Weaver, and easily outsell them, was Eugene "Buddy" Moss—who began as a harmonica player in the style of Eddie Mapp, but soon became a fine guitarist too. He learned guitar from Barbecue Bob, but he played more in the style of Blind Blake, a 6-string guitarist from Florida whose influence, via his records, was widespread. Blake's recording career lasted only six years, from 1927 to 1932. It yielded around eighty sides and made him more popular than any of his contemporaries, aside from Blind Lemon Jefferson. He was popular, as Tony Russell puts it, "less for his greyish singing than for his unequalled command of rag and blues guitar-playing," which was "effervescent and technically demanding."

According to Kate McTell, Willie knew Blind Blake, and once brought him up from Florida to Statesboro, but, in any case, Willie, always alert to records he could learn or profit from, was keenly aware of Blake's playing—and, on the 1956 *Last Session*, would reach back to his repertoire for 'That Will Never Happen No More', which Blake had recorded in 1927. Nevertheless, you couldn't really say his style influenced McTell's. No one we know of really did. It's one of the many remarkable things about him. He is by far the most significant of Georgia's pre-war musicians, and, though he could always fit in with, and even behind, other players, he created his style by himself.

By the early 1930s Willie had not only grown to know the Hicks Brothers, Curley Weaver, Buddy Moss, and many others in Atlanta and more widely around Georgia, but he had also met up with greater, further-flung figures, like the religious singer-guitarist from Texas, Blind Willie Johnson: "a personal friend of mine," McTell said in 1940.

As Michael Corcoran has it:

When Jack White of the red-hot White Stripes announced, "It's good to be in Texas, the home of Blind Willie Johnson," at Stubb's in June 2003, most of the sold-out crowd likely had never heard of the gospel blues singer / guitarist from Marlin, who pioneered a ferocity that still lives in modern rock . . . [but] The first songs he recorded, on a single day in 1927, are more familiar: 'Nobody's Fault But Mine' was covered by Led Zeppelin, Eric Clapton did 'Motherless Children', Bob Dylan turned Johnson's 'Jesus Make Up My Dying Bed' into 'In My Time Of Dyin'' on his 1962 début LP, and 'If I Had My Way I'd Tear This Building Down' has been appropriated by everyone from the Grateful Dead to the Staples Singers.

And "Johnson's haunting masterpiece 'Dark Was The Night (Cold Was The Ground)' was chosen for an album placed aboard *Voyager I* in 1977 on its journey to the ends of the universe."

Johnson and McTell were in the same temporary studio, for Columbia, in the same week in April 1930, Willie on Thursday 17th and Johnson three days later. They didn't record together, but they met up that week, probably for the first time. Over forty years later, Johnson's first wife,

Willie B. Harris, who had sung back-up on his session, remembered, unprompted, meeting Willie.

Like McTell, Johnson had been recording once a year since 1927, but, until now, his sessions had taken place in Dallas and New Orleans. His day in Atlanta would prove his last in the studio, though he had always laid down more tracks per day than Willie and this was no exception: Willie recorded two numbers that week, Johnson ten.

Outside the studio, Johnson survived another fifteen years and, at some point in the 1930s, McTell told John Lomax, he and Johnson traveled far and wide together: "from Maine to the Mobile Bay," as he put it with alliterative largesse. As with many of Willie's trips made with a musician companion, including those with Blind Lloyd in the narrower confines of small-town Georgia, the travels together of McTell and Johnson will truly have been a case of the blind leading the blind.

Willie's 1930 session resulted in one Columbia 78 record, 'Talkin' to Myself' coupled with 'Razor Ball'—a song that, once again, he had "jumped" from an earlier blueswoman's recording. Sara Martin's 'Down At The Razor Ball' is essentially a comic escapade story of genial bad behavior with cards and guns, delivered, as was customary in 1925, with an aura of matronly theatrical recital, sung as if the forty-one-year-old Ms Martin were wearing a fulsome ballgown on a stage festooned with heavy curtains. She and her combo take it at a pace utterly at odds with the supposed quick-fire chaos it describes.

For some reason, this concoction appealed to Willie, and he revisits it with surprisingly little alteration to the words, though he speeds it up to a bouncy medium pace and takes advantage of the acoustic guitar's natural informality. His playing is interwoven with remorselessly jocular spoken comments, as if to an imaginary second musician. It is Willie at his least appealing, but the other side of the same record, 'Talkin' To Myself' (on which he talks to himself far less), is lightweight but attractive, right from its opening couplet, a favorite of his, in which he sings to God and God replies: "Good Lord, good Lord, send me an angel down / 'Can't spare you no angel but I swear I'll send you a teasing brown.'"

This is the song in which the black man gives a dollar but the yellow wants 95 cents change, so that this blind singer's customary visual discrimination is much in evidence, though these are commonstock gradations and sit easily inside a lyric that puts a good many other such pre-assembled lines and couplets together. A railroad setting is used again too—"I even went down to the depot with my suitcase in my hand"—as is a more unusual fantasy about sailing on the ocean, walking "the sand of the deep blue sea," and seeing a shrimp dancing with a crab.

He also fantasises about crowds of women chasing him and begging him to be their man—"These here Georgia women just won't let Mr Samuel rest." Less innocently, perhaps, he decides that this is because "That new way of loving, mama it must be best": which, it has been suggested by white folklorists, means that all these women are enthusing about oral sex. It's pleasing, then, to see that the only known advertisement for one of Willie McTell's records ever taken out by the record company itself is Columbia's ad for this track in the important black newspaper the *Chicago Defender*, which has a comic pen and ink illustration of "Blind Sammie" running along a railway line, pursued by a gang of women, as a train's caboose pulls out of his reach up ahead. Strangely, this "Blind Sammie" looks like a balding white salesman, and several of the young women are flappers.

In 1931 Willie managed two more Atlanta sessions with Columbia, this time with Bob Miller acting as Frank Walker's assistant. The first of these sessions took place just two days after Barbecue Bob's death from pneumonia out in his homepatch of Lithonia on Wednesday, 21 October.

That Friday Willie recorded four numbers and two more eight days later—as well as playing guitar on both days on sessions by Ruth Willis (sometimes billed as Mary Willis), a thirty-two-year-old local singer with a day job as a domestic maid.

When Columbia released four sides from Willie's own sessions on their sister-label OKeh, he appeared under the pseudonym Georgia Bill, though the composer credit "McTell" was clearly written below each song title: 'Stomp Down Rider' coupled with 'Scarey Day Blues', and 'Low Down Rider' coupled with 'Georgia Rag'—this last a song in which Willie's lyrics ranged "all the way from Paris, France" to Atlanta's Harris Street and (as on his first-ever side, 'Writin' Paper Blues') the Virginia coast city of Newport News.

That same two-day session yielded a Blind Sammie record on the Columbia label too: the vengefully unpleasant 'Southern Can Is Mine' and Willie's 1930s masterpiece, 'Broke Down Engine Blues'. I think he must have known it attained greatness: he re-recorded it as 'Broke Down Engine' and 'Broke Down Engine No.2' in 1933, and yet again as 'Broke Down Engine Blues' for Atlantic Records in 1949.

As Bob Dylan says of the song in the liner notes to his own *World Gone Wrong* album of 1993, which includes a 'Broke-Down Engine' cover version on which he has no hope of matching the exquisite, transcendent McTell original, "it's about dupes of commerce & politics colliding on tracks." Er, yes. Actually he has a point here. By 1934, one-third of all US rail mileage was in bankruptcy. (The last time most rail companies made a profit was in the 1950s, when they carried the concrete that built the interstate highways that killed them off.)

The "field trips" of the major labels into the South were killed off by the Depression. Not only was Willie's October 1931 session his last for Columbia/OKeh, it was the last time the company undertook such a foray. And when he came back to Victor and Ralph S. Peer for one last session for them a few months later, this would be Victor's last blues session in Atlanta too.

(Gospel was another matter: gospel music would keep on thriving all through the Depression and the whole of the 1930s. It was a lucrative slot to occupy, in church and on record. Preachers, as well as hot quartets, often made records. One of Atlanta's star preachers, the Rev. J.M. Gates, cut over 200 sides in the fifteen years from 1926, and had his own Streamline Baptist Church in Atlanta. When he died in 1945, his was the biggest black funeral ever seen in the city—a claim that held right through until that of Martin Luther King Jr over twenty years later.)

Something else was different about Willie's last Columbia session. On Hallowe'en he brought in another musician to play behind him on one of the day's two tracks—and that musician, who would play again with McTell on many a later recording, and who here plays guitar and speaks on 'Low Rider's Blues', was the delightful Curley Weaver.

Born thirty miles east of Atlanta on Sunday, 25 March 1906, on a cotton farm outside Covington, Newton County, he learned guitar from his mother, Savannah Weaver (as had the Hicks brothers) and is said to have settled in Atlanta a couple of years before Willie.

The two of them made a perfect musical partnership and became stalwart friends. At some point later in the decade they would share an apartment in the city, with Willie's wife Kate and Curley's partner Cora—with whom Curley already had a daughter, the future Cora Mae Bryant, born in 1926—yet, at the time of his début joint session with Willie, Curley seems to have been living five miles or so south of downtown, still inside Fulton County, but in the borough of East Point, lodging with a middle-aged man who was, like Curley himself, a "theatrical janitor." Like almost everyone but Willie, he had a day job—and this despite being a superlative 6-string guitarist.

He'd played with harmonica-player Eddie Mapp (Curley never played on Mapp's records but Mapp did play on Curley's), and with Barbecue Bob, and, as noted, he'd made his first solo record in 1928. The year after, he traveled to New York and recorded briefly (with Mapp) for the now-mysterious QRS label in Long Island City, and, on two days in December 1930, he also recorded back in Atlanta (and back with Columbia, this time in the Campbell Hotel) as one of the Georgia Cotton Pickers. The others were Barbecue Bob—it would be his last session—and the sixteen-year-old Buddy Moss.

Eugene "Buddy" Moss was born in Warren County on 26 January 1914, at Jewell, or as it's now known, Jewells Mill, less than ten miles south-west of Warrenton as you head towards Sparta, in that corner where Warren County and Glascock County meet on the border of Hancock County to the west. He was one of twelve children, his parents sharecroppers, and he was in Atlanta by the age of fourteen, playing harmonica on the streets. Five years later, he would be a recording artist in his own right, now playing guitar and, all too briefly, looking like a star in the making.

Before Moss, Weaver and McTell all came together on record—for the sessions they secured with Vocalion in New York City in September 1933—Willie and Ralph S. Peer co-operated one last time, starting horribly early on the morning of Monday, 22 February 1932. Victor's recording equipment was installed inside Atlanta's Egleston Auditorium this time, and Willie brought a new musical partner along, the mysterious Ruby Glaze.

Four songs resulted, and all four were put out on records—on Victor in 1932 and later on the subsidiary label, Bluebird: 'Rollin' Mama Blues' was coupled with 'Mama Let Me Scoop For You' and 'Lonesome Day Blues' with the beautifully titled 'Searching The Desert For The Blues'.

I wish I could report that I'd solved the mystery of who Ruby Glaze, or "Ruby Glaze", was. Decades later, Kate McTell claimed to have been Ruby, and Bruce Bastin argued in the 1970s that Kate and Willie had already met by this point, and that she might have been in Atlanta at the time and could have been Ruby Glaze. The 1980s edition of the "bible" of pre-war blues listings, Dixon & Godrich's *Blues and Gospel Records 1902–1943*, offering a rare opinion, ventured that "Aurally, Ruby Glaze sounds very much like Kate McTell." The 1990s edition, Dixon, Godrich & Rye's *Blues and Gospel Records 1890–1943*, has colder feet on the matter, offering instead that "Aurally, there is some similarity between Ruby Glaze and Kate McTell."

I don't think so. We're able to compare singing *and* speaking voices here, since Ruby in 1932 and Kate three years later in Chicago both include little spoken asides on a couple of tracks—and you might say that these sound reasonably similar, though it seems to me that Kate sounds self-conscious and a little coy; Ruby does not sound self-conscious, but unapologetically sexy. And, when they sing, the difference seems incontestable. Ruby's voice is warm, relaxed, professional—Kate, on, say, 'Ain't It Grand To Be A Christian', is shrill, uncertain, and close enough to amateurish for us to suspect that she is only there because she's the main performer's wife.

I haven't found any other Ruby Glaze. There are many Glazes, black and white, on the 1930 US Census for Atlanta. No suitable Ruby Glaze appears on the Social Security Deaths Index. But, as the old saying has it, absence of evidence isn't evidence of absence.

Ralph S. Peer went on to publish Hoagy Carmichael and build up both the Peer International and the Southern Music companies, with fingers in the rock'n'roll pies of Little Richard and Buddy Holly, but his serious interest was in growing camellias, about which he became an international authority. When interviewed about the blues stars he'd recorded back in the 1920s, he couldn't call to mind a single one of their names.

Willie, Curley and Buddy went to New York City together in September 1933, recording copiously. Productive as these studio days were, only Buddy Moss gained future sessions on the strength of them. Curley and Willie returned to Atlanta.

Four months later, Willie married Miss Ruthy Kate Williams, and a more turbulent Atlanta life began.

# THIRTEEN

THE PRODUCER OF the 1933 McTell-Weaver-Moss recording sessions was the forty-three-year-old Arthur Edward Satherley, who had grown up in Bristol, in the west of England, and arrived in the States in 1913 hoping to see a land full of cowboys and indians. Finding himself in Milwaukee with disappointingly few of either type in sight, he had drifted into the record business in 1918 and enjoyed a long and agreeable career within it. At the beginning of the 1930s, he was living in a very mixed, well-to-do immigrant neighborhood on West 140$^{th}$ Street in New York City, and commuting downtown to produce and vet talent for the newly formed American Record Company, ARC. It was here that Willie McTell and friends recorded for this Englishman in September 1933.

Six 78rpm records by "Blind Willie" were duly issued on the company's Vocalion label, with no particular success, plus further records on various labels by Buddy Moss, Curley Weaver, and the so-called Georgia Browns (Moss and Weaver plus the more shadowy Atlanta guitarist Fred McMullen).

Willie's sessions were artistically patchy this time, and he would never again give us recordings with the shivering radiance that glows off the earliest sides. He had also become inclined to record more songs of garrulous, jolly inconsequence and fewer chiseled blues. The 1933 sessions did not reverse this drift—yet one day out of the four, the splendid second session, on Monday, 18 September, catches McTell on fire. He sounds a bit drunk but wonderful.

The first number, 'Lord Have Mercy If You Please', sends no signal that the rest will be so torrid, and might as easily have been logged as a Curley Weaver performance. Curley is strong, too, on the second number, 'Don't You See How This World Made A Change', but McTell comes storming through here, fusing great feeling with an intimate looseness of delivery that he has never captured on record before. It is thrilling to hear—and this is what he keeps up as he moves on to the marvelous 'Savannah Mama', where, right from the magnificent opening moments, his guitarwork is so concentrated and precise, so felt and so assertive (*this* is what inspired The Allman Brothers' slide style), while his vocal lines flow across all this precision with the grace of heartfelt risk-taking. He sings with an experimental mannered fluidity somehow freed from artifice by open ardor.

Three revisits to 'Broke Down Engine Blues' follow, and, by the time he reaches the second, he is blazing—an artist up on the high wire, inventing leaps and bounds as he goes, his voice deliriously free yet emotionally charged. So often with his recordings you can tell he's a wonderful mimic and he's selecting the particulars of his voice for that day or that song—but here he seems to set his soul free as he sings.

One more track follows ('My Baby's Gone'). McTell, Weaver, and Moss return to the studio on the Tuesday and Thursday that same week but, though these yield fine material, like the lovely 'Death Room Blues', Willie never quite hits those moments of incandescent reverie again.

After Willie returned to Georgia, he lost no time in finding a wife. Perhaps he felt time creeping up on him. Barbecue Bob was not the only one he'd connected with who had died since the decade began. His grandfather Elbert's wife, Judie, died in McDuffie in July 1930 after a heart attack—"There being an eyewitness, no inquest was necessary", as it said on her death certificate—and, in January 1933, Elbert himself died, from lobar pneumonia, at seventy-three. Without ever moving far, what a long journey his had been: from being the slave baby of Reddick McTyeir and Essey, through a lifetime of farm laboring, to a death in the deepest trough of the Depression.

The woman Willie married was Ruth Kate Williams, one of the children of the Rev. Andrew W. Williams and his wife Sarah, *née* Gilmore. She often claimed to have been one of the youngest, but actually she might well have been the oldest. The official version of the family story is, as so often, less tidy than the truth. The two children older than Kate in Andrew and Sarah's household were born before these two set up house together. If they were Andrew's children, Sarah bore both of them while he was still elsewhere in the district and living with a wife named Sallie.

We know little of Andrew's background, except that he was born in February 1885, almost certainly in Spread, and, by the age of fifteen, he was a farm laborer there, living with his widowed mother, Emily. He remained a farmer after joining the ministry.

His future wife, Sarah Gilmore, was one of a large number of children—their names included Annie, Inez, Hezekiah, Jacob, Amanda, Joe, Rose or Rhoney, Jewel or Julia, Clinton, Claudie, and Pleas. This last was also the name of their father, Pleas Gilmore Senior, born in slavery in 1863, whose own parents were from South Carolina.

Again, the family story is not the truth. The official version is that he marries a woman named Alice Whigham, supposedly born in 1867, and that their daughter Sarah is born in November, 1886.

Sarah is indeed born then, but not to Alice. In 1900, when Sarah is thirteen and her older brother Joe is seventeen, Alice Whigham is the twenty-one-year-old boarder in the household of their parents, Pleas Gilmore and his wife Fannie, who are both in their late thirties. Later, Fanny disappears and Alice becomes the wife—and, in due course, Kate's supposed grandma. (When Alice is buried in the cemetery at Spread Chapel in 1970, the official story has slipped her birthdate back from 1878 to 1867, and we are to conclude that she'd lived to be 103.)

In 1907 Sarah Gilmore has her own first child—and calls her Fannie, in remembrance of her real mother. Three years later she has a son, Arthur. Both appear with her maiden name as their surname on the 1910 census. Ruth Kate is born next, on 22 August 1911, and by now her mother and the Rev. Andrew have set up house together. Kate's younger siblings duly arrive: Emma, Sarah Belle, an obligatory Pleas, Marion, Hez, and Andrew Junior.

Keen country blues fans have heard a great deal of Kate's version of events—and especially of her whole life with Willie, comparatively brief though it was—because she was "found" by folklorist David Evans' parents in the mid-1970s, interviewed by all the Evanses, written up by David, and then interviewed several times more by other local white writers in Georgia. But, while there is no possibility of hearing Willie's side of the story, we can access another side of things from Kate herself— because, in 1979, luckily for us, she talked at great length to a *black* interviewer. The preacher's daughter gives a sometimes rather different account of life with Willie here.

The interview was conducted by E. Bernard West for that great book of oral history, *Living Atlanta*. West was one of its three main editors, and the gatherer of most of the testimony from black Atlantans. Little of the Kate McTell interview was used in the book—though it does include her account of how she and Willie were dealing in bootleg whiskey in the city in the mid-1930s—but the rest of the interview is available to be heard by appointment in the basement of the Atlanta History Center, out in Buckhead: the suburb where the New York to New Orleans train calls, and where, eighty years ago, Robert Hicks was working at that barbecue.

Today, much of Buckhead is absurdly swanky. Almost as soon as you pull off the Interstate and head uphill through woodland, the houses on either side of the road are, like those of Hollywood, fantasy mansions of brute immensity, their extravagant solidity challenging you to scoff at, or choose between, their jostling of styles. What do you covet: the Victorian gothic? the French chateau? the Tudor palace? They'd be squaring up to each other, spoiling for a fight, if they weren't so set back, each in its spacious grove of golden trees.

This route led to the undistinguished building housing the History Center archives. Inside, in a windowless, rather cramped library, Reading Room and Reference Librarian Mike Brubaker had set up an ancient, large reel-to-reel tape recorder and a pair of huge headphones heavily cushioned in black leather. Wires trailed across the floor and a table blocked off access to many of the bookshelves. There were two sets of four big tapes. I sat down and started playing through the master tapes, transcribing their contents.

There was a very partial transcript typed on blue copy paper, but this proved inaccurate, and, as I discovered going through the tapes, there were also bits of tape missing. Sometimes these had been transcribed, but sometimes there was no way of knowing whether the transcript covered all a missing section or not. I wasn't allowed to record the tapes onto my own minidiscs. The only permitted option was to transcribe it all there and then, which meant playing a few moments of tape, stopping the machine, writing down what I'd just heard or thought I'd heard, and then winding the tape back slightly so as not to miss a bit when the machine restarted. Every switch on, off, backwards and on again produced a loud clunk that must have irritated the many other people using the library at the time.

It took two days. The first day I wandered off at lunchtime in search of pleasant food but could find only the building's pathetic retro "diner," jumping with phoney 1950s ads and offering food taken straight from the freezer to the microwave. The second day I knew better and worked on through.

Even then, it was a race to write it all down before closing time—and when, right at the end, I realised that the copy tapes *didn't* have the gaps that the master tapes had, it was too late to play them through to check if there were bits I'd not heard. Nevertheless, it had been thrilling to me to listen to Kate McTell's voice: a voice Willie used to know so well—a very beguiling, girlish, lively one, though she was sixty-seven years old when the interview took place.

There was a good deal about how their mothers had known each other as children, and how she and Willie then met up, though it was all vague on dates and had Kate's usual ring of unreliability to it. She tells West she finished high school at fifteen: "My mother was a school teacher and she couldn't leave me at home, she had to carry me to school, and I was too far in advance. I started off in the fifth grade, so that's why I finished so early." Then, in her account of meeting Willie, she says she was graduating from Augusta's Paine College, or Paine College's high school—though the Paine College archivist cannot find her name on any list of those who did so—and Kate further muddies the story by having told the Evanses that she "went to Morris Brown College" in Atlanta and "finished there." Either way, she is concerned to lay the ground for her claim to have been the Ruby Glaze of the 1932 recording session.

"Willie was playing for our Christmas concert," she tells West, "and I sang, and he said 'The girl that sang—I would like to meet her,' and the principal said 'OK. When she finishes I'll have her come down and talk to you': so I did, and he asked me where I was from and ... he said 'I want to take you to Atlanta—I'm doing some recording pretty soon and I would like for you to go along with me.' I said 'I'm just a kid! My mother wouldn't let me do that!' "

If, as she suggests to the Evanses, this was the Christmas of 1931, this kid was twenty years old at the time—and this is the only December when Willie was indeed "going to be doing some recording pretty soon."

Kate goes on: "He said 'Well, where is your mother? ... Would you take me out to meet your mother and daddy?' I said 'Yes' and he asked me what my mother and father's name was. I said 'My mother's name is Sarah Gilmore Williams and my father's name is Reverend A.W. Williams.' He said 'Oh! your mother gave you to me when you was a baby! I *know* you're gonna be mine now! I'm gonna ask her for you again!'

"So I brought him out and sure enough he did. And my mother she said, 'Well, listen.' She squatted right down . . . and she said: 'Do you think that my daughter would make you a good wife?' He said, 'Yes I do, Ma Sarah, because you was always a good person. My mother always said it and ever since, I knowed you was a wonderful person.' And so she said, 'I wouldn't want you to marry my child knowin' that you were blind and she would ever mistreat you.' He said, 'I don't believe she would.' And she said, 'Well, if y'all wanna get married, ain't nothin' I can do about it. She's in Augusta goin' to school and you're gonna slip off and get married anyway.' Said, 'It's left up to you two, whatever you decide to do.' So we spent a week out here and then we went back to Augusta and I went to Paine College and signed out. Then we got married!"

All this might seem a little odd. We know they married in 1934 from their marriage certificate—the only document Willie McTell couldn't avoid appearing on in his lifetime—but, had she been Ruby Glaze, their "week out here" in Atlanta would have been in February 1932. West actually asks her age when they met and she replies, "How old I was when I first met Willie and we started off? I'd say—seventeen years old."

Then she adds: "Well, he was ten years older than me, so that'd be twenty-seven, right?"

Had Kate really been only about seventeen, this would have been around 1928, the best part of six years before they married, and she and Willie would have been together in Atlanta for almost as long as he'd been there at all—for which there is absolutely no evidence, and no one but Kate has ever suggested it.

Not even Kate suggests it consistently: later in the same interview, she says she first visited Atlanta in 1930, and then went back in 1934, and, asked where they lived in Atlanta, she says, "The first place I went to was 160 Hilliard Street. That's where his Aunt Mattie was livin' when we got married."

She also tells the whole story of their meeting as if they went straight from the Christmas concert to Wrens, secured her mother's blessing, and, after spending "a week" in Atlanta or somewhere else, went off to Augusta to get married. What might make this more plausible is that 1933 was the school's fiftieth anniversary, so that the Christmas concert would have been a bigger event than usual and a booking of Willie McTell as an entertainer more likely. Yet, had this been the real timing, Kate would have been a woman of twenty-two when saying she was just a kid, and this first encounter with Willie would have been the best part of two years after Willie's recordings with Ruby Glaze.

It's a highly peculiar parental blessing they receive, too. No consultation with the Rev. Williams at all, and a mere "I-guess-I-can't-stop-you" from this minister's wife. Kate makes it clear that neither of her parents attended her wedding, and neither did her aunt in Augusta, and the fact is that she and Willie crossed the state line into South Carolina to marry.

She tells Bernard West: "I was with mother's sister then. I call her my livin' mother now. And we had went to Aikens and got married, and we came back and we was layin' 'cross the bed and she said, 'What you mean layin' up in my house with a man?!' I said, 'Aw!!' and Willie hand her the license and she said, 'Aw, y'all mean to tell me you *really* got married?!' She said, 'Oh, Willie, Lord have mercy, you gon' take my child away?!' He said, 'Yes I am. I'm gonna take her to Atlanta—but I'm gonna continue to send her on to school.' Which he did."

Why did they cross the state line to marry? Was it just because of disapproval on the Williams family's part? Or because Willie had been legally married before? Or even because Kate had been married before? It's a source of great regret to me that I have failed to find answers to these questions.

But cross the state line they did. Giving their names as Willie S. McTell and Rutha K. Williams, they married in Aiken, South Carolina. They crossed the river from Augusta, Georgia, (which both claimed as their place of residence) to obtain affidavits on 10 January 1934, and next day their marriage license was duly granted. They took this to a Notary Public in North Augusta, who conducted a brief civil ceremony and issued them a certificate. Kate would say later that a cousin, one Lula Habersham, had to "stand as a mother" for her at the ceremony.

North Augusta is a miserable little place just across the Savannah River from Augusta itself, but Aiken, a few miles further on, is a lovely old town with gracious, wide boulevards—and, it follows, a vast amount of free parking space right on the leafy streets, and, therefore, a downtown that is still alive. I drove there in Willie's footsteps, sixty-seven years after the event, one Monday in early November 2001. The courthouse still stands, looking up one of the broadest and leafiest boulevards of all, where everything was autumnal browns and I walked through layers of pine needles, nut husks, and leaf-mold crustiness to approach it.

The building's elegantly proportioned exterior of pale gray stucco was festooned with notices and printed arrows, all refusing access by any of the front entrances and directing you round the side. I passed a happy, lumberjack-shirted bum sitting on a low wall conferring with a pasty, abstracted lawyer, and a number of disaffected young people who may as well have had the words "Awaiting Sentence" stamped on their foreheads.

It was just two months after 9/11, which explained but hardly justified the excess of security precautions for admittance. It proved harder for me to walk into the Aiken County Courthouse than to enter the United States. Inside, the staff were too busy for any prolonged investigation into what documents might be retained from the 1930s and you couldn't look things up yourself. Unlike the generous level of data held in Warrenton on anyone wanting to marry in Warren County, the notoriously lax pre-war South Carolina authorities had required no real information at all. Willie and Kate had told them nothing extra, and, probably on principle, both had lied about their age. Willie had claimed to be twenty-eight, and was one or two years older; Kate had claimed to be twenty-three and was a year younger.

I ate lunch in a downtown Aiken restaurant where a comical extravagance of affluent, smart women of a certain age poured in, singly and in twos, bearing elaborately gift-wrapped packages. There was a mutual coo of greeting between them and the proprietor, who was not a local but knew every one of their first names. He sat down with me to chat and told me that, when he plays a particular compilation CD in the restaurant, he has to skip the track with Martin Luther King Jr's "I had a dream" speech set to music because it's too Uppity Blacks for his clientele. In return I asked him to guess what year Aiken County's public schools had integrated. He guessed too early. Anyone would. The right answer is 1970.

Back from this South Carolina resort after their wedding, Willie and Kate began, or resumed, their Atlanta days. It was a busy life, mostly if not always in decent apartments and often with a telephone, which Willie needed for bookings as a musician, and which they both used for other business.

"Willie's uncle," Kate tells E. Bernard West, "he run a big whiskey still at that time, and he'd give us all the whiskey we wanted. And we'd carry it back on the train, come down with a great big suitcase and load it up, carry it back.

"I would tell several of my friends, 'I'm giving a party tonight, having a fish fry or a chili supper.' And I'd invite so many people in, you know. We'd always close the kitchen off with chairs. Willie said, 'Now I'm going to play. You sell the sandwiches and plates and things, and the drink. We sold scrap iron: that's where you made your money, selling scrap iron liquor.

"A lot of people, they's superstitious, they would tell me, 'You taste it, I don't want nobody's scrap iron liquor unless they taste it.' I said, 'I don't drink.' Willie'd say, 'I'll taste it. Ain't no poison in it.' He'd turn it up and

he'd say, 'Now you pay her for that one, and buy you another one.'"
Kate always collected the money.

"Who could come to these parties?" West asks.

"Anybody that wanted to! If you pass by, say, 'Hey, man, are you having a party?' 'Yeah, come on in.' That's the way they did it back then. 'Who's havin' a party?' they'd say. 'This is Willie McTell's house: they're having a party here tonight. Come on, man!'"

The police caught them with liquor only once. "They said, 'Where you got your whiskey at?' I said, 'Who told you we had any?' They said, 'We got the word, we see the crowd hanging around.' I said, 'Well, if you got the word, you can look for it. It ain't my place to tell you where it's at, if you think we got any in here.' And they just found a small little glass, that Willie had left just a little in, not in a bottle or anything.

"They said, 'Willie, we're going to have to carry you down.' He said, 'I'm going, baby doll, because they can't make me work. I'm blind. I can sit out my ten days.' I said, 'No, I'm going, and they're going to turn me loose.' So I went. The judge told them they didn't have nothing on us, because they didn't catch us with the whiskey and they didn't catch us selling it. And that was it, they let me go."

West asks her if they were white police.

"Yeah, there wasn't no black police then. In New York you'd find 'em, but not down here . . . I remember [when] they say, 'We got black policemen!' and I said, 'I don't believe it!' And they say, 'Yeah, they're gonna have a route, and the Ku Klux Klans is gonna take 'em out and everything.' But there wasn't nothin' to it. [And then] I saw my first black policeman in Atlanta—I think he was the first one hired. He was directing traffic at Five Points."

Then there was the numbers (unlicensed gambling lotteries), which everyone had always played—but Kate also seems to have dabbled in "running numbers": selling and distributing them.

"Willie's mother would always buy him a good number. He said she'd always bring him good numbers. He was lucky with the numbers. But the numbers was good. You could catch 'em better back then than you can now. Lot of people would play 'em. Anybody that could put a penny on it would play it. My aunt hit for about $6,000. I don't know how she did it, [and] when I was in Atlanta I hit enough to buy a Model-T car."

Kate says people went to hoodoo women for many reasons (including to Ma Sutton, whose Auburn Avenue restaurant became famous), among them to "go get luck for the numbers." She mentions an uncle of hers from Augusta: "I went with him down there one time. I drive for him. I was younger. I did most of the driving. Except picking up numbers, and I'd pick 'em up when I wasn't working. 'Cause they would think nothing of me, dressed in white, with my cap on. Wasn't supposed to wear the cap unless I'm in the hospital, but I wore it."

She talks of the places they lived and worked.

"We lived at 381 Houston Street, and then we lived 183 Fort Street for a long time; then we lived out on Highland Avenue in front of the Stone Bakery. But the first place I went to was 160 Hilliard Street. That's where Willie's Aunt Mattie was living when we got married.

"I worked at Grady's [Hospital]. You know they had a tunnel at the old Grady's. I imagine they still have it, where, if nobody claims the body, they got a train that carries all that stuff out to Marietta River and dumps it over in there: the bodies and everything. After they get through practicing on that body, that's where they dump them at. It's a tunnel, what we'd call the underground subway, and they just had something like on a little railroad track thing that would pull all this waste down there and just dump it over in the Marietta River. It was something terrible.

"I lived a better musician life than I did a nursing career life, specially with the Army. You get cursed, you get spit on, you get slapped, women's husbands be overseas, you know, and they'd be all juiced up, and they'd bring them in the ambulance, you get cussed and spit on and you're not supposed to hit a patient back.

"Saturday evenings we'd have about two hours at 81 Theatre on Decatur Street. They had these stage shows. It would be packed in there. Mostly black, because it was in the black area, but it was run by white. I'll tell you about Willie: he always would have him a contract. He'd say 'I'm not going to pick my fingers off for nickels and dimes.' He would tell them exactly what he was going to play so many hours for. And they'd guarantee him that he'd get it too, and he'd get it."

Willie McTell was never a headline act at this theater, which was part of the powerful T.O.B.A. syndicate (the Theater Owners Booking Association, though widely said to stand for Tough On Black Asses); star performers were booked with its contracts. Willie never obtained one, and, though he may have charmed the management into paying him an agreed fee for performing there, he could not have toughed out anything serious at a venue that had spent a breathtaking $10,000 on a new theater organ in 1925.

Kate more or less concedes that she might have been over-pumping the tire here, because she says that what happened after they left the 81 was that "then he'd just be walking the street and playing . . . The Silver Slipper was on the corner of Fort and Jackson Street. And on Houston Street, he used to play up there sometimes."

His best earner, and the one place he did have some kind of contract, was "at Pig'n Whistle out on Ponce de Leon Avenue and Fort Street, just above Sears Roebuck—and the stadium used to be out there too. Baseball stadium. And he would play blues, classical, spirituals, hymns, anything you could name, he'd hit it.

"They call them car hops, you know: from one car to another, and they'd say 'I want Willie. I want Willie next.' And he would make. We walked away from out there during the Depression many a night with $100. That's right. Which was marvelous . . .

"I used to go out there to sing at night with him. Me and him would be the only black there, unless Curley come along and played with him. He would go every night through the week, and Saturday . . . it would be during the summer season, too, not the winter season, 'cause he would always travel south of Florida in the winter season. Very seldom he'd spend the winter in Atlanta. He always liked to go to Florida, and he never took me."

When he was in Atlanta, they'd sometimes take little trips out. Despite its KKK associations, they went out to Stone Mountain some Sundays by streetcar: "just sightseeing." This is a natural-enough way of putting it but must also confirm how little Willie was hindered by his blindness.

At home they often played records: "Bessie Smith's records, Memphis Minnie's records, Joshua White. Buddy's records and Curley's records,

Fred McMullen, Blind Blake, Blind Lemon Jefferson. And he had his own study room—play room—'cause he had a lot of Braille records and a lot of Braille books and things."

Any white records?

"Yes, he liked it. He'd buy 'em. At the 81 Theatre we did our thing together. There were no separation. Like if Willie was going to play, if I was going to Charleston, if there were white girls there, they'd all Charleston along together. We mixed it at the 81 Theatre."

West asks how she and Willie had fun, and Kate says: "We'd go out and have a ball. He'd get drunk and I'd drag 'im home . . . He go out and a lot of times when we'd leave Atlanta and go to his uncle's house in McDuffie he would get drunk. But he'd always have me right by him, his hand layin' over me and one leg throwed over me. That's just the way he was . . . He'd never get sick off it, I tell you that. And I know he could drink a lot of whiskey."

West asks naïvely if Kate ever met any "ladies of the evening," and, after a little blustering denial, she gives a reply that hints at some knowledge of the business, and seems to support the claim Gold Harris' daughter Sally Cramer made to me, which was that Kate, who made money in many ways, ran a couple of housefuls of these "ladies of the evening":

"Oh yes, I'd see them, sure," said Kate. "Mostly Decatur Street. Well, that was where—we call them the houses. The trick houses. You know, like man say, 'You want to see a girl? I got one up here.' You go up there, and that was it. If you liked her, OK; if not, you come on back down. And a lot of the ladies liked it there. If you treat them nice, they would get through doin' their work and they'd come over your house or your apartment and help you clean your house up. So I never did have no trouble out of 'em. Stayed over there in their apartment and I stayed over in mine. Willie played for them. I'd be over there havin' fun with 'em. Didn't make no difference with me. 'Cause he was makin' the money. And The Man say all he want for his house was his rent, didn't make no difference who stayed in it. Said if they didn't like what was going on they could move out. So that settled that part of it."

She is also asked about the place that was the subject of Willie's songs

'Bell Street Lightnin'' and 'Bell Street Blues': "It was down. They claimed if you go down there you didn't come out alive, you know. But me and him would go down there most anytime, in Black Bottom, and he'd play. That's where they were selling it all on the sidewalks. Police was scared to go down there. We'd go down there any time of night, any time of day. Made a lot of money down there too. Come out. Nobody ever interfered with us in Atlanta. Never had any trouble. Black Bottom was rough, down on Bell Street. You had to let them know when you walked through there—because if you didn't they'd knock you out. Willie go through there with his pistol in his hand like he was the police. [Black Bottom was] the low end of Bell Street: from, I'd say Houston Street on back towards Ponce de Leon.

"Back then, some people lived good and some didn't. Because some people just didn't care whether they had anything or not. They didn't care whether they eat or not, whether they had anything in their house to eat or not—they just didn't care. But they didn't beat me like that, 'cause Willie could always get his food in the house and I'd always have his food cooked. And he'd tell 'em 'Man, I'm getting' sleepy now: you all gonna have to get out of my house . . .' He put 'em out of his house, lay down to go to sleep. And he'd eat his food. He'd say 'I can't feed them folks! I gotta work for my livin': let 'em get out and work for theirs. I'm working my fingers off every night tryin' to play: I ain't feedin' 'em.' "

West asks her about Depression times. Her first recollection is about furniture repossessions, which Willie came close to experiencing first-hand: "Like that furniture—if you miss one payment, if you don't owe more 'n $50 or $75, they'd want to come and take it back, and they gonna take it over and sell it for the same price. So Willie told 'em, 'If you put your foot inside that door—the man gonna come in my door is gonna have to have a warrant.' Say. 'If I have the money, I'll pay you, and if I don't, you don't.' So they gone about their business."

West says approvingly: "Willie was pretty cocky, wasn't he?!"

"He sure was! He was straight, and he'd tell it right out to 'em."

Asked if she remembered the soup lines, she says "I remember it very well, but we never did get in it . . . Food was cheap: fatback I think was five cents a pound 'long then. And it was that thick kind, too. About five pounds of fatback would last you a month: two people. They didn't eat this high-price food like we eat now. Steaks, chickens, pork: we didn't have all that. You had stew meat. You'd have chicken, but mostly fatback."

West says: "We want to go back to the '30s and I want to walk down Auburn Avenue with you. You describe to me what's happening . . . Saturday night . . . nine o'clock in the evening."

"That's a little too early. Round eleven o'clock: that's when they're falling out of the joints and clowning. Somebody walk up to you and say 'Hey, which way you goin'?' Say, 'Man, you don't know who you're talking to, do you? That's my wife! You don't ask her which way she's going. I'm going to take her wherever she's going.' 'OK, don't be smart.' 'One of these .22s hit you, you'll think I'm smart enough.' And he had his pistol in his hand then. He carried a .22 all the time. That's right! He was a mean man. That's right! He'd blast once or twice at several guys that's trying to get smart. 'Man, you don't need that girl. That's a baby you got.' He'd say, 'That's what I know. I call her Baby Doll. Whether I need her or not I got her, and I got her for law.'

"Come on down at Yates' Drug Store, go in there, they'd say 'Hey, Willie, play me a piece.' 'Man, I ain't got time: I got to take my wife home so she can get some rest. She just left that hospital. OK, I'll play you one little piece. Come on Yates, you making plenty of money, give me a couple of dollars.' You'd lay it on 'im. So, he'd play it for a few minutes, get a box of candy or something or other, come on out. Keep on down to about Fort Street, about Fort Street to Houston, cross Irwin, go up by the Barbecue Grill. They're really breakin' it down, there.

"He said 'I'm gonna take you home now and let you go to sleep, and I'm comin' back down here and make some money.' It would be around twelve o'clock."

In this one regard, the account Kate gives the Evanses is less romantic than that she gives to E. Bernard West. She tells the Evanses: "Then we had a little music room . . . And most of the music and his instruments and everything stayed in there, and a couch. And if he'd come in—he liked his little toddies. And if he'd come in, and he knowed I didn't want to be bothered, he would lie down on this couch in his music room, and didn't disturb me, when he'd go out and play late at night or something."

Yes. We can quite imagine Kate having made it clear that she "didn't want to be bothered" when he came stumbling home. But to West she offers a different ending: "He'd come on back, and I'd hear him the next morning, just about the break of day, singin' [and here she sings], 'Wake up, mama, don't you sleep so sound . . . These old blues walking all over your yard. Blues grab me at midnight, didn't turn me loose till day . . . I didn't have no mama to drive these blues away.' And I'd hear him and I'd get up and open the door."

This song was, of course, 'Mama, 'Tain't Long Fo' Day': a favorite of hers, from his 1927 début session, which she seems to have thought was "their song" Perhaps it did become that. He never re-recorded it.

Kate's younger brother, Andrew, came to stay the summer with his sister and Willie sixteen months after they married. He outlived Kate as well as Willie, and he was interviewed in 1992 by David Fulmer (the Atlanta-based journalist who subsequently bought and installed Willie's replacement gravestone out at Jones Grove in Happy Valley). Fulmer "found" Andrew, who had long since become the Rev. W. Andrew Williams and ran a barber's shop in Atlanta during the week. Fulmer was making a video about McTell, *Blind Willie's Blues*, and "Rev", as the family still calls him, proved a charming interviewee, if a little constrained by the formality of being filmed.

The side of Willie's Atlanta life that *he* saw was all honorable uplift. Like his testimony, his style of delivery is a contrast to Kate's.

I lived with him in the summer of 1935. I came to Atlanta and spent that summer from May through August—with he and Ruth . . . they lived a very normal life, had a beautiful little three-room apartment, there at 381 Houston Street, and he supported his wife and himself with his employment, basically from Pig'n Whistles. This was his greatest source of income and his support was quite unique. Very unique. He had the things for all of the needs of life. He had no other, no social services or assistance from any source. All he had to depend on was what he could earn—and, of course, frequently he would be called to do concerts at various churches even then. I went to a couple of churches with him to do concerts. And that was, you know, a bit of substitute income, but Pig'n Whistles was his basic income, and he lived a very good life.

He often talked about his opportunity to broaden his income and perhaps widen his acquaintance. He had contacts here and from here to Chicago and maybe to New York. And, of course, he felt that it was a better opportunity for me, and of course now I know that he was right. The opportunity for schooling and for future employment, to say the least of living conditions. He was not exactly selfish: whatever he could find that was good for him, if it could be shared he chose to do that. And not having any children, you see, and my sister, somehow I fitted into their life very beautifully.

He could take me about places in Atlanta . . . we would walk from block to block and he would tell me, "This street is such-and-so", and I would look up on the sign—and there it was. And we'd get on the streetcar, and he'd tell me the car that we were to ride. I remember very distinctly one day we went downtown to the post office. We caught the car on Auburn Avenue, and we got off at Five Points and he said, "Now we will walk to the Post Office," and of course he named five different streets as we turned, and we did arrive at the post office. And as a fifteen-year-old boy that was quite amazing to me.

One of the things that always struck me about him, as you can see he wore a very unique moustache. He shaped that moustache himself, he never allowed a barber to do that. And, believe it or not, he did it with a straight razor. He was . . . always neat. He never allowed himself to believe that he was dressed until he put on his necktie. He taught me how to tie a necktie, believe it or not. Very seldom would he let anybody shine his shoes, he did that himself. And he was always very neat. He never allowed himself to be laxed in his appearance.

He was very, very conscious of that. Medium-sized man, not a big man, and, em, he dressed himself always. He might ask the color one time and there was something about the texture of his suit, he would know the color the next time. I have seen him hang his brown, his black, his blue, in the closet, and when he went to the closet, if he put them in then he would always come out with the one that he wanted, and if it was not, he had a keen sense of telling you, "This is not my brown", "This is not my black—where is it?" Very unique.

Williams was impressed not just by Willie's skills and pride in himself, but by his receptiveness to others:

He had a keen sense of understanding your approach, about most any subject you wanted to discuss. He could do that. He liked to discuss bible, and of course he had a bible. That was interesting too. He was the first person I ever saw read Braille. He had a keen sense of scripture . . . and he liked to discuss scripture, and above all he liked to discuss people. He had a keen sense of politics. He listened to radio. Very keenly.

Musicians were always around too: "I knew Buddy Moss real well back in '35. Once I knew him, he was the kind of feller, he'd be around with Willie, oh my God, almost daily! Buddy Moss, Bumble Bee Slim—and I remember Josh White coming through, twice—once he came through going to Chicago and he came back through going to Memphis."

Fulmer asked Rev. Williams when his sister and Willie separated.

"I would think maybe something like 1940, or '41 at the latest, I would think that. She attempted to go to New York and she thought maybe she wanted a career, to work there, and she did go there but it didn't prove to be desirous."

Gold Harris' daughter, Sally Cramer, spent some time staying with Willie and Kate McTell in Atlanta two or three years closer to this separation than Andrew's long stay with them, and she saw a different side to their relationship—and perhaps to their characters. When I met her, she was eighty-one years old. After living and working in New York from 1941 to 1983, she had returned to McDuffie and was living back at Sand Hills Road in Happy Valley—on a lane called Cramer Street, in fact—just

242

across from the house where Bo-Rat and Hazel McTear took care of Willie in the last months of his life.

I was taken out there by Dot Jones, the retired Thomson tourism officer whose level of interest in Willie as a local figure was hugely greater than I'd expected. She had visited Kate McTell twice, and, back in 1992, she had interviewed Gold Harris, and had met Sally Cramer before.

We found her—a large swollen woman (as she said herself) who looked nothing like her age, with lively eyes, large glasses, a small lopsided green net on her head, and one leg amputated around the knee. She was sitting on a porch closed in by a series of glass panels that a teenage boy was cleaning with a good deal of perfumed spray-on gunk for much of the hour and a half we were there. A radio played plaintive jazz trumpet music softly, far off in the background. The room was broiling hot.

Sometimes Sally would drift off into monologues about her health in general and her leg in particular. There were interruptions to pay the teenage boy, and to answer a very tall, elderly man who came round enquiring about saucepans. But mostly she kept up an animated conversation, even when regaling me with the trials of being a woman who had moved far away from rural Georgia and then come back: "The Jewish people I worked for in New York, they treated me like one of the family, and they taught me things—they taught me what I know. They were good people. Now when I lived in New York and came back visiting here they treated me like a queen. But when I moved back . . ."

She made a pushing-away gesture. She feels resented back in Happy Valley. "I don't think I'd have come back at all if it hadn't have been for my daddy. I don't believe my leg would have come off if I'd stayed in New York."

She feels a strong loyalty to that wider world she'd moved in, and gratitude for it, and part of her obvious enjoyment of our conversation came from a relishing of my being from that wider world too. Her strong fondness for Willie McTell—she called him Doogie throughout—was the stronger for feeling she had breadth of experience in common with him: that he too had stretched himself beyond the end of Sand Hills Road.

She also admired his sense of purpose—"He looked after his guitar *real* well."

I asked if she recalled him playing the harmonica.

"Well he played harp," she said, "I don't know nothin' 'bout no Monica!"

We got to talking of Kate McTell. Sally Cramer is one of the very few people left who remember the days when she was Willie's wife. Sally was taken up there when she was about fifteen years old, which would probably make this around 1938, when Willie and Kate were in their fifth year of marriage. They were living on Highland Avenue.

"I never will forget, because a streetcar used to run past the house, and I wasn't used to that kinda thing. The streetcar rolled by there, and the Stones Bakery was right in front. Parkway Drive and Jackson ran into Highland right where I lived. They met right there. The house had a basement—that was an apartment down there, and then we lived on the first floor and somebody else lived upstairs.

"You'd walk up them steps to go in the house, and you turn one way to our door and turn the other way to another person's. That's the way of the whole street. We didn't have no hallways. The front room was the bedroom, and then the next room was, I guess, the dining room, and then next the kitchen and on the end of the porch was the bathroom. I remember that because Doogie came home one night and caught his wife with another feller." She laughed.

Sally had liked Kate at first, but soon started agreeing with her girlfriend, Rosalee, that Kate wasn't all that nice to Willie and was running around behind his back. (Rosalee was older, and married to Sally's Uncle Bus, Gold Harris' younger brother, who had been, and at this point may still have been, a truck driver with the Southern Cattle Co. They had a baby now and lived in a rooming house on Tanner Street, a good few blocks south.)

"I liked Kate at first, because she was nice to me, and I didn't think they was up, but Rosalee, she said it was wrong for her to be doin' Doogie like that. 'Cause she would take all of his money—he was getting a check, you see—and she was giving it all to this young man TC. And, well, she did talk to Willie right bad. She talked to him off, and everything: Kate didn't act like she cared nothin' about him. So we just didn't like it. He was getting a check and he would give her what he made playin' at all these places, and she would take everything—and that's what made us so angry, 'cause if he asked her for *anything* it would make her mad. And she rarely would give it to him.

"This TC was the only one I knew about, 'cause he was over there every night and Doogie was gone to play at the Pig'n Whistle. Doogie could walk over there from Highland to Ponce de Leon. I guess it must have been around ten o'clock, I don't know, when he would leave."

Eventually, Rosalee and Sally decided Doog should know what was going on.

"We put a chair right by the window, right between the two houses. And he sat out there by that window and he heard everything when he came in. And we left the back door open, and he came through the room where we were sleeping and right in there, and tore that front room *up*. He beat that boy and blood was comin' from everywhere.

"I've never seen a blind man beat up a young man like that in all my life. And then he tore up the mantle in the bedroom there. See they had a fireplace in there. He broke the lamps. I mean, he was beatin' up that boy, he was just running around in there. I think he was scared to fight him because of us, and he was just running and skidding everywhere. It was just like Doog could see what he was doing. He hit that boy the side of his head and beat him up. He actually whupped the man: a young man. He was swingin' his stick.

"I ran in the kitchen and got the butcher knife—I was young, but I had sense. I had to let him know that if he bothered my cousin we were gonna fight him. And he ran out and he was standing there in the yard—I mean, he was out there bleeding every which way and he didn't have on no clothes! It was cold, too. And when he was standing out there he told me he had to have his clothes, and I said, 'If he *says* you can come back in and get 'em you can come back.' He said he would come in and get 'em, but I had that knife.

"So, when Doogie left he was going to work singing and playing the guitar—he left singing just as loud as he could. 'Singin' the blues!' After he left, Kate was in there washin' the blood and stuff offa him. So that's when I left, and I ran all the way down Jackson to Tanner Street, to tell my Uncle Bus what happened. And my cousin Johnny McNair answered the door and he wanted to know what I was doin' running around over there at that time of night, because I was too young to be runnin' around out there by myself—but I didn't want to tell him, 'cause he had a hot temper, so I told him I was just lonesome and wanted to see Uncle Bus.

"So I just went on upstairs—and Johnny eavesdropped me and heard me tellin' Uncle Bus what was goin' on over there, and when Uncle Bus and I came downstairs to go back over there, he had *gone* already. And when we got back, John had beat us over there, hiding outside. Kate was inside, and John made me knock on the door. I didn't want to get in the front door, but he made me, and I was scared of him because he had such a temper. I knocked and she asked who it was and I told her it was me, and she went to open it and he just *knocked* it open. She went to run for the telephone and he snatched all the wires out of the wall. She ran upstairs to the neighbor's to call the policeman, and we all left.

"Rosalee and me, we stopped at the Silver Slipper. It was a small little place. We went on in there to use the telephone. Kate had called the law and, when we went to come out, she was in the car with the law, and she said *I* was the one: because, you know, I had the butcher's knife. And they had spotlights at that time, and we ran, and while they was gettin' John, me and Rosalee went around the corner to get out the way. So, when they started shinin' that light round that way, we just went up on somebody's porch like we was knockin' on doors."

They got away, slipped back down to Tanner Street very late that night and stayed in John's room.

"They had carried him over to the jail and they had him locked up. And I hated that I had went over there, but I didn't know what else to do. I'm from way down here in the country and I'm scared! But he did something down here in McDuffie. He and my other cousin, Toby Moss, well they had stole some man's car down here"—Sally laughed and said, "This is getting good!"—and then resumed the story:

"Well, Kate had a letter belonged to him. Somebody had wrote him up there and she had got a hold of that letter and knowed he was in trouble down here and he was runnin' from 'em. You used to be able to do stuff down here and then run over to another and the law couldn't come for you and get you—so Kate had been holdin' that letter and she gave it to the cops, and that's how they found out that they had been wantin' him down in Thomson. Do you know, he had to come back here and do that time? He sure did."

The butcher's knife was long, Sally said, because Kate sold sandwiches and stuff too. "She was smart. They did a lot of things. Willie played for whites over there at that place on Ponce de Leon. That was a wealth-end place. And our neighborhood on Highland was nice. Kate liked that, you know. And she had two houses over on Jackson. You know: rooming houses. She was smart. She had girls working for her."

I said, "She did? And you saw all this when you were fifteen or sixteen?"

"Oh yes!"

"And she owned these rooming houses?"

"Yes she did, at that time. 'Cause she would charge 'em whatever, 'cause they were her houses. What you call 'call girls'!

"Afterwards I didn't stay with her no more. That was the end of me with her."

And was that when they split up?

"No, they was still together, but I came back home. And I didn't get the chance to see him again. When I came home from New York, he was dead and buried. And he never came to New York to see me."

She closed her eyes, remembering those Atlanta days.

"He would play guitar at home too," she said. "I just remember how he would hold his head, but, d'you know—I can't remember a single one of his songs. And I thought I *never* would forget the one he sang that night when he left that house singing."

"Kate told me something," said Dot Jones, at the end of the conversation. "Kate told me: 'Willie was better to me than I was to him.'"

"Ain't that the truth," said Sally.

# FOURTEEN

'MA RAINEYS BLACK BOTTOM' is the name of a recording this tremendous Georgia blues singer cut in about December 1927 in Chicago, but *Ma Rainey's Black Bottom* is also a 1984 play by August Wilson about the humiliations of a typical early blues recording session. In the play the artist suffers under a white producer, but Rainey had a black producer, Jay Mayo Williams, a handsome man with an early receding hairline, small ears, and a slender moustache. He was no saint towards his artists and their royalties either, but no worse than most. A black record producer was a rarity back then, and it may say something about attitudes that his nickname in the business was "Ink." On the other hand, this may have been because he signed such a large number of blues stars to recording contracts in the 1920s and 1930s.

Born in Monmouth, Illinois, in 1894, he became a star athlete and entered Brown University, Providence, Rhode Island, in 1916. The third college to be founded in New England and the seventh in the United States, this Ivy League university was, despite the name, very predominantly white. He played in its football team during the 1916 and 1917 seasons, served in the Army during 1918, returned to Brown for the 1919 and 1920 football seasons, and that year was one of only three black players in the National Football League's first season (Paul Robeson was another). Williams had also shown a flair for business: he was a "junior partner" in a college clothes pressing service operated from another black player's dorm room. He received his degree in 1921.

After Brown, he played professional football in Hammond, Indiana, but by the time he was thirty he was installed in a Chicago office in charge of the recently formed Paramount record label's "race" series. After signing Ma Rainey and Ida Cox, Blind Lemon Jefferson and Blind Blake, he created a music publishing company for the label, paying flat fees rather than royalties to its artists.

He left Paramount in 1927 to form his own label, Black Patti, named after the black nineteenth-century classical singer Sissieretta Jones, who had herself been nicknamed "the Black Patti" to compare her to the white opera star Adelina Patti. The label collapsed in less than a year, but Mayo Williams bounced back, working with Brunswick and Vocalion, achieving two of the biggest hits of the late 1920s. He quit music in 1932 to become a football coach at Atlanta's black Morehouse College before returning to the record biz in 1934 to work on the new American Decca label as a producer and talent scout.

Perhaps he saw Willie McTell performing in Atlanta during his Morehouse College days—Kate says he saw her and Willie performing together at the 81 Theatre—but, at any rate, soon after Williams landed his job at Decca he came back to Atlanta, signed up Willie and various others, and took them all by car to Chicago for a week of intermittent sessions there in the spring of 1935. The forty-year old Mayo Williams was at the wheel of his large black car as they left Atlanta around five o'clock on Saturday evening, 20 April, for the 710-mile drive to Chicago. The occupants of the front passenger seats were Curley Weaver and perhaps the beautiful Georgia White, a thirty-year-old singer-pianist from Sandersville, mid-Georgia, while Kate and Willie McTell and the guitars sat in the back. Willie wouldn't let the guitars go in the trunk with the luggage.

Mayo Williams drove all night, with one stop on the highway when he was starting to nod off, and they arrived around ten o'clock on the Sunday night. They staggered into their hotel on Lake Michigan Avenue and had the Monday to rest before Willie, Kate, and Curley recorded on the Tuesday, 23 April. The Wednesday and Friday were also free, with a second McTell session on the Thursday.

Altogether they were in Chicago one week before Mayo Williams drove them home again. It was a glamorous, exciting time in a city that had so recently seen Al Capone's heyday. The St Valentine's Day Massacre had happened only six years previously. From 1925 until five years before the McTells' visit, Capone had controlled the majority of the vice industry there and his income was said to have been $100 million a year. He had gone to prison only three and a half years earlier (and been transferred to the Atlanta Penitentiary in May 1932).

According to Kate, every night at their hotel, very likely the Metropole at 2300 South Michigan Avenue, "they'd have a big ball downstairs, different musicians playing there. Free . . . There were plenty of white there. And we danced together. It was mixed there, in Chicago."

Willie and white musicians mixed here too: "The white musician would say 'Play it for me: I want to see if I can play it,' and Willie would play it for him and he'd catch it and learn it, and Willie would say 'OK, give me that hillbilly,' and he'd get on the hillybilly and give it right back."

Kate also says that, while they were in Chicago, they went to a basement club run by Jack Johnson, the great black ex-heavyweight boxing champion: "We was just up the street from him . . ." She says she and Willie went there and met him, and sang at the club.

This must have been a most interesting encounter. Both these black Americans were widely traveled men whose lives and careers had involved much negotiation with white America in times of the most brutal racism. The similarities ended there.

McTell was in his early thirties, had achieved little worldly success or fame, and though he may have listened to radio news broadcasts, he had always kept entirely quiet about politics and steered himself through the tribulations of the system with his head adroitly down. Jack Johnson was fifty-seven years old, with a career of historic achievement in his field and a lifestyle of flamboyant extravagance, both rather a long way behind him; he was a man whose success had provoked years of savage racial attacks and persecution, and who, far from keeping his head down, had jumped it up and down above the parapet over and over again. And the music he liked was not Willie's kind, but light opera.

By 1935 Johnson was hanging on with little money and few friends left, but the city's black newspaper, the *Chicago Defender*, was one, and would always give him a plug in its pages. The day Mayo Williams, Willie McTell, and the others set out for Chicago, the *Defender* ran this small item on page eight:

Jack Johnson, former heavyweight champion of the world, will entertain members of the press and tavern owners with a 6 o'clock cocktail party Friday April 26 at his club, 3831 Michigan Avenue. At the same time the former champion will introduce his own whiskey labeled "Old Champ" for the approval of his friends.

Willie McTell would have enjoyed that "cocktail party," and could have gone, too, since he was still in Chicago that Friday evening. But which day he and Kate dropped in on Johnson we don't know.

Nor can we be absolutely certain of the name of this club, but, five months previously, the *Defender* had given the same address for the Standard Motor Club—and Jack Johnson was certainly fond of motors. Added to which, Johnson's most recent biographer, Geoffrey C. Ward, thinks it unlikely that the "Old Champ" actually owned his own club, and that he was probably just on pin money as a meeter and greeter—so it does seem odds on that this was the club Willie and Kate McTell stepped into one April night in 1935.

The building itself is, for other reasons, a Designated Chicago Landmark: a house built for a grain merchant in the 1890s by architect Gustav Hallberg, and converted into an art center in 1940 as part of the Works Progress Administration's Federal Art Project (and now the only continuous survivor of more than 100 such centers established all across the States in the 1930s and '40s as part of the New Deal's good works).

Jack Johnson, the Muhammad Ali of his day, died as he might have wished to, crashing his car and overturning it on US 1, just south of Franklinton City, near Raleigh, North Carolina, on 10 June 1946. He was sixty-eight. He is buried at North Clark Street's Graceland Cemetery (a name with other, Memphis connotations). The headstone with the word "Johnson" really refers to his second white wife, Etta Terry Johnson—but that's where he is.

I didn't visit the site of Jack Johnson's club in Chicago, though it was by visiting the Chicago Historical Society's premises that I first found the *Defender* item about it: the only snippet that seems to exist to confirm a basis for Kate McTell's claims.

It was in their archive, too, that I found there had been no mention of

Willie McTell's visit to Chicago in the pages of the *Defender*. Its tone and range of interests was an odd mix, but Willie was operating on a level just below what might have fitted in. That month there were ads for a new record by Kokomo Arnold (a left-handed bottleneck guitarist from Georgia by now based in Chicago—and whose huge smash hit 'Milk Cow Blues' had been recorded for Decca and produced by Mayo Williams just six months previously) and the editorials were strongly pro "Negro rights," but the society pages were just as silly as the white ones in small-town Georgia, full of froth about the Jolly Wives Bridge Club, a Musical Tea, the Dancing Ladies Club, and so on.

The news pages veered between the arming of Ethiopia against Mussolini, "Plan Probe On Dope Evil In Schools," and a report of race progress in the film industry, which explained that Hollywood colors were to be natural from now on, so that octaroons would no longer be banned as too pale.

I tried to work in the main public library too, but they only let you use a computer for half an hour at a stretch, which is too short to get anything much done, and you can't get back on till you've waited another half hour. The result is rows of frustrated people being pulled from the machines and constantly replaced by others.

Extraordinary building, the library. The basic brick square of it takes up an entire block in each direction, and lowered onto the top of it is a ferocious French rococo roof in livid verdigris, looping and swooping off the edges on all sides in a monstrous outdoing of Paris, and sticking out so far from the tops of the walls that they have to have sandwich-board signs all along the sidewalks warning you to Beware Falling Ice.

But the architecture of the city is its glory. To come up out of Union Station onto the street and take a taxi to the Magnificent Mile (Michigan Avenue, up around Ohio) is to take an exhilarating cut across the river through a vast and majestic panorama of buildings symphonic in its chance cohesion, great edifices of every era soaring upwards together, the old set off by the modern, the brick by the stone, the squat by the slender, glass by concrete—a cathedral for giants, the sky its roof, assembled by innumerable craftsmen and death-defying workers over a hundred years and more.

My cab driver looked like the comedian Lenny Henry and sounded West Indian, but he was from West Africa and an enthusiast for Chicago. The 600 homicides a year, he says, all happen in the parts of the city you'd have no reason to go. He urged me to believe that people walk the streets, strolling safely, even in the early hours of the morning.

Not in January. I'd come in by overnight train to breathe in the atmosphere of the city and walk along Willie's patch of Lakeshore Drive to the building where he'd spent two days in the Decca recording studio almost seventy years earlier. As the train had waited for the signal to go ahead and roll the last 300 yards into the station, tiny snowflakes had drifted slowly down between the coach and the shining lights, and ice sat inside the tracks. On the river, sheets of dirty ice had been shouldering each other about like disgruntled manta rays.

At midday people hurried along in big coats or pneumatic jackets wearing weird black earmuffs that look like huge headphones. I stepped out of my hotel and turned left onto Ohio to walk the four or five blocks down to Lake Shore Drive. The sun shone and the extraordinary cold swirled around inside the legs of my trousers. This was a novel sensation. It was far colder here than December in Newfoundland. The lake was partly frozen.

I found the old Decca building at 666 Lakeshore. Brunswick had built a state-of-the-art studio here on the sixth or eighth floor in 1928, and all Decca's masters from 1930s Chicago were made here. The building is condominiums now, and exceedingly expensive. The lobby is vast, and all polished marble, with a stone galleried landing all around, carved with elaborate gothic tracery. Ruskin could have occupied himself sketching it. When you raise your eyes above the ground level of desk clerks and parcel store and lawyers' offices, the whole great place swaggers with the classy hush of some richly endowed and indulgent seminary dreamed into being by a refined and corrupted church. Willie McTell, of course, could have seen none of this, but he would have absorbed the feel of the place, and I could picture him standing there.

It was to be his last time in any real studio for a major record label: and the five Blind Willie McTell 78s Decca issued afterwards would be his last new records to see release for close on fifteen years.

★    ★    ★

253

Back in Georgia, Willie resumed his usual rounds, dividing his time partly between Atlanta, Statesboro, and Happy Valley but traveling more widely too, sometimes with Curley Weaver and sometimes, as we know, with other blind musicians. On 26 January 1936, up in McDuffie, Uncle Coot's son Bo-Rat—Eddie McTier—married Hazel Samuel. Eddie was an illiterate farm laborer of twenty-six; Hazel had turned sixteen two days before they obtained their license, though she'd said she was eighteen when applying for it. She was the daughter of Mary Lou Samuel[s], who was black, and Cleveland Story, who was white and lived in his white household next door. Mary Lou was the mother of his children. Hazel's younger sister, now Annie Jackson, told me: "Momma and Daddy had eleven, I think. Yes, six girls and five boys. I got obituaries somewhere . . ."

By 1930 there were already five girls and four boys. Mary Lou Samuel was thirty-seven, single, head of the household, and bringing up these nine children. Right next door was the forty-five-year-old Cleveland Story and his white fifty-year-old wife, Belle, and no children at all (though they did have two septuagenarian lodgers).

Whether the maiden name Hazel took from her mother's family was Samuels or Samuel is very unclear—it's Samuel on the 1930 census, and on her 1936 marriage application and license. It's of interest because the singular form is also Willie McTell's middle name, which may have been chosen to indicate a connection somewhere a generation or two back. The names McTier, Moss, Story, and Samuel(s) appear in profusion on the Happy Valley census pages, and the cemetery of Mount Aldred church, about 150 yards into Warren County, is full of these Mosses and Samuels. (It's an odd coincidence, but nothing more, that Eddie and Hazel both had fathers with the first name of Cleveland.)

It would be Bo-Rat and Hazel who, twenty-odd years down the line, would give Willie McTell his last home. In early 1936, while they were newlyweds, Willie was writing a song called 'Married Life's A Pain'. He might even have written it the previous year, since it was recorded by no less a figure than Big Bill Broonzy in April 1936 and it's a strong possibility that he was offered it while Willie was in Chicago, or that Mayo Williams heard it then and gave it to Broonzy soon afterwards. It's a pleasant record with a sparkling piano part by the still-unidentified Black Bob, and a lyric that includes the verse "I laid down lucky, I woke up, I had to take the blame / Yes I'm broke, down and out, Man ain't married life a pain."

Not only was Willie McTell credited as the song's composer on Big Bill's record, but he went on to try to record it himself that same year. In late June 1936 he was called to Augusta to record for Art Satherley's junior colleague, W.R. Calaway, for Vocalion, the label of the New York sessions of three years earlier.

William Ronald Calaway, originally from Orlando in Florida, was one of those producers who tried to steal his artists' work, and sometimes succeeded: he did so with Gene Autry's 'Dallas County Jail Blues', failed with Roy Acuff's 'Great Speckled Bird', and claimed, ludicrously, to have written everything from 'My Rocky Mountain Sweetheart' to 'Jesus Gonna Make up My Dying Bed'. But he had also been responsible, in 1934, for springing the great Charley Patton from jail in Belzoni, Mississippi, and taking him by train to New York for what would prove his final two days of sessions, so that, like most of the music industry's wheelers and dealers, Calaway did some good as well as bad.

There was no proper studio in Augusta, and Willie's sessions were held at radio station WRDW (later owned by James Brown, who came from Augusta: Kate claimed she "knew him when he was a shoe-shine boy"). Bruce Bastin claims that "Calaway and Art Satherley's wife owned a motel" in Augusta, and that this might have been why this location was chosen for the sessions, but he notes that Willie and Kate McTell stayed instead with her aunt, as they had immediately after their marriage, and that Vocalion paid her for providing Willie's accommodation. This time, Kate McTell's singing was not required, but Calaway put Willie together with Piano Red for the recordings.

This did not work out well. Red said later that it had been Willie who'd brought him in on the sessions, but the intention had never been that they play together. Willie, as usual, was simply encouraging a fellow musician to seek out session opportunities for himself. They had not rehearsed together and, when Calaway insisted on recording them as a duo, Willie was not pleased.

Bastin writes that perhaps Calaway hoped to produce a piano-guitar duo to replace the hit team of Leroy Carr and Scrapper Blackwell (Carr had died a year earlier), and adds: "For the only time in McTell's recording career he was teamed with a pianist, and a none too subtle one at that. However enthusiastic one might be about Red's playing, it would be difficult to select a rougher pianist to team with McTell."

Twelve sides were recorded: six listed as by Piano Red alone, two by Piano Red and Partner, and just four—and these included 'Married Life's A Pain'—as by "Blind Willie and Piano Red." No wonder Willie was unhappy. None of the twelve sides was ever released and none survives. Red said later that the masters had melted in the summer heat.

Within weeks, Calaway went back down to Mississippi, met up with ARC's talent-spotter supreme, H.C. Speir, in Hattiesburg, and recorded a large number of people Speir had found. Calaway, apparently, never paid Speir, but the company ended up with some successful artists and with the unknown young Robert Johnson—who would not be successful in his own short lifetime, but has long since become the white world's *most* revered blues artist. Meanwhile, Willie went back to his habitual activities and to the base he and Kate shared in Atlanta.

It was there, and at about this time, that the much-vaunted Aunt Mattie died (I have searched for her paper trail entirely in vain). Kate has given no real account of her death, but perhaps what she says about Willie's reaction when death was imminent throws light on an unexplored part of his character.

Kate reports: "He said, 'I don't want—you all know I can't cry, and I don't want to go around . . . You and [Aunt] Lillie going to be up there whooping and hollering, "Oh, Amen, Amen".' And he say, 'I don't want to hear it myself.' And at that time a telegram man came, and he said, 'I have a telegram for Willie McTell, or Mrs Willie McTell.' And I said, 'Well, where is it from?' And he said, 'The hospital.' And I went to screaming then.

"[Willie] said, 'What I told you? I'm going out of here. I'm leaving right now. I can't stand it.' He left out. And it was her. She had passed."

This is one of the few times Kate lets slip anything that might detract from her idealised story of their relationship, but there's a hint of criticism here—for in her next breath she says this: "He never took anything too seriously. Now he got a cousin that got killed in Atlanta. Aunt Lillie's son—got stabbed on the corner. And he loved him very much. His name was Tom Kelly. And he took that pretty seriously."

You can quite see that Willie might find wailing melodrama hard to take, but you can quite see too that great impatience with anyone's unhappiness might be all of a piece with Willie's policy of unremitting cheeriness. Insistent sunny optimism has its limitations.

At any rate, it sounds as if Willie was generally happier out and about than at home with Kate, but in the second half of the 1930s, she often traveled with him. She said they even went back to New York together and met the singer Josh White there, and sang with him, at "Small Paradise"—a more pleasing name than the slightly different real one, Small's Paradise, a Harlem club on 7$^{th}$ Avenue near 135$^{th}$ Street, famous as a hang-out for whites who liked black music.

The writer Elijah Wald says that while it certainly made sense for Willie to have met up with White, because he was the only Piedmont region player living there and was in touch with Buddy Moss (they recorded several duets), it strikes him as surprising that they should have performed at Small's Paradise: "It is possible that someone would have taken them there and presented them for a song or two as a novelty," he told me, though he had heard no report of Josh White ever playing there, and, at least in the late 1920s, it was very upscale, with a "symphonic orchestra" and "full-dress onlookers."

More certainly, Willie and Kate played the 600-seater Morton Theatre in Athens, Georgia, even though it was, like the 81 Theatre in Atlanta, part of the TOBA circuit. Unlike the 81, it was black owned, founded by the remarkable Monroe Bowers Morton (and, since his mother was a half white ex-slave and his father white, he was known as Pink Morton). He was a property speculator, bought *The Progressive Era*, one of three local black newspapers, and at one time served as the Athens Postmaster. He built his theater in 1909–1910 as part of a larger building, its offices and black-owned stores originally rented out to subsidise his showbiz.

Morton died in 1919 but his theater became a key stop on the circuit for stars like Bessie Smith and even Duke Ellington when they were touring, and a significant black vaudeville venue, where you could catch such exciting novelty acts as Wilton Crawley The Human Worm (from Chicago) and the sixty-strong Mastodon Colored Minstrels. But the Morton also held live shows that were more like local talent nights with one big-name top of the bill, such as Butterbeans and Susie, sometimes simply called Midnite Shows. Kate remembers some called Midnight Rambles, and it was at these that Willie sang and played guitar while Kate danced the Trigger Toes. The whole theater was dark wood, lit by gas lamps, with narrow passageways and stairs that Kate says Willie found hard to negotiate, while the dressing rooms were merely a curtained-off backstage area with no washrooms.

Kate claimed that their bookings were sometimes for as long as six weeks, and that "sometimes we would play for four hours, and then we would have some recreation, and then we would come in and play for four more hours," though she may have meant that this was the pattern of the overall show, which included a house band.

It's doubtful whether Willie's name ever made it onto a printed program. When the theater began to be renovated in the late 1970s, no bill with McTell's name on it was found—but Dot Jones, the retired Thomson-McDuffie press officer, said that the annual Willie McTell Blues Festival was created there after an Augusta newspaper writer, Don Rhodes, saw McTell's name on such a program and encouraged them to do something to celebrate Willie and the fact that Thomson had been his birthplace.

Kate herself claimed that she'd kept one of their contracts from the Morton, but that the Evanses had taken it away. The theater's archives include many contracts and much correspondence about contracts, but none includes McTell's name. Similarly, she says that she and Willie would perform at the black-owned Douglass Theatre in Macon and at the Delmont in Augusta.

In Athens they stayed, perhaps, with Sister Fleeta Mitchell. Willie used to visit her there, anyway, in the years between her moving in to 820 Reece Street at the end of 1936 and the birth of her child there in 1944. Fleeta doesn't mention Kate, but recalls Willie's visits. He was, she said, "such a friendly ole man, just as friendly as can be: keep you smilin' all the time. Every time I seen him he's full of joy."

Willie and Kate also spent a couple of summers, probably 1937 and '38, touring with a medicine show, up through Florida but mostly in Georgia, though they stayed with it as far as Kentucky, where they could stay with Willie's aunt, Annie McNair. The show was owned by a white couple from Tennessee who sold rattlesnake liniment, and it played mostly around courthouse squares, though sometimes in a tent, with comedians, novelty acts, and so on. Kate McTell "Charlestoned and Black Bottomed" and tap danced, and Willie produced his usual musical magic: the finest 12-string guitarist of his generation, bar none, playing hokum songs for small-town rural audiences.

Kate told Bernard West that their travels within Georgia took them to all their home stomping grounds: "Burke County, Jefferson County, Richmond County, Warren County, Glascock County, McDuffie County—all the way back up."

They even played in little Keysville, which is not far from Kate's hometown of Wrens, for a man named John Garrett, who ran a funeral home down in Louisville, the Jefferson County seat. "Me and Willie used to play there when he give those big dances down there . . . And this medicine show would come there and put up."

To drive to Wrens and Keysville today is to travel back in time almost to these medicine show moments. I pull into the gas station at Wrens and ask where downtown is. "You're in it," the middle-aged redneck woman answers, as I knew she would. Everyone likes their little joke, and in small towns that is their joke—a defensive disparagement. They like to get it in quick, before the outsider can.

The countryside out east from Wrens towards Keysville is especially bucolic, full of picturesque decay and soaked in old-fashioned atmosphere. There's a big old cotton gin with all its rust-red trucks still there in a row like giant kiddie-toys. On the map, Keysville looked no more of a place than, say, Brickstore, which isn't really there at all anymore, but, after Boggs Academy Road (where Willie's brother-in-law, Rev, went to school), you arrive at tiny Keysville: a crossroads with a functioning gas station and shop, and a wide grass area just beyond, on both sides of the road—the perfect place for a medicine show or a circus to set up.

In the gas station shop I was lucky enough to bump into Mr Samuel Powers, a sixty-year-old cool black dude with one gold tooth, a black beard, and denim cap. He was very tickled to find that I was enquiring about John Garrett. "How d'you hear 'bout *him*?"

He remembered him from when he was a small child, six or seven years old, going around with his grandma. "He was a big fat man," he told me. "He seemed old to me then. Probably be about a hundred if he was still around." He said he was well-to-do for a black man in the country in those days. He took me out to show me the spot on the red dirt road where he reckoned Garrett's funeral home had stood. It was about a mile off from the crossroads. There's nothing there but woodland now: open, pleasant woodland in which the pines are scattered between deciduous trees. It's private property and, on the opposite side of the road, it was for sale.

Samuel Powers told me that Garrett had sold up and moved to Louisville to open his funeral home there instead—going up in the world—and that he still has grandchildren there, he thought, and that they used to run some kind of restaurant.

I'd followed him in his old Cadillac to the spot where Garrett's place had been, and we stood in the road chatting. He's lived here all his life and used to walk along here with his grandma. That's when I asked his age, to get a better idea of when he remembered Garrett from. I said, "If you're sixty, how come your beard's still black? Look at mine, it's gray!"

"Yeah," he grinned, chewing on the cigar he'd bought at the gas station, "but you can git stuff to fix that!" He turned his car around in the sand and drove off. We gave each other a wave.

I went down to Louisville too and there met local historian Leroy Lewis. He told me that the whole story of the town being a center for slave sales was completely untrue: slaves were sold here, as everywhere, after being brought in from the coast, but these were pre-arranged sales—there was never a big market for them, and they never stood under the town's much-photographed market hut being auctioned in the way people think. He said this story was invented in the 1920s by local businessmen who were campaigning (successfully) for Highway 1, "from

Maine to Miami," to run through Louisville. They also moved the "historic" marketplace building: it used to be off at one side of the road, not placed grandly in its center.

Willie continued to travel with Curley Weaver, from time to time, and we know that the two of them spent at least a week busking in Nashville, Tennessee, in the summer of 1939. Someone named Bill Love (and there have been many of that name with Nashville connections) wrote in to the weekly paper *Jazz Information* early in 1940 to say that he'd "run across" Willie and Curley "beating the streets. They were so good, both solo and duet, that for a week last summer I got them to play for me every night." Mr Love also chatted to Willie, asking him about other blues musicians. This was at a time when the information available to enthusiasts was scanty, but Willie was knowledgeable, of course, and told him that Bessie Jackson was a pseudonym for Lucille Bogan, and that the pianist on her sides as Bessie Jackson was Walter Roland. This was right on both counts.

On another occasion, Kate McTell said that Willie had returned from Nashville with a photo of him and the Grand Ole Opry comic star Minnie Pearl standing together; she also claimed that Willie had once recorded in Nashville. Despite much searching, no such photo and no such recordings have come to light.

Back in Georgia, as the 1930s were ending, Willie and Curley knocked around with the usual crowd of musicians. With one exception: Buddy Moss. After coming back to Atlanta from making records in New York in August 1935 (with Josh White as his accompanist), Buddy Moss killed his wife in a fight, spent time in Atlanta awaiting trial, and was then convicted of murder and given a long sentence. He duly served time in the newly built prison on West Gibson Street in Warrenton, and then about thirty miles further north-west at the Greene County Prison Farm outside Greensboro.

Here, in May 1941, still aged only twenty-seven, he was photographed by Jack Delano, a Ukrainian immigrant born the same year as Moss, for the Farm Security Administration (part of the New Deal program). He's pictured playing guitar alongside three other prisoners, one of whom is dancing and snapping his fingers. Two are wearing classic striped convict uniforms; Moss is in civilian clothes, looking cool and wearing a Willie McTell-style hat. (One of these photos appeared on the cover of a blues compilation LP in 1969, but it had been chosen for its general subject matter: Moss was not identified.)

After extended efforts by Art Satherley and J.B. Long, manager of the recently deceased Blind Boy Fuller, to get him freed, Moss was paroled later in 1941 and did odd jobs for Long in Elon College (the town), North Carolina, where he met up with Sonny Terry and Brownie McGhee and, that October, went back to New York with them to record.

In Atlanta, Curley Weaver often played as part of an informal trio with a reputedly fine guitarist called Jonas Brown and the minor legendary mystery figure Bo Weevil, with whom McTell was also friendly, and who seems to have arrived in Atlanta in the 1920s from Macon. Bruce Bastin says that Bo Weevil "lived in a shack made of old boxes on Houston and Butler . . . He was murdered in 1957 by a local whore."

You have only to read Rebecca Wells' 1996 novel set in the 1930s, *Divine Secrets of the Ya-Ya Sisterhood*, to breathe the air of another Atlanta of Willie McTell's era: one from which he and his musician friends were as wholly excluded as if they inhabited another planet. This Atlanta came out in force for the film premiere of *Gone With The Wind* on 15 December 1939, with Vivien Leigh, Clark Gable, Olivia de Havilland, and the other stars of the movie arriving by train to be there at Loew's Grand Theater, its front decked out to look like Tara.

The novel the film was based on, by local heroine Margaret Mitchell, would go on to become, it's claimed, "the world's top selling book, next to the Bible," and Mitchell's Atlanta home, at the corner of West Peachtree Street and 10$^{th}$ Street, is open to the public. She became a full-time Red Cross volunteer and gave medical school scholarships to fifty black students before meeting her early death.

The one star who wasn't at the film premiere was Hattie McDaniel, who played the Mammy. Clark Gable threatened to boycott the event if she wasn't invited, but, in fact, she declined to attend because of the climate of race relations in Atlanta at the time. She became the first black American to win an Academy Award—she won "Best Actress in a

Supporting Role" for *Gone With The Wind*—and, in February 1940, was therefore the first black person to attend the Academy Awards ceremony as a guest rather than as a waitress.

She was to die of breast cancer in 1952, aged fifty-seven; in 2006 the US Post Office issued a 39-cent Hattie McDaniel Commemorative Stamp. Her name has long been prominent in politico-academic analysis of race, film, and the Mammy figure—including by Cheryl Thurber, in her long essay 'The Development of the Mammy Image and Mythology'—but McDaniel merely said, with nice brevity: "I'd rather play a servant than be one."

The night before the film premiere, there had been a *Gone With The Wind* Costume Ball at City Auditorium after a parade along Peachtree. I like to picture Willie standing on Peachtree as this parade passed him by, giving his super-tuned ears an overload of extravagant oohs and aahs and braying.

# FIFTEEN

ON THE EARLY evening of Monday, 4 November 1940, Willie was standing with his guitar outside the Pig'n Whistle on Ponce de Leon, encouraging fun-seeking customers to drive into the parking lot as usual, when a car pulled in and he heard himself addressed by an elderly, strong voice with an unmistakeably white Texan accent. No, the man said, he did not wish to patronise the Pig'n Whistle. He wished to know the musician's name.

Thus did Blind Willie McTell, now thirty-eight, meet the redoubtable septuagenarian John Avery Lomax and his second wife, Ruby Rochelle Terrill Lomax, fifty-four. It was Ruby who had spotted McTell on the street.

"Look," she'd said, "there is a Negro man with a guitar," and they had swung their car back into the Pig'n Whistle yard. They were surprised and pleased to hear that this was McTell, since someone had mentioned his name to the Lomaxes only two hours earlier. They impressed upon him that they represented the Library of Congress in Washington, DC—

the government of the United States of America, no less—and they had a proposition to put to him: that they might record him at their hotel the following day. But Willie surprised them by volunteering.

"Business isn't so good. I'll go along with you to your hotel right now."

So they guided him to their car, and then told him they didn't know the way to their hotel.

"I'll show you," said Willie, and he did, amazing them in the process. As John Lomax wrote afterwards: "Between us and the hotel there were six or seven right-angled turns and two places where five or six streets crossed. Chatting all the while with me, Blind Willy called every turn, even mentioning the location of the stop lights. He gave the names of buildings as we passed them. Stored in his mind was an accurate, detailed photograph of Atlanta."

When they arrived, Lomax proposed that, should Willie agree to return to play and sing for them in their room next morning, promptly at nine, he would be paid one dollar plus his taxi fare: in exchange he would have the privilege of being interviewed and recorded for the Library of Congress Archive of Folk Song—and hence for posterity.

"Blind Willie," said Lomax, giving the musician an early demonstration of how firmly he could expect to be patronised in the course of their encounter, "Uncle Billy Macrea in Jasper, Texas, says that the colored folks are a promising race. Don't fail me."

Willie "chuckled," Lomax said later, "in instant understanding." No doubt he did.

John Lomax was enjoying an extraordinary Indian summer. This was a man born only two years after the Civil War ended, at Goodman, Mississippi, whose parents had set out for Texas in two covered wagons when he was less than two years old, partly because his father didn't want his family to be "raised in contact with the Negro."

Lomax grew up on a branch of the Chisolm Trail and, thrilled by the cowboy songs he kept hearing, started writing them down while still an adolescent. He went into teaching, then to business college and, after that, already twenty-eight, he attended the University of Texas. He graduated in 1897, stayed on as an administrator, married in 1904, won a scholarship to Harvard, resumed collecting cowboy songs—he heard 'Home On The Range' from a black bartender in 1908—and published his first collection in 1910.

Seven years later, Lomax was forced out of the University of Texas by State Governor Jim Ferguson (who was, as Chris Smith wrote in an entertaining book review, "clearly several longhorns short of a cattle drive"). Lomax, at fifty, went to Chicago and became a bond salesman and banker. He was long since back in Texas and the father of six children when their mother, Bess, died in 1931. Three years later, now aged sixty-six, he married the forty-eight-year-old Ruby Rochelle Terrill, a woman smart in every sense, with record-breaking student scores, degrees, and years of Latin teaching behind her.

The Archive of Folk Song had been founded in 1928, and, after resigning his job as a banker at the height of the Depression, John A. Lomax regained his energy for folksong, and, with his son Alan, then a youth of eighteen, began a series of excursions and recordings on the Archive's behalf in June 1933, at first carrying old-fashioned cylinder recording equipment through Texas until a more modern disc recording machine was delivered to them in Baton Rouge, Louisiana, that July. For the next two years, the father and son team made arduous field trips through nine southern states, using Lead Belly as their driver for much of this time, before starting separate, and essentially rival, folklore careers.

In March 1939, Ruby accompanied John Lomax for the first time on one of his field trips. A year later, he put in a request to the Library of Congress "to finance another recording trip for himself and his wife . . . through the South," as the Assistant in Charge put it. That assistant, two years into the job and on a salary of $1,620 a year, was son Alan, who added: "In addition, Mr Lomax wishes to come to Washington and work for fifty days annotating the hundreds of records he has made for the Archive."

Despite the difficulties of their relationship, Alan was pushing hard for all this to be appreciated and financed, and he drew up a detailed breakdown of the monies his father and stepmother would require for their 5,000 mile trip: $5 per day expenses for six weeks on the road; 5 cents a mile for gas; 200 12-inch acetate discs at 75 cents each and six sapphire needles at $3; plus the 50 days' work in the Library at $5 per day each; and $50 miscellaneous expenses—all told, $1,178.

With a little argy-bargy they got it, and set off—and however much emphasis you want to place on Lomax's overt and unthinking racism, or on his brusque and quarrelsome temperament, you might concede that he collected a great deal of invaluable material that would otherwise have been lost to us all, and worked himself extraordinarily hard to get it. (By 1945, when *Time* magazine noticed them for the first time, it reported that between them, John and Alan Lomax had "recorded 10,000 songs, many of which had never been heard more than five miles from the prisons, corrals or lumber camps where the Lomaxes found them.")

He was coming up to seventy-three years old when he and Ruby left home in San Antonio and began their 5,000-mile expedition on Sunday, 8 September 1940. Their energy was extraordinary, and, on that first day, after loading the equipment into the car, they drove a hundred miles to Glenrose, Texas, "recorded until near sundown," and, in the evening, listened to someone else performing *and* wrote down the lyrics and made detailed notes. By the beginning of November they'd worked their way through Texas, Louisiana, Mississippi, and Alabama.

The day they met up with Willie McTell they had started out from Livingston, Alabama, in the morning, recorded a group of men at the Cherokee County Camp near Canton that afternoon, loaded their heavy machinery up again, and then driven the best part of fifty miles south on poor roads to reach Atlanta, arriving there at 6.30pm. They'd have been excused if they'd given the "Negro man with a guitar" a miss that evening and driven on past.

Willie, of course, reported on time next morning. He entered the Robert Fulton Hotel on the corner of Luckie and Cone Streets, listened to the big clock tick above the heads of the reception desk staff while he waited, and was taken up, no doubt with many an eyebrow raised by guests and staff alike, to the Lomaxes' rooms. The hotel, named after a man wrongly claimed to have invented the steamboat, was a sixteen-year-old solid oblong in brick and stone, designed by Emil Charles Seiz (who had built the Rufus M. Rose House for a "medicinal whiskey" magnate in Atlanta at the start of the century, and died the year Lomax and McTell met). It was considered a highrise at fifteen storeys. Its 300 bedrooms were matched by 300 baths, with "Servidor Service, Circulating ice water and ceiling fans in each room," an air-conditioned coffee shop, and meetings rooms. It would be re-named the Georgia Hotel in 1951 and demolished twenty years later.

A photograph shows Willie inside the Lomaxes' quaint-looking room, the big microphone visible in front of the dresser and, seen in the mirror, the curtain blowing in at the open window. The shot was taken by Ruby while Willie performed and John Lomax sat listening, one watery eye on the disc recording equipment.

Willie "sang and played his 12-string guitar vigorously for two hours," though only a minority of the whole was recorded. The cumbersome machinery recorded performances directly onto acetate discs, which were in short supply by this point in the trip, and not to be "wasted", and each could hold only a few minutes' worth of material.

Despite these constraints, the Lomaxes drew a fine series of performances out of this articulate, knowledgeable man, winning from him a wider range of repertoire than the commercial record companies had wanted, and letting him talk. The songs included a variant of a black folklore hero ballad, a folksy railroad song, Willie's version of the pop hit 'Baby It Must Be Love', religious numbers of differing ages, including a version of 'Amazing Grace' that melds into his friend Blind Willie Johnson's wordless 'Dark Was The Night', the beguiling old ballad 'Delia', and a couple of blues numbers, one being what would turn out to be the first of three recorded versions by McTell of 'Dying Crapshooter's Blues'.

The questions and answers that top and tail some of the songs give us the first interview with McTell ever captured either in print or on record—and this from a man whose recording career with major labels now stretched back well over a decade. This, then, was the first time on any level that the public world was offered such basic information as that Willie had been born in Thomson, Georgia, had grown up in Statesboro, and had attended the Georgia Academy for the Blind in Macon. It was also the first indication that, unlike most musicians, Willie McTell had a most precise turn of mind, volunteering that Thomson was "134 miles

[east] of Atlanta, thirty-seven miles west of Augusta," rattling off the exact date of his 1927 début recording session, the correct order of the labels he went to, and the names and exact business addresses of several of their producers, and then specifying the years of his blind school attendance and the name of the principal at the time.

Curiously, for someone so profligate with facts and figures, he builds several untruths into his account, perhaps just so as not to feel too pinned down. He tells Lomax he's had a letter from Blind Willie Johnson's wife saying Johnson had died; he says that he gave up playing music for a "period of eight years" before attending blind school; and he tells Lomax he's forty-two years old—surely a deliberate error, especially from someone who six years earlier had claimed to be twenty-eight on his marriage certificate.

There are some tense moments too—especially when, far too early on in the proceedings to be unthreatening, Lomax asks: "I wonder, I wonder if, if you know any songs about colored people havin' hard times here in the South?"

"Well," says Willie circumspectly, hoping to head this off but floundering a bit in response—itself an indication that he feels ill at ease—"that—all songs that have a reference to our old people here, they hadn't very much stuff of the people nowadays, because they're—"

Lomax interrupts: "Any complainin' songs? Complainin' about the hard times and sometimes mistreatment of the whites? Have you got any songs that talk about that?"

It's often been claimed that Lomax is overbearing in tone here as well as alarming in his line of questioning—but actually he asks in a gently earnest tone to start with, and immediately after dictating a respectful summation of who McTell is onto the recording, which might have been expected to offer some reassurance. But this is all being recorded at a time and place where even Willie's presence in a white folks' hotel room is fraught with tensions and deep unease.

Willie says quickly, and outrageously, really: "No sir, we haven't. Not at the present time, because the white peoples is mighty good to the Southern people—" and here there's a telling pause, and then, "—as far as I know."

"Mm hmm. And you don't know any complainin' songs at all?!"

"Well . . ."

"'Ain't It Hard To Be A Nigger, Nigger'—do you know that one?"

You can feel the air in the room threatening to burst.

"Er— that's not in our time," says Willie, "and—well—now—as for spirituals down here, 'It's A Mean World To Live In'—but that still don't have a reference to the hard times." At this point Willie gives a feeble, apologetic laugh.

Lomax, not recognising this as a song title but taking it as a philosophical remark, or a politically evasive one, presses Willie further.

"Why is it a mean old world to live in?"

"Well," says Willie, jiggling about in discomfort, "it's not altogether. It has reference to everybody."

"It's—it's as mean for the whites as it is for the blacks, is that it?"

"That's the idea."

"You keep movin' around like you're uncomfortable," says Old Mr Tact. "What's the matter, Willie?"

To which Willie, without hesitation, gives an answer that sounds just as untrue as his claim that the whites had been mighty good to the coloreds.

"Well, I was in an automobile accident last night: little shook up. No one got hurt, but it was all jostled up mighty bad: shake up. Still sore from it, but no one got hurt."

He delivers his "no one got hurt"s as if reading the lesson in chapel. It brings a memorable dialog to a surreal conclusion.

Off the recording, McTell then agrees to play "Boll Weevil". Folklorists like Lomax had not yet arrived at the notion that they should collect what was there, rather than try to dictate it, and, therefore, father and son (and others too) constantly prompt people to sing songs they have a collector's bee in the bonnet about, so that we get a far from spontaneous number of 'John Henry' and 'Delia' and 'Boll Weevil' renditions, and I'm quite sure 'Boll Weevil' was Lomax's idea, not Willie's. That said, it's delightful to have on record his eccentric and charming version.

Perhaps, too, there's a subtext of local loyalty to Atlanta and Georgia here, and some resistance to the Texan interrogation—because the version of 'Ain't It Hard To Be A Nigger, Nigger' that McTell would have known would have been the one that runs: "Ain't it hard to be a nigger in Atlanta? / The police ride from door to door / They pick up the niggers and let the white man go / That's why it's hard to be a nigger anywhere in Georgia." And when Willie starts to sing 'Boll Weevil', straight after this interrogation, he doesn't hesitate to blame Texas outright, and perhaps mock its mindset slyly too.

"Boll weevil, boll weevil, where you get your great long bill? / I got it from Texas, I got it from the western hills."

Willie runs through the rest of his two hours without further recorded trouble, and to listen to him now is to marvel at his undiminished, deft dexterity on the 12-string guitar and at the always alertly nuanced beauty of his voice. In these testing circumstances it's a quiet, remarkable triumph.

Lomax concluded his notes: "He sang some interesting blues. His guitar picking was excellent. Declining to let me order a taxi to take him home ('I'll have that much more money,' he said), he shuffled away from me across a busy street in the downtown district. I watched him until he was out of sight. The face of a blind person always tightens my heart strings."

Afterwards, Lomax gave some of these recordings highly eccentric titles. The entire section starting with his introductory speil about Willie, followed by the interrogation about "complainin' songs," is titled "Monologue On Accidents", though it is plainly not a monologue and not about accidents.

A little over seven years later, Lomax died in Greenville, Mississippi, on 26 January 1948. He was eighty. He had published his autobiography, *Adventures of a Ballad Hunter*, the year before. Ruby outlived McTell, dying three days after Christmas 1961 in the Christian Home for the Aged in Houston, Texas. She was seventy-five.

A year before her death, one of the so-called New York blues mafiosi, Larry Cohn, arranged to buy a tape recording from the Library of Congress. The charge at the time was $10 per reel of tape. Librarian Rae Korson suggested that, if a few chunks of speech were shaved off what was sent out to him, they could squeeze it onto one tape. Cohn went ahead and bought this cheap edit. Six years later this was the version issued on LP, as *Blind Willie McTell: 1940*. Unbeknownst to Dick Spottswood, the man behind the album, when he ordered his copy from the Library of Congress, the edited-down version was the one they sent.

This penny-pinching distortion of the historical record has continued with every reissue for the last forty years. For the sake of saving $10, what is still the circulated version, and now on CD as the *Complete Library of Congress Recording*, has never been complete at all.

The information excised includes Lomax introducing 'I Got To Cross The River Jordan' with "which he says he used to sing and play with Blind Willie Johnson," and Willie then adding that "This is a song that I'm gonna play that we all used to play in the country—an old jubilee melody". At the end of 'Kill-It-Kid Rag', Ruby asks: "When was that composed, do you think? When did you first hear that?"

Willie replies: "Around 19 . . . that music's old, but that's the words was made last year, last year this fall of the year."

John Lomax: "Who made the words?"

"Well, myself and several of the boys gathered it up."

"Down at Miami, Florida?"

Ruby: "And how old do you think the tune is?"

"Oh, the tune is something like thirty years old, I guess."

We also lose this substantial introduction Willie gives at the start of 'Amazing Grace': "old days of songs. Now then, I have another small one—just about two lines, givin' you a reference on how the people used to play guitar back in them days that, that, um, are over now. All people played church songs on the banjo. They was scared to play any kind of real songs in them days. They played old church songs, old hymns. I ain't gonna sing this, but I'm gonna play it. It's just a line of it. The name of it is 'Amazing Grace, How Sweet It Sounds'. It's an old hymn, but I'm gonna sing it in the colored form: how they played it back in the country. It's kinda like this. Listen here."

Ruby asks, "For parties?" and McTell says, "No, ma'am, not for parties, for church! Back in them days." Only then does he say the one sentence we hear on the so-called "complete" recording.

At the end of his brief and beautiful rendition of the song, moreover, we are robbed of this glimpse of McTell expressing his feelings, perhaps articulating nostalgic longing for the past, and admiration for a lost style of musicianship. It's beyond all reason that this rare and touching moment should have been excised.

"You think about back in them days," says McTell, "olden times, how you can't get stuff now to sound like that."

Lomax responds here, coaxing: "Well, can you hum like your mother or father did, and sort of play your guitar?"

"Sure," says Willie, "I can hum that way. Here's some of it—" He seems about to resume, but Ruby says, "Wait a minute—" presumably as a disc is close to its end, and the moment for any reprise of the performance is gone.

Not only is this recurrent deletion absurd in having misled so many people for so long, and in having kept off the public record several nuggets of information, but actually it has warped our sense of the atmosphere in the room for most of the time Willie was there. The whole feel of the occasion has been changed by snipping off these bits and pieces. On the fuller recording, we hear Ruby speak—several times: it's obvious that she's a presence, she's part of what's going on. You hear her laugh: she's relaxed and friendly and makes it all less formal.

John Lomax, too, sounds less fierce, less peremptory, on the fuller version. Early on, he calls Willie "Mr McTell" in a wholly respectful, polite tone of voice; ahead of 'Kill-It-Kid Rag' he says casually to Willie "It's a rag, isn't it?" and Willie replies easily, "Let's call it a rag," and lights straight into the piece. And at the end of his performance of 'Chainey', John Lomax laughs and says "That's great!"

So, the widely sold version of the McTell-Lomax session deletes conversation and information, removes Ruby Lomax from the room almost entirely—making John Lomax seem to monopolise things and keep her silent, which he doesn't at all—and robs Lomax of several touches of warmth and humanity.

All these deletions distort, and they're an impertinence—and to be perpetuating them is exactly the kind of interventionism John Lomax is so scorned for by today's folklorists, whose hands are supposedly so much cleaner. It leaves Lomax more sinned against than sinning.

As for his racism, well, yes, he was a typical racist of his time and place. But, unlike almost all others, he devoted much time and energy to collecting black song and to asking black people questions for posterity— questions that assumed they were people with information and a history and opinions to offer. It's easy to take all this as read today; for a white Southerner born in the 1860s it was remarkably progressive.

You might as reasonably criticise Willie McTell for the obsequiousness of his response to Lomax about race relations. The point has often been made that Willie's ambivalence on the matter has to do with the fact that, as a musician, and a very personable one, his own experience of whites was comparatively benign, and certainly very different from how it was for the average field hand, tenant farmer, city laborer, or maid. Cheryl Thurber put this to me in a particular, perhaps quirky way:

> He's encountering other people mostly at the point where they're giving out money, not asking him for money . . . I don't think he encountered that same sense of whites trying to take advantage of him that other people would have.

She added, discussing the Lomaxes' recording too:

> Willie knew how to play whites: he knew how to get along with them and he had had whites looking out for him at various points in his life . . . And he *was* a professional musician, he was making a good living. And he was making a good living off whites: he was not taken advantage of most of the time.

This comes across strongly in all the testimony about Willie's tobacco-season visits to Statesboro. As we know, a lot of Willie McTell's traveling had been in a set seasonal pattern. Any notion of incessant wandering, or even of epic journeys to faraway states of the union, seems a romanticising of how it was. Willie followed the money, and one consistent flow of money came from tobacco. He followed the tobacco markets, so that he

274

moved with the season, and stayed mostly within the south-eastern States: Georgia and the Carolinas. So it was that his revisits to Statesboro were both regular and predictable. Blind Lloyd's recollections of time spent in the tobacco warehouses with Willie suggest that, from his own lowlier perspective, Willie played the whites almost absurdly well:

> They was a fool about him, all them white folks around there in Statesboro. Man, they used to have us . . . they had them old bar-rooms up there, you know. "Come on, come on, Doogie and Lloyd." That was some old white people. "By God, we got to have a little tune today!" We'd go in that bar-room in there. Different boys'd be having half a pint. Ha ha. Get us keyed up. Have a chicken supper.

He remembered, similarly, the two of them playing at a cane mill outside nearby Millhaven:

> Willie say, "I'm done drunk enough now. I want to eat something now." ... I think it was chicken, rice, and biscuits and things. Come out there and serve us . . . I said, "Mr. Tom," I said, "it's mighty late to go into town but I declare, I ain't got me no tobacco now." He said, "Well I'll be damned, ain't got no tobacco." Went into the store and got me a packet of George Washington and a plug of Bull of the Woods . . . Doog, he never did smoke. He'd chew this here Beech Nut. That's what he wanted. Tobacco, chewing tobacco.

Outside the Jaeckel Hotel, when Willie was playing to the tobacco salesmen (the "drummers") and to wealthy businessmen, he was similarly well treated, from the black perspective of the times. The Jaeckel, after all, was absolutely *it*, the Ritz of the region, and Willie McTell was an accepted, welcome feature on its frontage: this was a privileged position.

It was the first brick hotel in the area, it had steam heat, electric lights, hot and cold running water, a ladies' parlor, a gentlemen's parlor, a dining hall, and twenty-eight rooms. The foyer led to the dining room, which led to the kitchen. The porch on which Willie entertained the clientele was forty feet long and eight feet deep. By 1935, after several changes in ownership and management, the Jaeckel had fifty rooms.

Naomi Johnson remembers it all from the 1940s, when she worked there: "Oh. But they had these big chandeliers, and then the dining room when you sit down to eat . . . and you had a waiter, that waiter had that towel on his arm, and . . . if he sit your glass down, he didn't sit your glass down overhand, he sit your glass down like this. And you had the finest crystal you could buy. And you had tea glass, water glass, wine glass."

Naomi Johnson was a cook: "I used to get Florida lobsters here—you don't get 'em no more. I don't know what happened. And they had a big tail and a big gill. And I'd boil that lobster. I'd go to Savannah and get 'em by the cases. I'd boil them and put them in the freezer, and as I'd get an order, I'd take 'em out, I'd split em half in two and then I'd stuff 'em with crab dressing. I had a dressing. It was delicious.

"I wasn't even cooking and shook hands with the President: President Carter. And my sister went to the inauguration and she danced with Kennedy. Now we was poor little old children raised in the country with no learning. And the governors of Georgia, well I think I cooked for about twelve or fifteen of them.

"But mostly the peoples was from North Carolina: the salesmen would all eat there. There was a lot of salesmen then. See, we had the tobacco season then, and Willie would come, and all the tobacco men would gather round him—and he could really play. And that's why I knew him. He would be here about a month."

She also remembers that Willie would get taken elsewhere sometimes by these customers. "They used to have big fish fries out for the tobacco men, the farmers, and I think they would invite him out there to play . . . they had ponds with fish houses on it, you know, houses out there where they going fishing. If they wanna stay all night, they stay out there. Magnolia Lodge—that's back out on the Millen side. All over . . . See, they want to get away from home on the weekend, they go out to the fishponds. Some of them got houses over the pond."

Mildred Bouie Harville, born in 1912, remembered going on overnight fishing trips with her father, a postman who "had a big old boat: it would seat six or seven people," paddled by Willie's great Statesboro friend, Tom Cuthbert: and she remembers Willie coming along. "Willie'd sit at the camp and wait till they came back and start fryin' the fish. He would either sing and play for 'em, or he would get the little twigs and break 'em in two and use them for firewood. He'd get him a bunch of twigs and sit there and feed the fire . . . This was at the St Augustine Bluff on the Ogeechee . . . We fried fish and hush puppies, and maybe someone'd bring a potato salad.

"We'd spend the night. We had a cabin down there. Tom and Willie would spend the night too. They slept on the porch." Breakfast would be eggs, grits and coffee.

She, too, remembers Willie at the Jaeckel: "He could make a lot of money. Merchant salesmen . . . they were real generous. That was a big deal when the tobacco market came."

Cheryl Thurber also argues that, when it came to dealing with the Lomaxes, Willie probably felt valued by the white world in a further way:

"I think Willie was seeing it in that sense that he was helping out, providing information . . . that he was doing something to contribute to an understanding of music history—probably a sense of music history rather than black culture. He had respect for libraries, he did read Braille and he did get Braille books from libraries, so I think there was a sense in which he was pleased to be [asked]: that this was a little bit different. So I don't think he felt like he was being ripped off by John Lomax and his wife."

I think, though, that there's another aspect of Willie's general race ambivalence. Did he know he had white ancestors? He knew something: some of it. He knew his grandfather—Elbert was still alive and around till Willie was in his early thirties. There were a lot of mixed-race people in his neck of the McDuffie woods: not just McTiers but Samuels, Mosses, and Storys, and so on, and Willie was aware of the unreasonable racism that went on *within* that community.

When Coot's wife Mary Belle drank she got "chitsy," Hazel McTear's sister Annie Jackson told me, and then she'd be one of the people who'd pick on her daughter-in-law's family, the Samuels:

She was all right when she didn't have any in her. When she had any in her, she got wild. I never forget the time she jumped on me. She just didn't like our color. I got her back there. I hit her with something in the head. She was chokin' me and I hit her.

We know we were mixed up a little. I think the doctor in Augusta see, he wouldn't believe I was this color ... he said they couldn't tell him I wasn't white. And he said I didn't have but about a eighth of black in me. They didn't like us when we were growin' up—the whites didn't and the blacks didn't either.

It seems to me, therefore, that perhaps it isn't only from wariness that Willie declines to offer John Lomax "any complainin' songs." Perhaps part of his discretion here is from some knowledge of his own family's complexity of complexion—some sense of the untellability of the "lies that life is black and white."

And as Willie McTell moved on from his encounter with the Lomaxes, he was coming to the end of his relationship with Kate McTell—who went off to spend 1941 in New York City—and beginning what would prove to be a far longer, more solid relationship with Helen Edwards: a woman who was herself, as it happens, at least half white in appearance.

Helen was descended from Broughtons and Hintons. Her paternal grandfather, Moses Broughton, had been born in 1828, her grandmother, Amanda, in 1835, and they had produced at least seven children, several born into slavery and then Floyd, born in 1866. They were farmhands, living around Brickstore, just east of Covington along old Highway 12 in Newton County by the time Floyd was an adolescent in 1880.

There were Hintons living in the same patch of countryside, and Floyd married Henrietta Hinton, seven years his junior. One of their handful of children was Helen, born on Rutledge Road, Brickstore, on 1 April 1905. By the time she was fifteen, still living at home with her mother, her parents had split up and her father, Floyd, was living down the road with her older sister Florence and her family, the Franklins. By 1930, Helen's mother, Henrietta, had moved to Atlanta, and was living in Howell Street in Ward 4—the same patch as Willie and friends—in the household of one of her sons, Helen's brother Joe, a molder in a foundry, and his wife, Mary, a maid in an electrics plant.

We don't know when Helen moved to Atlanta—we can't find her on the 1930 census, unfortunately: but then we can't find Willie on there either. They probably met in Atlanta, though a connection through Curley Weaver's Newton County group of friends is possible: certainly Curley's daughter, Cora Mae Bryant, was acutely aware of her when she spoke to me in 2001, hissing at me that she didn't care what anybody said, she knew Willie's wife was white.

By the time Willie and Helen met, she seems to have had two children by other men: a son named James Newsome and a daughter, Alice. Perhaps Alice's father was the mysterious Mr Edwards whose name Helen had taken by the time she and Willie got together. When he vanished we don't know.

James Newsome was born in September 1921, when Helen was sixteen, and Alice two years and one month later. Neither seems to have been living with Helen by the time she and Willie started living together in the early 1940s, though they seem to have remained in contact throughout their mother's life.

We know regrettably little about Willie and Helen's life together, except that, even though he was never monogamous, they stayed together from the early 1940s right through till her death in 1958—and that she had no ambitions to be a singer, dancer, or musician—and that at least one of her sisters and her mother were around a good deal of the time while Willie and Helen were sharing their Atlanta apartments. Willie most definitely considered Helen his wife, though he doesn't seem to have divorced Kate and there is no extant record of any marriage between the two of them.

By late 1944 they were living together in Willie's usual neighborhood, and their addresses here included 248 Houston Street and 262½ Ellis Street. But Willie often took Helen to Statesboro and to Happy Valley, and she is the wife that almost everyone still alive knew. She was widely liked, and, though her photographs give no indication of it, she was widely regarded as a beauty.

Statesboro resident Barbara Davis remembers "Cousin Doog" bringing Helen to her mother Mamie's house for the first time: "I had seen her in Statesboro, 'cause he had brought her for the family to see, too. Uh huh.

My grandmother and all had seen her, my mother, everybody had seen her."

I asked what they'd thought.

They thought that she was pretty, but they were surprised, you know, that he had married a white woman! In those days and times, that was just something that wasn't commonly done. They said "white," but let me put it this way, knowing now what I did not know then, it's possible that she could have been mixed, and just very, very fair. But she had some white ancestors somewhere, if it was her mama or daddy or somebody very, very close—because she was whiter than any black person we knew at that time, you know. Now, the only other people that I knew that might have been that white but were black were the Van Burens . . . the Van Burens were very, very light people. And even Mrs Van Buren, I think Helen was lighter than she was. So she had very fair skin, very beautiful skin.

Willie had told them about her on a previous visit, though Barbara doesn't remember him saying anything about how they'd met.

No, the only thing he told us, and he was talking to the older folks when he was saying this but, of course, I was listening—he came to Statesboro and he was telling them that he had gotten married to this beautiful woman, and they all, of course, was teasing him, sayin' how was he going to see how beautiful a woman was, and all this. They was sayin' how could he pick somebody so beautiful when he was blind! That would be the gist of the conversation: not putting her down because he had married a white woman, but just kinda sayin' to him, "How did you find her?!", you know. And the men would say, "I got both eyes and I can see, and I ain't never found nobody like that!" and all stuff like that, you know . . . Cousin Doog now, he was a brownskin man, he was not dark complexioned. He was brownskin.

In 1944, meanwhile, tiny Thomson saw the birth of another future minor celebrity, Millie Jackson (though she would move away to New Jersey in her teens), and the following April, in Warm Springs, Georgia, President Franklin D. Roosevelt died at sixty-three. The next day, the funeral train carrying his body back to Washington, DC, stopped in Atlanta to change engines en route; thousands turned out to bid a last goodbye to the president who had given them the New Deal (which for most was the only deal they'd ever been offered).

Six months later, Willie's friend Blind Willie Johnson died in Beaumont, Texas. The kind of music he and Willie McTell played, acoustic country blues, had also passed. Buddy Moss was scuffling away up north, Curley and friends were living fairly hand to mouth, and there were no record deals in prospect for Willie. As Peter B. Lowry saw it, looking back from the 1970s:

> The Piedmont blues had a long reign—1926 to 1941—that far surpassed any other form of black music . . . There were many reasons for its decline, including World War II, a ban on recording by the musicians' union from 1942 to 1944, as well as changes in taste. By the time the recording industry was back in full swing after the war, the audience clamored for new things, and amplified instruments and tape recordings altered things completely.

The so-called Petrillo ban on recordings, which came into effect on 1 August 1942, was nothing to do with the war-time rationing of the material 78rpm records were made from, which was shellac, but was a total ban on new recordings imposed by the American Federation of Musicians and named after its leader, James Petrillo. The ban was, in Paul and Beth Garon's words, "an attempt to stifle the competition that jukeboxes represented for working musicians, and in order to collect royalties from the major labels." The ban achieved very limited success, and was, as so often with musicians' unions, wrong-headed. Jukeboxes did not necessarily threaten the livelihoods of working musicians, and Willie McTell was, like most of his audience, happy to live with them.

The Atlanta of the early 1940s was the scene of other struggles. The *Constitution* had made ex-sports writer Ralph McGill its leader writer after he'd filed uncompromising coverage of Hitler's seizure of Austria in 1938;

from that summer onwards he wrote a daily column, he became editor in 1942—and all through the decade his was a progressive voice, savaging the shortcomings of the "separate but equal" policy and arguing that black voters would have to be accommodated and would wield real influence in future times.

This could not be taken for granted. In 1944 black Georgian voters were prevented from voting in the Democratic Party's primaries—which, since Georgia was a Democratic Party fiefdom, meant that blacks were effectively disenfranchised altogether. That 4 July the Reverend Primus King of Columbus, Muscogee County (like Willie's brother-in-law, "Rev", he was a barber as well as a preacher) demanded a ballot in the primary, and when this was refused him, he filed a lawsuit. It reached the US Court of Appeals in 1946. The judge asked King whether he wanted $5,000 in damages or the right to vote. King replied simply: "I want the right to vote—for me and my people." The court ruled in his favor, though, even after changing the state of Georgia's electoral processes, gaining the vote took years of further struggle. Primus King died forty years later; another fourteen years on, the state honored him by naming a section of Macon Road after him in his home county.

The music that had not rolled over by the early 1940s was gospel music, which had thrived all through the Depression and enjoyed a continuous healthy life, hindered by the Petrillo ban but hardly threatened by it.

In and around Atlanta it wasn't only the prolific Rev. J.M. Gates whose church was packed out and who was able to keep audiences, on record and in person. After the pioneering Wheat Street Female Quartet, which recorded in the mid-1920s, a whole cluster of successful gospel groups were created in the 1930s, most prominently the Starlight Spiritual Singers, the Echoes of Zion, the National Independents, and the Reliable Jubilees. The Golden Gospel Singers formed (in Decatur) in 1942, followed four years later by the Five Trumpets: a group that would cut twenty sides between 1949 and '55—by which time, disc jockey Zenas Sears had long been putting out black gospel music on Atlanta's radio stations.

Gospel music has been much ignored by most blues-fan writers—like me, they tend to be on the atheistic left and often find the whole gospel agenda essentially a turn-off—but it had always been a part of Willie McTell's working life, however lightly he might have worn the scriptural message.

Statesboro resident Mrs Lillie Mae Brown's first memory of hearing McTell goes right back to about 1925—before he ever recorded blues—and it is the memory of being taken, as a five-year-old child, to a Revival meeting in the town:

My father died in 1926, so it probably was 1925. It might have been 1924, I don't know: it was one of the two. Everybody was havin' a Revival up there at Philadephia AME Church off Johnson Street, and they took me to the Revival: and I was small. They had a minister there who were preachin'. I don't know who he was, but they had a blind boy there, and his name was Blind Doog. And the church was crowded, but he was playin' his guitar—and the song was 'The Little Black Train Is A-Comin'': and I got frightened, and I asked my mother when the little black train was comin'. And she said, "Well, we don't know when it's comin'," so I said, "Well, what is the little black train?"—and she told me it was *Death*! And I said, "Well, Mama, I don't wanna go on that black train." But he were playin' that song, that young man. And I was real small. I didn't know he was Willie McTell: all I knew was he was Blind Doog. Everybody in town called him that.

Later on in life, about 1927, we moved near him and he and my brothers were good friends . . . Everybody knew him, and they just loved him—he could play that guitar: it was like *talkin'*.

Similarly, Naomi Johnson speaks of Willie making his guitar talk, and the song she has most vividly in mind is again not a blues:

Oh yes. I have heard him play. It's beautiful. It was beautiful. I never heard nobody play a guitar like he could. And he could play 'Amazing Grace' on there and make you cry. Oh, make you cry. You just couldn't hardly take it. That's why I think he learned to play for the church—I think that's what he said. But he could really play the church songs.'

She remembers him singing 'When The Saints Go Marching In', too.

Willie had already started to record some religious material at the sessions in New York and Chicago in the mid-1930s, and, as we've seen, he performed several such pieces, including 'Amazing Grace', for the Lomaxes. It's easy to assume that it was only in the 1940s that he reached more and more for such material, yet if folklorists were less blues-inclined, they would probably have found more evidence that Willie was already taking church opportunities to perform all through the 1930s.

It is from the 1930s, rather than the '40s, that "Rev" remembers Willie giving church concerts and performing religious repertoire. He told David Fulmer:

> He played spirituals quite frequently. In my community he would come at night, like on weekends, and on Sundays, and he had many concerts in the area. I was privileged, as a twelve-, thirteen-, fourteen-year-old boy, to accompany him: that is, to get him there, and see the huge number of people that would gather. Normally we would be in an area so thickly populated we could walk on Sunday nights. He was tremendous with his entertainment there, with his spiritual and gospel song. This was in places like Wrens, Matthews, Keysville, and what we called the Stellaville area. Churches, black churches, were very, very thick in that community, and those were the ones that would use his services . . .
>
> One of the things that I have not heard anybody say too much about: he blew a harmonica as well as he played a guitar—now he had a contraption on his guitar where he could put that harmonica to his mouth while he played his guitar. That is correct . . . and this was the thing that was striking in his religious programs: where he would use that harmonica and, oh my! it could change the tune of the gospels and the spirituals that he were playing, so dramatically until it would just make you up and listen. I think this is what caught our attention in the rural areas so greatly . . . and the playing of that 12-string guitar: something that I've never seen anybody else with, and I think this would be true with the people of the area which both of us come from.

That 12-string guitar was just literally eye- and ear-catching: we had just never seen anybody play one of those.

Willie had never been one of those troubled-soul musicians who had agonised over the divide between the music of the Devil and the music of the Lord. As "Rev" explained,

> ... he often said that no one taught him: he felt like it was a divine gift . . . that only the Almighty could have given him the talent to do this, and that he did not use them in any destructive manners whatever. I think of that very strongly, because he believed that strongly—that he was not against the will of God when he went even for blues. And that always lived with me.

Besides, if he were, with his usual facility, following the money, then perhaps it was no wonder that he was leaning towards the church. "Rev" describes him switching from secular to church performances as naturally as Saturday nights turned into Sunday mornings:

> He would come down ... and those areas had, as you know, general stores. They would make provisions for him to sat on their front just like Pig'n Whistles, and it was almost unbelievable the crowd of people would be around, and they would constantly put nickels and dimes in that guitar. This would last till ten, eleven o'clock at night, every Saturday night: his audience was tremendous . . . And then on Sunday he would find himself in various churches in the community—and there again it was a freewheel nickel and dime.

The church services he attended also gave him extra repertoire.

> If he heard a song one time, and you could do this going from church to church, he could sit down and put music to that song and play it! . . . he would go to church and sit down and hear them do them a capellas, and then he would go back home and he'd sit down sometimes ... and he could put music to whatever a capella song that he heard . . . by ear.

In Athens, as we know, he would visit Sister Fleeta Mitchell and her husband, the Rev. Nathaniel Mitchell, and naturally the three of them would perform religious songs for their own pleasure as well as for others. 'You Better Mind [How You Walk]' is one of the songs she says they used to sing together, and they would also perform on a program at the University of Georgia. Sister Fleeta doesn't remember which society or club this was for, but she remembers the practicing at her house, and that her husband sang, she played piano, and Willie played his 12-string and sang too. In Statesboro, Willie had long been a member of the Tabernacle Baptist Church, where he sometimes performed and received some of the proceeds of the collection. "He used to do a lot of singing in Tabernacle Church," Robert Owens said. Willie was also a member of a Mount Olive Church, out in the surrounding countryside.

Around the mid-1940s, Willie joined forces with a whole group of religious singers, and they toured around giving concerts in churches—by no means only on Sundays. These were organised appearances, and took place on weekday evenings. The first time Willie McTell's name was ever published in a Statesboro newspaper was in this small news item from the editorial page of the *Bulloch Times & Statesboro News* for 19 September 1946:

BLIND SINGERS WILL GIVE SERIES CONCERTS.
Willie McTell, long known blind musician former resident of States-boro, requests notice that he is here again with a group of other blind singers who will join him in a series of concerts opening Friday night, September 20, at Bethel A.M.E. Church; at Thomas Grove on the night of Tuesday, Sept. 24th; at Register on the night of Wednesday 24th [sic], the hours being 8:30. The public, white and colored, is invited.

This group doesn't seem to have had a collective name, but it included at least one woman pianist. Robert Owens remembered them as all females, and remembered them coming to stay with him:

Sometimes he'd have four and five girls with him, him and Blind Lloyd . . . They used to have a van, some kind of coach. They came down and spent one night with me on the farm, the whole group of 'em . . . They were all blind. Every one was blind—except the driver.

Back in Atlanta, though, just before the end of the decade, as Willie was playing on a street corner, another man would accost him to ask if he would consent to record.

This was a very different person from folklorist John Avery Lomax. Ahmet Ertegun was a Turkish immigrant from a rich diplomatic family, a jazz fan who'd learned about the blues from hanging around in the black clubs of Harlem, and he had recently co-founded Atlantic Records, the New York upstart label that would soon launch the careers of a younger generation of stars, including Georgia's Ray Charles: a label dedicated to the sort of commercial music that was anathema to Lomax.

Willie was getting on for fifty years old when Ertegun asked him to record. Such an invitation was unlikely to come again.

# SIXTEEN

A HMET ERTEGUN WAS twenty years younger than Willie McTell. He'd been born at the end of July, 1923, in Istanbul, and he arrived in America in January 1935, an eleven-year-old boy and precocious jazz fan. He had already seen and heard Duke Ellington and Cab Calloway at the London Palladium.

"My brother had played me a lot of jazz records," he told me, "and we had all the pop records in the house, because my mother bought pop records: the big hits, you know. We were music fans in London—my father was the Ambassador in London for about two or three years—and I listened to orchestras like Ambrose and Ray Noble and Lou Stone and Jack Hylton. So I was aware of the English orchestras and they all had some jazz players in them.

"And then my brother was going to school in Paris and, after we came to America, he continued to study in Europe, and so he would send me the records that came out on the Swing label, recordings with Django Reinhart and the Hot Club of France, and they had musicians like Coleman Hawkins and Benny Carter, who were ex-patriot musicians.

"But once I got to America I started collecting records, you know, buying old, used records."

They were in Washington, DC, and Ahmet and his brother, Nesuhi, would go round black areas, going from door to door, asking if they had any records for sale: "And they all had some old records in the basement."

This would have been from 1936 onwards. "That's when I began, became interested in the blues records. And the blues records were also collected by almost all the jazz collectors. All the jazz collectors also collected Bessie Smith and some of the other girl blues singers. But then from that we went on to, you know, buying Big Maceo and all the other male black singers who recorded in the '20s and the early '30s. You know, Blind Lemon Jefferson, Blind Willie Johnson . . . Blind Willie McTell, of course, had a lot of records on RCA Victor."

Ertegun's first encounter with McTell was on these records, and he "had a lot of his records," but McTell was just one small part of an immersion into all this music, and more highbrow excitements too: "I would, once in a while, be allowed to come to New York for two or three days. And all that time my days were spent doing two things. There were two jazz havens: one was the Commodore Music Shop and the other was the HRS—Hot Record Society—Music Shop, which was on 7th Avenue and 53rd Street or 54th Street. It was run by Steve Smith, and Commodore Music Shop was run by Lou Gabler. And my time was split between going to those places, just to try and buy a couple of records, and the rest of the time was spent going to the Museum of Modern Art or the Metropolitan."

Atlantic Records got started—but "it was hard to record funky blues music in New York, because all the musicians and singers were graduates of Big Bands and ... they did not have the inclination that gospel and blues people had to do music that the general public wanted. And we knew that and we had a very hard time finding anybody approaching that."

Before signing Ray Charles, who became a kind of blueprint for the funkiness quotient they were determined to create and capture on record, the Erteguns made a number of trips to the South. On one of these, Ahmet found Willie McTell (who was, of course, nothing like Ray Charles at all): "I didn't know it was McTell. But I was walking around the streets of the black section of Atlanta and there was this blind man, you know, with a guitar singing on the corner with a cup, you know, and singing some sort of gospel song. And I stopped by to listen to him. And he *kinda* sounded like what I remembered, you know, McTell sounded like. But I wasn't sure.

"So I said, 'Did you ever hear of Blind Willie McTell?' to the man. So he says, 'Aw,' he says, 'I *am* Blind Willie McTell.'

"I said, 'I cannot be*lieve* that!' I said 'Really?!' He said, 'Yeah! Who are you!?' So I said, 'Oh, I run a record company in New York.' So he said, 'How's everybody at RCA?' I said 'Well I'm not with RCA, I'm with this little record company.' So I said I would love to make records with him, but he didn't want to make any blues records. He just wanted to sing gospel music.

"So I said, 'Well, I really want to make—'

'If you make blues records,' he said, 'I don't want anybody to know that I'm making blues records, so we'll change my name.' So I said what would you like me, what shall we call you? He said, 'Call me Barrelhouse Sammy.'"

He just said that straight off?

"Yes."

And what shape was he in?

"He was in good shape and, er, good spirits. You know, I think that he sang at churches, and he seemed to be, I mean, living a life he'd been leading all along anyway, and singing on a corner was not—he was not sad doing that."

After Willie agreed to record, it was all sorted out that same day, if Ertegun recalls it right: "Yeah, I think, if I remember, that we said 'Great!', you know, whatever, and there was a studio nearby there, and we went to the studio and they were not doing anything and they obliged us: and he just played the guitar and sang and recorded a whole bunch of songs.

"We were traveling, you know, we weren't staying anywhere, and I think that we were just there for one day. And it just happened accidentally. I had no idea whether these records would ever be releasable, you know, but having stumbled upon a great, a person whom I knew—not many people I met had even heard of many of the people that I knew. I mean, I don't know how many people at that time there were in the *world* who knew who Blind Willie McTell was! I don't know how many collectors collected his records in 1948, you know.

"And we didn't have any money in those days. On that trip, I was only able to make that trip because a girl I knew who was going to Sarah Lawrence graduated, and she lived in Texas, her father was a big lawyer in Texas, in the oil business, and when she graduated they gave her a Ford convertible, and she called me and said, 'I don't know how I'm ever going to get this car to Texas!' So I said, 'Listen, I'll drive it there for you!'

So that was the only way that we were able to make that trip. And I think I must have put 20,000 miles on that car, just driving it around!

"Of course today, if I were to stumble upon someone like that, I would be able to afford to, you know, to do a lot for them, and do an album, do preparation, but in those days it was quite something for me just to be able to put down for posterity somebody whose work was forgotten."

I was curious as to how this Turkish ambassador's son could say he had no money at the time: "Well," he told me, "we had a lot of property in Turkey, you know, land and so on, but my father was never in business. We were never in trade. My father represented Turkey at all the peace treaties after the First World War. He was Mustapha Kemal Ataturk's legal advisor, he was an international lawyer—and he died very young: sixty-one years old. You know, we lived very well: my parents sent us off to very good schools, and we lived, you know, in embassies in a grand style, we had chauffeurs and butlers and nannies and governesses and all of that, but my father left very little money, and all of that went to my mother and my sister. My brother and I took nothing. And my mother went back to Turkey, and my sister also. And my brother and I decided to temporarily stay in America.

"Nesuhi was in Los Angeles at the time my father died, and he was married to a girl who owned the Jazzman Record Shop, and the Jazzman record label. And he started a record company called Crescent Records, prior to—before I started Atlantic. I had no inheritance whatsoever. And I started Atlantic with a loan from a friend. And it wasn't a loan, it was an investment. And the man who invested $10,000 got over three million when he left the company.

"So I had no money. When we started Atlantic Records I was living on $50 a week, out of which I had to pay rent and food and everything else. So. And having left living in a huge embassy, I now was living in a tiny bedroom in a broken-down hotel. The living room or the bedroom was the first Atlantic office, and I shared my bedroom with my cousin, who was a young Turkish leftist poet."

Was it the local distributor who found the studio: a radio-station studio?

"We must have located that studio for some other reason: I'm trying to

291

remember. There must have been maybe somebody else that we were thinking of recording down there. But I somehow seemed to know where there was a studio."

Ertegun, who was still in his twenties, produced the session.

"What astounded me was the power of his guitar. He really played, put down a rhythm track that was powerful, you know. He was a great player. Great player, great singer."

And what kind of deal did they have?

"We had no deal! I think we paid him a few hundred dollars, you know—that day. And I told him, you know, that, if the record sold, I'd pay him royalties."

Ertegun then claimed, somewhat inaccurately: "But he didn't know what that was. You know the independents are blamed for having cheated black artists? The reality is that the independents did cheat, most of them cheated the black artists—but they paid something, you know. The majors never paid them anything. Columbia and RCA, they didn't pay black artists, and most country artists got no royalties. They only recorded for a flat fee and they made their money by personal appearances when their records were a hit."

This session turned out to be the first of two returns to so-called commercial recording. Both took place in radio-station studios in Atlanta, and neither brought Willie any latter-day success. It used to be believed that the other session had happened earlier in 1949 than the Atlantic one, but eventually the Ertegun visit was pinned down to October 1949, and the session for Regal, always thought to have been held earlier that year, actually took place in May 1950. So, after thirteen years' total absence from record company sessions, suddenly Willie found himself brought back for two more in the space of less than eight months.

At both, his material was a mix of the secular and the religious. For Atlantic he revisited 'Broke Down Engine Blues', 'Little Delia', 'Kill It Kid', 'The Dyin' Crapshooter's Blues', 'I Got To Cross The River Jordan', 'You Got To Die', and 'Ain't It Grand To Live A Christian', but he also gave them 'Pinetop Boogie Woogie', 'The Razor Ball', 'Blues Around Midnight', 'On The Cooling Board', 'Motherless Children Have A Hard Time', 'Pearly Gates', 'Soon This Morning', and 'Last Dime

Blues'. All of this remained unreleased until long after his death, except for two tracks put out on a 78rpm by Atlantic in January 1950: 'Kill It Kid' coupled with 'Broke Down Engine Blues', by Barrelhouse Sammy.

That May, he was one of a group of musicians who responded to ads placed by Fred Mendelsohn for people to record for his Regal label at a session to be held in Atlanta. Mendelsohn was a figure not so dissimilar to Ertegun, except that he was almost a decade older and had grown up on New York City's Lower East Side. In 1949, in Linden, New Jersey, he co-launched the Regal label with David and Jules Braun, and made frequent scouting trips to the South.

In Atlanta, Willie and Curley Weaver were among those who turned up—and the generous amount of studio time they were given yielded some of their most delightful recordings. Altogether they made twenty-five sides: twenty are by McTell, with some guitar and vocal accompaniment by Weaver. They revisit much earlier material, but also give us one of the most endearing records you will ever hear: a vocal duet on 'Wee Midnight Hours', a re-working of an old Leroy Carr song, on which Curley's voice leads and Willie sticks close behind him with a tender falsetto. It is utterly beautiful. And remained unissued in both musicians' lifetimes. Curley, but not Willie, lived to hear the release of 'A To Z Blues' on *Living With The Blues*, a compilation LP issued in about 1960 on Savoy, for which Fred Mendelsohn found gospel acts.

In the early 1950s, Willie went on to sing spirituals on radio station WGST in Atlanta and on WEAS in Decatur, and later, on what must have been Willie's last visit to Kentucky, the remarkable lifelong Wobbly and hobo artist Utah Phillips heard him sitting on the porch at a street party in a suburban neighborhood of Knoxville, singing the Rev. Gary Davis' number 'Twelve Gates To The City.'

The same year as the Regal session, Willie was phoned up by an Atlanta librarian of slender build, neat appearance, and thinning hair, Alma Hill Jamison. (Some would claim Willie could tell all that from her voice.) The daughter of a Methodist Episcopal Church minister, Ms Jamison had attended the University of North Carolina and Emory University and, having graduated with honors, had gone on to the Emory Library School and begun her career with the Carnegie Library in downtown Atlanta in 1930. She worked at various times as a reference librarian, a cataloguer, a school librarian, and again as a reference librarian before becoming the Assistant Director of the Atlanta Public Library in 1942.

By the time she spoke to Willie, she was handling personnel records, interviewing job candidates, and selecting the library's books to be bought on philosophy, psychology, religion, and bibliography. Unfortunately, she was not a pre-war blues fan and her questions related only to securing information about other singers for a third party, Ms Martha L. Shoemaker, who had herself been enquiring for a fourth party, Ed Paterson, a writer on the London-based popular music weekly *Melody Maker and Rhythm*. He was interested only incidentally in Willie and mostly in the history of Barefoot Bill's two obscure Atlanta recording sessions from 1929 and 1930.

Nonetheless, at least Ms Jamison tracked Willie down, and could report this:

I have ... talked over the telephone with Willie McTell, who is still living here and playing on the streets. He is totally blind and moves from place to place, so a second attempt to reach him at the same address brings out the fact that he has moved on to another and unknown address. I am still trying to locate this.

Mr McTell gave me quite a bit of information, however.

She cites a couple of facts about the Columbia producers and assistant producers he'd known, and repeats the list he'd supplied to the Lomaxes of his own pre-war recording history, and then adds that:

Other coloured singers he remembers were Hudson Whittaker of Savannah, Georgia, known as "Tampa Red" and Arthur Phelps, known as "Blind Blake"; also Georgia White, of Sandersville, Georgia, made records for Decca, but McTell did not remember under what name. Whittaker also worked for OKeh, then later for Victor, using a Tampa, Florida, address at this time.

That, unfortunately, was that.

This snippet of interview was published on 26 May 1951. It was, as far as we know, only the second time he'd ever been asked for an interview, and it was over a decade on from the meetings with John and Ruby Lomax. It was a tremendous missed opportunity, combining only dull facts on other people with Ms Jamison's romanticised notion of Willie as a homeless wanderer.

He may have moved house in the middle of her attempts to contact him, but he was never of no fixed abode, and he was, as she proved herself, still on the end of a telephone when at home. (Even in their last listing, in the 1958–1959 *Atlanta City Directory*, Willie and Helen had a phone number; it was PL3–4717.)

No doubt times were toughening up, though. Whatever money Willie received from his last "commercial" recordings cannot have been much, but, his income augmented by Helen working as a "domestic," he was still doing better than many. The same year Willie was recording for Regal, Big Bill Broonzy was taking a janitor's job at Iowa State College in Ames, at $1.10 an hour.

Perhaps Willie had always managed money well—though it sounds as if Kate had been its manager for some years. Now this may have been part of Helen's role, along with looking after Willie's health. Robert Owens got this impression. Asked, in the 1970s, if he knew how the finances had been handled, Robert replied: "I really don't. This wife he had here—the last wife—I think she looked after the most of these things."

I was thrilled, thirty years later, to be put in touch with Barbara Davis—because here was someone able to tell me that she had spent time with Willie and Helen in their city apartment. This was a piece of tangible testimony—the only piece out there, half a century later—about their life together in Atlanta. And Barbara could put an approximate date to it—1953—because she was there at the end of her schooldays, to look into whether she wanted to go into nursing.

Even though she was a very young woman herself (she was born in 1936), she's amazed to hear that Willie must have been fifty by this point and Helen almost that age: they both seemed younger than that to her. That's how good a shape they were in then.

"I guess I must have been about sixteen, and I went to his home. He

295

lived in Atlanta, Georgia, with his wife: and at that time I'd heard rumors that he was married more than once. That I don't know. The only wife that I met was named Helen. And I went to their home and I was able to stay with them a few nights. I went during the summer to check out the nursing school, to see if this was gonna be the career that I went into, you know, when I finished high school, which was gonna be that next year. They had it open during the summer: if you thought you wanted a career in nursing, at Grady School of Nursing, you could go there and check out the dormitory and see what they had to do and all that stuff.

"My mama and them had talked about it once on one of his Statesboro visits. And he had said, 'Well you know, you could stay with me while you check it out.' I didn't know anybody, and at those times those ole folks didn't trust you away from home unless it was somebody who was gonna kind of be over you where you were going to be staying. So anyway I had an opportunity to stay with them in their home. And I got to know to her, real well. She was a beautiful person—a very beautiful person, in personality and in her looks: and she was very kind."

I said I was glad to hear it, but that the couple of photos I had seen of her—albeit rather badly reproduced—were not flattering at all.

"Uh huh, well she was very beautiful. She was not a blonde, she was not a brunette, but she had a beautiful color hair. She was tall, she was slender, and she was very kind. And my cousin, I used to tease him, I'd say 'Now how in the world you gonna pick out a woman so beautiful and you cain't even see her?!' And she used to laugh, and he'd say, 'Yeah, but I can feel her!' And he used to feel her face, you know, and he would tell me how beautiful she was just from feeling her face. And he'd say, 'I know how you look, too': this was what he'd tell us."

I asked how Helen dressed.

"Well, they wasn't like, sexy clothes, if you would allow me to use that word. They were just normal clothes. And they were dark. They wasn't light. I remember seemed like it was a kind of dark green type dress that she had on that day. It was a one-piece sort of dress. But it was not, you know, flowers or loud or fancy or nothing like that.

"I've been trying to remember the address of where he lived in Atlanta when I went to visit him—the only thing I knew, it was upstairs and it had a long bannister across the front of the porch, you know. It had like a porch all the way across the apartment, but it was upstairs, I do remember that. I remember us walking to the bannister, talking—and when I would leave they would stand there and wave to me when I would go.

"I think I found it on my own. They gave me directions, and there were buses. I can remember taking a bus to this corner of some street, and I don't know what street it was, but I remember that they said, when I got off the bus, if I looked up I could see their apartment. And I found it.

"Inside, I guess—at that point I wasn't really into decorating and all that stuff, but the room that I slept in was like in the living room: I slept like on a cot, or whatever. When you went in the door you went into the living room, and you went through their bedroom and it was like a passage and you went on through to the kitchen. And I forgot exactly, but the bathroom was sort of like on the side away from the kitchen. I don't remember paying that much attention, except that, in the living room, you know, it was nicely furnished. There was a cot over by the window, and the rest of the room it had like just regular furniture: chairs and a sofa."

What part of Atlanta was this?

"I can't tell you: I don't even know where Grady Memorial Hospital was in reference to where he lived. I don't know if this just wasn't that important to me or what, but I don't remember enough about it to try and tell you."

I asked what kind of age Helen was then. Barbara's answer was surprising.

"Now I can tell you only about what I perceived her to be. 'Cause not knowing for sure, but she was younger than he was, let me put it that way. She was younger than he was. And not knowing that much about age in those years, but I would say that, if she was forty, she was just forty. I perceived her to be, you know, a young person. She did not look old. Her skin was not wrinkled, you know what I'm saying? It wasn't long. I probably was there a couple of nights. But it was long enough to really get to know her."

Barbara never saw Helen again. Soon after she stayed with them, Willie and Helen moved house—and this time to an entirely different part of

Atlanta. Instead of being in the north-east, they were now on Dimmock Street, in the south-west: first at 1005 and then next door. The building was owned by Emmitt Gates, apparently a relative of the famous Rev. J.M. Gates. Willie taught Emmitt's teenage son to play guitar.

Gates was still around in the 1970s, when Peter B. Lowry found him: "I happened to find Willie's address," said Lowry, "and a fellow named Emmitt Lee Gates lived there—and he had lived there when Willie lived there, and he told all kinds of stories. He was a wonderful guy. Very forthcoming, you know. I just went to this house that Willie had once lived in, and he happened to be home. He was an older guy, and was more than willing to talk about Willie.

"He told me that Willie would have a pocketful of bottlenecks— he'd use different bottlenecks for different songs. That Willie would get up dressed up nice, walk down to the end of the road, turning left leaving the house, and picking up a tram there, and he never took the wrong tram to where he wanted to go: traveled around Atlanta that way."

The house was two storeys: four apartments, two up and two down. "Standing on the sidewalk looking towards the house, the land slopes down, so—let me put it in English terminology—the first floor is a little bit above road level and the ground floor is below that, but it's not a basement apartment. It's just that the land slopes down, or else the road was built up, which is actually more likely."

It was a wooden building. "Clapboard. Not shingled. Blank strips. Willie lived in one of the downstairs quarters of it, and Gates lived in one of the upstairs quarters, above Willie."

David Fulmer told me the house is still there: "That house is still standing. As a matter of fact, you can see it from the MARTA train, if you go to the airport . . ."

There's a hint of one more fragment of interview given by Willie to a newspaper, though the article, in Hugh Park's 'Around Town' *Atlanta Journal* column in March 1956, is so filled with blandly stated flagrant untruths that we can't be sure he really spoke to Willie at all. The piece starts:

Blind Willie McTell, who strummed a guitar at the Peacock Alley and Pig'n Whistle for 18 years when both had curb service, has been located at last. He is still following his profession of wandering in and out among the parked cars of a drive-in, this time the Blue Lantern, playing his music to whoever asks him and taking what they give him . . . The Negro troubadour still makes his way about with the help of a cane, strumming his guitar softly as he moves slowly among the cars, waiting for the voice of a patron to call him . . . He and his wife live at 1003 Dimmock St., SW, and when night begins to fall she tells Willie goodbye and he catches a bus. He makes the transfer by himself and gets off by himself.

We get to the quotation from Willie soon afterwards: "Willie at 56 is stout and growing a little gray. 'But not from worrification,' he says."

Park implies that Willie also tells him that tips aren't as good as they used to be, but he offers no more direct quotation (until the end of the piece, which is a risible regurgitation of the story behind 'Dyin' Crapshooter's Blues'). He does add a lovely, if untrustworthy, story—the implication is that Willie has just told him this story himself—about the good old days:

Oddly enough, the most Willie ever made in one night was during the tail end of the depression. The weather that New Year's Eve of 1936 was bitingly cold with the thermometer holding around 20 degrees. But Willie played until his hands became too numb. Then he would go and warm them by the kitchen's gas heater (it was at the Ponce de Leon Pig'n' Whistle) and come out and play some more. As voices shouted from car to car, "Happy New Year!" Willie sat down and counted his money. He had $50.

The house on Dimmock Street is where the record shop owner who recorded the *Last Session* later in 1956, Ed Rhodes, says he took Willie back to in the station wagon: when Willie was, according to Rhodes, drunk much of the time.

Drink, as with so many people, brought out a more malevolent side of

Willie's character. On the full recording Rhodes made, when Willie speaks about women he has known, he is by no means the radiant and graceful soul that "Rev" would have recognised from the 1930s, nor even Barbara Davis from just a couple of years earlier.

After he sings 'Don't Forget It', he offers this account of the song's origins: "I rigged up that one off a old gal that I used to like—you know—you know, just an old primitive gal I was hangin' around, you know: just messin' around with her."

He's asked what he means by a "primitive gal," and he says:

Just primitive. Little primitive gal, you know. Old—old idle broad. Just—this idle old broad, just get out and get drunk and everything, you know how it is. You get out and you get that old broad late at night, you know. They just don't . . . they just don't analyse, you understand. They just don't—just don't come up to the standard.

You just out with 'em, you know—you ain't, you don't mean 'em no good, you just out with 'em. You don't mean 'em no good whatever in the world. No more—just go-they-come-day-God's-in-Sunday: you just out with 'em, you don't care nothin' 'bout 'em, just dry long so. Just, you know, messin' around.

Nor was Atlanta perhaps the ideal place to be sinking. Wages and salaries were still much lower than in the North, while the US Supreme Court ruling in the case of Brown v. Board of Education in 1954 ("in the field of public education, the doctrine of 'separate but equal' has no place. Separate educational facilities are inherently unequal") had intensified and given a focus to racial antagonisms all over the South. The city seethed with incipient, and often actual, violence. While Ralph McGill's editorials still gave eloquent voice to (relatively) progressive opinion, the notorious future state governor Lester Maddox spoke the message of reaction—and segregation at any price—to a threatened and squeezed white working class. He'd long been publishing political opinion through adverts for his Pickrick Restaurant on Northside Drive (which, via "Pickrick Says . . ." tirades, used this alter ego to articulate his views) but, in 1957, he began to stand for political office in the city, challenging

300

the incumbent in the Atlanta mayoral race. He lost, and did so again the year after, but he was a loud, atavistic campaigner and did great harm in a city that might have been far more civilised without him.

Sam Charters, drawn there in search of the likes of McTell in the 1950s, remembers it without affection:

> Atlanta was hard. It was not an easy city to get into. Some cities, people were more open than others. There was a great divide between white and black, and this was still before the Civil Rights battles, so that I was very uncomfortable working in Atlanta. Also, Atlanta and Memphis were church-dry cities, which people don't realise. They'd really shut down. Yeah, the churches had closed down the clubs, so that you really—you couldn't hear music. St Louis was still fairly open, New Orleans was wide open, but in Atlanta and Memphis, you walked into the Southern Baptist church atmosphere. And particularly, there I was, the scruffy New York kid, and whatever I said there was the license plate of the car anyway, and things were very tense and it was often uncomfortable. Atlanta was not a city I could work in.

There's an unexpected cameo of these tensions in action from the middle-of-the-road country singer George Hamilton IV. He told British interviewer Spencer Leigh:

> Sam Cooke and I got into a taxicab in Atlanta and this policeman stopped the cab and wrote out a ticket for the driver . . . I said to the driver, "Did you get a speeding ticket?", and he said, "No, it wasn't for speeding, it was a citation for breaking the law. I was using this as an integrated cab." He was given a ticket to appear in court and pay a fine: this was in the land of the brave and free in 1958. It's hard to believe it happened, but it did.

If Willie's deterioration was swift in the mid-1950s, it accelerated in the fall of 1958. Two deaths coming hard one upon the other shook him badly. On 12 October, the uncle who had been the solid rock through-out Willie's life, Cleveland "Coot" McTier, died, after an eight-day stay

301

in the University Hospital in Augusta, from septicemia, an infected wound brought on by the diabetic mellitis he had suffered from for the best part of thirty years. Twelve days short of his seventieth birthday, he died at 3.25pm that Sunday afternoon. He was buried exactly one week later, in the little unenclosed graveyard of Jones Grove Baptist Church at the side of Happy Valley Road. When Willie received the news, and whether he and Helen came out to Thomson for the service, we don't know. Coot's death was registered that 3 December; the informant was "outside child" Willie Shelton, a son.

Less than three weeks after Coot's death, Helen died. She had been suffering internal bleeding for two or three months, but suddenly collapsed from heart failure. She was rushed to Grady Memorial Hospital but died within minutes, at 7.50pm on Saturday, 1 November. She was fifty-three years old.

On Monday the 3$^{rd}$, a preliminary obituary notice appeared in the twenty-eight-page *Atlanta Constitution*. At the bottom right-hand portion of the 'Obituaries, Funeral Notices and Death Reports' page, in the small section labeled 'Funeral Notices (Colored)', the eleventh person listed was Helen: "McTELL—Mrs. Helen McTell of 1003 Dimmock St., SW, wife of Mr. Willie McTell passed Nov. 1, 1958. Funeral announced later. Haughabrooks Funeral Home."

'Georgia Deaths' was a category that clearly applied only to whites. (In the same paper two days later there was a story about some injured miners being offered a free vacation at Jekyll Island, Georgia, but reporting that then they had discovered that one of them was "part colored"—so he was told his vacation would be segregated . . .)

Willie registered Helen's death on Wednesday, 5 November, and, on the Saturday, published this obituary in the *Atlanta Constitution* '(Colored)' columns:

McTELL—Mrs. Helen McTell of 1003 Dimmock St., SW. Funeral services will be held Sunday Nov. 9, 1958, at 2pm. from the Fort Street Methodist Church at 562 Boulevard NE, Rev. Strickland officiating. Interment in Aikens Cemetery at Covington, Ga. Survivors are a husband, Mr. Willie McTell; son, Mr. and Mrs. James Newsome of

Detroit, Mich.; daughter, Mr. and Mrs. Oliver Beasley of Philadelphia, Pa.; mother, Mrs. Henrietta Broughton; four grandchildren, three sisters, two brothers, several nieces, nephews and a host of other relatives and friends are invited to attend the funeral. Haughabrooks Funeral Home.

When I went to Skyline Drive that day in February 2003 to buy my copy of Helen's death certificate, and then found the obituary notice on microfiche at the public library, there was one trivial puzzle and one that was more intriguing. The trivial one was that, back in 1958, the pastor listed for the Fort Street Methodist Church in the Atlanta City Directory was the Rev. G. Wesley Thomas, not a Rev. Strickland. I let this go: presumably either Rev. Thomas was away at the time, or Rev. Strickland was better known to the McTells.

More puzzling was: where was Helen buried? On the death certificate, in the box marked 'Name of Cemetery or Crematory', the single word "Covington" was written, but the address box was filled in with "Covington, DeKalb, Ga." But Covington is and was in Newton County, not DeKalb—DeKalb County lay between Atlanta (Fulton County) and Newton County. Perhaps, people suggested, it meant that the cemetery was out on the old Covington Highway, but still in DeKalb as you headed out that way. I could find no such place on any map. To increase the puzzle, the obituary says "Aikens Cemetery at Covington, Ga." I could find no such place as this either. I looked everywhere.

Coming out of the DeKalb County public library when it closed that evening—a neo-classical building set back amid lawns with well-tended shrubs in a little bijou suburban setting, its interior all soft furnishings, white pillars, airiness and calm, a generous supply of computers (two or three specifically for "guests") and polite help—I went along the street to the Java Monkey coffee house and wine bar, and, supplied with a glass of red, I was going through my notes when, with striking serendipity, the sound system played Bob Dylan singing 'Blind Willie McTell'.

Back in Atlanta next morning, I was walking the windy street from my hotel towards the heart of downtown when, almost surreally, a minibus marked THOMSON GEORGIA drove past me and disappeared down Ralph McGill Boulevard. I felt that the spirit of Blind Willie must really be with me.

I went to Haughabrooks Funeral Home, on Auburn Avenue near Edgewood (where Willie and Curley Weaver had recorded the Regal sessions in a building that now stands empty), to see if they could solve the mystery of where Willie had buried Helen. This funeral home was one of the success stories of businesses set up by black women in Atlanta. It was founded with $300 in 1929 by Geneva M. Haughabrooks, who had been a cook for one of Georgia's state governors, and a teacher, before learning the mortuary business and then setting up her own. She had moved it to Auburn Avenue in 1937.

A committee chairwoman of the Atlanta Negro Voters League, she was still in charge at the funeral home when Helen McTell died, but long gone by now, as was the man who had embalmed Helen, Samuel Pierce. (Geneva Haughabrooks died in 1977, Pierce soon after Helen.)

The company's ad in the 2003 *Bell South Real Yellow Pages* said they had been "Serving Atlanta For Over 70 Years", had "Financing Available", "Pre-Need Arrangements", and that theirs was a "Newly Renovated Facility Located In The Historic MARTIN LUTHER KING, JR HISTORIC DISTRICT". I hoped this last didn't mean that they would have just thrown away whatever meager supply of old paperwork they might have had before the renovation.

This is still a poor and black section of town. I'd driven down the streets where Willie had once lived—Fort Street, Ellis, Courtland, Hilliard, Butler, and Bell Street. Nothing is there anymore. Haughabrooks remains, on a shabby patch of street.

It was very hushed inside: an old building revamped at no great expense, and a small firm, still independent. Inside the front vestibule a corridor ran straight ahead, and off it, on the right, were several offices, their doors open. Inside the first, behind a large solid desk, a large smartly dressed man in his forties sat facing the open doorway. This was Marcus Wimbey, CEO. He was on the phone, so I went to the next doorway. In that room sat Mrs Elaine Maddox-Weaver, Mortician, a very smart woman in her thirties, looking like a younger, smoother-skinned Oprah

Winfrey. She was dressed in a faultlessly groomed black suit, to which not a speck of dust or hair was attached.

She was immediately sympathetic—of course she's trained to be anyway, but this was a relaxed, self-confident sympathy alert to the situation, not done by rote. She was doubtful that they would have an answer. Nowadays they keep a copy of each funeral program, but back then she thought there would only have been a logbook with the same information as on a death certificate.

She, too, was puzzled by the cemetery having been stated as Covington but in DeKalb County. She found the one man still working who had been at Haughabrooks since 1959, but he knew of no such place either. But another "old-timer" was sent to retrieve the logbook "way down in the basement"—and though it didn't solve the mystery of Helen's last resting place, it did give me unexpected, unlooked-for detail about the funeral that Willie had given the woman he had lived with for at least the previous fourteen years.

It had not been done on the cheap. He had paid $35 for the embalming, $25 for Professional Services, $400 for the casket, $20 for the burial garment, $10 for the headstone, $10 taxes, $35 for the casket coach, $120 in vault charges, and there had been two limousines (at $30). He had paid $315 in advance on the Tuesday, 6 November, and the balance by the 13th in five installments. The advance and the last payment were by checks, paid by Life of Georgia Atlanta Life Assurance. Mrs Maddox-Weaver was able to give me a couple of corresponding figures today, suggesting that Willie had spent the equivalent of $500 for the embalming alone, and about $2,500 for Helen's casket.

"He gave her a pretty good funeral," she said.

The mystery of her burial place was solved for me later by a very supportive local amateur historian, Gary Doster. I had phoned around all six Covington funeral homes, and, at one of them, a Mr Goolsby had suggested that Aikens Cemetery was an old place out on the Elks Road, off the old Highway 12: not in DeKalb at all, but firmly in Newton County. Gary Doster and his wife Faye went out looking for it, and, at their second attempt, after much searching, found not only the cemetery but Helen's grave.

State Highway 12 (US Highway 278) runs right through Covington in an east–west direction. If you drive east past the intersection with State Road 142 on the eastern outskirts of Covington, just over a mile and a half further on you cross two bridges close together over the Alcovy River swamp. Immediately after the second bridge, you turn right (south) on Elks Club Road. A mile and a bit down here, you turn right onto a dirt road into what was a large wooded area that is now a grown-up clearcut, probably waiting to be replanted with pine trees. After a couple of hundred yards there's a locked metal gate straight ahead and the road bears right. Take this right curve and the cemetery is a couple of hundred yards further ahead on the left. On the map it is identified as Echols Cemetery, not Aikens at all.

The first time the Dosters found the place, they couldn't see Helen, and Gary reported back to me that they "both thought it was unusual in that there were a large number of nice tombstones in relation to the number of graves marked with field stones. In most black cemeteries there usually will be several unmarked graves to every grave with a tombstone but that was not the case . . . There were a few old funeral home markers on some graves without tombstones, but none with legible data. I did not see any from Haugabrooks." There were, he added, well over fifty tombstones, all dated in the twentieth century, mostly from the 1920s or '30s, but with at least one from the 1980s.

On 9 December 2004, Gary e-mailed again, with the subject-heading "I found Helen McTell!" He wrote: "I don't know how I overlooked her on my first visit, but yesterday my wife and I went back to the cemetery in Newton County and found Helen McTell's gravesite." They attached several photographs.

The top of her gravestone is broken off, but can be set back in place. A rudimentary floral relief design loops across the rounded top, and the lettering below reads simply this:

HAUGHABROOKS
MRS
HELEN
McTELL
NOV–1–1958.

The one cheap touch to Willie's send-off for Helen was that $10 gravestone. It is made of concrete, the lettering crudely carved into its surface before the concrete dried. But it's still there, about 750 feet above sea level, set amongst the tree stumps and close to other members of her family, including the mother who outlived her.

# SEVENTEEN

O NE MONTH AFTER Willie lost both Coot and Helen, Robert and family moved to the North: to Plainfield, New Jersey. Emmitt Gates told the Evanses that Willie had soon moved a new "wife", Josie, into the apartment on Dimmock Street, but this was small compensation for great loss. She may even have been one of them ole primitive gals.

Willie had already become diabetic before Helen died, and without her to help him through, limit his drinking, give him a good reason to come home at night, and love him, his health took an immediate dive.

In the early spring of 1959 he suffered a stroke. It was "minor," but it slurred his speech and further affected his dexterity—and, therefore, his playing and his ability to make enough money to live on. Someone, possibly Josie, contacted Eddie McTear in Happy Valley and Robert in

New Jersey. He and another relative, Alfred Story, known generally as Uncle Boo, drove over to collect Willie from Atlanta and arrange for a van to fetch over his furniture too. "And he had some nice furniture," as Robert noted later, when he saw it stored in a barn that Eddie had cleared out and cleaned to accommodate it.

Eddie had conferred with Robert about who should look after Willie now that he could no longer look after himself. Eddie told Robert that if he wanted to take him up to New Jersey, that was his business—but that he didn't have to. Eddie told him he'd had a lot of experience of dealing with diabetes: his father, Coot, had been diabetic for thirty years, so he knew how to handle it. And he was already giving Willie his shots by then, and he reassured Robert that he'd keep in touch about how Willie was doing. Robert agreed.

So it was that Willie almost hung up his travelin' shoes. Almost but not quite. Ola Ivey, Gold Harris' granddaughter, who was born in 1950 and brought up by Gold and his wife Margaret, saw a lot of Willie in these last months, and remembers that, even towards the end, Willie would disappear now and then. He made a partial recovery, and could play the guitar again and move around. In fact, as Ola remembers it, it was *Gold* and Uncle Boo who went up to fetch him from Atlanta.

"They'd notified Daddy—I used to call Gold Daddy—so Daddy and Uncle Boo went to get him. I remember Mama (Margaret) sayin', 'Now be careful.' And he stayed around us for a while—in what they called the Panhandle, which is lower Warren County—and then he went up to Cousin Bo-Rat's and Cousin Horace. And then he was gone again. He'd walk anywhere. 'Cause Daddy used to get at him about leavin' and not tellin' anybody where he was goin', and he would always laugh and say 'Ha ha! I *got* my senses!' I never heard him say he got lost, either."

Her memories here may be fused with earlier ones, because, as a child, it seemed to her that Willie was around much of the time.

"He always had on that old hat, that little hat; and there was a black coat, I guess like an old suit coat, with some suspenders and a shirt. I remember the suspenders 'cause they were always too big, to me. When him and Daddy would be sittin' under that tree and he didn't have that jacket on, it would always be those suspenders, and a old shirt, and he'd be turning the brim of the cap around. But on Sundays when he went to church he'd have on like a man's brim hat: black and wide.

"Cousin Doogie would be up singin' and praising the Lord and stuff like that. Daddy would just laugh and say 'You praisin' the Lord on Sunday and devilin' Saturday night!' They would tease each other a lot."

Annie Jackson remembers Willie's last months too, when he was staying at Hazel and Bo-Rat's place and recovered enough to play guitar at barbecues Hazel ran to make money: "My sister and them, they had some kind of little old place they ran, up there at the house, and he would sit out in the yard and be playing his guitar, and everybody just go up throwin' in money. Throwin' him dimes and quarters all the time, and he'd be sittin' there playin' them boogie songs.

"She used to cook stuff in the house and sell it—all kinds of stuff. Sold beer all the time. When I was there it was mostly beer. And she would cook all kinds of stuff in the house—chicken, and cakes: she made cakes and things.

"He would [be] out there all the time—he wouldn't be under the tree, he'd just be sittin' out there in the middle of the yard where the crowd wasn't at. Yeah, I liked to hear him play—he really could play that guitar. When he played up there it would just be high in his arms—he'd just stick it up in his arms and play.

"But I didn't see him till he got real sick. I know they built a room on there, on the side of the house back there, back thisaway. They built a room up there onto the house I think they put him in. He didn't look that old then. But got sick."

Ola didn't know anyone who didn't like him. But most of her memories are of being enthralled by how skillful a blind man could be—"You could try to slip up on him: you never could. He'd always hear you, and you could just walk in the room, he'd know who you were"—and of him and Gold "playin' and drinkin' and havin' fun. They'd be up at Cousin Bo-Rat's. They were always messin' around with the guitars. They'd just sit out under that pecan tree with that jug of whiskey, and they'd sing 'Bring My Baby Back To Me' or something. That's what they'd sing when they'd be drinking. But there were so many songs they'd sing. I used to think Cousin Doogie made 'em up as he went.

310

"Doog took that guitar everywhere he went. If you saw him, you pretty much saw that guitar."

That had always, always been true. So much so that it was when he went off without it that Robert knew something was going wrong with Willie. This was in the short space of time between Helen's death and the Owens' departure for New Jersey.

"I could tell there was something bothering him," Robert said, "... Because he did something he never did before. When her [Robert's wife, Catherine] and me taken him to the train at Dover, Georgia [for him to catch the fast train back to Atlanta], he had done got out of the car, boarded the train, the train had pulled off, and I was fixing to pull off, and I looked in the back seat, and his guitar was back there. He'd never leave that guitar nowhere."

Ola remembers Willie's health declining further in Happy Valley near the end, though of course she didn't understand what was going on. "I remember there was one incident. It was at Cousin Horace's, I think. They were havin' a barbecue and I remember Daddy telling Cousin Doog he shouldn't eat some barbecue and hash. And as a child you just think 'Why are you telling him not to eat that?'"

On Monday, 10 August, or possibly the day before, Willie had a second stroke. Horace told the Evanses: "He was out there under that pecan tree. I give a barbecue . . . And I just filled him up a plate and give him all he could eat. Yeah, he loved his barbecue . . . and he had another stroke that night."

He didn't seem so bad until they put him in the bath and he couldn't get up again. He said to Hazel, "I can't stand up": and that was almost the last thing he said that made sense.

Next day, Tuesday, 11 August, they took him into the local hospital in Thomson, giving his name as Willie McTier. Gold Harris, Eddie, and Horace McTier obtained, on advice, a Petition For Commission Of Lunacy With Ten Days Waiver from the Sheriff of McDuffie County, L.J. Norris. Since there were three relatives stating that Willie was "mentally sick," the petition was granted by the Court of Ordinary that same day. Two physicians and an attorney formed the jury that put their names to it at two o'clock, and, because Judge John F. Watson was satisfied that Willie was a Georgia resident and had not been "introduced into the State or County for the purpose of being sent to the Milledgeville State Hospital," he was sent there. A "writ of lunacy" was certified against him.

A Treatment Permit for Milledgeville State Hospital staff to treat him was signed by Gold Harris (with a cross, "his mark"), as witnessed by the judge, and a History Blank filled in which described Willie McTier as sixty-one-year-old colored male and a widower.

It makes poignant reading. The patient's financial condition was "Dependent." The patient had not made a success in business. His disposition before becoming insane had been "Sociable." The patient had never had syphilis, tuberculosis, or cancer, was not addicted to alcohol and/or drugs and had never been insane before. His attack was "Gradual." The symptoms that caused Eddie McTier to think the patient's mind was affected were that he "Talks out of his head", "Thinks he is in distant places" and "Talks to members of his family who have been dead for years."

Whether Willie was taken into Milledgeville by ambulance or train we don't know, but he arrived on Wednesday, 12 August, without any luggage or money, and, after a partial examination, he was placed on the ward for acutely ill patients. The doctor who saw him found him "poorly nourished." He had no strength in his right hand, and, after being asked several times how long this had been the case, he said it had happened the previous night. He could not stand up unaided, and, in the days that followed, he had to be cared for in every way. He remained "always quiet."

I drove to Milledgeville from Macon, as it happens, choosing the old Highway 49 North. It was dusk almost at the outset, but I could see enough to feel that this whole stretch was a delight. It felt like, looked like, Kenya, and came on strong: jaunty vegetation, lush green, old wooden houses like big shacks with big porches, sitting on their small plots of cultivated land twenty yards or so back from the edge of a road fringed with little old-fashioned telegraph poles. Some buildings were collapsing; some had tin roofs. There was sometimes cattle, and little goats.

And then Milledgeville. I won't push the Kenya resemblance too far, but a British colonial town in the South is not so different from one in East Africa. The road took me right into the center, where I was surprised, on Hancock Street (the main street), to see at least two bar-restaurants open, and three young students of the sports-team pudgy-white-drunk variety laughing in delight as their rented stretch limo arrived and double-parked on the street. The black chauffeur held the door open for his guests and they piled in after much guffawing and shouting.

North Columbia Drive was hushed plush residential, but kept widening out until the railroad track ran across it. The barrier was down (a rare occurrence all trip), so I sat there by the soft red lights, car window down, in the dark, hot air, hearing that whistle blow as the locomotive approached. I began to count the trucks, each the length of a passenger carriage, as they dawdled past sounding like slow, giant knitting needles. I wondered if the train would be sixteen coaches long. Sixteen passed, and on and on they rumbled. It was 108 trucks long.

Next morning, back in the blazing heat of Hancock Street in August, the Welcome Center opposite the old county courthouse sold me a $6 discounted Historic Tour fee and I got on the bus. The only other punters were a thirty-something couple from elsewhere in Georgia. We began at the old Governor's Mansion, which dated from the short time when this was the state capital and the interstate of the day was the river. A young history graduate gave a substantial intro in the hallway and then talked us around the rooms (in every case beginning with "I'd like to welcome you to the — Room"). We ended at St Stephen's Episcopal Church, which Sherman blew the roof off. Today it has a Heavenly Gifts giftshop. Later I made my own tour, visiting Flannery O'Connor's grave in the oldest cemetery, Memory Hill, where also lies a genius of a domestic architect, John Marlor, who, in a short life (born in England, 1789, died in Milledgeville, 1835), designed many of the ingenious, musty houses of the town.

Just down from the decaying art deco Campus Theater is the new county courthouse (built to look like the old, but simpler and larger), where I called in to find the Probate Judge's office to apply for Willie's death certificate. There are entrances on all four sides of the building, creating four pale gray corridors that meet in the middle, with a series of rooms off on each side, and this pattern is repeated on the floors above.

Nothing is explained but everything is clearly labeled—with, Willie would be surprised and I hope pleased to find, Braille writing on every office plaque. No one ever looks at you as if they don't think you should be there. The room I needed had a counter area about twelve foot long at chest height, and, behind it, a huge area with several enormous desks ranged around with large distances between them, each occupant identified, and several doors and partitions opening off them, and, at the right-hand end, a wide open doorway into the large area where the files are kept and photocopies made.

I gave the short, near-retirement-age lady my request, she filled in a few details (asking, "What year did he die?", for instance, rather than what date), charged me $10, and issued a receipt. She went away and searched, and came back with a weary, I-don't-like-foreigners truculence to say, "Sir, we don't have his death on record for 1958."

"It's 1959," I said, not for the first time. She gave me a look and plodded off again. On my side of the counter a shaven-headed young Army cadet who had been delighting these ladies with his aw-shucks charm and his Georgian normality went away with his gun permit form, and was replaced by the splendid, glowing figure of Mr Oscar Davis Jr, Vice President of the People's Funeral Home on North Clark Street. He was one of those portly people who holds himself so well you feel you wouldn't want him any other way (like Fats Domino). The death certificate arrived, and I asked why they always had to be white writing on black—a negative—and the lady across the counter didn't know. She said they were all like that and always had been.

By now she had softened up. As so often, initial suspicion—if not plain muted hostility—is melted away if you just keep talking, letting people in a little to what you want, so that they end up pleased that a foreigner should be taking such an interest in, and be so well-informed about, one of their own. And she and her colleagues softened further when Mr Davis and I got into conversation and he was so well dressed and respectable a figure (white shirt, tie, tie-pin, cufflinks, cuff-chains, black trousers and shoes) and so engaged by what I was doing that we looked through the details of the certificate together. I came away with everybody's warm good wishes and a request from Mr Davis that I tell him when this book became available.

I had seen Willie's death certificate reproduced before—David Evans had included it in the booklet to the *Atlanta Blues 1933* LP in 1979—and I had long ago noted all its detail (though, in Willie's case, "detail" is a grand term for it), but it always feels sobering and faintly unseemly to be holding such things in your hand.

The "informant" had been Records Milledgeville State Hospital; they had not bothered to write any State File No. at the top, and they had written down "Gold Harris" as Mortician, because he was first on the list of those who took Willie's body away—but they had not asked him for any of the information he could have given about Willie.

Hence we get not only Date of Birth "not given" and Birthplace merely "Ga.", but Married? "UK" (meaning "unknown", not "yes, he was married in Britain"); Ever in Armed Services? "UK"; Father's Name? "UK"; Mother's Maiden Name: "UK"; Name of Cemetery: "UK"; and, to add insult to mortal injury, Usual Occupation? "Patient."

People were paid a salary to be that bad at their work. Except for Willie's birthdate, Gold Harris could have answered all those questions, had anyone asked.

Back in the Welcome Center, Bill Williamson told me more about the Milledgeville of 1959, when he was a young adult here.

"In the 1950s, the State Hospital had 13,000 patients," he claimed. "It was the largest mental institution in the world." I thought of the old Soviet Union and wondered. I thought of it again later when I read that, from 1962 until 1992, Milledgeville State Hospital boasted "the world's largest kitchen."

People in the town inevitably called it "the funny farm," but Bill thought they were more afraid of it than disparaging. "The patients could earn walk-out privileges, and they could come downtown. It was a pretty good program: to try to reintroduce them to the society."

The size of the place made it Milledgeville's biggest employer, too. "It still is one of the largest employers," he said. "The prison system has taken over several of these buildings. There are five prisons now. They took over and renovated buildings—but some of the old buildings are still used by the present hospital population and they've added new ones too."

Did you only end up in the hospital if you were poor?

"Last measure. Yes, sir, last measure. There were some people that were not poor, but I would say the majority of 'em were."

Bill made one scary visit to the place himself back in Willie's day, when he was about twenty-three years old: "We had a Hallowe'en carnival at my Youth Development Center and the staff came in costume, and I thought I'd get an old prison uniform with the stripes: and I knew they used them out there (they did then: they don't now). I went out there to borrow a uniform, and a friend who worked there carried me over to the Criminally Insane ward. We went through about three different locks to get into the building, and he introduced me to the warden—and then my friend left: he said, 'I gotta get back to work,' and he left. Now I'm getting a little apprehensive, y'know, and then the warden turns around and says, 'Now Bill, I can't find so-and-so: I'm just goin' over to the other building.' So he left me in the ward, with prisoners walkin' up and down the aisle. The first one who came up to me and said, 'You got a cigarette?' I gave him the whole pack. That warden left me about thirty minutes. I often wondered what would have happened to me if he'd had a wreck and got killed. I'd be: 'I don't belong here: let me out!', and they'd be 'Yeah, we heard that one before.' That was terrifying."

All the same, Bill went out there often.

"We used their medical facilities. We didn't have a doctor when I worked at training school. Anytime a boy got sick we would send him out there. Plus I had teams, table tennis, basketball—many teams—and we would play each other. Usually they were the staff, not the residents. They would get up a team and we'd play each other, so I had been out there a lot."

I thanked Bill for his information and went for something to eat—and a man by the splendid name of Wayne Hammock told me he remembered the basketball out there, from when he was a ten- or eleven-year-

316

old boy in 1958 or '59. He said they had a basketball court out there and there was a black patient called Archie who used to throw the ball up, let it fall on his head from a great height, and laugh like a drain. Everyone else laughed too. He asked did I know that he lives in the best place in the world, although it used to be a whole lot better back in 1959? He strongly contested Bill Williamson's idea that there would have been more black patients than white: he was very definite on the point. It reminded me that I should always seek more than one witness.

I went out to see what is now called the Central State Hospital. In 1837 the legislature appropriated the vast sum of $20,000 for a dormitory near Milledgeville—yes indeed, the vast institution it became, and where Willie McTell drew his last breath, was built not *in* Milledgeville but safely outside it, at the village of Hardwick. Here the state's mentally ill could receive custodial care. A four-storey building was opened in 1842 and, with later additions, became known as the Center Building. Originally serving only pauper patients, its services were soon extended to all bona fide mad citizens.

And there it is still, the old Center Building, looking like a Southern White House, with fountains in the middle of the drive and big old pecans and magnolia trees, seventy to a hundred years old, on the lawns. This now houses the administrators.

Beyond is a great sprawl of buildings of all sizes and many eras, some small and shabby, some big old four-storey brick ward buildings; it wasn't always clear if they were still in use. Everywhere the internal roads split off into different little feeder roads, past acres of grass, well maintained. In the afternoon sun the whole place looked enormous and orderly and as un-sinister as anything institutional can.

I drove past the old train depot building where supplies used to roll in and people's bodies used to roll out again, unless they were buried on site, which many were. I parked by the fountains, where the moderate grandeur of the building loomed over me. The person I was told I wanted no longer worked in the Release Information Dept. in the basement, and the woman on the foyer desk down there had already phoned in vain for two different alternative people who could help me.

We decided between us that it was five o'clock and I would have to come back tomorrow.

Up on the ground floor again, in the big dark-wood lobby with its sofas and chairs and lavish, formal flower arrangements, I had a frisson of panic. There was no one around, and a big notice by the heavy, dark front doors declared that they'd be locked from 5pm till 8am. Luckily it wasn't true.

Outside, as I took photographs, a quiet young student type I had noticed pushing a trolley of files around earlier on came up and chatted. She said she used to play on the lawns once a week as a small child on her lunch break while attending some special class for Gifted Children. She said this wryly, but she said it. Perhaps everyone here feels a need to explain that they are not a patient. (And, of course, I had wondered.)

Next morning I asked for Information Release and Sara Greene agreed to meet me in the lobby. While I waited in its large mahogany spaces, I looked at the small display cabinet on one side wall, in which artefacts of the hospital's past were on view. They were mostly photos of old dignitaries, but it showed me that they used to publish a little magazine, *The Bulletin* (monthly). I don't suppose anyone read it aloud to Willie in August 1959, but I wanted to look at the latest issue of the time.

Sara Greene arrived to deal with me, a kindly if routinely suspicious middle-aged woman with gray eyes and wispy hair, wearing a raspberry-pink sweater with a neutral jacket and skirt. We shook hands, and she stood in wonderment, as some Americans do, at the very notion that Abroad existed, and that I was a proof of it, and had come all the way from so mysterious a part of the globe. In the solemn hush of the lobby, I told her what I wanted, which was, essentially, the medical records for the week Willie spent here in the hospital—the last week of his life.

I told her he hadn't been a mental patient, he'd simply had a (second) stroke, and that Milledgeville had been the only place that would take him in free, it being 1959 and him a black man. She marveled at my knowing all this about her neck of the woods, and wrote down a detail or two.

"You can't have them," she said. "I can't give you them if you're not a direct relative. They're less than seventy-five years old."

I had anticipated some such obstacle.

"In any case," she added, with some hestitation, "I think that's the period where we have no records. There's a period around then—I think it's 1955–62, something like that—they got destroyed."

I hadn't anticipated that.

"But, anyway, you can't have them." She looked me in the eye, and then suddenly added: "Unless you get a Court Order."

I was thrilled, intrigued.

"And can I get one, d'you mean?"

"I really can't say." She paused. "But, if I were you, I'd go back into Milledgeville and go see Superior Court Judge Hulane George down at the courthouse. She might give you one. And her secretary's name is Jennifer."

I thanked her warmly. But what about the very possible non-existence of any such records for 1959? Could she check first to see whether they existed? There'd be no point trying for a Court Order if there was no information it could order her to divulge.

She conceded this and went off to see what she could find out. When she returned it was to say that, *if* she was reading the system aright, it was only the Discharges records that had disappeared. Thrown away in error. And, since Willie died in the hospital, he wasn't discharged, and his records might well be on file—but not at the hospital itself: they're all at State Records in Atlanta. But, if I could get my Court Order and pass it on to her, she would forward it with the Information Release Request to Atlanta and they would mail the records back to her. She could then supply them, by mail or in person, to me.

I thanked her again and drove back to Milledgeville, this time parking my car in the courthouse lot. After all, I was here on business now.

The top floor was clearly the right place for Superior Court Judges. There was the Superior Court itself, and a Media Room, and rooms in which clients and lawyers could confer, but I looked in vain for a label reading Judge Hulane George. The whole place seemed empty until a woman with strawberry blonde hair and a flowery dress came out of one door and moved away from me towards another. This was Jennifer.

She took me into her office, I explained myself, and she eyed me circumspectly. She told me Judge George was not in the office at this time, that she might or might not be in later on, and that, if she did come in, she might or might not have time to consider my request and make a ruling.

"Anyway," she said, "you have to start by swearing an affidavit. I can do that with you now." She pulled the affidavit template onto her computer screen and began asking me questions and typing in my answers.

This was so bizarrely instant, compared to the protracted equivalent in England. I had turned up the day before, paid $10 and been given a death certificate on the spot; now I was getting an instant affidavit created and sworn, with no hanging around in lawyers' offices—and this as the preliminary to acquiring an almost immediate Court Order. I hoped.

I had to swear that I was who I said I was. This was a bit like the Visa Waiver application form you fill in on the flight over to the States, on which they ask solemnly, "Do you plan to engage in any terrorist activity while in the US?"

I swore that Willie had no surviving direct relatives.

"So far as you know," said Jennifer pointedly, giving me a firm look.

"That's a good idea," I said, "Yes, please put that in."

She typed it in.

"I have actually spent some time," I said, "checking into whether he does have surviving relatives."

"That's a good idea," she said, "I'll put that in." And she did. (It would be another couple of years before I found that Robert Owens had surviving children, half-nieces and -nephews to Willie.) I added that McTell had been interviewed for the Library of Congress in 1940 and was Georgia's pre-eminent blues artist.

When we'd finished, I asked if Jennifer thought the judge would grant the order. "Why don't you phone me at 4 p.m.?"

At three o'clock I was passing the building anyway, so I went back up. Jennifer was there; Judge George wasn't.

"Oh hi," she said, in a ruthlessly neutral tone: and started walking away from me across the room, so that she had her back to me as we walked along, which made me feel doomed. At best, I thought, the judge hasn't been in.

"Judge George has been in," said Jennifer. "I showed her your affidavit." She paused. "And she said she had heard of him, your blues guy."

"Yes?"

She turned round to look at me.

"And she's given you your order."

I lit up, then breathed out a long, ruminative sigh. I was so *grateful*. Jennifer was amused by how much I cared. She probably savored the novelty of seeing an Englishman show some emotion.

From the gray corridor downstairs I used a payphone to ring Sara Greene.

"Oh hello," she said in her kindly voice.

"I've got it!" I said. "And thank you so much for your help!"

She asked if I wanted to mail it to her or drive out there. Then she surprised me again.

"Since your visit," she said, diffidently, "I've looked him up here and I've found a card filled in by the doctor when he died."

It takes about twenty minutes to drive out on North Wayne to the hospital. Sara Greene came to meet me again in the lobby, and, before I'd even produced the Court Order, she showed me photocopies she had made of two dark gray, discolored-looking medical cards about six inches by four, with rounded corners, comprising printed boxes for sub-divided information. One was a slightly expanded version of the other and demanded Name, County, Hospital No., Nativity, Age, Sex, Race, Civil Condition, Duration, Diagnosis, Admitted, Furloughed, Discharged, Died, Cause of Death, Name of Guardian or Relative, and Ward.

The answers had been typed in. The old typewriter's lettering danced in front of my eyes, but I could see that I was being given about five completely "new" pieces of information about Willie's last days and death. Among them was the fact that he had died in the Ingram Building: this was newly specific stuff.

I handed over the Court Order and she said she'd send it right off to Atlanta. We parted amiably. Afterwards I thought many times of how trusting she had been to give me the photocopies before she'd seen the Order, simply because I'd said I had it. She had obviously become interested in McTell's case, too, or she would not have gone looking for these bits of information in the meantime.

The Hospital's museum offered a truly excellent level of statistical detail on the history of the place, making possible a very specific reconstruction of how it was when Willie was a patient, as well as painting the general backdrop. LaShunda Dennis, the very young PR woman, walked me over there in the broiling heat, her thin bare arms giving off no hint of perspiration as I sweated away like a tractor. We crossed the lawns to the big hall where they hold dances and concerts for the patients. She wanted to find the caretaker, to see if his memory went back far enough, but, of course, being a caretaker, he wasn't around. The inside of the hall, 1950s concrete, was like a huge skating rink without the ice. We moved on to the little building that was once the train depot, and now houses the museum.

She let me in and she let me wander, and I did. It was unremarkable: no ghoulish mementoes. Even the exhibition of old equipment, beds, surgical knives and rubber tubing merely looked like those in any current British hospital. I could get no sense here of all the pain and wretchedness, injustice and terror that must have been part of the history on display.

The first admission of black patients was after the Civil War. This is a hospital which, in American terms, goes back a long way. The Powell Building dates from the 1850s, and used to have a lavish greenhouse, almost on the scale of Kew Gardens, near the depot. The Holly Building had been erected 1949–50 specifically to house Colored Patients.

There were many telling statistics. The earnings of Attendants in 1891 made very clear the different strata of society. All received full board, plus monthly pay as follows: White Males, $25; White Females, $16.65; Colored Males, $12.50; Colored Females, $10.

LaShunda foraged on my behalf too. She found me Annual Report no. 117, the very issue I needed to see, covering July 1959 to June 1960. It bulged with detail about what was going on around Willie in the hospital. He was one of only eight black male patients and eleven black females who died of Cerebral Hemorrage in the period, out of a total of 273 black patients who died. The largest number died from arteriosclerosis, followed by acute myocarditis. The Jones Operating Room had performed 410 major operations and 520 minor. They applied 365 casts and treated 196 minor lacerations. Electric shock treatment had been given to only ten patients; of these, two had "improved" after it.

And Wayne Hammock had been right: there were far more white patients than black. The total admissions for the year were: White Male, 1,538; White Female, 1,248; Black Male, 487; Black Female, 499 (grand total, 3772).

The list of Classified Occupations of all patients did not include Musician; Willie was either one of the forty-two black male admissions whose occupation was Not Given, or one of the fifty-seven who had none.

Ms Dennis also found me the newspaper cuttings file for 1959. This was not flattering. The Atlanta *Constitution* for 27 August, exactly a week after Willie's body left the hospital, quoted the Executive Director of the Georgia Association for Mental Health as saying that Milledgeville was "large, unmanageable ... completely outmoded and obsolete." He proposed its abolition and replacement by nine regional mental health centers. Another paper's reporter was more shocked by what he'd seen inside.

Since his report was too long for me to copy out on the spot, I asked LaShunda if she could photocopy it for me—expecting, as I stood trying to sound casual about it, that an alarm bell would surely now ring: that even someone new to PR would register that giving out newspaper reports headed something like SHOCKING TRUTH BEHIND MILL-EDGEVILLE ASYLUM BARS was not quite part of her brief. However, all credit to her, she clearly took the view that she was helping me in a worthwhile project and that a stance of having nothing to hide in 2001 was better than getting coy about the bad old days of fifty years ago.

It had been such a good day. All I needed now was to drive round to the Ingram Building, where Willie had spent his final days, and take its photograph. As I drew near it, I saw that the twelve-foot tall chain-link fences surrounding it were swathed all along the top with dazzlingly bright silver loops of razor wire: miles of it in loops the size of dinner-plates. It was hard to see the three-storey brick building inside. I could just make out the heavy plainness of the brick, colored like cheap liver pâté and gashed by rows of narrow, tall windows.

There was a tall, chain-link gate wide enough for one person at a time to pass through, in the front of the fence, with several locks. Beyond it a chain-link and razor-wire corridor pushed towards the front wall of the building. A small wooden noticeboard read "Frank Scott State Prison."

There was no one around. I sat in the car making notes, and was just considering whether it would still be OK to take photos, and how hard it would be with the sunlight bouncing off all this wire and mesh, when a purple and white Georgia Dept. of Correction Perimeter Security Service patrol car pulled up. A sturdy, pleasant-faced woman of about thirty leaned out.

"Pardon me, sir—can I help you?"

"Thank you. Am I allowed to photograph this building?"

"No sir. No photography. You'd have to ask permission at the gatehouse."

"Where is the gatehouse?"

She pointed further off down the bleak road. "It's that white building there on the right. I'm gonna radio you in."

"OK, but I'll be a minute." I had notes to catch up on.

"No problem," she said, and her car moved forward slowly and quietly, like a placid shark, and I got back to my notebook. I was still squinting up at the windows behind which Willie McTell had died, when she re-presented herself.

"You taken some photographs?"

"Not at all. I've been making notes."

"Uh huh: would you follow me now please?"

I followed her car and, after a hundred yards, we turned into a parking lot inside high fencing. I was accompanied to a very small white gatehouse, like the entrance to an old-fashioned seaside pier.

Beyond its bare concrete floor and white painted brick walls was a twirling metal gate, the sort of turnstile you find in a zoo, its horizontal arms slicing between stationary ones so that no one unauthorised can pass.

Three men in pale blue, immaculately ironed uniforms came through

324

this from some inner courtyard beyond which more of the prison lurked. Summoned by walkie-talkie, they filed in primed to look me up and down and deal with me. The senior officer was bulky, his face squashy. He smiled unpleasantly and spoke in an insinuating, faintly mocking tone.

"What's your name, sir?"

I told him.

"What's your purpose here today?"

I said I was looking at the State Hospital because I was writing the biography of the Georgia blues singer Blind Willie McTell, and I had just found out from the hospital records that he had died in the Ingram Building over there where I'd been parked.

"He died here in August 1959."

From the world of my successful day, with a court order in my pocket and the hospital's co-operative interest behind me, somehow I had stumbled through a hole in the dazzling air into the brute world of a state prison's security system, straining at the leash and fingering its weapons. It was a small taste of how every black American had stood in relation to white power all through Willie McTell's lifetime.

The senior officer and one of the others stared with blank eyes. Their policy was never to believe someone brought in from the outside. They heard the defensive tone they had themselves induced, and let the truth of the story bounce off them. The third, looking nervous, took in what I'd said and murmured, as if he knew he shouldn't show human interest: "Really?! Blind Willie died here?" He was shyly thrilled.

"Yes," I said, taking this cue and addressing them all. "He was here a week, in the Ingram Building"—you could just see it through the window—"so I drove along from Hospital Administration, to see if I could get a picture of the building he died in—for the book."

The one who'd been interested let his face close down now, and looked away, leaving me to his superior officer and silent sidekick.

"You bin takin' photographs?"

"No. I haven't. But I didn't know the Ingram was part of the prison till I stopped outside it. It used to be part of the Hospital. It was for black patients."

The dead-eyed stare.

"So I asked the perimeter guard if I was allowed to take pictures and she said come down here and ask permission."

"You can only get permission from the warden. He's not here right now: you'd have to write to him."

"Ah. But I'm visiting, from England. I'm only in Milledgeville till tomorrow."

On a whim, he softened, momentarily. "Just a minute," he said, and went back through the turnstile. A few yards away I could see him talking to another large figure in pale blue. He came back.

"Sir, you can't have permission. We're going to ask you to leave now, but the warden will meet you in the parking lot."

They escorted me back towards my car in the burning sunlight. Suddenly there were three more uniforms, surrounding a pacing figure in civilian clothes. He was in his fifties, with a weatherbeaten, tough face, mean as hell and relishing the caprice of his authority. He wore a Texan hat, brown jacket, charcoal trousers and big boots, and strode around, confident his "boys" would follow, in formation, nervously loyal to the unchecked powers he exercised.

He stepped up and guffawed at me under his hat, which kept his face always in shade. His eyes were hard blue. He looked like a cowboy film cattle boss, openly corrupt and enjoying it.

"You cain't take photographs here. What's your name?" And he made me dance the whole dance over again. By the time I'd finished, two police cars had arrived, placing themselves quietly between me and the parking-lot exit behind the warden.

"I'm sure these gentlemen will take care of you," he grinned, striding away, closed off by his posse. Two police officers ambled over. I was a suspect now. The prison authorities had handed me over to the cops and now I was theirs.

"Move away from the car please sir, and give me the keys." Moving forward meant stepping up close to him. "Let me see your driver's license and insurance."

I handed them my British driving license, which did not have photo ID. It was exotic and suspicious. They unfolded it, turned it this way and that, and passed it back and forth between them.

They needed photo ID. I produced my passport. They riffled through pages with Arabic stamps.

"OK, now tell me what it is you're doing here, sir."

They ask questions not to hear the answers or understand the situation but to watch you squirm through the interrogation. The sun was ferocious. I was drenched in sweat. I felt smelly.

They handed me back my documents. The cop knew I was wondering if he'd finished with me. He stepped closer, hands on his belt, with his badge and bits of uniform glinting in the sun.

"You know this is State Prison property."

"Yes, I do now, but as I explained, I didn't know that when I drove down the road. This used to be part of the hospital."

"Uh huh." Almost as an afterthought he asked: "Have you been drinking?"

"Drinking? No!" I said, immediately remembering that over lunch I'd been sitting downtown having a Killian's Red.

"Well," I added, like George Washington, "I had one beer several hours ago."

"You had a beer?!" he said, as if I'd confessed to a significant crime.

"Yes. One beer."

"You shouldn't be driving. Don't you know we have a no-tolerance of alcohol policy here in the state of Georgia?"

This was bizarre news to me, since where there are any bars at all, pick-up trucks are always parked in clusters outside them.

"You say one beer?"

"Yes."

He pointed to the painted line marking off a parking space.

"Can you walk straight?"

"Can I *walk* straight? Of course I can!", I said, trying to get him to recognise his over-reaction. Futile, of course.

"Go ahead."

I walked the line, turned, walked back. It was obvious I'd done this with absolute sobriety. He scowled at me long and hard, and said, "OK, sir, you can go. Get into your car and leave this area. And drive carefully." He got back in his car.

Sweat pouring off me, I searched my pockets and failed to find the keys. I looked around the floor and felt under the seats. I looked in my bag. The cop sat with his motor running, waiting to watch me leave. Suddenly he used his loudhailer, so that his voice was very loud, mechanised and bizarre:

"I want you to hurry up and leave right now, sir."

I walked back over to him to tell him I couldn't find the keys, though he already knew this from watching me.

"Uh huh," he said, "I suggest you hurry up, sir. I mean it. If you can't leave right away, I'm gonna have to take you away myself."

"Oh, come on!"

"Sir, one more minute and I'm gonna have to remove you from this area."

"I'm trying to leave. I don't understand where I can have put the keys. I'll look again."

I went back to the car, rummaging unhappily through my pockets and then crouching down to feel under the driver's seat again.

He walked up behind me and said sharply, "Sir! Are these yours?"— and handed me my keys. They'd been in his pocket all along.

I started the car, backed it out and drove off the way I'd come. The road had a 20mph speed limit, which is almost impossible to achieve and feels crazy when you're being followed. We crept along in this artificial way and I felt some relief at being off prison terrain and back in the grounds of a mental hospital.

I was still moving slowly away when he set his light flashing. Jeez! Now what? I stopped and he came over to the window.

"Let me see that photo ID again please sir. I forgot to phone in some details."

He radioed them in to HQ, machine held tight against his mouth, and, speaking for my benefit, added: "He has been escorted off the property and advised not to return."

He handed back my passport.

"OK sir. Let me see you leave altogether now." He followed me all the way to beyond the last sideroad down which I might have been planning to double back into the hospital grounds, and then disappeared.

I kept on going till I was back downtown. I certainly needed a drink after that.

That shocked 1959 reporter had spent two days inside the hospital, on a visit alongside forty-one members of the Georgia State legislature. What they saw was "almost unbelievable." As they walked through one building, Lt Governor Garland Byrd "turned to me and remarked, 'This is as bad as those at Germany's notorious Dachau prison camp during World War II.'"

The Lt Governor made this comparison Monday during the first tour of the Dupree Building, a three storey frame structure housing some 550 Negroes . . . Mrs Byrd, who accompanied her husband, wept freely as she watched the pitiful sight of the patients sitting on the floor . . . The nurse conducting the tour through the ward told me that 112 women were on the ward, and that one bathtub services them all, as well as only two commodes to care for the entire group . . .

In the 10th ward, an old dilapidated one storey wood building, which was labeled fire trap, housed a group of elderly men, who had no other recreation than to just sit and hold their hands all day. "How is the food here," I asked one patient. His reply was, "You wouldn't eat it." Walking through one of the buildings, a representative noticed the foul smell of urine soaked floors and said: "I don't see how they stand to sleep here."

In Ward 4 and then Ward 2 of the Ingram Building, Willie was spared all this by being, it would seem, unconscious much of the time. He seems to have been conscious when he arrived—his admission record notes that he was "quiet"—and it's possible he had periods of wakefulness, even as late as the day before he died, but, for the majority of the time, he was apparently no longer aware of his surroundings.

But in any case there is also a striking contrast between the descriptions of neglect, lack of recreational facilities, and general unwashed abandonment, and the very close medical attention that Willie clearly received.

The medical notes obtained from Atlanta show that his condition was monitored constantly, and in great detail. There was no question of his just lying there, conscious or otherwise, unattended. On admission, he was given a "partial physical" examination by a doctor, whose report was typed up that day, and his temperature, pulse, and respiration were measured. Relevant aspects of his "blood chemistry" were measured at least once daily, and the results logged. A sheet of doctor's orders included putting him on a salt-free diet, fitting a catheter, and prescribing tablets on the day of his admission, and making changes in his medication two days later.

A serological report was typed up and he was given a Wasserman Test the day after he arrived, and, by the next day, his chest X-ray had been developed, analysed, and written up. The day before he died, the "lab girl" was told to check things every four hours (though she seems to have skipped two of these). His breathing, pulse, and temperature were measured and logged twice daily throughout the week; his medicine, quite rightly, was specified item by item, daily.

His severe deterioration on 18 August was noted promptly—the medical note "get stat blood sugar" implies that they were worried he was going into a diabetic coma—and they put him on a drip twelve hours before he died. Presumably to cover themselves, a letter dated 18 August was sent from the Director and the Clinical Director to Gold Harris, saying, "This is to advise you that the above named patient is being treated on the ward for acutely ill patients and . . . We regard his condition as potentially critical and such that he is likely to make a sudden change for the worse and the end come abruptly."

Willie died at 4.25 next morning, Wednesday, 19 August. It was the same day of the year as the death of his white great-grandfather over half a century earlier. The death certificate gave the cause of death as cerebral hemorrhage. The hospital's more detailed notes were that Dr M.E. Smith "offered a diagnosis in this case, of: CBS (Cerebral Brain Syndrome), associated with circulatory disturbance, other, cerebral hemorrhage, left side, with psychotic reaction."

Today, the diabetes would be better managed, and we would term it

Cerebral Vascular Accident rather than CBS. The hemorrhage was on the left side of his brain, so that it was the right side of his body that was impaired. He might well have had cerebral vascular disease for some time, and the earlier stroke may have been part of that: clearly from the medical evidence here, something had happened around nine months previously —that is, at the time of Coot's and Helen's deaths—that propelled him into much greater illness. By the time he arrived at the hospital, the nerve endings in his leg were impaired by blood not reaching them properly.

There was one more significant fact in the medical records. The Wasserman Test result showed that Willie had syphilis. His "very small eyeballs" and their "opacity" therefore suggests that there may have been—may have been—congenital syphilis. This, passed through the placenta from the mother, can reveal itself in many other physical abnormalities, which Willie did not have (commonly, an odd bridge to the nose), but congenital syphilis could certainly account for underdeveloped eyeballs and, perhaps, their congenital cataracts. And it would have been perfectly possible, even had Minnie still been suffering from syphilis herself when pregnant again with Robert, for him to have been born free of infection.

So it might be that this information from the very end of Willie's life tells us something about its very beginning.

Gold Harris collected his old friend's body from Milledgeville State Hospital the next day, Thursday, 20 August 1959. Willie was put onto the p.m. train at the Central Supply Warehouse depot for one last train ride, back to Warrenton. From the station here, Willie was taken to Haynes Funeral Home to be embalmed.

This funeral home still exists. The black side of the tracks in Warrenton is strongly reminiscent of the West Indies, and the Haynes Funeral Home sustains this picture. It's a pretty little building, old but cleanly painted, with an unusually venerable clock outside above the canopy where they back the hearse up to the door. On the verandah are several doors, one marked "Chapel", one "Office", and a third signed "If Office Closed Call At House Next Door."

Next door is a more modern small bungalow, brightly painted and with a pretty, neat front garden: short stubby grass and an old white plaster birdbath with two white plaster rabbits grazing its edge, jaunty hanging-basket plants hung in a fringe along the top of the verandah, and lovely tall canna lilies guarding the corners. The path and steps up to the door are lined with that bright green artificial grass you sometimes see in strips around the poolside in hotels. Two tiny wrought-iron chairs and a two-seater bench sit on the verandah—whereas, on the more solid porch of the funeral home, a few beautifully 1950s chairs are ranged against the wall, as if for pleasure-lounging on a cruise ship.

When Willie was embalmed here, Haynes was owned by the current Mrs Haynes' husband, while he and his brother co-owned the Haynes & Peterson Funeral Home in Augusta. Mrs Williette Elizabeth Haynes (everyone calls her Elizabeth) has been here only since 1962 and can find no paperwork from earlier. Nor does she know when the business started; her father-in-law, Girard L. Haynes, who founded it, was granted his Georgia State Board of Embalming license in January 1930 (the certificate is on the wall), but there's an old lady, now ninety, who told Mrs Haynes she could remember, as a seven-year-old child in the schoolyard opposite, watching bodies being carried in and out. Girard Haynes died at seventy-three in April 1961, and he was running the business right through till he needed its services himself.

Mrs Haynes' house was built in 1963 after an old one was pulled down—"I wanted to pull it down before it fell down," she said—and gained her own Georgia State Board of Funeral Services Certificate in July 1968.

That schoolyard is long gone, and so is the blacksmith's shop out the back where they made the headstones as well as shoeing mules and horses. The funeral parlor itself used to be next door to where it is now, but that was before the 1940s.

Mrs Haynes showed me into the office, which is tiny, and sweetly reassuring in its old-fashioned undesignedness. It has a green carpet, little khaki rugs, a cane rocker, an ashtray stand, and an old TV holding up some flowers on a table behind the door. Certificates and photographs crowd the mock-wood walls, an old doctor's desk sits in one corner with an interview chair alongside, and a three-seater cane-backed sofa takes up the far corner.

We talked as Mrs Haynes rummaged in vain for paperwork from 1959, and then she showed me through to the little chapel-cum-viewing room off to the left of the office, and the embalming room, and a newer room added on to the right where new coffins are stored waiting to be chosen. In Willie's time, all but the rich bought cloth caskets. I inspected a "cloth" one of today, which felt as if it were made of sculpted papier-mâché with a covering of thin felted material in muted duck-egg blue. This is still the cheap option, but makes no concession to simplicity: its lines are grandiose and florid, and it sports heavy-duty metal handles, as if designed by Cadillac.

The little chapel stays dark and hushed, the windows covered in thick plush red curtains, curiously rolled over like a doorstep sausage across the top. There are rows of chairs, not all a match, perhaps seven to a row; a moveable red-curtained screen at the front with a cream central section on which Jesus stands nailed to a brass cross; an old standard lamp in each opposite corner; and an old gas fire on one wall.

Behind a screen is the door to the very small embalming room, with a warning notice about formaldehyde. Inside here a high metal table on wheels has replaced the wooden one on which Willie would have been laid out. There is one small basin and much rubber tubing.

Back in the office, Mrs Haynes found a photograph from the 1940s, with the hearse, her father-in-law, and his two assistants, Lamar Cody and Robert Thomas, stood in front of the current building, the clock above them. The car was the home's newly acquired Buick Super 8, which has a straight-8 engine—which means that its eight cylinders are all in one long line, demanding a monstrously lengthy hood (or bonnet, as we English say)—and it was probably made between 1947 and '49. This huge, solid vehicle would have given Willie his last earthly ride.

Mrs Haynes, a warm and good-humored old lady, generously offered me the loan of this vintage photograph and I promised to bring it back with a larger, laser-print photocopy. Next morning I found her strimming in the garden, with a wonderful '50s tropical sun hat on, quietly pleased to have her photograph back and saying she would put the laser copy on her office wall. I headed out for Thomson again, where Willie was taken for his funeral and burial at Jones Grove Baptist Church.

According to Kate, Willie's funeral was on a Sunday morning, which would make it 22 August 1959. But since she tells many contradictory lies about these events, it's hard to trust even that small detail. It's very clear, though, that she was determined to rain on Willie's last parade. It's a shame these squabbles have to be logged at all.

She hadn't lived with Willie McTell for almost twenty years, yet she tells the Evanses that "instead of them getting in touch with me, and they knew I was nursing at Fort Gordon, they just rushed him on to Mill-edgeville without my consent," and that she only found out about the funeral at the last minute because, when Robert arrived, he said, "There ain't gonna be no funeral then unless she's here." Then she says that when she got there on the Sunday morning, she reached the church to find "no preacher—no obituary—no nothing. It was just a mess." She says she had to get the preacher.

It is true, as we know, that somehow the gravestone supplied to the Happy Valley family turned out to bear the wrong name—though this would have been much less of a big deal in such a community back then than for those of us for whom the written word is entwined in our DNA—but the idea is risible that no one but Kate could organise anything for Willie, and that the others wouldn't have bothered, or that their hearts weren't in it.

Kate admitted in a follow-up Evans interview that she hadn't even known Willie wasn't still living in Atlanta. She seemed to think this was someone else's fault, not hers. Yet interviewed later by Vinnie Williams for the *Augusta Chronicle*, Kate had changed her story. Willie was still in Atlanta, and still singing when he died: "That was in 1959 . . . I brought him home and buried him in Happy Valley, at Jones Grove Cemetery. His grave is marked Edd McTier but it is Blind Willie McTell. The family sometimes spelled the name McTier. Only I put the slab on it."

Indeed. I asked Sally Cramer about this. Did she think Kate was only told about the funeral at the last minute, if she was, because his relatives around Happy Valley weren't keen on her?

"There's a possibility," said Sally, "that she wasn't keen on them."

When Robert was interviewed, he said he had only met Kate once. He spoke of being notified by Eddie when Willie first had a stroke, and he no more thought of notifying Kate then than Eddie did. And when he talked about coming to Willie's funeral, he neither mentioned her name nor made any complaint about the arrangements.

Willie was laid to rest in a tranquil, pleasant spot close to where he was born. He was only fifty-six years old but he had packed plenty in and left behind a rare combination: a large number of friends and relations who had loved, valued and admired him, and an enduring body of work for us all.

# EIGHTEEN

A FTER WILLIE'S BURIAL, Robert Owens returned to New Jersey. In Happy Valley shortly afterwards, the building holding all Willie's possessions burnt down. According to David Evans,

> Kate had been offered Willie's guitars at the time but didn't want to pick them up then. She was upset because Willie had wanted his twelve-string guitar buried with him and this wish was overlooked . . . Willie had left three guitars when he died, the twelve-string, a six-string, and an electric guitar with an amplifier. His brother-in-law, Clarence McGahe[e], took the twelve-string, but his grandchildren tore it up ... and the pieces were thrown away. Another cousin of Willie's named George Harris got the six-string, but Harris died a few years ago, and the whereabouts of the guitar are now unknown. No one seems to know what happened to the electric guitar.

He added that Gold Harris had retained Willie's metal tipped cane.

Ola Ivey still has that cane of Willie's, passed down to her from Gold, and she keeps it by her bed—but she says it is an ordinary walking cane.

She also reports that Gold used to own one of Willie's guitars, and kept it out at his house on the borders of Warren and Glascock, but that, when he tried to find it after Willie's death, it had disappeared. Aside from Willie's pew from Jones Grove Baptist Church, now owned by Cora Mae Bryant, that's about all we know of what became of Willie's physical possessions.

As noted right at the start of the story, Samuel B. Charters' book *The Country Blues* was published less than three months after Willie's death, and 'Statesboro Blues' issued on the accompanying album. It was seized upon by the folk revival movement and his work began to be re-issued on the relatively new and handily less breakable format of the vinyl LP. Had he lived and been in adequate health, he would certainly have been among those with a new career on the coffee-house circuit. Playing to gatherings of keen white people would not have been a problem for him at all.

Ralph S. Peer died in Los Angeles five months to the day after Willie, and Ruby Lomax the following December. In March 1962, the singer Willie had accompanied on record back in 1931, Ruth (Mary) Willis, died in Atlanta, aged sixty-four.

Six months later, on 20 September 1962, Curley James Weaver died at Almon, Covington, back in Newton County where he had started out. He, too, was only fifty-six.

Curley died just as the political mainstream of the United States was starting to face the need for desegregation, and though it was a long time coming down in the South, some of those who had been contemporaries of Willie and Curley lived to see changes for the better, while some of those who had been musicians also lived to find themselves "rediscovered."

Buddy Moss, in a disappointingly modest way, was one of these, and he became one of the very few drawn into active participation in the Civil Rights Movement. Buddy had sloped around doing odd jobs through much of the 1950s and beyond—he worked on a tobacco farm, as an elevator man, and as a truck driver, among other things—and, in 1964, went backstage to see his old musical partner, Josh White, who was giving a concert at Emory University. The folk-blues enthusiasts around White thus "rediscovered" Buddy Moss. By this point he had remarried, to a large and lovely woman called Dot.

Eleanor Walden (then Mrs Bill Hoffman) was among those young white Georgia residents who were active in the Civil Rights Movement, and drew Moss in. "We started out just knowing him. We were involved in the folk movement and we had parties. His wife was wonderful: just a dear person. She was a large southern lady with a light soprano voice, and when they sang together, the heavens rejoiced."

Buddy appreciated her too. Eleanor remembers him saying once: "If I was out all night and came stumbling in the morning, that woman would say 'Are you hungry? What can I fix you to eat?'"

Dot must have been aware that this was rare forbearance, for Eleanor also recalls: "One night when Bill had left me home alone with the kids once too often and gone to a party at Bud Foote's house with Buddy and Dot I had seriously had enough: I walked over to the house, proceeded to take a coffee mug and smash it on Bill's head. And I remember Dot saying, 'Are you sure your wife is white?'!"

It was still dangerous then, mixing black and white: "One time Buddy and Dot and a blind cousin were stopped leaving our house—we lived in Clarkston, a segregated town just outside Atlanta—and they were taken to jail. Black people driving down this little road at night were targets."

What she remembers of Buddy is "his wonderful playing and his humor, and he had the *most* patience teaching young white musicians. Buddy was big: he was a large person, but I was around him a great deal and I saw his gentle side. He was somebody who shared his talent."

He also gave his time to the cause. Eleanor's father had been a Wobblies organiser ("He was one of the men who brought Joe Hill's body back from Utah to Chicago in 1915; my lullabies were the songs from the Wobblies' *Little Red Songbook*") and she had met Pete Seeger and others in Washington Square Park in Greenwich Village in the late '40s. In Atlanta she was inevitably involved in the Civil Rights struggle. She helped organise the Atlanta Folk Music Society and a festival that brought in Greenwich Village figures like Pete LaFarge and Len Chandler—and Buddy Moss too.

"He didn't involve himself in the politics, and he had been around the

338

block a few times—he'd seen things come and go, but he was extremely cordial and he never put himself outside what we were trying to do. He was there, he was present, he was as involved as he could be, with his music, and in integrated performances, which was dangerous for him. We didn't realise how, at the time."

Bill Hoffman remembers Buddy a little differently: "Buddy was a complex man. There was a lot, a *lot*, of burning resentment underneath. He knew what had been done to him. He also had great trepidation about getting involved with us. And when the record John Hammond made with him wasn't released, he said, 'Same old same old.' And he could fly off the handle. Buddy could be a dangerous person. But he was very gentle with our children."

It was not the gentle side of him that the British blues researcher Bruce Bastin and the American Peter B. Lowry encountered in the 1970s. They were on their third blues-adventure trip together, spending a good deal of time in Georgia and the Carolinas, researching the blues, meeting musicians, recording them, and living quite dangerously at times. Bastin would eventually synthesise these researches and more into his large book *Red River Blues*, first published in 1986. But it was a copy of Bastin's small, earlier book *Crying for the Carolines* that he and Peter B. Lowry took round to Buddy Moss' house to show him.

Bill Hoffman told me that "if people mentioned his time in jail, he denied it; he never mentioned that"—and he certainly didn't like reading about it in Bastin's book, even though Lowry and Moss knew each other well by this point: they had first met when Moss played a set at a New York City club in the summer of 1969, and not long afterwards Lowry had visited Buddy's Atlanta home.

Now he was there again, with Bastin:

Buddy was half pissed. He spent a lot of time drinking. And he was upset by what Bruce had written, even though Bruce I don't think had written very much in his book, and he went into one of his tirades. He went on about how the so-called white man liked to talk about the poor downtrodden black man, and I was fed to my teeth and I said "Look, Buddy, I took enough shit from the cracker this morning" [the

Newton County police had almost jailed these outsiders for "consorting with Negroes" earlier in the day] and I said "I don't have to listen to any more," and I got up and left. And apparently Buddy then went to his dresser and got out his pistol and started after me. And his wife, who outweighed him by a factor of about three, managed to get in the way, and Bruce managed to get the offending book and got out and into the van and said, "Drive! Now!" So off we went.

Buddy Moss survived until 1984: long enough to read about himself all over again in a text by Bruce Bastin, and to listen to himself too, when an institution called the John Edwards Memorial Foundation (the JEMF) issued its compilation of previously unreleased recordings from 1933 by Willie McTell, Curley Weaver, and Moss, in 1979. According to Curley's daughter, Buddy didn't have a record player and went round to see her with it, saying "Cora Mae, play that doggone thing, let me see how it sounds."

It sounded terrific, and, even though it was now twenty years since Willie's death, this LP's very substantial accompanying booklet was the first major attempt to tell his story. And because it was first, and came from respected academic David Evans, it became the formative official version of the Blind Willie McTell story.

It never claimed to be the whole truth, but it was all too readily taken for nothing but the truth.

Writing of Kate in the period long after McTell's death in 1959, he acknowledges that she was born in 1911 and then says, "Some years later she remarried to Johnny E. Seabrooks, a career army man, and has had two children. The youngest was born in 1975, quite a remarkable event in medical circles since she was sixty-four years old. Her family, however, has always had an unusual medical history. Her mother was one of twenty-five children, and her grandfather lived to the age of 120. When he died in 1945 he was the oldest American citizen."

The truth is, of course, that Kate McTell Seabrooks' grandfather had *not* lived to 120, her grandmother had not been one of twenty-five children and, more to the point, she had not miraculously defied medical science and avoided the attention of the media by having a baby at the age of sixty-three. Nor had she given birth to the older of the two children in the house. She had adopted both children.

Hazel McTear lost her husband Bo-Rat on 6 March 1973; he died of bronchial pneumonia in the hospital in Thomson, aged sixty-four. Hazel herself died of a heart attack nine years later, on 21 March 1982, and was buried alongside Eddie at Mount Aldred. Her sister told me she had applied for support: "She was tired of doin' what she was doin' and she wanted to come out of it. But she got a letter from the Social Security administration saying she had been turned down. And she had a stroke when she read it. And when they found her, the letter was layin' on the floor next to her."

By this time, Robert Owens was also dead. He and his wife had long been back in the Statesboro area, and when he died in the Memorial Medical Center, Savannah, on 5 April 1978, aged sixty-one, he was buried at Eastside Cemetery, where Minnie had been laid to rest over half a century earlier. (Clarence McGahee also died in 1978.)

Robert was survived by his wife, Catherine, six daughters, two sons, thirty grandchildren, fifteen great-grandchildren, and several nieces and nephews. Catherine died at seventy-nine in June 1989.

Several of his children have passed away since, though Willie's nieces Kathleen Edwards and Shirley Ann Allen (Robert and Catherine's daughters), still survive, as do two further children of Catherine's, Irene DeLoach and Mildred Smith. Jay Mayo Williams survived until 1980; he died in Chicago that 2 January, aged eighty-five. Art Satherley lived to a still greater age, dying in Fountain Valley, California, on 10 February 1986; he was ninety-six. Ahmet Ertegun died 14 December 2006 in New York, aged eighty-three.

On 7 October 1983, at the age of eighty-seven, Gold Harris formally married Margaret Burnett—because, granddaughter Ola Ivey told me, his first wife Nellie, up in Philadelphia, had applied for a widow's pension, which led to the realisation that she and Gold had never been divorced. Through the good offices of Judge Lucy Bryant in Warrenton, a divorce was obtained and Gold married the seventy-eight-year-old Margaret.

Gold outlived Margaret, but died a victim of Alzheimer's Disease at the age of ninety-eight, in January 1995. Like Willie, he is buried at Jones Grove in Happy Valley. Gold's brother, Tom, and Cousin Horace, had both died a decade earlier, and Horace's wife Doretha five years before that.

Gold's daughter Sally Cramer died of heart disease, aged eighty-six, at home in Happy Valley on 12 August 2006.

And Kate? Well as we know she lived to be interviewed many times, but also to outlive second husband Johnny Seabrooks, to see her adopted son Ernest Bernard grow up and to see the adolesence of April Seabrooks, the adopted daughter she'd claimed she'd given birth to. With April, she maintained this story to the end. She died in a coma in hospital in Augusta on 3 October 1991—and only at Kate's funeral did April learn the truth.

Bernard and April remained in Augusta, but seemed close only geographically. Both were generous to me with information, and each had a story to tell.

Bernard was sixteen years old when Kate told him he'd been adopted:

I remember—it was in the summer of 1980, 'cause she bought me a car for my birthday, that's the reason I can remember, and we were sittin' out and she was tellin' me about this, because I had questions about her bein' my mother, actually—I had been hearing things, y'know, rumors and stuff, about me bein' adopted, and I never knew this, and I started talkin' to my mother, and she started tellin' me—she was honest with me.

She said, "Yeah, baby," she said, "Yeah, I wanted a child so bad." She said, "Your mother wasn't takin' care of you; I was standing in the kitchen and your mother was standin' right behind me and I heard you screamin' and I went out my back door, I was nursin' at Fort Gordon at the time, I had just got off work and I heard you screamin' and I went over in the back door, and your mother was alcoholic."

She was drunk somewhere and had left me in the house for a couple of days, looked like, 'cause I were wet, pissin' wet and diapers needed changin' and I had pneumonia. So she actually just took me out the house. And took me over to her house and kept me for, like, three days, and this woman never did show up lookin' for me. And she went back over to check the house, the woman hadn't been back, so what she did . . . I couldn't have been no more than a week and a half old, she told me, so she ... drove around with me on her lap and gave me to her mother, Sarah Williams. And they nursed me and I like died 'cause I had pneumonia, and, uh, she went back and, uh, when she did find the woman she ... told her she didn't care, she didn't want no children nowhere. And so my mother knew that she was an alcoholic, she wanted to catch her when she was straight, and she got her when she was sober, and I think my mama said she gave her $25, *after* she got to stay sober and signed the papers.

When Bernard came to start school, they obtained a Delayed Certificate of Birth: "And, on that, they entered Willie as my father and quite naturally my mother as Kate, and my grandmother signed it as a witness and all of that."

Only a couple of years before we talked, Bernard found out his biological father's name, and went to meet him:

And when I went to him to meet this man, he ask me what I want, and I said, "Well, y'know, I just wanted to meet you." "Well why? I ain't got no money," and I said "It ain't about no money: I just wanted to know who my father was." And it hurt me so bad, the conversation he and I had: that was my first and only time of meeting this guy. So I really claim that I have no family at all now.

Bernard was twenty-seven when his mother died:

The last of July '91 she acted kinda strange, but I didn't really pay it no attention, but she would talk out her head sometimes: like, "What we doin' up here in Atlanta: why y'all got me up in Atlanta?" I thought maybe she'd been drinkin' beer, you know, 'cause she like a drink of beer every now and then, from time to time, you know—and [I'd say] "Mama, stop that, you scarin' my sister."

But September the 7th—that's the night that everything changed. Actually, my whole life changed that night. My sister came up cryin', she say "Bernard, you need to come see about Mama, there's somethin' wrong with her." So I remember I helped my mama to the bedroom, and I kept watchin' her that night, and she would stop breathin': and I didn't know nothin' about how strokes and stuff happened.

Next morning Kate was diagnosed as having had a light stroke, and taken into the hospital for tests. They told Bernard they'd keep her in over-night, but they were pretty sure she was going to be all right.

Bernard and April went back to Wrens. Next morning a physician phoned, saying, "Mr Seabrooks, we need you up here at the hospital immediately: your mother just suffered a major setback. She had a stroke and her brain's swellin' up. You need to get up here." When they got there Kate had been moved to Intensive Care:

There was maybe four doctors standing around, brain surgeons, you know, and several nurses round my mama's bed, and when we walked in my mother was strapped to the bed—they had both arms strapped to the bed, and maybe fifteen nurses around her bed, holdin' her down, and she was just screamin', and her eyes had turned completely gray— and my sister, she fainted just like that, out of fear . . . And this doctor, this brain specialist, he said "There's nothing we can do for her whatsoever." And they gave her forty-five minutes to live, and that was September the 9$^{th}$: and her heart was so strong that she stayed alive almost a month.

Drama attended the funeral too, as Bernard recalls just as vividly—in an account that indicates that "Rev", his uncle, was not always seen as so high-minded:

My sister didn't know she was adopted till on the day that my mother's funeral—right after my mother's funeral. My uncle Andrew, Rev, they had a big mess over there at the house. That's why I've never been close to none of those people after my mother's death, because I feel that they really destroyed everything that I had, that my mother worked so hard for. I felt that, if they had really been friends to my mother or really

344

loved my mother, that they wouldn't have did what they did after my mother died. There was a bunch of people there eatin' and stuff right after my mother's funeral, and my sister was there frantic, man. I mean she was just cryin'. She say, "They talkin' 'bout my mama adopted me, and me and you was adopted and Sharon my mother"—which was her real mother, and I knew, 'cause my mother had told me this, I knew all about it. And she pointed to Sharon, which *was* her biological mother, said, "They sayin' she my biological mother and they lyin'!" I said, "Come out, let me talk to you. Lawd, I told mama she need to sit down and talk to you about this."

First of all I went back in the house and I put everybody out—and my uncle had a pistol in his pocket. My uncle Rev. He had a pistol, he had a gun. And they got real out of hand, he was like, "Well, this is my sister's house and you ain't nothin' but a drunk an' a dope addict and you were the reason my sister she in the shape she were in"—and my cousin went in the kitchen and called the police. So the sheriff came down there, and he had knew me all my life. He said, "This Kate's son, and as far as I'm concerned, this his home, and if there's any problem y'all take it to court." He said, "They botherin' you?" I said, "Yeah, I want *all* them, not only them but everybody that's here"—it might have been 120 people—I said, "I want everybody to leave!"

But everything fell apart, April moved in with a cousin, Bernard let the bills pile up, Rev acquired the house after all, and by the time I was interviewing Bernard, he was inside the jail on Phinizy Road, Augusta. He was out by 2007, and hustling hard for whatever back royalties there might have been on Blind Willie McTell's song compositions and records. In our last email exchange he told me, if I wanted to know why he wasn't putting April's name forward along with his own for any such monies, I should phone him up. When I tried, his line had been disconnected by the phone company.

April too would have liked those monies, but she wasn't hustling for them and she wasn't trying to cut Bernard out of his share. April was born on 28 June 1975, so she's eleven years younger than Bernard. She grew up in Wrens, finished high school in 1995 and when I met her in Augusta in

2001, she'd completed a year's Child Development course that qualified her to work as a teaching assistant, and had spent her first year working with three-year-olds. She had a daughter herself, aged four.

April surprised me by telling me that her Great-Aunt Inez was still alive: the aunt that Kate and Willie had stayed with just after they got married back in 1934 . . . She took me round to meet Inez, and I did, and she let me take her photograph, and told me that, if she lived to see 25 February, she'd be ninety-nine years old—but she wouldn't answer any questions: "I don't remember nothin'," she said, with some finality.

April would despair of Bernard. "It's all me-me-me-me-me with him." She says she always had to be more grown up than him. She took to seeing her biological mother, and Bernard would tell her, "It's all right for you, you got your mama and everythin', and I ain't got nobody." She'd say, "And your point is?" (April's mother Sharon died suddenly in July 2007.)

The money that might have been paid to Blind Willie McTell in back royalties remains unpaid, so far as I can discover.

In 2004 the Chamber of Commerce people in Thomson passed on to me a query they'd had from the Peer International music-publishing company about whether McTell had any heirs. I duly contacted the executive at Peer International and explained to him that this was a subject I had spent the last three years looking into (among much else) and that, in due course, I might be able to enlighten him on the matter. We had a series of exchanges in which it became clear that this guy was very impatient to find someone to pay—someone who could make a plausible claim to be a McTell heir—but he absolutely refused to say what the hurry was.

"You're an intelligent guy: you can work it out," is all he'd say. When pressed, he indicated that, if someone wasn't paid soon, the money would go "somewhere else": either to some indifferent large corporation, or the tax man, or "bad guys."

I was left to puzzle out what this might mean. I couldn't understand how Peer International was going to lose by some McTell money going to one recipient rather than another—yet, since he was so pushy and unpleasant and unbending, it was clear that it wasn't out of the goodness of his heart that he wanted to find a McTell heir.

And then, around the same time, the Thomson people also forwarded me a very similar enquiry from Scott Cameron, who handles Muddy Waters' estate and a number of others. He was a much nicer man—surprisingly olde-world courteous and human, in fact. So I mentioned to the Peer International executive that Scott Cameron was also interested, and said that really it was nothing to do with me, but I was curious that these two queries had come along at much the same time—and the Peer person grew very abusive and accused *me* of not having McTell's heirs' best interests at heart, and washed his hands of me, threatening to make it very expensive if my book was going to quote any of McTell's lyrics. Nice guy.

I asked around as to why such an executive would be so anxious to offload some unspecified but supposedly significant amount of McTell publishing money onto someone so fast. What was the alternative he was so anxious to avoid? The best response I had was an informal answer passed on from a lawyer friend of another manager of old blues musicians' music estates, who speculated that, if monies held by Peer on McTell's work weren't paid out quickly, then, under New York law, they'd have to hand them over to the State Escheat Fund: a law that the ambitious State Attorney-General, Eliot Spitzer, had been using to go after all the big publishers and record labels (until his fall from office in March 2008).

The lawyer's comment was that if the McTell monies were substantial—"large enough to attract attention if word gets out, which it would if they [had] to pay [them] over to the State," and, if Peer hadn't paid anyone on the account for decades—"probably since McTell's death in 1959 and maybe even before that"—then "This combination could be a professional black eye to Peer; indicating they couldn't be bothered finding someone they owed lots of money to. That's not the kind of attention to detail that potential co-publishers are looking for. Add in the obvious racial overtones and the cultural importance of McTell's work, and you have a nasty publicity problem for Peer."

I learnt later that Bernard told people Peer had paid him a six-figure sum (while ignoring April). He was in as big a hurry to spend it as they had been to pay out. Within a year it was gone.

347

As for who might have had a legitimate claim to such money, or might rightfully claim other past and future royalties – well, that's not my business, and I can't pretend to know.

The David Evans account of McTell's life mentions, though only vaguely and in passing, several other supposed wives and children of Willie's: First, "Emmett [sic] Gates ... remembers Willie marrying a girl named Taylor in Senoia around 1922, though the union did not last long." But Emmitt Gates only knew Willie in the 1950s and Peter B. Lowry, the first to speak with Gates, doesn't believe he'd know anything of the sort.

Second, there's a supposed son in Florida, also from a supposed marriage predating that with Kate—which Kate mentions not only to the Evanses but to E. Bernard West also, though telling both she never met or found out anything about him. Neither, unfortunately, even tried to press her for detail.

Third, "One white man in Savannah claims that Willie had a son, born around 1931, who swept up at the Silver Moon. Willie would help him out occasionally when he was in town. The boy's mother was from New Jersey and eventually brought him back there."

Fourth, "He is also said to have had a 'wife' at Midville named Ethel"—the first of a tangle of people called Ethel, apparently: "Robert Owens also reports that Willie had a daughter named Ethel . . . and that Willie persuaded Robert and his wife to name their own daughter, born in 1948, Ethel after her." Willie is "said to have an 'ex-wife' still living in Decatur," and "Possibly the woman named Rachel in Decatur was Ethel's mother." Then again, "Sometime around 1950 Willie and Helen 'adopted' a little girl, who may have been Ethel or some other child of Willie, though it is not clear whether the girl lived with Willie and Helen on a regular basis. A picture exists of Helen with the girl and the girl's mother. Willie and Helen's landlord Emmett Gates remembers the girl's mother's name as Josie."

Evans adds: "These facts are confusing and contradictory and indicate a need for further research into McTell's domestic life." You might think it would have helped to show a bit of interest at the time, and to have asked around while people were still alive to know, instead of changing the subject back to guitarists every time these matters arose in interviews. (You might also think it would have helped had Evans provided any notes on his sources, or given the rest of us access to whatever he holds.)

He concludes: "At any rate, it is clear that ... between 1944 or earlier and 1958" Willie "had at least one daughter by another woman. His daughter is now [1970s] said to be a pianist in Atlanta, but it is not known whether this is Ethel or the adopted daughter or whether these two girls were, in fact, the same."

Next, after Helen's death, "Helen's daughter, Alice, took the girl that Willie and Helen had adopted, and Willie went off to Statesboro to visit his brother . . ." And then, after Willie brought Josie to live with him, "Willie called her his 'wife', and she had a daughter by Willie who was about six years old at the time. Whether this was the girl that Willie and Helen had adopted is not known." (On this last point, a six-year-old child in late 1958 would have been a very young baby indeed when adopted by Willie and Helen "around 1950," as Evans says.)

All my own efforts to trace any Florida son have failed, and I have run out of time trying to contact descendants of Helen's—those whom no one has claimed were Willie's children—though I came tantalisingly close to finding one, Josephine Cook, who stated on an online profile of herself that her foster mother had been Alice Beasley (Helen's daughter). This online posting was when Ms Cook was promoting a business enterprise that has long since gone bust, leaving behind it only a discontinued phone number. All attempts to track her down have so far failed. I wish they hadn't—if she could talk about growing up with Alice, she might be able to say at least something about what Alice said of Helen, about whom we still know so little. Alice Beasley died in Philadelphia in 1999.

Nevertheless, there's one overall thing that's striking about all these stories of Willie's other children. They're all mere rumor—and it's surely odd that not one of them, nor their children in turn, has ever shown enough interest in their connection to Blind Willie McTell to come forward. It's also noticeable that so many of them are supposed to have been adopted children. (And, in the case of the Ethel that Willie mentions—only mentions, mind—to Robert, it's surely odd that he should want his brother to name a newborn child after one he had himself, unless his own had already died. That's the normal circumstance in which people hope that one person might be named after another.)

What we seem to have here then, at best, is an adopted child who had already died in Willie's own lifetime, and rumors of other children, mostly adopted rather than fathered by Willie. And therefore it strikes me that the strong likelihood is the *opposite* of the impression the Evans account gives: that instead of Willie having children all over the place, he had none—because he couldn't have children.

He liked the image of the "born to ramble" minstrel with women and children everywhere—it's part of the macho, girl-in-every-port self-portrait that goes with the territory—but since he did have plenty of women, I think there's a noticeable absence of children. Helen definitely could have children: we know she had two before she met Willie, and that she was still under forty years old when they first shared a home. They had no children together. Willie and Kate had none together. And though we know that Kate adopted Bernard and April, she was in her fifties and sixties by that point. We don't know that she never fell pregnant after she left Willie and went to New York in 1941. She was a nursing assistant: she had easy access to abortion if she wanted it.

Most significantly, *Willie* seems to have assumed that he and Kate had no children through his failure rather than hers. Kate told E. Bernard West: "[Willie] said 'If I should die, and leave you a young woman, I want you to marry again, and raise a family.' Said 'We are not going to have any children—I see that now. All these years we been together we didn't have any.'"

My amateur assumption would be, then, that sorting out Willie's estate is relatively simple—and that, if Willie died intestate and without having ever divorced Kate, then what's rightfully his should have passed to her children, even if they were adopted with less formality than most legal régimes would demand today. (Kate did not die intestate: she made a will and Bernard was the executor; the lawyer she instructed, John Pilcher, still runs an office in downtown Wrens.)

But in June 2008 the question of the unfairness of Bernard receiving monies and April receiving nothing became academic: for that month Bernard died suddenly, at the age of forty-three.

If April doesn't have the basis for a reasonable claim, then the alternative rightful heirs would surely be the four surviving children of Robert Owens and/or his wife Catherine, in Plainfield, New Jersey and at Portal, just outside Statesboro. It doesn't appear to have ever crossed the mind of any of them that such money should be coming their way, and no doubt they've lived happier lives for not having worried about it in vain. Anyone who's read *Bleak House* knows how that works.

But there must be money, and it certainly ought to come through to someone with a family connection to Willie, rather than sit around inside a music-publishing company that is extremely lucky ever to have had any rights at all in works that they acquired only through Ralph S. Peer's sharp-operator deals in the 1920s and '30s—works that they did nothing to create and nothing to promote or add value to for Willie's benefit at any point (and which, in any case, were often songs that even Willie would have been hard put to argue he'd really written in the first place).

And, if Peer *did* hand over monies to Bernard before attracting the bad publicity they'd feared, then any legitimate claimant can surely claim more, so all is not lost.

As so often, somebody needs a good lawyer.

Meanwhile, there are the spoils of Willie's "heritage" to be fought over, now that the world of tourism has woken up to the potential dollar power of African-American history in general, and not least of the history of the blues.

In Willie's case he's not a big enough blues fish for Atlanta to need to fry him corporately. The city boasts only the small private enterprise of Blind Willie's, a pub with live music out on Highland Avenue, still a funky part of Atlanta: a pub where, until early 2002, their bar was often propped up by an old friend of Willie's, the fine vocalist and guitarist Frank Edwards, a man born in Washington, Georgia, on 20 March 1909 and who was still enjoying the blues till the very end.

I met him there four months before he died. Described in a 1970s blues magazine as "a dark, taciturn man," I found him good-humored and approachable, with kind eyes. When the live act played, he was attentive, smiling, and applauding each number. He was also by far the most nattily dressed person in the crowded room. He came in several nights a week, and had his own mug, from which he poked bits of foam up with a red straw and sucked them appreciatively as we chatted. He could still play guitar, too. I asked if his fingers were still OK and he said yes, looking down at them with the quiet smile of a man who knew he was lucky.

He'd been in Atlanta since 1937 and first met Willie there in the '30s. "Knew 'im well," he said. He knew Kate too, but had nothing to say about her. I told him she'd said Willie always carried a pistol.

"Heh heh! No, I never seen that. Never carried one myself. Never did."

Did he ever see Willie get in a fight?

"Nope, never seen 'im fight. But he could take care of hisself all right." A pause, and another chuckle. "He used to *lead* other blind people around! He did! I seen that. Heh heh!"

Frank Edwards had first recorded in 1941, and he had been one of those who turned up alongside Willie and Curley for the Regal sessions in Atlanta in 1950. But the chance to ask him more about his old friend Willie was gone. The live performance by Carey Bell and his white-boy band took a break and Carey came over. In any other company he would have been an old man. After the initial charming greetings and grins, Frank Edwards asked how he was doing, and Carey said, "Well, I'm gettin' tired, man. Sometimes I jes' get tired, man." Frank made solicitous, understanding noises. I guess Carey Bell could have been seventy but he was probably younger than that. A good twenty years younger than unflappable, dapper Frank, anyhow.

I left him in Blind Willie's, Atlanta's only place of tribute to his old friend.

In Statesboro and Thomson it's different, though. They are both small enough to want to own Blind Willie McTell, so they are rivals nowadays in making him their tourist attraction. Thomson always had the grave, but its heritage efforts got it the Georgia State Historical Marker and a blues festival named in his honor. Statesboro got the award from Willie's induction into the Georgia Music Hall of Fame (Macon gets the Hall itself), and recently opened a Willie McTell Trail that takes you alongside the railway tracks where Willie and Minnie lived almost 100 years ago.

The Historical Marker is set back from the road at the Happy Valley

Crossroads, by the old wooden store, where the road south to Wrens meets the Happy Valley Road that takes you out to Willie's grave. Its text was written by Dot Jones, tourist officer for the town at the time. It reads:

BLIND WILLIE McTELL

MUSICIAN

Willie Samuel McTear (1901–1959) was born between Big and Little Briar Creeks in the Happy Valley community. In 1911, he and his mother moved to Statesboro, where he began his life of traveling and performing. Although blind from infancy, Willie developed a lifelong independence based on his acute sense of hearing, remarkable memory and versatile musical genius.

Willie performed and recorded under many names but favored 'Blind Willie' McTell. Best remembered for his blues, McTell had a remarkable repertoire of blues, spirituals, gospel, rags, folk ballads and popular music. McTell played from 'Maine to Mobile Bay', and at theaters, taverns, road houses, churches, medicine shows, train stations, barbecue joints, house parties and on the streets. His blues feature his trademark twelve-string guitar played in rapid and intricate patterns of jagged, shifting rhythms accompanying his clear tenor voice. He started recording in 1927 for RCA Victor and went on to record for Columbia, Okeh, Vocalion, Decca, Bluebird, Atlantic and the Library of Congress. He last recorded in 1956 and returned to McDuffie County shortly before his death and is buried in the Jones Grove cemetery. Blind Willie was inducted into the Georgia Music Hall of Fame in 1990.

Which is pretty good, considering. It was erected in 1993, and they had a small ceremony. Dot Jones remembers:

It was a terrible Saturday morning on a rainy, rainy, rainy day. They had installed it for us the day before and they put a cover over it, and then we had a dedication for it. A nice group of people came out from down there, some relatives, and a group of men and women, family or church members. We really had a bigger crowd, but some of the older people just couldn't stand it when the rain got too heavy. But some people came from Atlanta, and everyone just sort of stood around the marker and there was a little presentation.

Annie Jackson's son, Teddy, remembers that a small choir sang—which was a nice touch: "Yeah, I think it was the choir from Jones Grove, because they had a program at the church that Friday night, and then the Saturday morning they come and unveiled it, and it rained. And they were doing the ceremony while it was raining. And I think it was the choir from Jones Grove that sang that morning."

The Georgia Music Hall of Fame inducted Willie at the same time as Ronnie Milsap, Chips Moman, Wendy Bagwell, and the Sunliters:

William Samuel McTell. On September 22, 1990, Blind Willie McTell was inducted into the Georgia Music Hall of Fame in the posthumous category. Blind Willie is known as the King of Georgia Blues Singers. This 'Georgy Award' was created by Tiffany & Company. The front of the 3-sided prism is the Seal of the State of Georgia, while the back contains the music and lyrics to the state song, 'Georgia On My Mind'. All of this is hand etched.

There is scandal here, however. Not only has Willie's Georgy Award now disappeared, but the handling of the presentation was a disgrace at the time. It came down to the politics of the Thomson-Statesboro competition for Willie's heritage dollar. The head of the Georgia Senate Music Committee, which oversees inductions, was Senator Nathan Dean, and he had been pushed to recognise Willie McTell by the woman then in charge of PR for the Statesboro Convention and Visitors Bureau, Virginia Anne Franklin—whose own side of the story I cannot give, because she has repeatedly avoided talking to me, and she no longer works for the CVB.

Dot Jones' side of the story—the Thomson side, in other words—is that she was at the ceremony, and though she couldn't see Kate McTell when she took her seat, she assumed she was up at the front and going to receive the award on Willie's behalf: that this was less than a year before Kate died, and it was rather gratifying that someone like her, who did at least have a real connection to Willie, was to be a focus of attention and collect the award. Kate had told Dot in advance that she'd been told her ticket to the event would cost her $50; Dot said she would sort this out—that obviously a recipient shouldn't be charged.

She had therefore phoned either the Hall of Fame itself or the PR woman, and had been told that *she* would take care of it and also send Kate her travel money, and for Dot not to worry. When it came to the moment of the presentation itself, it was Virginia Franklin who got up from the front table and accepted the award—and Dot was shocked to find that Kate had not even been there.

She spoke to a very hurt Kate later, who said that, well, this woman had been related to the person who'd sent Willie to the Academy for the Blind, so that family had been owed something . . . (In fact, Virginia Anne Franklin is the daughter of the Mr Franklin who ran the downtown Franklin Drugstore for about fifty years. I never heard it suggested that he paid a cent towards Willie's schooling, even if anything of the sort would justify the ceremony débacle.)

Nothing justifies this—but what explains it is that Kate represented Wrens, and Jefferson County, next to McDuffie. She represented up there in Thomson, and not Statesboro.

David Fulmer felt stuck in the middle of this when he was making his documentary *Blind Willie's Blues* in the early 1990s:

Dot Jones had sort of her own agenda, and that made it sort of difficult for me, because she ... tried to steer me to people that she knew and so forth. I don't know what kind of spin she was trying to put on all this, but anyway. I went down there and I did spend time there with Dot Jones and with the woman at the CVB in Statesboro: I don't remember her name. But she was in the middle of this, and she was trying to claim McTell for her. So that feud was going on and I never quite could keep straight who was giving me the real story and who was steering me towards this or that.

The then Curator of the Hall of Fame, still in place in 2001, was Joseph R. Johnson, a great enthusiast for the music. He felt very clear about the subsequent disappearance of the Georgy itself. He told me:

> The award was accepted by Ms Virginia Ann Franklin, and we have a letter on file from Senator Nathan Dean thanking her for accepting the award on his behalf. When I approached Ms Franklin about the Georgy Award, she told me that she gave it to the Georgia Music Hall of Fame Curator. I told her I was the Curator and that I don't have it.
>
> She acted very oddly and wanted to end the conversation—and then stated that it must have been lost in the mail. She was not friendly at all. I have not pursued the issue because we can always have another made if we choose. They cost about $1,000.

Willie would be amazed. There he is in 1940, singing on the street, he hasn't made a record since the doomed session with Piano Red in 1936, and then John Lomax's wife hones in on him and, for $1 plus his taxi fare, he's recorded for the Library of Congress—and, in the course of the interview, he happens to say "But Statesboro was my real home": and sixty years later this remark is the motherlode for corporate Statesboro and Bulloch County to promote themselves as players in the tourism they want to get off his name. In the early 2000s his larger-than-life cutout stood up there on the second floor of the Jaeckel Hotel, where he would never had been allowed to stand in his own lifetime.

And meanwhile, because he was born in Thomson and buried in Thomson, where they never bothered to fill up a birth certificate for him at the time and where he would have been discriminated against and wholly unnoticed and unvalued by every layer of officialdom in the city at both ends of his life—here, they now have a website, *www.blindwillie.com*, run by the CVB, which shares its offices with the Chamber of Commerce, and they have a festival to celebrate their local hero's name, and in the process they too can bring in the bucks.

But there is a difference between "heritage" and the past it sometimes sullies, and there are individuals in both communities who did not know

Willie McTell themselves but respect his achievements and his grace and character in the face of great adversities, and who are genuinely proud of his connections to these Georgia places. And there are still individuals in both communities who did know Willie, and whose memories still illuminate his life and work for us.

That work did not lead forward, like that of his Mississippi contemporaries, to the electric modernity of Chicago and beyond. Instead, like his life, it points back into times of both affecting quaintness and of terrible difference. The past, as we know, is a foreign country we cannot reach, but we can stare across at it, appalled and in wonderment, from the shores we stand on now.

# APPENDIX: BLIND WILLIE McTELL
## CAREER DISCOGRAPHY

This discography covers the work on which McTell was the primary artist, or shared at least equal billing with other artists. There has been no thorough Career Discography of Blind Willie McTell's work until now. All dates are given the British way round, i.e. day / month / year, and, of course, all years so cited refer to the twentieth century. So for example 5/11/40 means 5 November 1940.

## 1: The Recordings:

McTell's own recordings were made in four periods.

**The early work**, cut in Atlanta, New York City, Chicago, and Augusta, Georgia, for a number of labels, starting with Victor (he was their first Atlanta-based blues artist), dates from 1927 to 1936. (David Evans' invaluable notes on McTell, published with the LP *Atlanta Blues 1933*—see *Section 3: The Releases*, below—and based on research work by him, his parents, his then-wife, Cheryl [Thurber], and Bruce Bastin, say that ". . . beginning with his first session, McTell made commercial recordings at least once every year till 1936," but, in fact, he made none in 1934.) These recordings are:

'Writin' Paper Blues', 'Stole Rider Blues', 'Mama, 'Tain't Long For Day' and 'Mr. McTell Got the Blues' [2 takes] (Atlanta, 18/10/27).

'Three Women Blues', 'Dark Night Blues', 'Statesboro Blues' and 'Loving Talking Blues' (Atlanta, 17/10/28).

'Atlanta Strut', 'Travelin' Blues', 'Cigarette Blues' and 'Come On Around To My House Mama' (Atlanta, 30/10/29); 'Real Jazz Mama' and 'Kind Mama' (Atlanta, 31/10/29); 'Death Room Blues', 'Drive Away Blues' and 'Hard Working Mama' (Atlanta, 26/11/29); 'Blue Sea Blues', 'South Bound Georgia Blues', 'Mr. McTell's Sorrowful Moan', 'Weary-Hearted Blues' and 'Love Changing Blues' (Atlanta, 29/11/29).

'Talkin' To Myself' and 'Razor Ball' (Atlanta, 17/4/30).

'Southern Can Is Mine', 'Broke Down Engine Blues', 'Stomp Down Rider' and 'Scarey Day Blues' (Atlanta, 23/10/31); 'Low Rider's Blues' and 'Georgia Rag' (Atlanta, 31/10/31).

'Rollin' Mama Blues', 'Lonesome Day Blues', 'Mama, Let Me Scoop For You' and 'Searching The Desert For The Blues' (Atlanta, 22/2/32).

'Lay Some Flowers On My Grave', 'Warm It Up To Me', 'It's Your Time To Worry' and 'It's A Good Little Thing' (NYC, 14/9/33); 'Lord Have Mercy If You Please', 'Don't You See How This World Made A Change', 'Savannah Mama', 'Broke Down Engine', 'Broke

Down Engine No.2' [2 takes] and 'My Baby's Gone' (NYC, 18/9/33); 'Love-Makin' Mama' [2 takes], 'Let Me Play With Your Yo-Yo', 'Hard To Get', 'Death Room Blues' [2 takes], 'Death Cell Blues', 'Lord, Send Me An Angel' [2 takes] and 'Snatch That Thing' (NYC, 19/9/33); 'B And O Blues No.2' [2 takes], 'Weary-Hearted Blues', 'Bell Street Lightnin'', 'Southern Can Mama', 'Runnin' Me Crazy' and 'East St. Louis Blues (Fare You Well)' (NYC, 21/9/33).

'Ain't It Grand To Be A Christian', 'We Got To Meet Death One Day' [2 takes], 'Don't Let Nobody Turn You Around', 'I Got Religion, I'm So Glad' and 'Dying Gambler', 'God Don't Like it', 'Bell Street Blues' and 'Let Me Play With Yo' Yo-Yo' (Chicago, 23/4/35); 'Lay Some Flowers On My Grave', 'Death Room Blues', 'Ticket Agent Blues', 'Dying Doubter Blues', 'Cold Winter Day', 'Your Time To Worry', 'Cooling Board Blues' and 'Hillbilly Willie's Blues' (Chicago, 25/4/35).

'Undertakers Blues', 'Mama Keep Steppin', 'Maybe Some Day' and 'Married Life's A Pain' (Augusta Georgia, 1/7/36).

**Next** comes the one-day songs-and-talk session taped in an Atlanta hotel room for the Library of Congress by John A. Lomax and Ruby Lomax on 5 November 1940. The titles given for the songs and interview-answers from this session are as they were assigned by John Lomax; this explains the oddness of the title 'Monologue On Accidents', for instance: McTell did not set out to "perform" a 'monologue on accidents.' Hence, too, the third-person title 'Monologue On Himself'. Likewise a song he performs twice during the session is once given as 'I Got To Cross The River Jordan' and once in minstrelised form as 'I Got To Cross De River O'Jordan'. The session comprises:

'Just As Well Get Ready, You Got To Die', 'Climbing High Mountains, Trying To Get Home', 'Monologue On Accidents', 'Boll Weevil', 'Delia', 'Dying Crapshooter's Blues', 'Will Fox', 'I Got To Cross The River Jordan', 'Monologue On Old Songs', 'Old Time Religion, Amen', 'Amazing Grace', 'Monologue On The History Of The Blues', 'Monologue On Life As A Maker Of Records', 'Monologue On Himself' 'King Edward Blues', 'Murderer's Home Blues', 'Kill-It-Kid Rag', 'Chainey' and 'I Got To Cross De River O' Jordan' (Atlanta, 5/11/40).

(A far more detailed sessionography of McTell's work in these first two periods resides in the bible of pre-war blues listings, *Blues And Gospel Records 1890–1943* by Robert M.W. Dixon, John Godrich and Howard W. Rye. This multi-indexed, cross-referenced update of 1997— the fourth edition—includes, as for every other artist in the book, not only a listing and dating of every track McTell laid down, including recordings unreleased at the time, but also naming all accompanying musicians and, in each case, listing the original studio matrix number, 78rpm record label, and catalog-number, where applicable, plus any artist's pseudonym used on a 78rpm release. However, it doesn't list vinyl issues, let alone CDs, except for tracks that happened not to achieve 78rpm release in the first place. Nor, of course, does its session-listing look beyond 1943. Equivalent books for the post-war period got as far as *Blues Records 1943– 1966* by Mike Leadbitter and Neil Slaven, 1968; Leadbitter's premature death in November 1974 stymied what was to have been an updated three-volume set of listings of *Blues Records, 1943–1970*. What emerged instead was a revised version of the manuscript of volume one: i.e. *Blues Records 1943–1970: A Selective Discography, Volume 1: A to K*, Leadbitter and Slaven, 1987. Neil Slaven hoped to complete and publish *L to Z*, plus a revised Vol. 1, but was pre-empted by a rival updating, commissioned by the publisher of the earlier volumes, *Blues*

*Records 1943–1970 "The Bible Of The Blues' Volume Two L–Z* by Mike Leadbitter, Leslie Fancourt and Paul Pelletier, 1994. This, however, is a much less careful work: in many cases it has not corrected earlier "information" proved incorrect by more recent research results, and in McTell's case it misdates one of his post-war sessions, that for Regal, detailed below.)

**The third period of McTell recordings** is that marked by his return to commercial recording in 1949–1950, with sessions for Atlantic and Regal, both recorded in radio-station studios in Atlanta.

Only with the reissue of some of the Regal material on a Biograph CD in 1993 has come the suggestion outside specialist magazines and books that the Regal session took place not in 1949 but in 1950. This is particularly interesting because it reverses the order in which these two sessions were thought to have been made. It used to be believed that the Regal session had happened earlier in 1949 than the Atlantic one. The pinning-down of the Atlantic session to *October* 1949 comes from an Atlantic Records' ledger, as transcribed in Peter A. Grendysa's book *Atlantic Master Book # 1*, self-published in 1975; the Regal session was believed to have happened earlier the same year. Indeed, when the short-lived fanzine *Pickin' The Blues* published a Post-War Years Discography of McTell and Curley Weaver in issue #10, Edinburgh, 1982, it still believed the Regal session date to be August 1949, though actually the re-dating of the session to 1950 had first appeared in print in 1980, in French discographer Michel Ruppli's book *The Savoy Label: A Discography*, its re-dating of the McTell session being the inevitable consequence of its re-dating the Fred Mendelsohn field-trip for Regal during which McTell's session was held. Thus Howard Rye's McTell listing in *Collector's Items* #15, Walton-on-Thames, 1982, referred in passing to "the 1950 Regal session," and this "new information" was then slipped in as an undeclared revision to the Don Kent notes accompanying a Biograph CD, which claimed to reproduce the notes to the original LP issue. The further pinning-down of the session to *May* 1950 was achieved by Bill Daniels in 'A DeLuxe And Regal Feast, Part Two—Regal Records 1949–1951', in the now-defunct *Whiskey, Women and . . .* #10, Haverhill, Maryland, November 1982.

We can now say with some confidence, therefore, that the Blind Willie McTell material recorded in this period comprises, in chronological order, the following (with the Atlantic session first):

'Broke Down Engine Blues', 'The Razor Ball' [2 takes], 'Little Delia' [2 takes], 'Kill It Kid' [2 takes], 'The Dyin' Crapshooter's Blues', 'Pinetop Boogie Woogie' [2 takes], 'Blues Around Midnight' [2 takes], 'On The Cooling Board', 'Motherless Children Have A Hard Time' [2 takes], 'I Got To Cross The River Jordan', 'You Got To Die', 'Ain't It Grand To Live A Christian', 'Pearly Gates', 'Soon This Morning' [3 or 4 takes] and 'Last Dime Blues' (Atlanta, October 1949). NB: There are, additionally, false starts for 'The Dyin' Crapshooter's Blues', 'Blues Around Midnight', 'Motherless Children Have A Hard Time', 'Ain't It Grand To Live A Christian' and 'Soon This Morning'; these would not be worth mentioning except that one of them—of 'Blues Around Midnight'—runs as long as 58 seconds.

'Don't Forget (It)', 'A To Z Blues', 'Good Little Thing', 'You Can't Get That Stuff No More', 'Love Changin' Blues', 'Savannah Mama', 'Talkin' To You Mama', 'East St. Louis', 'Wee Midnight Hours' [though it is Curley Weaver's lead vocal on this track], 'Pal Of Mine' [2 takes], 'Honey It Must Be Love', 'Sending Up My Timber' [2 takes], 'Lord Have Mercy If You Please', 'Trying To Get Home (Climbing High Mountains)', 'River Jordan', 'How About You?', 'It's My Desire' and 'Hide Me In Thy Bosom' (Atlanta, May 1950).

Last comes the one-day songs-and-talk session recorded in Edward Rhodes' Atlanta record shop in 1956. (Again, CD-reissue of the material from this session that has been released has brought about a quiet refining of previously known fact: in this case the recording date for this last session, never more pinned-down than as from "the fall of 1956", has now been fixed at "September 1956". This may have emerged—but, if so, it did so somewhat belatedly—from another Michel Ruppli book, the equally massive and expensive *The Prestige Label: A Discography*, 1980, an update of Ruppli's own *Prestige Jazz Records 1949–1969*, published in Denmark in 1972.)

The session comprises conversation (mostly monologue), which on the LP issued from this material is separately designated on only one occasion (i.e. as "Early Life"), plus songs; however, the full "session", in order and as logged, is as follows:

'Warm Up', 'Baby It Must Be Love', 'The Dyin' Crapshooter's Blues' [NB: This is logged as 'Talk About Dyin' Crapshooter's Blues' and 'Dyin' Crapshooter's Blues', but clearly the talk is an integral part of the performance in this case: indeed, it's what makes it the best version of the song], 'Early Life (Talk About Early Life)', 'Pal Of Mine', 'More About Life', 'Don't Forget It', 'Talk About Kill It Kid', 'Kill It Kid', 'Talk About That Will Never Happen No More', 'That Will Never Happen No More', 'A Request For My Blue Heaven', 'My Blue Heaven', 'Some Talk About Drinking', 'Beedle Um Bum', 'Talk About Salty Dog', 'A Married Man's A Fool', 'Talk About A To Z Blues', 'A To Z Blues', 'Talk About New Orleans', 'Goodbye Blues', 'Basin Street Blues', 'Talk About People In Room', 'Salty Dog', 'Wabash Cannonball', 'Talk About St. James Infirmary', 'St. James Infirmary', 'Talk', 'If I Had Wings' and 'Instrumental' (Atlanta, September 1956).

# 2: The Lost Recordings:

A number of takes from 1927–1936 were never issued, on wax or vinyl. By the nature of the industry practises of the day, many tracks never issued in the first place tend not to exist at all. You never know: astonishingly, forty-two Paramount test-pressings by various artists were found in Illinois in November 1985, some of them helping to hold up a roof and others put out in the snow as garbage. They turned out to include previously unknown takes by Tommy Johnson, Son House, and Charley Patton (the story is told in 'Paramounts In The Belfry' by Bob Hilbert, *78 Quarterly* Vol.1, #4, Key West, Florida, 1989). But barring similar unforeseen discoveries, the following McTell recordings are therefore lost forever:

'Cigarette Blues' (Atlanta, 30/10/29); 'Real Jazz Mama' (Atlanta 31/10/29); 'Death Room Blues' and 'Hard Working Mama' (Atlanta 26/11/29); 'Blue Sea Blues', 'South Georgia Bound Blues', 'Mr. McTell's Sorrowful Moan' and 'Weary-Hearted Blues' (all Atlanta 29/11/29); 'Lay Some Flowers On My Grave' (NYC, 14/9/33); 'Let Me Play With Your Yo-Yo', 'Hard To Get' and 'Snatch That Thing' (NYC, 19/9/33); 'Death Room Blues' and 'Dying Doubter Blues' (Chicago, 25/4/35).

The four blues sung by McTell backed by Piano Red, made in Augusta GA in 1936, were also never issued and pretty certainly no longer exist: 'Married Life's A Pain' (26/6/36) 'Undertakers Blues', 'Mama Keep Steppin' and 'Maybe Some Day' (1/7/36). This means that no McTell recording from 1936 actually exists.

On the other hand, a further scattering of recordings from these early years, also unreleased at the time, *have* been found to exist and have, therefore, enjoyed their initial release on vinyl—and even on CD: three of McTell's 1933 outtakes were released for the first time in 1994 and a fourth in 1995. These recordings are specified below.

However, there are almost certainly further lost recordings, this time from the third McTell recording period, i.e. 1949–50. First, 1949 alternative takes of 'Kill It Kid', 'Razor Ball' (originally logged by the record company as 'Raise A Ball'!), 'Pinetop Boogie Woogie' and 'Soon This Morning', all from the Atlantic Records sessions. Two sides recorded for Regal in 1950 were long thought to be lost—a revisit to 'River Jordan', and McTell's only recording of Thomas A. Dorsey's 'How About You?'. Though reportedly issued as a 78rpm, Regal 3280, no copy has ever been found and the tracks were assumed to be non-extant till 2002. (See The Releases.)

## 3. The Releases:

I avoid here 78rpm wax releases. Throughout this discography, unless otherwise stated, "issued" means "issued on vinyl." Second and third generation vinyl reissues are not listed, except where they offer something different or hold historic significance of their own. Key CD re-releases are also listed.

Most of **McTell's early work** was compiled on two Yazoo and one Roots LPs: *Blind Willie McTell: The Early Years (1927–1933)*, Yazoo L-1005, NYC, 1968 (though the first six of this company's releases, among which was this McTell compilation, were on the Belzona label; this was then re-named Yazoo and the LPs swiftly re-issued as such); *Blind Willie McTell 1927–1935*, Yazoo L-1037, NYC, 1973; and *King of the Georgia Blues Singers: Blind Willie McTell (1929–1935)*, Roots RL-324, Vienna, Austria, 1969. The Roots LP, on which the sound quality is very poor, includes some 1935 tracks featuring McTell with his wife Kate also singing. She can't sing. (The Roots label, active in the 1960s–70s, has no connection with the oddly punctuated Columbia Roots 'n Blues Series.)

Yazoo L-1005, NYC, 1968 comprised 'Broke Down Engine Blues', 'Mama 'Tain't Long For Day', 'Georgia Rag', 'Love Changing Blues', 'Statesboro Blues', 'Stomp Down Rider', 'Savannah Mama', 'Travelin' Blues', 'Drive Away Blues', 'Warm It Up To Me', 'Three Women Blues', 'Writin' Paper Blues', 'Southern Can Is Mine' and 'Talkin' To Myself'. Yazoo L-1037 (issued in stereo!) comprised 'Ticket Agent Blues', 'B&O Blues No.2', 'It's A Good Little Thing', 'Cold Winter Day', 'Kind Mama', 'Experience Blues' [Ruth Day with McTell, guitar], 'Southern Can Mama', 'My Baby's Gone', 'Painful Blues' [Ruth Day with McTell, guitar], 'Razor Ball', 'Stole Rider Blues', 'God Don't Like It', 'Scarey Day Blues' and 'Atlanta Strut'.

Roots RL-324 comprised 'Come On Around To My House Mama', 'Razor Ball', 'Rollin' Mama Blues' [with Ruby Glaze], 'Lord Have Mercy If You Please' [with Curley Weaver], 'Don't You See How This World Made A Change?' [with Curley Weaver], 'My Baby's Gone', 'Weary-Hearted Blues', 'Runnin' Me Crazy', 'We Got To Meet Death One Day', 'Dying Gambler', 'God Don't Like It' [with Kate McTell], 'Bell Street Blues' [with Curley Weaver], 'Lay Some Flowers On My Grave', 'Ticket Agent Blues' [with Kate McTell], 'Cold Winter Day' [with Curley Weaver] and 'Your Time To Worry'.

Virtually the same compilation offered by Yazoo L-1037 was also released as *Blind Willie McTell: Death Cell Blues* on Biograph BLP-C14, NYC, 1973. Likewise, the Roots collection was partly duplicated years later on *Blind Willie McTell 1929–1935*, Document Records

DLP531, Vienna, 1983/4, though this latter was significantly different in offering the first-ever issue in any format of a second take of 'We Got To Meet Death One Day' (Chicago, 23/4/35).

Some early work lies outside these releases: 'It's A Good Little Thing' (with Curley Weaver, NYC, 14/9/33) was issued ahead of all the rest, by Sam Charters—and unknowingly—on an LP for Folkways in 1957: that is, he included tracks by various other artists to fill out his accessible Blind Willie Johnson tracks on *Blind Willie Johnson: His Story* (Folkways FG 3585, NYC, 1957), and one such track was McTell's 'It's A Good Little Thing', billed as by "Blind Willie (?) and partner", giving this track vinyl release some ten years ahead of its emergence on Yazoo L-1037.

Then 'Statesboro Blues' (Atlanta, 17/10/28), was issued, again by Charters, on the various-artists LP *The Country Blues*, RBF Records RF-1, NYC, 1959, alongside his pioneering book of that name (*The Country Blues*, NYC, Rinehart, 1959)—before re-appearing on Yazoo L-1005. Next, 'Dark Night Blues' and 'Loving Talking Blues' (Atlanta, 17/10/28) plus 'Mama Let Me Scoop For You' (Atlanta, 22/2/32) and 'Ain't It Grand To Be A Christian' (Chicago, 23/4/35) were issued on the early compilation *Kings Of The 12-String Guitar*, Piedmont Records 13159, Arlington Virginia, 1963. One first-session track, the first of two takes of 'Mr. McTell Got The Blues' (Atlanta, 18/10/27) was issued only on *Travellin' This Lonesome Road: A Victor/Bluebird Anthology*, RCA International RCA INT-1175, London, 1970 (and RCA 731.046 in France). And the wonderful talking blues 'Travelin' Blues' (Atlanta, 30/10/29) became better known than most in Britain when, a couple of years after its release on Yazoo L-1005, it was included on *The Story Of The Blues*, a double-LP (CBS Records [M for mono] 66218, London, 1969) compiled by Paul Oliver and released in association with his book of the same name (*The Story Of The Blues*, 1969; paperback 1972).

Of his four sides from 1932, all vocal duets with Ruby Glaze (who can sing), only three achieved release on album before the 1980s. 'Mama Let Me Scoop For You' is on the 1963 Piedmont LP and 'Rollin' Mama Blues' is on the Roots LP (both detailed above); 'Searching The Desert For The Blues' appeared on the early compilation *Bluebird Blues*, RCA Vintage Series, LPV-518, NYC, 1965, released simultaneously in the UK as RD7786. (It is a possibility that this track might have been released first on the oddity *Country Blues and Gospel*, Heritage Records H.302, Australia [?], 1964–5: a 6-track 33rpm EP.) All four of the 1932 recordings subsequently appeared on *Blind Willie McTell: The Remaining Titles (1927–1949)*, Wolf Records WSE 102, Vienna, 1980s. This LP filled gaps left by the original Yazoo releases of McTell's early work.

Two 1933 tracks ('Broke Down Engine', NYC, 18/9/33—his first revisit to this song—and 'Death Cell Blues', NYC, 19/9/33) were issued on LP only on *The Atlanta Blues*, RBF Records RF-15, NYC, 1966. Previously unissued tracks from 1933, having been found to exist, appeared on the similarly titled *Atlanta Blues 1933*, JEMF-106, issued by the John Edwards Memorial Foundation, Folklore & Mythology Center, UCLA, Los Angeles, 1979. These tracks, actually made in New York City rather than Atlanta (the LP title referring to regional style rather than recording-location), were as follows: 'It's Your Time To Worry' (NYC, 14/9/33); 'Broke Down Engine No.2' (NYC, 18/9/33: a second revisit, made the same day as the first); 'Love-Makin' Mama', 'Death Room Blues' and 'Lord, Send Me An Angel' (all NYC, 19/9/33); 'B And O Blues No.2' [2nd take], 'Bell Street Lightnin'' and 'East St. Louis Blues (Fare You Well)' (all NYC, 21/9/33). This left still unissued (until CD releases in the mid-1990s) the alternative takes of 'Broke Down Engine No.2', 'Love Makin' Mama', 'Death Room Blues' and 'Lord Send Me An Angel'—all of which exist on test-pressings, which are now stored at the John Edwards Memorial Foundation (no longer at UCLA but at the University of North Carolina at Chapel Hill).

Of McTell's seventeen recordings from two days in late April 1935, just one, 'Hillbilly Willie's Blues' (Chicago, 25/4/35), was on the relatively early reissue LP *The East Coast States Vol. 2*, Roots RL-326, Vienna, 1969–70: a Various Artists compilation. The sound quality here was very poor, especially bearing in mind that Decca's original recording was immaculate, but this track had not been issued on vinyl before.

Those April 1935 recordings that were unreleased on 78s at the time but were subsequently found to exist were issued as follows: 'Don't Let Nobody Turn You Around' (Chicago, 23/4/35) and 'Cooling Board Blues' (Chicago, 25/4/35) on the Japanese MCA (Blues Tradition Series) album *Blind Boy Fuller / Blind Willie McTell*, MCA 3523, Tokyo, c.1975; 'Let Me Play With Yo' Yo-Yo' (Chicago, 23/4/35) was issued both on this Japanese album and on an LP within the German box-set *Blues Box One*, MCA-Coral 6.30106–3, Hamburg, 1975. 'I Got Religion, I'm So Glad' (Chicago, 23/4/35) was first issued on another Japanese LP, *Gospel Music Vol. 1 (1926–1940)*, MCA 3530, Tokyo, 1976. As already stated, the second take of 'We Got To Meet Death One Day' (the first is on the Roots LP) was released in the 1980s on Document DLP531.

A general selection (twelve tracks) of these 1935 recordings—not aiming to highlight rarities—was released on *Blues In The Dark*, MCA Records Jazz Heritage Series MCA 1368, Universal City, California, 1983. When released, this was the first time that a whole LP of McTell's pre-war work had ever been issued on vinyl by the record company that had itself issued the relevant 78rpms in the first place. (These had been on Decca; MCA owned Decca and thus its McTell masters.) In other words, the earlier vinyl releases on Yazoo and Roots had in effect been bootlegs, selling material taken from 78s whose copyright ownership lay elsewhere: mostly with corporations that had never even heard of Blind Willie McTell, let alone contemplated reissuing his material.

Of all the vinyl listed above, the following were subsequently issued on CD: Yazoo L-1005 as Yazoo CD-1005, NYC 1990; Yazoo L-1037 (now subtitled *Doing That Atlanta Strut*) as Yazoo CD-1037, NYC 1991; and the Wolf Records album as *Blind Willie McTell 1927–1949*, Wolf Collectors Series Special Edition WSE-102CD, Vienna, date unknown. The 1969 Paul Oliver compilation has also been CD-reissued: *The Story Of The Blues* 2-CD set, Columbia 468992–2, NYC, 1991. However, all McTell's extant early-period work (1927–1935), re-compiled into chronological order and including all the extant rare tracks except the four outtakes deposited at JEMF (as detailed above), is now available as follows: *Blind Willie McTell Vol. 1, 1927–1931*, Document Records DOCD-5006, Vienna, 1990; *Blind Willie McTell Vol. 2, 1931–1933*, Document Records DOCD-5007, Vienna, 1990; and *Blind Willie McTell Vol. 3, 1933–1935*, Document Records DOCD-5008, Vienna, 1990.

It is recurrently alleged that Yazoo offers better sound quality than Document/Wolf. I wouldn't rush to say so myself. In any case, in 1995 came a Blind Willie McTell set featuring almost all his early work for Victor in superior sound quality. This was the McTell set in the *Blues Collection* magazine-plus-CD series (no.43, April 1995, incorporating the CD *Blind Willie McTell: Statesboro Blues*, BLU GNC 043, The Blues Collection/Orbis Publications, London: notes by the present writer; German language edition April 1996), which re-issued every extant track from McTell's first two sessions except for one outtake (take 1 of 'Mr. McTell Got The Blues', Atlanta 18/10/27), as well as issuing both extant tracks from his last sessions of the 1920s and all his work with Ruby Glaze.

Ahead of that, in 1994, came a Blind Willie McTell set in the Columbia Roots 'n Blues

Series, *The Definitive Blind Willie McTell*, Columbia/Legacy C2K 53234, New York. (In fact three McTell tracks, none of them rarities, had already appeared on earlier Roots 'n Blues issues: 'Southern Can Is Mine' [Atlanta, 23/10/31] on the *Beauty Of The Blues* sampler CD, Columbia Roots 'n Blues 468768–2, NYC, 1991 and on the compilation *Legends Of The Blues Vol. One*, 467245–2, NYC, 1991; and 'Georgia Rag' [Atlanta, 31/10/31] and 'Warm It Up To Me' [NYC, 14/9/33] on the compilation *Great Blues Guitarists: String Dazzlers*, Columbia Roots 'n Blues 467894–4, NYC, 1991.) The 1994 McTell set collates *all but one* of the extant sides recorded by McTell for Columbia and its sister-label OKeh in Atlanta in October 1929, April 1930, and October 1931, plus the Vocalion sides from the sessions done in September 1933 (the second paragraph below deals with the much-heralded outtakes from these last sessions).

This collection adds a small number of further tracks on which McTell is not the main artist. The present discography excludes recordings on which McTell was merely a back-up guitarist for Harris and Harris, Buddy Moss, Piano Red, Curley Weaver, or Ruth Willis. But, in the case of the last two artists on this list, a few tracks were made on which you might argue that McTell gets equal billing, and the Columbia set includes some of these, as follows: 'Rough Alley Blues', originally billed as by "Mary Willis, vocal, accompanied by Blind Willie McTell, vocal & guitar" (Atlanta, 23/10/31); 'Experience Blues' and 'Painful Blues', as by 'Ruth Day' [same woman], with McTell down as 'Guitar Sammie' in Columbia's original files (Atlanta, 23/10/31); 'Low Down Blues', as by "Mary Willis, vocal, accompanied by Blind Willie McTell, guitar, and Curley Weaver, 2$^{nd}$ guitar" (Atlanta, 31/10/31): surely a track on which McTell *is* merely a back-up musician (the set omits the same session's 'Merciful Blues', which featured the same line-up, because though the two were issued as a 78rpm, Columbia were unable to find a copy to take it from); 'You Was Born To Die', as by "Curley Weaver & Partner' and 'Dirty Mistreater', ditto (NYC, 18/9/33). On the first of these two, the "Partner" *is* McTell: he sings on the choruses and plays guitar throughout; but, on the latter, the "Partner" is Buddy Moss, who plays the second guitar: McTell's contribution is off-mike comments barely audible during the hummed third verse. Both of these were tracks that had been LP-issued on the JEMF-106 album, 1979, already mentioned.

The fully fledged McTell recordings on the *Definitive Blind Willie McTell* set that derive from the Vocalion sessions of September 1933 include, at last, three of the four still-unreleased outtakes, i.e. the alternative takes of 'Love-Makin' Mama', 'Death Room Blues' and 'Lord, Send Me An Angel'. A note in the set's booklet claims that 'all of the artist's known extant recordings' for the Columbia labels are included, but in fact the set still omits one of the four Art Satherley alternative take test-pressings, namely the never-issued first take of 'Broke Down Engine No.2' (NYC, 18/9/33).

This last outtake finally sees release in 1995 on the Various Artists compilation CD *Too Late Too Late Volume 5 (1927–1964)*, Document DOCD-5411, Vienna, 1995: one of the tidying-up CDs at the very end of Johnny Parth's mammoth project of issuing every extant pre-war blues recording.

(NB: These four alternative 1933 McTell takes are not listed at all in the first three editions of Dixon & Godrich's *Blues & Gospel Records 1902–1943*; they were omitted from the 1982 edition despite having been documented as extant in the substantial McTell 1933 sessiono-graphy published with the notes to the JEMF-106 LP in 1979. However, these takes are included in the listings in the 1997 edition *Blues And Gospel Records 1890–1943* by Dixon, Godrich & Rye.)

**The 1940 Library of Congress recording** was first trailered by the release of an excerpt from McTell's performance of 'Boll Weevil' on a Library of Congress Archive of Folk Song album *The Ballad Hunter Vol. 3*, AFS L51, Washington, DC, c.mid-1950s: one of a series of five LPs (AFS L49–53) comprising audio-illustrated talks by John A. Lomax that had first appeared as radio broadcasts as early as 1941. The LP series title alludes to Lomax's book *Adventures of a Ballad Hunter*, 1947. The side of the LP on which McTell's 'Boll Weevil' is excerpted features a talk on the song itself, with extracts from other versions by people from Guthrie to Lead Belly.

The whole recording of the McTell 1940 "session" (nineteen "tracks") was then issued on *Blind Willie McTell: 1940*, Melodeon MLP-7323, Washington, DC, 1966 (and on Storyville 670.186 and SLP186 in Europe [Storyville Records is Danish-based, and nothing to do with Storyville Publications]). I've heard it rumored that this has been CD-issued by Biograph (Melodeon became a subsidiary of Biograph in 1972 or 1973) but I can't find anyone who has actually seen it. It certainly is on release as *Blind Willie McTell: Complete Library of Congress Recordings In Chronological Order (1940)* on RST Blues Documents BDCD-6001, Vienna, 1990. However, as noted in Chapter 15, the issued version has always been shorn of some introductory speech by McTell and bits of comment by John and Ruby Lomax in response to his performances and conversation. These omissions were made when Larry Cohn requested the material in the mid-1960s and the librarian was concerned to fit the material onto one reel-to-reel tape. I'm grateful to Todd Harvey at the Library of Congress for urging me to listen to the version they hold there, and to Jas Obrecht for his transcriptions, proving that there is more here than has ever been released.

**The 1949 session for Atlantic** remained unreleased except for two tracks put out on a 78rpm issued in January 1950, which comprised 'Kill It Kid' c/w 'Broke Down Engine Blues' as by Barrelhouse Sammy (Atlantic 891). Later, these two tracks were, perhaps unsurprisingly, the first to appear on vinyl. They were issued on *Country Blues Classics—Vol.3*, Blues Classics BC-7, Berkeley, 1966. The rest of the extant session (except for four alternate takes: i.e. one take each of 'Little Delia', 'Blues Around Midnight' [and that 58 second 'false start'], 'Motherless Children Have A Hard Time' and 'Soon This Morning' still lurking unissued) was first issued on vinyl (thanks to Peter B. Lowry) as *Blind Willie McTell: Atlanta Twelve String*, Atlantic Records SD 7224, NYC, 1972 (with sleeve notes by Mike Leadbitter and Simon Napier). This has been issued on CD with the same title as the album version, on Atlantic 7 82366–2, 1992.

**The eighteen 1950 Regal sides** long thought to be the extant total were all issued, but distributed between one Savoy and two Biograph LPs, none of which offered all eighteen:
*Living With The Blues*, Savoy MG 16000, Newark, New Jersey, c.1960, was an early LP selection of Savoy's post-war country-blues material (Savoy owned Regal by then) and it includes just one of the McTell Regal sides, 'A To Z Blues'. This LP was issued considerably later in the UK by the endearing little Oriole company on their Realm label: *Living With The Blues*, Realm Jazz Savoy Series RM209, London, 1964.

The first of the Biographs was *Blind Willie McTell 1949: Trying To Get Home*, Biograph BLP-12008, Brooklyn New York, 1969. This offers eleven sides: 'Hide Me In Thy Bosom', 'Honey It Must Be Love', 'Sending Up My Timber' [2 takes], 'Lord Have Mercy If You Please', 'It's My Desire', 'Trying To Get Home', Don't Forget It', 'Good Little Thing', 'You

Can't Get That Stuff No More' and 'Pal Of Mine' [take no.2]. When this album was first issued, a sleeve-note claimed, wrongly, that it represented the complete output of McTell's Regal session. Its selection, augmented by more of his Regal tracks, has been CD-issued as *Blind Willie McTell: Pig 'n' Whistle Red*, Biograph BCD126, USA, 1993.

The other Biograph LP combines some McTell sides with some by Memphis Minnie from the same year: *Blind Willie McTell—Memphis Minnie 1949: Love Changin' Blues*, Biograph BLP-12035, Canaan New York, 1971. The McTell sides on this album are: 'Love Changin' Blues', 'Savannah Mama', 'Talkin' To You Mama', 'East St Louis', 'Wee Midnight Hours' and 'Pal Of Mine' [take no.1]. There has been no CD-reissue of this LP: its material has been divided up and re-compiled. The Memphis Minnie tracks have been CD-issued on a compilation putting her Regal material alongside tracks by Jimmy Rogers, St Louis Jimmy, Sunnyland Slim, L.B. Montgomery, and Pee Wee Hughes; the Blind Willie McTell tracks have been put alongside material by Skip James and Bukka White on the curiously titled *Three Shades Of Blues*, Biograph BCD-107, NYC?, 1992.

All eighteen of these Regal sides were CD-issued on *Blind Willie McTell and Curley Weaver: The Post-War Years 1949–1950* on RST Blues Documents BDCD-6014, Vienna, 1991, but for legal reasons to do with the Weaver material this was later deleted.

The two further Regal sides long thought to be lost—'River Jordan' and the Thomas A. Dorsey song 'How About You?' (the latter not recorded by McTell at any other session)—were suddenly released, without any statement of the importance of their discovery—on a 2002 compilation album *The Back Porch Boys*, mostly featuring Alec Guitar Slim Seward and Louis Jelly Belly Hayes, on Delmark DE-755, Chicago. The Regal 78rpm on which these two tracks had reportedly been issued, had still not been found, but the masters were unearthed when Regal had been sold to Piedmont and Piedmont had passed them across to Delmark. Thus all twenty extant Regal recordings had finally been made available, the last of them not till the twenty-first century.

**The 1956 "Session"** has not yet been issued in full (though when the edited-down version of the session was issued, it was never made clear that this was not the full session).

*Blind Willie McTell: Last Session*, originally issued on Prestige Bluesville 1040, Bergenfield, New Jersey, as early as the autumn of 1961, and reissued on Prestige PR 7809, Bergenfield, New Jersey, 1966 (and in the UK for the first time then, as *Blind Willie McTell: Last Session*, Transatlantic Records, PR1040, London, 1966) has also been CD-reissued, in the USA (and as a cheap import in the UK), on Prestige Bluesville Original Blues Classics OBCCD-517–2 (BV-1040), Berkeley, California, 1992. This CD has been digitally remastered, and is astonishly "clean" and crackle-free—which is especially useful when it comes to hearing McTell talking—and yet, and yet, the clean-up process does take a slight edge, or bite, away from the singing voice. This CD-reissue is padded out with a couple of "bonus tracks" (as if it were an Elvis movie soundtrack album), which prove to be the two Atlantic 1949 tracks issued as a 78rpm single in January 1950.

NB: Any of these may also get secondary release on other companies' cheapo CDs, just as Robert Johnson's material has been issued on Charly Blues Masterworks (rather a nasty series) as well as on Columbia. Such duplications usually offer inferior sound quality and very inferior documentation. In McTell's case, the Bob Dylan Effect can also be detected in the emergence of two such sets on the previously unknown American-based Blue Planet label, which CD-issued the Library of Congress session and the Last Session as *Nobody Sings The Blues Like Blind Willie McTell Volume 1*, BPCD1002, USA, 1993 and *Volume 2*, BPCD1003, USA, 1993 respectively.

Meanwhile, the following titles from Blind Willie McTell's last session remained unreleased: 'Warm Up', 'More About Life', 'Request For My Blue Heaven', 'My Blue Heaven', 'Some Talk About Drinking', 'Talk About Salty Dog', 'Talk About New Orleans', 'Basin Street Blues', 'Talk About St. James Infirmary', 'St. James' Infirmary', 'Talk', 'If I Had Wings' and 'Instrumental'.

(This information was first revealed in the article 'Blind Willie McTell—A Last Session' by Samuel B. Charters, *Record Research* magazine #37, Brooklyn NY, August 1961, and was restated in Leadbitter and Slaven's *Blues Records 1943–1966*. However, since the record sleeve never mentioned the incompleteness of its contents, this was generally forgotten, though the existence of an unissued part of the session was hinted at subsequently by David Evans in his JEMF-106 notes: these mentioned 'St James Infirmary' and 'Basin Street Blues' as part of McTell's last-session repertoire, and in re-telling the story of the unearthing of the session, state that Charters "arranged to have most of it issued'). NB: 'Don't Forget It' as issued was an edited-down version of the full recording.

In 2005 it was announced that the complete recording was to be issued, as part of a limited-edition package *Blind Willie McTell: The Box Set* (details tba) but this has not yet happened.


## 4. Early Vinyl Releases in Sequence:

Abstracting a history of when which McTell tracks first emerged on vinyl, we find a most interesting sequence. If you had no access to 78s, but were vigilant for Blind Willie McTell on vinyl, you could first have come across his work in this order:

1: Mid-50s: excerpt from 'Boll Weevil', cut 1940.
2: 1957: 'It's A Good Little Thing', cut 1933.
3: 1959: 'Statesboro Blues', cut 1928.
4: c.1960: 'A To Z Blues', cut 1950.
5: 1961: *Blind Willie McTell: Last Session*, cut 1956.
6: 1963: 'Dark Night Blues' and 'Loving Talking Blues', cut 1928.
   'Mama Let Me Scoop For You', cut 1932.
   'Ain't It Grand To Be A Christian', cut 1935.
7: c.1964: 'Searching The Desert For The Blues', cut 1932.
8: 1966: *Blind Willie McTell: 1940*, cut 1940.
   'Broke Down Engine Blues' and 'Kill It Kid', cut 1949.
   'Broke Down Engine' and 'Death Cell Blues', cut 1933.
9: 1968: *Blind Willie McTell: The Early Years*, cut 1927–1933.
10: 1969: *Blind Willie McTell 1949: Trying To Get Home*, cut 1950.
    *King of the Georgia Blues Singers*, cut 1929–1935.
11: 1969/70: 'Hillbilly Willie's Blues', cut 1935.
12: 1970: 'Mr. McTell Got The Blues', cut 1927.
13: 1971: 'Love Changin' Blues', 'Savannah Mama', 'Talkin' To You Mama',
    'East St. Louis', 'Wee Midnight Hours' and 'Pal Of Mine', cut 1950.
14: 1972: *Blind Willie McTell: Atlanta Twelve String*, cut 1949.
15: 1973: *Blind Willie McTell 1927–1935*, cut 1927–1935.
    *Blind Willie McTell: Death Cell Blues*, cut 1927–1935.
16: 1975: 'Let Me Play With Yo' Yo-Yo', cut 1935.

17: c.1975: 'Don't Let Nobody Turn You Around', cut 1935.
   'Cooling Board Blues', cut 1935.

Oddities of this chronology of McTell's vinyl releases include the facts that the first whole album of his work to appear was taken from his last-ever recording session, and that 1933 and 1949 versions of 'Broke Down Engine [Blues]' were issued before the consummate first version from 1931.

# NOTES

INTRODUCTION

**Atlanta, Georgia—summer 1956 . . . September 1956. McTell and Rhodes . . .**
phone interview with Sam Charters, Stockholm, 8 Aug 2002, e-mail exchanges with Jan
Cox, Dec 2004, plus the Ed Rhodes interview in *Blind Willie's Blues*, David Fulmer,
Lawrenceville, Georgia; Missing Lenk [sic] Video, 1996.

**Pittsburgh-born . . . Samuel Barclay Charters . . . Mary Lange . . .** phone interview
with Sam Charters, ibid.

**On the LP that he issues alongside the book . . .** *The Country Blues*, RBF Records RBF
1, New York, 1959. RBF stood for Record Book & Film Sales Inc., and was a subsidiary of
Folkways. Before this he had released compilations and his own field-recorded work on
Folkways (e.g. *Blind Willie Johnson: His Story*, FG 3585, NY, 1957 and the important
acoustic session *Lightnin' Hopkins*, FG 3822, NY, 1959).

**Paul Garon . . . recalls the prices . . .** e-mail to the Pre-War Blues e-mail discussion group
*pre-war-blues@yahoogroups.com*, 21 Oct 2002.

**sold on eBay for $4,495 . . .** item no. 4058689006, auction ended 19 Dec 2004.

**Paul Oliver ['s] . . .** *Blues Fell This Morning* . . . In the US its title is *The Meaning of the Blues*.

**Frederic Ramsey's *Been Here and Gone* . . . in search "of what might still remain of
an original, authentic African American musical tradition"**; quoted from the jacket
of the republished US paperback edition, 2000.

**Charters' critics . . . lightweight hokum . . .** The LP contradicts this claim: it is
deliberately wide-ranging but includes Blind Lemon Jefferson, Blind Willie Johnson,
Sleepy John Estes, the very raw Tommy McClennan, and Robert Johnson.

**When we come to ask how and when . . . McTell becomes famous . . . because he
isn't Mississippi, he isn't raw and dark.** Similarly, almost no one is much interested in
the gospel-song recordings of any of these pre-war artists—not even the ones from
Mississippi. Time and again journalistic, critical and scholarly attention ignores this part
of the canon, even when it's just as prominent as the blues in the repertoire of the very
musicians and singers they most admire.

**Skip James . . . like a ghost on stage at the Newport Folk Festival in 1964 . . .**
Guralnick, pp.113–4.

**Blind Willie McTell is one of those sought out . . . He dies eleven weeks and a day
before . . .** McTell dies 19 Aug 1959; Charters' book is published 5 Nov 1959.

**February 1960. Sam and Ann Charters . . .** 'Blind Willie McTell—A Last Session',
Samuel B. Charters, *Record Research* no.37, Brooklyn NY, Aug 1961, p.7; phone interview
with Charters and e-mail exchanges with Jan Cox, op.cit.

**hunched over an old Pentron tape machine** . . . this detail from Charters' *Sweet as the Showers of Rain*, p.130.

**a portrait taken in the late 1920s in the Kelly Studio . . . in Atlanta** . . . the exact date is unknown; the name of the studio is legible on the excellent copy seen in the files of the Folklife Center, Library of Congress, Washington, DC, 26 Feb 2003. On the reverse someone has written "Blind Willie McTell c.1925", though I think it unlikely that the picture pre-dates his first involvement with Victor Records, in 1927.

**The trashpile was in the basement** . . . information from John Reynolds, interviewed by phone, 26 Jul 2004, and by e-mail, 28 Jul and 7 Aug 2004.

**This privileged bohemian enterprise** . . . Rice was the founding editor. See 'Starting a Magazine: A Guide For the Courageous; the Short Happy Life of *Jubilee*' by Edward Rice, *The Merton Seasonal, A Quarterly Review*, Vol. 24, No. 1, Louisville KY, Spring 1999. Kerouac spent Xmas 1958 at home in Northport with Robert Lax, the magazine's Roving Editor, who had published some of Kerouac's poems. On Christmas Eve they drank wine and read from *Finnegan's Wake* and from Jack's unpublished manuscripts. The following year, Kerouac's Catholic poems were published by *Jubilee* in a volume entitled 'Hymn— God Pray For Me'. Kerouac also gave *Jubilee* his 1955 story 'Statue of Christ'. 'Visions of Tom—Jack Kerouac's Monastic Elder Brother', Angus Stuart, online 28 Jul 2004 at *www.thomasmertonsociety.org/kerouac.htm*.

**No one alive now knows how it came to be there** . . . information from John Reynolds as above. Re his involvement with Lead Belly's family, he says: "In the early '50s I made contact with Lead Belly's widow, Martha. We became fast friends and I visited her often in her 414 E. 10th Street apartment. Her niece, Tiny Robinson (daughter of Martha's twin sister, Mary), lived downstairs with her two young children. Martha and Tiny moved to Brooklyn in the early '60s and years later, after Martha died, Tiny moved to Nashville . . . Before moving Tiny invited me . . . to go through a trunk of Lead Belly memorabilia—a real treasure trove that included dozens of letters that Lead Belly had written to Martha from Los Angeles in 1946. That's when Tiny (sometimes called 'Queen' Robinson) and I decided to put together a Lead Belly scrap/picture book." [*Lead Belly: A Life in Pictures*, ed. Tiny Robinson and John Reynolds, Gottingen, Germany: Steidl, 2007.]

**Belzona . . . Yazoo . . . Nick Perls** . . . based on the Yazoo entry, by Steve Hoffman, advance typescript from Routledge *Encyclopedia of the Blues*, plus snippets on the Pre-War Blues e-mail discussion group 31 Jan and 2 Feb 2005.

**Transatlantic . . . releases by sex therapist . . . Cammeron** . . . online 11 Dec 2004 at *www.unionsquaremusic.co.uk/titlev4.php?ALBUM_ID=372&LABEL_ID=7*.

**Ralph McTell . . . "I was one of the lucky ones . . ."** phone interview, England, 24 Jan 2005.

**Both men are buried in the Carnation Ridge section** . . . online, 11 Dec 2004, at *http://gagen.i-found-it.net/carnationridge.html*.

**Hettie Jones** . . . e-mail from Alan Balfour, 17 Nov 2001 and brief Academy of American Poets biography online 11 Dec 2004 at *www.onlinepoetryclassroom.org/poets/poets.cfm?prmID=457*.

**Bob Dylan . . . "Blind Willie McTell"** . . . recorded NYC, 5 May 1983 [2 versions]. One version released *Bootleg Series I–III (Rare and Unreleased) 1961–1991*, 5-LP or 3-CD box set, Columbia Records 468086 1 [LPs] or 468086 2 [CDs], New York, 1991. Dylan first performed the song live in 1997 and has done so over one hundred times since.

**every track that Blind Willie McTell had recorded** . . . detailed in Apprendix: Career Discography.

ONE

**one of Georgia's smallest** . . . all current Georgia geographical and route information is taken and interpreted from the excellent county maps in *Georgia Atlas and Gazetteer*, 2000, used in conjunction with my own journeys, except where otherwise stated.

**and . . . poorest** . . . stated by Ms Sue Simons, Warren County Librarian, in situ, Aug 2001.

**His body was brought to Warrenton by train . . . on a late August day in 1959** . . . for this and all other statements about McTell and those he knew, sources are detailed later.

**The Chamber of Commerce, trying to promote tourism, says** . . . quoted in a 2003 *Savannah Morning News* found online, 16 Nov 2004, at *http://savannahnow.com/exchange/stories/010803/EXClocalbizbriefs.shtml*.

**Just 6,336 people live in this county now** . . . all contemporary statistics published by the US Census Bureau as extracted from the 2000 Census.

**Gold Harris lived here, on County Line Road . . . one side of the road is in Warren and one isn't** . . . stated from personal knowledge by Warren County Probate Judge Lucy J. Bryant, in situ, Aug 2001.

**"Georgia," as Tom Henderson Wells wrote** . . . *The Slave Ship Wanderer*, p.1.

**the land of the Lower Creeks and Chickasaws** . . . Wilhoit, 1976 (though clearly this is largely a reprint of a book from the 1930s).

**In the Warren County of 1800** . . . all general historical population figures for Warren Co. taken online, 18 Nov 2004, from the Carl Vinson Institute of Government, UGA's Warren County Historical Population Profile at *www.cviog.uga.edu/Projects/gainfo/countypop/warren-pop.htm*.

**"free persons of color"** . . . figure 19 attributed to the 1800 census "conducted by John Hopson and Hardin Pruitt" in Wilhoit.

**In 1815 the state decreed** . . . *Georgia Laws, 1815,* Vol. 1, p.143+, as posted online at *www.rootsweb.com/~usgenweb/ga/gafiles.htm* by Tara D. Fields, 14 Feb 2004.

**and in 1819 decreed** . . . *Georgia Laws, 1819,* Vol. 1, p.41+, as posted ibid. This was repealed 1824.

**in 1833 . . . illegal to teach a "free person of color" to read or write** . . . *Georgia Laws, 1833,* Vol.1, p.143+, as posted ibid.

**As slave states went, Georgia's totals were never huge** . . . all general slave figures are rounded from those found online, 18 Nov 2004, at the Geostat Center's Historical Census Browser at *http://fisher.lib.virginia.edu/collections/stats/histcensus*.

**The Savannah River was a crucial link** . . . the importance of the river connecting these cities (and transporting cotton before the railroads) is stressed in Flanders.

**Kendall McTyeire** . . . except as otherwise stated information is from *Kendall McTier Family*, Jan McTier, "looseleaf notebook of information and family trees . . . of the descendants of Kendall McTier (by any spelling)"; augmented by interview with Jan McTier, Dearing GA, 6 Aug 2001.

**by 1850, Kendall has built up his tally of slaves to ten** . . . *1850 Census of Georgia Slave Owners Index*, p.210: Kendall McTyre has ten slaves and Reddick McTyre has two. Details 1850 Slave Schedule, Warren Co., GA, Militia District Sub Division 90.

**Kendall . . . not been moved by . . . *Uncle Tom's Cabin*** . . . He's very unlikely to have read it: he probably couldn't read. We know that he couldn't sign his name. All extant documents bear an "X—his mark."

**the legal document that gives her to Reddick** . . . "Know all men by these present that I

Kendall McTyre give to my Son Reddick McTyre a negro girl by the name of Essey To have to hold to keep to which I do warreant [sic] and defenc [sic] against my right and titles . . ." *Warren County Deed Book Z, p.26*, recorded 24 Feb 1854, reproduced in McTier.

**William Zeigler of Crawford County** . . . text of his will found online, 19 Sep 2004, at *www.afrigeneas.com/slavedata/Zeigler-GA-1854.txt*

**You can even use a slave as a mortgage** . . . *Glascock County Centenary 1857–1957*, no details available, p.15.

**in the summer of 1860** . . . 1860 Census giving information as applicable 1 Jun 1860.

**"Mulatto" was a technical term** . . . information from a posting on the *GA-AfricaAmer-L@rootsweb.com* e-mail discussion group by Howard A. Griffin, 18 May 2003.


TWO

**Reddick [McTyeir] remained a bachelor** . . . except where stated, information is from McTier, augmented by interview with Jan McTier, Dearing GA, 6 Aug 2001.

**He owned a hundred acres** . . . Georgia Agricultural Census, 1860, extracted in McTier, ibid.

**His "real estate" was valued at $400 and his "personal estate"** . . . $2,200 1860 US Census, Glascock Co., GA, Gibson Post Office, 1168 G M District, p.12, enumerated 5–6 July.

**neighbors . . . named Kitchens** . . . census Glascock County, 1860, online, 23 Nov 2004, at *www.rootsweb.com/~gaglasco/g1860.htm* and Glascock County, Georgia, Deeds and Mortgages, 30 Oct 1858 pp.83–4, online 15 Nov 2004 at *www.rootsweb.com/~gaglasco/glasdeed.htm*.

**on the 4 July 1861** . . . all information *Augusta Chronicle & Sentinel*, 11 Jul 1861.

**Colonel Robert Harris Jones, a lugubrious-looking man** . . . photograph online, 8 Nov 2004, at *www.mindspring.com/~jcherepy/22d_ga/22d_ga.html*.

**Camp McDonald (just outside what's now Kennesaw)** . . . online, 28 Aug 2004, at *www.kennesaw.ga.us/history.aspx*.

**The winter was mild . . . The main enemy was mumps** . . . letter from Camp Blanchard, 5 Feb 1862, published *Rome Courier*, 21 Feb 1862, online, 7 Sep 2004, at *www.mindspring.com/~jcherepy/22d ga/feb21–62.html*.

**Reddick's early battles** . . . much general information taken from "Time Line of the Civil War" pages online, Nov 2004, at *http://memory.loc.gov/ammem/cwphtml*. All detail re soldiers in Reddick's Company B in *Roster of the Confederate Soldiers of Georgia 1861–1865, Vol.II*, Lillian Henderson, no details [Augusta GA library item 114438], pp.942–950.

**Seven Pines** . . . detail on individual battles mostly taken, Nov 2004, from online pages within *www.ehistory.com/world/WarView.cfm?WID=2*, plus letter from camp, 24 Jun 1862, online, 7 Sep 2004, at *www.mindspring.com/~jcherepy/22d_ga/jun24–62.html*, plus some general description of the war and detail re Fredericksburg from Welsh. [NB not all soldiers were men. A Mrs Irvin, aka Charley Green, disguised as male, fought in many battles. *Daily Intelligencer* [Atlanta], 18 Sep 1863, p.1. No doubt other cases existed.]

**Many men now had no tents** . . . letter from camp, 15 Nov 1862, published *Rome Courier*, 4 Dec 1862, online, 7 Sep 2004, at *www.mindspring.com/~jcherepy/22d_ga/dec4–62.html*. I have also drawn on *Washington Weather*, Kevin Ambrose, Dan Henry and Andy Weiss, *nia*, excerpt online, 7 Sep 2004, at *www.weatherbook.com/Mudmarch.htm*.

**There was a severe snowstorm on the night of the 22nd** . . . soldier's correspondence from camp, Guiney's Station, Virginia, 6 Mar 1863, published *Rome Courier*, 19 Mar 1863, online, 7 Sep 2004, at *www.mindspring.com/~jcherepy/22d_ga/mar19–63.html*.

**Stephen Crane's** *Red Badge of Courage* . . . first published 1895, this classic of American literature is thought to be based on the battle of Chancellorville, though its author wasn't born till after the Civil War was over. (Stephen Crane, b.1871, d. 1900.)

**Stonewall Jackson** . . . online, 30 Nov 2004, at *http://home.san.rr.com/stonewall*, except amputation detail and **"He has lost his left arm; but I have lost my right arm"** . . . online, 30 Nov 2004, at *www.civilwarhome.com/jackbio.htm*.

**Point Lookout prison camp** . . . details re its general position and population statistics online, 1 Dec 2004, at *www.clements.umich.edu/Webguides/Schoff/NP/Point.html*. Wagon-wheel shape from print of c. 1863 online, 1 Dec 2004, at *http://home.jam.rr.com/rjcourt52/cwprisons/lookoutn.htm*. African-American guard details online, 1 Dec 2004, at *www.plpow.com/Guards.htm*. Detail of weather, food, and hospital wards from prisoners' writings quoted in *Point Lookout Prison Camp For Confederates*, Edwin Beitzel, no details, 1972, quoted in McTier.

**Early in the war . . . an agreed procedure for exchanges** . . . general information from Russell Liner, Richmond Public Library, VA; e-mail to author, 3 Dec 2004.

**Grant's offensive began in the Wilderness** . . . battle details online, 3 Dec 2004, at *www2.cr.nps.gov/abpp/battles/va046.htm*.

**On 7 May . . . Spotsylvania Court House** . . . battle details online, 3 Dec 2004, at *www2.cr.nps.gov/abpp/battles/va048.htm*.

**The writer William Least Heat-Moon** . . . *Blue Highways*, p.405.

**Cold Harbor** . . . Reddick's regiment detail McTier; battle details online, 3 Dec 2004, at *www2.cr.nps.gov/abpp/battles/va062.htm*.

**Jackson Hospital had opened** . . . archive documents online, 9 Dec 2004, at *www.mdgorman.com/Hospitals/jackson_hospital.htm* and within its pages.

**Hatcher's Run, Dinwiddie County** . . . battle details online, 3 Dec 2004, at *www2.cr.nps.gov/abpp/battles/va083.htm*.

**The two generals met in . . . Appomattox Court House** . . . "Surrender at Appomattox, 1865" online, 1 Dec 2004, at *www.eyewitnesstohistory.com*, plus general sources including *www.mscomm/~ulysses/page45.html*, seen online ditto.

**Back in the upstairs parlor** . . . see 'Souvenirs of the Surrender' by Marie Kelsey, online, 8 Dec 2004, at *www.css.edu/usgrant/souvenir.html*. (Grant's table is in the National Museum of American History, Washington, DC; Lee's table is in the Chicago Historical Society's Civil War Room.)

**Surrender followed swiftly on all other fronts** . . . 26 Apr, Gen. Joseph Johnston surrendered to Sherman outside Durham, North Carolina; 4 May, Gen. Richard Taylor surrendered at Citronelle, Alabama; 2 Jun, Gen. Edmund Kirby Smith surrendered the Confederate Dept. of the Trans Mississippi; and 23 Jun, Gen. Stand Watie surrendered Cherokee forces in Oklahoma [*www.nps.gov/apco/surrend.htm*, online, 8 Dec 2004].

**In December 1865, Congress ratified** . . . details checked online, 9 Dec 2004, at *www.nps.gov/malu/documents/amend13.htm*. (The ratification was declared 18 Dec 1865, but in fact by then Oregon had become the 28th state to ratify it. Before year end California and Florida had come in. The rest followed in 1866. Only Mississippi refused.)

THREE

**to Thomson . . . by bus from Atlanta, something that Willie had done himself many times** . . . testimony of various witnesses, including Barbara Davis in Statesboro, GA, 13 Aug 2004, phone interview.

**Sister Fleeta Mitchell** . . . see later in the book for details.

**James Baldwin writes** . . . 'A Letter from the South', collected in *Nobody Knows My Name*.

**the Thomson Depot . . . built about 1860** . . . general historical information on Thomson and McDuffie County taken from Thomson-McDuffie Tourism CVB leaflets, undated but c.2001, and from *History of McDuffie County Georgia 1870–1932*, W.C. McCommon and Clara Stovall, Thomson, GA; Ida Evans Eve Chapter of United Daughters of Confederacy, typescript; no publication date given [Georgia Archives Call Number: F292.M13 M32].

**the young railroad engineer from Philadelphia** . . . this was J. Edgar Thomson.

**The veterans camp was disbanded . . . ". . . few veterans left and those being quite feeble"** . . . quote unattributed but posted online by James Malone and seen, 25 Oct 2004, at *http://ftp.rootsweb.com/usgenweb/ga/mcduffie/military/civilwar/svc.txt*.

**Jones Grove Baptist Church . . . I went to a service** . . . 4 Nov 2001.

**Atlanta film-maker and writer David Fulmer** . . . details given later.

**Martin Luther King Jr** . . . quoted from the final chapter of King's *Stride Towards Freedom*.

**In Statesboro . . . Naomi Johnson told me** . . . interviewed at her home, 31 Jan 2004.

**In Jenkins County, Georgia . . . a lone slave grave** . . . transcribed in *Jenkins County Georgia Cemeteries*, Vol. 4 [of 5], compiled Bonnie Gay, edited Mrs Lawrence B. Kelly; printed Statesboro GA, 1988, by Statesboro Regional Library.

**presiding bishop G.E. Patterson says** . . . *Augusta Chronicle*, 19 Nov 2004.

**Jeremy Hardy** . . . discussing popularising of gospel music, BBC Radio 4, 18 Oct 2001.

**Cora Mae Bryant's . . . "museum" . . . Oxford, Georgia** . . . as seen, 7 Aug 2001.

**the LP *Atlanta Blues 1933*** . . . sleevenotes by Bruce Bastin and David Evans; album details in Appendix: Career Discography.

**Cora Mae Bryant . . . $20 for a copy of a blues CD** . . . *Born With The Blues*, recording dates unstated; Music Maker CD MMCD22, Hillborough NC, 2001.

**Peter B. Lowry . . . "She was pleased at the time,"** . . . phone interview, 14 Sep 2004.

**Willie's original gravestone . . . David Fulmer . . . replaced** . . . Detail from David Fulmer in Atlanta, phone call, 28 Oct 1998, and e-mail, 29 Oct 2003. *Blind Willie's Blues*, David Fulmer, Lawrenceville, Georgia; Missing Lenk [sic] Video, 1996.


FOUR

**the Mount Pleasant Road route . . . Willie sometimes walked** . . . information from Dot Jones, retired tourism officer for Thomson-McDuffie, who had interviewed Hazel McTier and other relatives of Willie in the 1970s and had shown me this route, 3 Nov 2001.

**"I ain't goin' down that dirt road by myself"** . . . e.g. 'Ain't Goin' Down that Dirt Road (By Myself)', Howlin' Wolf, Chicago, Nov 1968, unissued till the 3-CD *The Chess Box*, MCA CHCD3-9332, US, 1991.

**an Act to define "persons of color"** . . . *Georgia Laws 1865* Vol. 1 p.239, as posted online at *www.rootsweb.com/~usgenweb/ga/gafiles.htm* by Tara D. Fields, 14 Feb 2004.

another that prescribed and regulated "the relationship of husband and wife" . . . *Georgia Laws 1865* Vol. 1 p.240, as posted ibid.

Sherman's burning of Atlanta and . . . March to the Sea . . . from 'General William T. Sherman: Would The Georgia Campaigns Of The First Commander Of The Modern Era Comply With Current Law Of War Standards?', Thomas G. Robisch, online, 6 Jan 2005, at *www.law.emory.edu/EILR/volumes/fall95/robisch.html*, and Sherman's route extrapolated from *Memoirs of W.T. Sherman*, as extracted online and seen, 6 Jan 2005, at *www.publicbookshelf.com/ public_html/The_Great_Republic_By_the_Master_Historians_Vol_III/generalsh_fb.html*.

Laura Smalley spoke for many . . . interviewed by John Henry Faulk, Hempstead, TX, 1941. This is one of many recorded interviews with ex-slaves that can be heard online on the Library of Congress website *www.memory.loc.gov*, 16 Jan 2004.

The *Georgia Encyclopedia* entry on Emancipation . . . seen online, 18 Jan 2005, at *www.georgiaencyclopedia.org/nge/Article.jsp?path=/HistoryArcheology/CivilWarandReconstruction/ Topics-12&id=h-1084.*

Chapter 10, titled "Negroes", begins: . . . Wilhoit, p.157.

And "Slaves were not necessarily unhappy . . ." ibid pp.159–160.

Georgia Historical Society . . . library . . . 501 Whitaker Street, Savannah, GA 31401. Chartered 1839, it claims to be the oldest cultural institution in the state. Visted, 1 Mar 2003.

Flanders . . . starts by noting . . . preface, p.vii. statements of this sort . . . p.270.

John Dollard's lovely landmark study . . . *Caste and Class in a Southern Town, 1937*; page references are to 3$^{rd}$ edn, 1957. Quotation here is pp. 56–59.

George McDuffie: speech . . . to the South Carolina legislature in 1835 . . . quotation reproduced on a history page on the website of Oakleigh Middle School, Junction City, Oregon, seen online, 24 Jan 2005, at *www.junctioncity.k12.or.us/Oaklea/breinmut10.htm.*

in Glascock. . . Reddick is living with. . . wife Mary and eleven-year-old Elbert . . . 1870 US Census for Glascock County GA, Gibson Post Office district, pp.16–17.

Silversmith . . . George Guimarin(e) . . . 1850 Census for Warren Country, Division no. 90.

the 1890 Census . . . all information from ' "First in the Path of the Firemen': The Fate of the 1890 Population Census" by Kellee Blake, US NARA Publications, Spring 1996, Vol. 28, No.1; seen online, 28 Jan 2005, *at www.archives.gov.*


FIVE

in January 1934, Willie and Ruthy Kate Williams . . . marry . . . details Ch.13.

As Cheryl Thurber has observed . . . day of interviews at her home in Baltimore, MD, 11 Nov 2001.

Cleveland "Coot" McTier . . . stood in line to register . . . registration card no.51, Precinct 13–2, McDuffie County, 5 Jun 1917, with Registrar's Report 10–3–24–A, ditto, held in a National Archives office in Atlanta GA. Registration was within the remit of the Provost Marshall General to the Secretary of War. (On the form, the registrar misspelled the name Cleveland; when Cleveland signed the form, spelling it correctly, the registar did not correct his own error.) That physical examination took place at 1917 draft process is mentioned in Dollard, p.161.

many didn't bother—including . . . Ed . . . concluded from detailed check of all possible cards, conducted by NARA SE Region Archives Specialist Guy Hall, Oct 2004.

*Black Marriages [of Lincoln Co., Georgia] 1866–1939* . . . compiled and edited by Judith Crow Wells, no other details; in Lincolnton Library, 5 Feb 2004.

**census indexes for each decade from 1850 to 1880** . . . compiled by Larry Raymond Butler and Janica Butler Turner, 1990s, no other details; Lincolnton Library, 5 Feb 2004.

**I visited black funeral homes** . . . Haughabrooks Funeral Home, Atlanta, 6 Mar 2003; Payne's Funeral Home, Warrenton, 2 Aug 2001; Hardwick's Funeral Home, Thomson, 5 Aug 2001; Payton's Mortuary, Statesboro, 30 Jan 2004.

**clipping from the *Augusta Chronicle* about Willie McTell's wife Kate** . . . by Vinnie Williams, 12 Nov 1980, p.3P.

**husband had helped the journalist** . . . statement by Mrs Josie A. West, Hardwick's Funeral Home, Thomson, 5 Aug 2001.

**In Statesboro . . . the newspaper ran no obituary column** . . . all this information from Delma E. Presley, Museum Director Emeritus and Professor of English Emeritus at Georgia Southern University, e-mails, 9 and 15 Feb 2005. (Dr Presley has read the entire archives of the Statesboro newspapers for his own research purposes.) As stated in the wonderful *Statesboro . . . 1866–1966 . . . A Century of Progress*, pp.62–78, the main papers of earlier eras were the *Statesboro Eagle, Georgia Farmer, Statesboro Star, Bulloch County Banner, Bulloch Herald, Bulloch Times* and *Statesboro News*, though several were re-namings and buy-outs. (*Bulloch Herald* ceased publication as a weekly end of Nov 1970.)

**In the 1970s, the Metropolitan Association for the Blind in Atlanta . . . information on Willie** . . . 'Blind Willie McTell,' David Evans, JEMF-106 LP sleevenotes, issued by the JEMF, Folklore & Mythology Center, UCLA, Los Angeles, 1979, p.6, based on info from Peter B. Lowry (unattributed).

**a tenor in their Glee Club in about 1950** . . . Bastin, p.137.

**the Center for the Visually Impaired** . . . 739 West Peachtree Street, NW, Atlanta GA 30308. Visited, 21 Feb 2003.

**we started with what we knew—or what we thought we knew** . . . i.e. from the general published accounts of McTell's life and work researched in the 1970s by Peter B. Lowry, Bruce Bastin, David Evans, Cheryl Evans Thurber, Anne M. Evans, and David H. Evans, as acknowledged.

**Willie himself says** . . . stated in *Last Session*, recorded Atlanta GA, Sep 1956.

**Marcel Lajos Breuer . . . asked to design a new Atlanta library** . . . library history from its website, 4 Feb 2005: *www.afplweb.com/z1/centennial/hist.html*; Breuer's details online same date from *www.design-technology.org/MarcelBreuer.htm, www.the-artists.org/ArtistView.cfm?id=8A01F17A-BBCF-11D4-A93500D0B7069B40* and *www.designmuseum.org/design/index.php?id=43*.

**Margaret Mitchell** . . . Summary of attitude as quoted on library website, ibid.

**AncestryPlus** . . . Detroit, Michigan; Thomson/Gale. Commercial firm charging by subscription, generally to educational establishments, libraries etc., for online access to genealogy databases including images of US censuses etc. Census records are available on microfilm at the National Archives, LDS Family History Centers and many libraries.

**Georgia Deaths Index** . . . database that is an index of deaths recorded by the state of Georgia, 1919–1998. Information per entry is often less than full, but, in theory, comprises name of the deceased, death date, race, gender, and age of the deceased, county of death, death certificate number and volume, and date the certificate was filed.

**Vital Records Office** . . . 2600 Skyland Dr. NE, Atlanta, GA 30319, (404) 679–4701; part of the Georgia Division of Public Health, responsible for maintenance, within stated date limits, of birth, marriage and death records plus an index of divorces.

**Cleveland's certificate was the key one . . .** Georgia State File no. 33379; copy obtained 24 Feb 2003.

**death certificate for Cleveland's father . . . "El McTear" . . .** no certificate number filled in, but filed in Militia District 152 (Mt. Auburn), McDuffie County GA, on 17 Jan 1933; the informant is one Mattie B. Cody. Copy obtained county probate court, 2 Feb 2004.

**Willie's aunt Annie Bell McTear . . . "delayed birth certificate" . . .** a "delayed birth certificate" is a certificate applied for retrospectively by the person herself. For this one no certificate number or State File no. is stated, but it is dated 9 Jul 1953 and signed by the Reviewing Official, the Clerk to the Court of Ordinary, McDuffie County GA, 27 Nov 1956; copy obtained county probate court, 2 Feb 2004. (She says she was born in 1888, which would have made her sixty-five, but we'd find that her year of birth was 1891. Another oddity: she signs herself Annie McTear McNair, but the affidavit of support sworn back in McDuffie county is signed "by Willie McNair, Non-Relative".)

**death certificate for El's later wife Judy/Julie/Julia . . .** no certificate number filled in, but filed in Militia District 134, McDuffie County GA, 26 Jul 1930. This states that she was a Story, born in McDuffie, and that she died of a heart attack, aged sixty-one, on 15 Jul 1930. Copy obtained county probate court, 2 Feb 2004. NB: In fact her name was Judy/Judie, not Julie/Julia. She had been born 1866 (1870 Census Warren Co. GA, Warrenton, p.106 enumerates Aug 1870.)

**he's "All MacTer" on the 1910 census . . . "Ell Metier" . . . 1880 . . . Elbert on the 1870 . . . back on the 1860 census . . .** 1910 Census: McDuffie Co. GA, Militia District 152, Enumeration District 47, sheet 12A. 1880 Census: McDuffie Co. GA, Militia District 152, Enumeration District 77, p.3. 1870 Census: Glascock Co. GA, Gibson Post Office, p.17. 1860 Slave Schedule: Glascock Co. GA, Militia District 1168G, p.3. This lists Reddick McTyeir's slaves as one black male ten-year-old, one black female fourteen-year-old [i.e. Essey] and one mulatto male aged nine months [i.e. Elbert].

**Nancy Barksdale . . .** the 1900 census for Mt. Auburn, McDuffie Co., gives her birth as Sep 1865; it gives her mother's birthplace as Virginia and her father's as Georgia. The 1920 census for 152nd Militia District [Mt. Auburn], McDuffie Co., GA, shows Nancy's mother Jane still alive, her age given as ninety and her birthplace now given as Georgia.

**By 1880, Elbert had moved out and Nancy was living with him . . .** 1880 US Census for Mt Auburn, McDuffie Co., GA, Enumeration district 77, p.3 (429C). Their children's birth years and months stated on 1900 US Census for Mt Auburn, McDuffie Co., GA, Enumeration District 41, Sheet 12 (though the census taker muddles up Cleveland and Elbert Jr, wrongly making Cleveland the younger boy). The 1900 census is uniquely valuable in recording the month and year of everybody's birth, rather than just asking them to state their age.

**"Mady", or Doll, is Elbert's child . . .** She's listed as a McTier on the 1910 US Census.

**Tom Harris . . . and Nancy will have three further children together . . .** i.e. G. Jesse, Buster, and Sallie.

**Cleveland . . . the 1920 census on which he appeared only as "Kute" . . .** McDuffie Co. Militia District 133, Enumeration District 63, sheet 4B. (On this census, all the family present—Cleveland, wife, Mary B, and children Mattie, Eddie, Irene, and "Horrice" are all logged as mulattos.)

Nancy's . . . parents and her brother . . . on the 1880 . . . 1880 US Census for Mt Auburn, McDuffie Co., GA, p.428B. (R.Barksdale, sixty-seven, farmer, birthplace Georgia, his parents' born Virginia; Nancy's mother Jane, forty-four, occupation "keeping"; her parents and herself born Virginia; their Georgia-born son, Magor, six years older than sister Nancy, is a twenty-one-year-old sawmill laborer.)

**Holland Nimmons McTyeire** . . . McTier, pp. 16–19.

**Jan McTier** . . . phone call and Dearing farm visit, 6 Aug 2001, augmented by e-mail, 13 Mar 2005, and details from Lindy McTier's unpublished stories of his childhood, written for his children, kindly lent to me and drawn on with permission.

**"history is history"** . . . McTier, p.37.


SIX

**Ed was a sixteen-year-old unskilled laborer . . . born in Happy Valley in or about August 1883** . . . 1900 US Census for Mt Auburn (152 District), McDuffie Co., GA, Enumeration District 41, Sheet 12, enumerated 25 Jun.

**Minnie Dorsey . . . born in October 1887 and now, in 1900** . . . 1900 US Census for Mt Auburn (152 District), McDuffie Co. GA, Enumeration District 41, Sheet 10B, enumerated 21 Jun.

**By the time of the 1910 census** . . . 1910 US Census for Jefferson County 1460 GM District, Enumeration District 35, Sheet [blank] B [the no. 3851 is written alongside], enumerated 16 Apr.

**Ed . . . reputedly by now a drifter and gambler** . . . "Ed McTear was a rather unsettled person, known to drink and gamble . . ." stated without supporting detail, but implicitly summarised from testimony of other family members interviewed in 1976, in 'Blind Willie McTell' by David Evans, JEMF-106 sleevenotes essay, 1979, p.6.

**So he was born when Theodore Roosevelt was President** . . . Teddy Roosevelt, the 26th President and the first born in New York City, held office 14 Sep 1901 to 4 Mar 1909.

**the specific date held temporarily on file by the Metropolitan Atlanta Association for the Blind** . . . ibid.

**In the McDuffie County Probate Court office . . . the old *Colored Marriage Books*** . . . Cleveland McTear marriage to Mary Bell Moss, 1 Oct 1916: Book 7, p.142; marriage of Eddie McTear to Hazel Samuel, 23 Jan 1936: Book 8, p.411.

**Illness was rife** . . . see 1880 Federal Census Mortality Schedule, Glascock County GA.

**In 1880 their acreage under cultivation** . . . Georgia Agricultural Census for 1880, extracted from the microfilm records in the Washington Library, Macon, GA in McTier, p.37.

**In 1867, black men in the South were enfranchised** . . . the specific information in this and the next nine paragraphs is taken from 'Race, Voting Rights, and Segregation: Rise and Fall of the Black Voter, 1868–1922', *www.umich.edu/~lawrace/votetour2.htm* to ditto *votetour7.htm*, author unidentified, seen online, 17 Feb 2005; 'Moving Onward: From Racial Division to Class Unity: The Stages of Development of the Ideology of Race in the United States: Reconstruction and After', authorship uncredited, Chicago, 1998; the League of Revolutionaries for a New America, seen online, 19 Feb 2005, at *www.lrna.org/texts/movingon/movingon.4.html*; and 'Atlanta in the Civil Rights movement', Atlanta Regional Consortium for Higher Education, online, 19 Feb 2005, at *www.atlantahighered.org/civilrights/essay_detail.asp?phase=1*.

**The KKK . . . 1865 . . . disbanded in 1869 and the Knights . . . 1870 . . .** *Statesboro: A Century of Progress 1866–1966*, p.426.

**Ida B. Wells-Barnett . . .** pamphlet 'Lynch Law in Georgia', cited without further detail ibid. Her work includes *Southern Horrors: Lynch Law in all its Phases*, with an introduction by Frederick Douglass, New York: Thomas & Duncan, 1931 [the year of Ms Wells-Barnett's death]. This is one of many works in the pamphlet *Lynching in the United States: A Selected Bibliography of Sources in the Auburn Avenue Research Library Atlanta, Georgia*, compiled by Henrietta Payne-Goodridge, Atlanta GA, Auburn Avenue Research Library, 2002.

**In 1945, Oliver C. Cox . . .** 'Lynching and the Status Quo', *Journal of Negro Education* 14, no.4, Fall 1945, pp.576–588. (Listed *Lynching in the United States*, ibid.)

**The last group lynching in the US . . .** see Wexler.

**The last lynching of a single individual . . .** statistics at the Archives of Tuskegee Institute, quoted in 'Atlanta in the Civil Rights movement', op.cit., give a date of 1968, but this overlooks the well-documented lynching of Michael Donald in Alabama in 1981. (In 1987 an all-white jury found the KKK responsible and ordered it to pay $7 million. It had to hand over all its assets, including its national HQ in Tuscaloosa.) This information seen online, 12 Mar 2005, at *www.spartacus.schoolnet.co.uk/USAlynching.htm*.

**on Sunday afternoon, 23 April 1899, in Newnan . . .** except where specified, all details of lynchings in the paragraphs that follow are taken from the eleven-column-wide, thirteen-page-long document 'Georgia Lynching Victims', seen, 9 Nov 2004, on the *Atlanta Journal Constitution* website, at *www.ajc.com/opinion/0402/28georgia_list.html*. Response to the 23 Apr Newnan atrocity, including by Du Bois, is the focus of Chapter 6 of Litwack (listed in *Lynching in the United States*, op.cit.)

**Millard H. McWhorten . . .** details from tourist leaflets read in Senoia, Coweta County, 23 Jan 2004.

**These murders . . . often planned . . . public spectacle . . .** the book *Without Sanctuary: Lynching Photography in America*, James Allen; Santa Fe, NM, Twin Palms Publishing, 2000, includes reproductions of such postcards, collected by the author, an Atlanta antiques dealer. (Listed in *Lynching in the United States*, op.cit.)

**'Strange Fruit' . . . Billie Holiday . . .** first recorded 20 Apr 1939, NYC [2 takes], with Frank Newton and his Café Society Orchestra, issued Commodore Records XFL14428 [take 1], and Commodore Records 526 [take 2].

**Bob Dylan . . . 'Desolation Row' . . .** first take 29 Jul 1965; issued take 2 Aug [instrumental overdubs 4 Aug] 1965; *Highway 61 Revisited*, Columbia CL-2389 and CS-9189, 1965.

**In Statesboro . . . Drew Holloway, was hanged in public . . .** *Statesboro: A Century of Progress 1866–1966*, pp.427, 431.

**Maude Brannen Edge . . .** ibid, p.442, 443 (reproduced from columns written 1957).

**Superior Court, first held in May 1797 . . .** *Historically First . . .*, Beth Crawford Parrish, Statesboro, GA; First Federal Savings and Loan Association of Statesboro, 1977, p.1.

**John Dollard . . .** on the general topic, see Ch. VII, 'The Sexual Gain', pp.134–172.

**"legitimate status" . . .** ibid, p.136; **"many, if not most . . ."** p.139.

**Bob Hammond . . . of the Burke County Museum . . .** notes made from conversation at the museum, Waynesboro, 29 Jan 2004.

**As Dollard puts it: "One might ask why . . . renunciation . . ."** p.143.

**"It may be again that . . . the psychic strain may be much less." . . .** p.144.

**Alan Lomax . . .** *The Land Where The Blues Began*, p.374.

'A-Z Blues'. . . shocks even seasoned blues aficionados . . . see Appendix: Career Discography for recording and release details. The comparable McTell song 'Southern Can Is Mine' was the subject of a long and troubled correspondence on the Pre-War Blues e-mail discussion group (*pre-war-blues@yahoogroups.com*) in Dec 2004.

the delight with which African Americans heard . . . of the sinking of the *Titanic* . . . this is widely documented; for a summary, including song examples, see Gray, *Song & Dance Man III*, pp.136–7, 358, 460. As noted there (p.358), it was not only black Americans who rejoiced. Russian symbolist poet Alexander Blok wrote that he was "indescribably happy. There is, after all, an ocean."

"We have seen white men guarding the border . . . Dollard, p.166.

Dollard sums up by observing . . . p.170.

Eric Millin . . . *Defending the Sacred Hearth: Religion, Politics, and Racial Violence in Georgia, 1904–1906*, M.A. Thesis, University of Georgia, 2002; summary of its argument quoted from the website of the Dept. of History, University of North Carolina at Chapel Hill, online, 19 Feb 2005, at *www.unc.edu/depts/history/gradstudents/millin.html*.

The Allen Sturgis case, in McDuffie . . . *Augusta Chronicle*, Jun 4 1888, p.1. Sturgis was a thirteen-year-old on the 1880 US Census for McDuffie County, Thomson, Enumeration District 75, p.13. When he was lynched for burglary, his mother Ann would have been fifty years old and his father, if still alive, sixty-eight. Sturgis also had a younger sister, Fannie, who would have been nine years old when her brother was murdered.

On Tuesday, 7 May 1907, east of Thomson . . . *Augusta Chronicle*, 8 May 1907, p.1.

Charlie was a month short of thirty years old . . . these details based on 1900 US Census for McDuffie County, Militia District 152, Enumeration District 41, Sheet 1A.

headline in the *Times-Journal* of Eastman, Dodge County . . . 19 Nov 1897, p.1.

Benny Richards . . . pamphlet 'Burning at Stake in the United States: A Record of the Public Burning by Mobs of Five Men During the First Five Months of 1919, in the States of Arkansas, Florida, Georgia, Mississippi and Texas', republished Baltimore, MD; Black Classics Press, 1986, p.13–14. *East Tennessee News* report, 15 May 1919, and letter from NAACP secretary, quoted in pamphlet. Race of its secretary specified by him in letter to Florida governor, quoted p.19. (The pamphlet description in *Lynching in the United States*, op.cit., states wrongly that he was tortured and burned alive. 'Georgia Lynching Victims', op.cit., lists his name as Denny Richards aka Denny Brown. Ancestry.com's search engine, 17 Mar 2005, can find no one by any variant of the name on the 1910 US Census for Warren County or the surrounding counties.)

From the *McDuffie Weekly Journal* . . . extracts copied Warrenton library 3 Aug 2001.

". . . a lynching town" . . . *McClure's*, New York, author and date unstated; reprinted *Statesboro News*, 2 Jan 1905. *McClure's* was a monthly, published from 1893; it attracted writers including Conan Doyle, O. Henry, Jack London, Joel Chandler Harris, Stephen Crane, and Rudyard Kipling. This story was probably by Ray Stannard Baker (1870–1946), who turned some of his articles into *Following the Color Line*, 1908.

That 28 July, a Thursday night, a forty-six-year-old farmer, Henry R. Hodges . . . ages of Mr and Mrs Hodges and daughter and names Claudie and Kittie, 1900 US Census for Bulloch County, Militia District 1320, Enumeration District 95, Sheet 4B. Kittie's middle name and boys' names from 'Hodges Family History', which offers variant crime details, online, 14 Mar 2005, at *www.rootsweb.com/~gabulloc/histories/hodgeskids.html*. Social status of the Hodges, and descendants still in Bulloch, from reseacher Delma E. Presley, e-mail, 10 Mar 2005. Inquest details, wives' accounts and contemporary news coverage from *Statesboro: A Century of Progress 1866–1966*, p.428 and *Statesboro News*, 05 Aug 1904.

**"County's great tragedy was in July, 1904."** . . . *Statesboro: A Century of Progress 1866–1966*, p.428.

**picture postcards . . . copyrighted to T.M. Bennett** . . . seen online, 14 Mar 2005, at *www.rootsweb.com/~gabulloc/histories/hodgeskids.html*.

**Judge Daley, a cadaverous man . . . the ornately-carved backdrop to his judicial chair** . . . description based on a photograph in the invaluable book *Statesboro*, Delma E. Presley and Smith C. Banks, p.24.

**soldiers deployed from Savannah and Statesboro took no action** . . . information, and the account of the lynching and its violent aftermath, from *McClure's Magazine*, op.cit.

**both men were turpentine farmhands** . . . 1900 US Census for Bulloch County GA Statesboro Town, Enumeration District 94, Sheet 32B (Reid) and Worth County GA Sylvester Town, Militia District 867, Enumeration District 102, Sheet 4A (Cato).

**An old man and his son, in their cabin** . . . op.cit. This is listed as a lynching on website *www.jimcrowhistory.org/scripts/jimcrow/map.cgi?city=statesboro&state=georgia*, seen online, 19 Feb 2005: "Albert Roger and his son were lynched at Statesboro, GA., 17 August, for being Negroes. A number of other Negroes were whipped for no other offense . . . Before the rampage ended, numerous blacks were assaulted and their homes destroyed. Law enforcement officials never attempted to prosecute any of the rioters or mob ringleaders. Many blacks moved out of Statesboro in the wake of the riot."

**The third man to die was Sebastine McBride . . . 17 August** . . . This date is calculated from the contemporary *McClure's* account. It's more credible than the date of 27 Aug, as listed in 'Georgia Lynching Victims', op.cit., suggesting that 27 is a misprint for 17.

**The Methodist minister . . . Whitley Langston** . . . statement approved 1 Sep 1904. *New York Evening Post* quoted in the *Statesboro News*, 16 Sep 1904.

**written by . . . James Alonzo ("Lonnie") Brannen** . . . Delma E. Presley's judgment, e-mail, 10 Mar 2005.

**As Charles Moseley and Fred Brogdon wrote** . . . 'A Lynching at Statesboro: The Story of Paul Reid and Will Cato,' Charles Moseley and Fred Brogdon, *Georgia Historical Quarterly*, LXV, Oct 1981, pp.104–118. This is also the source for the following information: 1 Aug Augusta and Savannah newspaper details, Before Day Clubs story and details, length of inquest jury deliberations, editorial demanding public hanging, date of jury selection, date set for hanging, sheriff unlocking cell door, identification of Portal as McBride's home, *Statesboro News* quote "If the Negroes really think . . .", Methodist Church expulsion and withdrawal figures, and 18 Aug citizens' meeting.


SEVEN

**a special generation was being born, in Georgia and elsewhere** . . . except where otherwise stated the dates and places of birth in the lists that follow are taken from the assiduous Eric LeBlanc's detailed listings as posted daily on the Pre-War Blues e-mail discussion group; his listings are available online, organised by date, at *www.bluesworld.com/bluesdates.html*.

**Mamie Smith, whose first record can be said to have "started" the blues** . . . 'Crazy

Blues', NYC, 10 Aug 1920, OKeh Records OK 4169. Its million-selling success spurred other record labels to record blues for the previously unaddressed black market.

**unknown date, that fragile genius Tommy Johnson** . . . that it was some time in *January* 1896 was "new" information found by Bob Eagle on 1900 Census Hinds County, Mississippi, Enumeration District 71, and posted to the Pre-War Blues Group (op.cit.), 26 Mar 2005.

**the "Rip Roarin', Snortin'** . . . **Skillet-Lickers** . . . Russell, *Blacks, Whites and Blues*, p. 15.

**'The Darkey's Wail'** . . . ibid, p.42. Recording details (2 Apr 1927, Atlanta; issued Columbia 15163-D) Russell, *Country Music Records: A Discography, 1921–1942*, p.718.

**the Georgia Academy for the Blind in Macon** . . . Puckett's attendance dates, e-mail from Tony Russell, 16 Oct 2004; segregated buildings information, interview with Sister Fleeta Mitchell, Athens GA, 14 Apr 1998.

**Emmett Miller** . . . *www.takecountryback.com/features/blues2.htm.*, 29 Jul 2004.

**Zoar United Methodist Church** . . . 9889 Zoar Church Road, Stapleton GA 30823; visited 5 Feb 2004.

**Roosevelt appointed a Commission on Country Life** . . . Kennedy, ch.1, p.6, as reproduced online, seen 20 Feb 2005 at *www.washingtonpost.com/wp-srv/style/longterm/books/chap1.*

**By 1910 Willie was six years old** . . . **in Spread** . . . 1910 US Census for Jefferson County 1460 GM District, Enumeration District 35, Sheet [blank] B [the no. 3851 is written alongside], enumerated 16 April.

**Spread is the old name for Stapleton** . . . Jefferson County map, 1899, and Jefferson County map 2001, the former seen online, 28 Feb 2005, at *www.cviog.uga.edu/Projects/gainfo/histcountymaps/jefferson1899map.jpg.*

**Spread changed its name to Stapleton around 1916** . . . interview with James Lee Hobbs at his home, Stapleton GA, 5 Aug 2001.

**the Augusta, Gibson & Sandersville Rail Road** . . . stated in the unsigned railway buffs article 'Branchville and Bowman Railroad: Problematic Minutiae' seen online, 28 Feb 2005, at *www.geocities.com/joedbart/content/cc/bb/bbproblems.htm.*

**In 1913 an American Ford took fourteen hours** . . . **By 1925 a Model T** . . . **there were twenty-six million** . . . Kennedy, ch.1, p.9, as reproduced online, op.cit.

**Railroad Street, Thomson, in 1908** . . . old photographs of Thomson described from scans of old postcards kindly sent to me by local collector, Gary Doster.

**The 1933 State Highway Department map of Georgia** . . . map dated July 1933, published by the Department, Atlanta GA, available in libraries 2001.

**Stapleton's railroads died in the Depression** . . . interview with James Lee Hobbs, op.cit., plus local observation, 2001.

**Minnie played** . . . **guitar** . . . **according to Kate McTell** . . . 'Blind Willie McTell', David Evans, notes to *Atlanta Blues 1933*, JEMF-106 LP, JEMF, Folklore & Mythology Center, UCLA, Los Angeles, 1979, p.8.

**Memphis Minnie made her first record** . . . details, as always with discographical information of this type, is taken from the "bible" of listings and discographies for the old blues, Dixon & Godrich, now superceded by Dixon, Godrich & Rye.

**David Evans' parents gave her** . . . **Paul Oliver's book *The Story of the Blues*** . . . *Blues Unlimited* no.125, Jul/Aug 1977, p.4, confirmed by day of interviews with Cheryl Thurber (Evans' wife at the time) in Baltimore MD, 11 Nov 2001.

**Gold Harris** . . . **recalled** . . . undated interview quoted in 'Blind Willie McTell', David Evans, op.cit., p.8.

**Uncle Harley, logged as Elbert H. McTier on the 1900 census** . . . 1900 Census for Mt Auburn (152 District), McDuffie Co. GA, Enumeration District 41, Sheet 12A.

**the Ellises . . . son Henry . . . said later** . . . undated interview with Henry Ellis, quoted in 'Blind Willie McTell', David Evans, op.cit., p.8.

**Bulloch County had been formed from . . . St Philip's** . . . *Statesboro: A Century of Progress*, pp.2–3.

**Archibald Bulloch** . . . ibid, plus online article seen, 6 Mar 2005, at *www.georgiaencyclopedia.org/nge/Article.jsp?path=/HistoryArchaeology/ColonialEraTrusteePeriod/People-4&id=h-682*.

**foragers from Sherman's army** . . . *Statesboro: A Century of Progress*, pp.8–9.

**Statesboro became the county seat** . . . ibid, p.6 and *Statesboro*, p.7.

**It was only eleven miles but in the 1890s . . . the Engineer was E.E. Smith** . . . article by D.B. Turner, *Bulloch Times*, 24 Apr 1930, reprinted *Statesboro: A Century of Progress*, p.19.

**Willie McTell was . . . driven up by car from Statesboro to Dover** . . . interview with Willie's half-brother, Robert Owens, and his wife, Catherine, quoted without source details in 'Blind Willie McTell', David Evans, op.cit., p.21, but in fact from the interview recorded Statesboro 15 Jan 1976 by David Evans and Cheryl Thurber.

**the population of Statesboro** . . . all from census figures as given in *Statesboro: A Century of Progress*, p.425.

**Dr George Ross** . . . ibid, p.423. Details that follow on courthouse dates, Mrs Lee's hotel, turpentine, Mr H.S. Blitch, strikes, a portable saw mill, soda-bottling, mains water, the telephone, Bulloch Oil, the fire dept, street lights, guano trains, churches, egg-sized hailstones, cotton, and tobacco are all gleaned from the pages of the same volume.

**the Statesboro Buggy & Wagon Company . . . would take the body of Minnie** . . . Georgia State Board of Health Bureau of Vital Statistics death certificate file no. 33162, 21 Dec 1920, Statesboro; copy Georgia Vital Records Service, 24 Feb 2003.

**Naomi Johnson . . . says** . . . interviewed at her home at Elm Street, Statesboro, 1 Mar 2003 and 31 Jan 2004.

**the boll weevil** . . . "Atlanta Blues", Bruce Bastin, notes to *Atlanta Blues 1933*, op.cit., p.1.


EIGHT

**he could discern light through one eye, as several who knew him said** . . . 'Blind Willie McTell', David Evans, notes to *Atlanta Blues 1933*, JEMF-106 LP, JEMF, Folklore & Mythology Center, UCLA, Los Angeles, 1979.

**a little shack by the Savannah & Statesboro Railroad** . . . stated as fact, without any source offered, ibid, p.7.

**testimony recorded in the 1970s** . . . David Evans, ibid, pp. 7–8: this "incident is quite well remembered by older people in Statesboro"; as usual, he gives no detail or sources.

**the town's progressive character** . . . originally drawn to my attention by Emeritus Professor Delma E. Presley, phone conversation Statesboro, 1 Mar 2003; plus many conversations since.

**the outsider who became mayor . . . James Alonzo Brannen** . . . ibid, plus e-mail from Dr Presley, 23 Mar 2005.

**one of the first women newspaper editors in Georgia** . . . details this paragraph from Presley & Banks, pp.6, 115, 107, except . . .

**forty-six-year-old German immigrant Gustave Jaeckel** . . . US census 1900, Bulloch
Co., Statesboro Town, Enumeration District 94, Sheet 5B, and US Census 1910, Chatham
Co., Savannah City Ward 3, Enumeration District 59, Sheet 22B.

**Glenn Ford** . . . recalled by Naomi Johnson, who worked and met him there; interviewed
Elm St, Statesboro, 1 Mar 2003.

**In 1907 . . . the City Colored School** . . . *Statesboro: A Century of Progress 1866–1966*,
pp.266–270.

**William James was thirty-five years old . . . six foot, six inches . . . a large presence**
. . . Delma E. Presley phone call, op.cit.

**Minnie's alleged possible birthplace of Wadley** . . . David Evans, 'Blind Willie McTell',
op.cit., p.6; no source given.

**an instructor from the Tuskegee . . . New York State** . . . *Statesboro: A Century of
Progress*, plus detail online, 23 Mar 2005, at *www.nps.gov/tuin*. Tuskegee's reputation was
damaged hard in 1972 when the scandal broke of its complicity in a forty-year-long public
health service experiment in which 400 poor blacks with syphilis were neither given
diagnosis nor treatment.

**Anna Jeanes** . . . details online, 24 Mar 2005, at *www.fairhillburial.org/famous.php*.

**the Rev. C.T. Walker** . . . *Statesboro: A Century of Progress*; speech summary reprinted from
*Bulloch Times*, 31 Jul 1912.

**Earl M. Lee . . . Statesboro resident** . . . phone interview at his home, 8 Aug 2004.

***Bulloch Times* for the spring season, 1916** . . . pen and ink illustration from undated
paper "just before Easter" 1916, reproduced *Statesboro: A Century of Progress*, p.329.

**"my real home"** . . . said to John A. & Ruby T. Lomax for the Library of Congress, Atlanta,
5 Nov 1940.

**Harvey Van Buren** . . . 'The Life of a Hospital', Barry Turner, *Statesboro Magazine*, Vol.4
no.1, Jan/Feb 2003, ed. Karen Powell, Statesboro GA, p.70; *Statesboro*, p.115; and
*Statesboro: A Century of Progress*, p.430. (This last, written late 1960s, never mentions that
Van Buren was an African American. Its only hint is the phrase "has been a leader among his
people.")

**during the flu epidemic of 1918** . . . detail from Delma E. Presley, op.cit.

**from his drugstore . . . 3 and 5 North Main . . . to no.45** . . . detailed town maps
produced for insurance companies (here the Sorrier Insurance Agency: an unfortunate
name, you'd think) by Sanborn Map Co., New York. Their 1922 and 1930 Statesboro
maps seen local library, 3 Mar 2003. All detail of house interior, gazebo parties, car, meal
routine, baking and type of talk between Mrs Ellis and Minnie supplied by Dr Jack N.
Averitt, born 1922; former graduate school dean and history professor at Georgia Southern,
interviewed at his home, Circle Dr, Statesboro, 2 Mar 2003. His mother was close friends
with Mrs Ellis, he practiced piano in their house daily and remembers it as from age four.

**Nellie McQueen Ellis . . . William Hays Ellis . . . Annie E** . . . personal details collated
from *Index, Eastside Cemetery, Statesboro*, typescript, seen Jenkins Co. Library, plus 1900 US
Census Bulloch Co., Statesboro Town, enumeration District 94, p.1B; 1910 US Census for
same district, p.1B; 1920 ditto, p.4A; 1930 ditto, p.8B; plus information in situ from Ed Ellis
and his son W.H. (William Henry) Ellis, 30 Jan 2004, and from Jack Averitt, ibid.

**Benjamin Ellis, born in 1810 . . . Joshua** . . . US Census 1860, Bulloch Co., Bengal Post
Office, pp.9–10.

**oil seed mill . . . One of the investors . . . was Ellis** . . . *Statesboro Magazine*, Vol.4 no.1,
Jan/Feb 2003, op.cit., p.52.

**Mr Ellis . . . many Statesboro pies . . .** *Statesboro: A Century of Progress*, pp. 15, 24, 153, 306, 382, 386, 444. There are contradictory claims for when W.H. Ellis took over the drugstore. I've gone with 1908 in the main text, as ibid p.386, but p.313 suggests that he was running the business by Nov 1902.

**Henry told Evans** 'Blind Willie McTell', David Evans, op.cit., p.8.

**Lindy McTier . . .** e-mail reply to questions, 22 Mar 2005.

**the "new" W.H. Ellis . . . remembers . . .** conversation in his City Hall office, 30 Jan 2004.

**Willie the Statesboro child didn't just play marbles . . .** all detail on Willie this paragraph stated in "A Glance Back", Beth Crawford Parrish, *Historically First . . .*, Statesboro GA, 1977; 1ˢᵗ Federal Savings & Loan Assn. of Statesboro, pp.40–1.

**For $12 you could buy . . . the Vanophone . . .** *Statesboro: A Century of Progress*, p.323. Other detail this paragraph re musical instruments in Statesboro, pp.338–9.

**a man called Stapleton . . . remembered in the 1970s as Seph . . .** David Evans, 'Blind Willie McTell', op.cit., p.8. Joe and Eva Stapleton detail 1920 US Census, Bulloch Co., Statesboro City, Enumeration District 14, Sheet 8A.

**Willie . . . used to . . . listen to . . . Miss Annie, play the piano . . .** 'A Glance Back', Beth Crawford Parrish, op.cit.; all other detail 1910 US Census, Bulloch Co., Statesboro City, Enumeration District 11, Sheet 1B and 1930 ditto, Enumeration District 16–9, Sheet 8B.

**Ada and Ida Watts . . .** David Evans ('Blind Willie McTell', op.cit., p.8) refers to "a blind girl named Watts living down the street" who "read Braille and . . . encouraged him to receive an education"; no details or source given. Details 1910 US Census, Bulloch Co., Statesboro City, Enumeration District 11, Sheet 22B, and 1920 US Census, Bibb Co., Macon City Ward 3, Enumeration District 35, Sheet 15B.


NINE

**Lourie Owens (the spelling of "Lourie" is uncertain) . . .** This is the spelling on Robert Owens' death certificate (State file no. 011764, issued Savannah GA April 1978). On the 1910 census it is given as "Lurry", on the 1920 as "Lury" or "Lery", and on the 1930 as "Lura". He is a "Mulatto" on the 1910, "Black" on the 1920 and "Negro" on the 1930. (1910 US Census Bulloch Co. GA District 9, enumerated 29 Apr; 1920 US Census Bulloch Co. District 14, enumerated 7 Jul; 1930 US Census Bulloch Co. District 16–10, enumerated 14 Apr.)

**his mother, Adeline . . .** We find her as a fifteen-year-old on the 1880 US Census for Burke Co., District 65, described as a farm laborer, born in Georgia, black, and married to a Robert Owens, farmer, "Mulatto", aged twenty. Her fifty-year-old mother, Caroline Ashberry, lives with them. We find Adeline again on the later census pages as above.

**on Robertson's sideshow. He had an old plantation show . . .** McTell, Atlanta, Sep 1956. Full session given to me on cassette by David Fulmer, Mar 2003; transcribed 23–24 Oct, 2004. In his book *Sweet As The Showers Of Rain*, p.122, Sam Charters, who had edited down the full recording for the 1961 LP (see Appendix: Career Discography), extrapolated from it that McTell "was most closely associated with the John Roberts' Plantation Show in 1916 and 1917 . . ."; Bastin, p.131, picked this up and ran with it as "he was reported playing with the John Roberts' Tent Show in 1916 and 1917 . . .". However, no such outfit, whichever way you name it, has left any trace of any existence. Doug Seroff, co-author of *Out Of Sight*, has stated that the name that came to mind immediately was "the John Robinson Circus Show" (phone-call to this writer, 20 Sep 2004).

**the John Robinson Circus Show** . . . details from Thomas Deighan and P. Carter (e-mails to circus history group *www.circushistory.org*, 8 Jun 2004), John Robinson (no relation) at *www.sideshowcentral.com* seen, 19 Sep 2004, (now *www.sideshowworld.com*), and from *www.lawrencecountyohio.com/ironton/stories/circus.htm*, 20 Sep 2004.

**Bessie Smith** . . . **Ma Rainey** . . . *Encyclopedia of the Blues*.

**Georgia Tom** . . . statement by Thomas Dorsey seen quoted, 29 Jul 2004, on *www.honky-tonks.org/showpages/tadorsey.htm*. For a detailed study of this remarkable figure, see Harris.

**Georgia** . . . **prohibition** . . . **Bulloch County** . . . "largely dry since July 1880" and details re Augusta and Savannah dealers, newspaper ads and trainloads of jugs all from *Statesboro: A Century of Progress*, pp.431–2; all other details from Dr Delma E. Presley, e-mail to this writer, 25 Dec 2006: "Georgia allowed local communities to decide for themselves whether to permit the sale of alcohol. Bulloch County remained dry through the prohibition period . . . Until 1915 confederate veterans could sell 'near beer' as a means to supplement their meager war pension. So called 'locker clubs' (private golf clubs, social clubs, etc.) also operated until then. But the legislature voted for total dryness in 1915, and Georgians officially could not consume alcoholic beverages legally until voters repealed the eighteenth amendment. On May 15, 1935, both the state and county voted to repeal the prohibition amendment . . . Voters enacted a liquor ordinance in December of 1947, and to this day one cannot purchase packaged liquor in the county. Private clubs, like the County Club and American Legion, continued to serve liquor legally."

**In the 1930s, living in Atlanta** . . . **Willie would be selling bootleg whiskey** . . . see later chapter.

**Annie Jackson and her son Teddy** interviewed at Mrs Jackson's home, Thomson, GA, 4 Feb 2004. (Re "the farmland around Happy Valley": Teddy Jackson told me the terrain "had changed: Happy Valley was mostly farmland then, not pines—they're a post-1970s quick cashcrop.")

**Probate Judge Lucy Bryant** . . . conversation Warren County Court, Warrenton GA, 2 Nov 2001. Mrs Bryant retired in 2004 and died 1 September 2007, aged 71.

**Harper Myrick** . . . reported in the *Bulloch Times*, 17 July 1919.

**Willie Moore, a highly regarded Statesboro individual** . . . Delma E. Presley, e-mail, 25 Dec 2006.

**Interviewed in the 1970s, Robert Owens** . . . from transcript of interview by David and Cheryl Evans, at Owens' home, 130 Elm Street, Statesboro GA, 15 Jan 1976.

**Robert, interviewed in the 1970s** . . . transcript of interview by Anne Evans and David Evans Snr., at Owens' home, Statesboro, 22 Aug 1975.

**the death certificate obtained in Atlanta** . . . Georgia State Registrar File no. 33162, acquired 24 Feb 2003; see Chapter 5 for account of its acquisition.

**Jack Averitt** . . . interviewed at his home, Circle Drive, Statesboro, 2 Mar 2003.

**Dr Frank Forest Floyd** . . . full name and "blemished" ibid. (Jack Averitt added: "I do not remember him: he delivered me [*laughs*] but I do not remember him.") Detail re Floyd's arrival date and Sanitarium status from *Statesboro: A Century of Progress*, pp. 243–4. Floyd's age (he was born Jan 1875), wives' and son's names from the US Censuses for 1900, 1910 and 1920: respectively Bulloch Co. GA Briar Patch District, Enumeration District 92, Sheet 11B, enumerated 12 Jun 1900; Bulloch Co. GA Statesboro City Supervisor's District 1

(Enumeration District unreadable from scan) Sheet 2B, enumerated 15 Apr 1910; and Bulloch Co. GA City of Statesboro Enumeration District 14, enumerated 9 Jan 1920.

**Ethel [Floyd] . . . interviewed in the mid-1970s . . .** by either David and Cheryl Evans or Anne and David Evans Sr, 1975–76 (no details footnoted), quoted in Evans, booklet to the LP *Atlanta Blues 1933*, JEMF-106, LA, 1979, p.8.

**"Statesboro Buggy & Wagon Co." . . .** The company sold large numbers of mules, horses, saddles, and hardware; they also opened a mortuary and traded as the Statesboro Undertaking Co. But the genealogy librarian in the Regional Library in Statesboro found me an ad in their newspaper archive in which the Statesboro Buggy & Wagon Company presented itself directly as "Funeral Directors and Embalmers", published 16 Dec 1920: just six days before Minnie's burial.

**the black section of Eastside Cemetery . . .** the death certificate states "Stateboro Cemetery"; there is no such place: the main (white) city cemetery is Eastside.

**Mr O.L. McLemore . . .** He is pictured in c.1910 in Presley and Banks, p.111; Dr. Presley tells me McLemore worked for the company through most of the 1920s (phone-call, Jun 2004).

**Mrs Herbaline Rich . . .** interviewed by phone at her home, Statesboro GA, 14 May 2004. The detail re the wooden marker also from her testimony.

**Thomas Grove [Baptist] Church . . .** date organised given in *Statesboro: A Century of Progress*, p.49. McTell concert date from *Bulloch Times and Statesboro News*, 19 Sep 1946 (first mention of him in the city's papers).

**Jack Averitt too remembers a story his father told . . .** interview op. cit. .

**"My mother died and left me reckless . . ."** is followed by "Papa died and left me wild, wild, wild." The closest similar use seems to be in Bessie Smith's 'Reckless Blues' (NYC, 14 Jan 1925), where it is not parental death but complaint that yields the epithets: "My mama says I'm reckless, my daddy says I'm wild".


TEN

**Willie's father is said to have taken up with . . . Pearl Hill . . .** David Evans, who seems to have assumed this was after Ed's liaison with Minnie; booklet to the LP *Atlanta Blues 1933*, JEMF-106, LA, 1979, p.7.

**Ola Moss, was born around 1901 . . .** maiden name from McDuffie County Probate Court general marriage index listing marriage to Clarence McGahee 23 Dec 1916; age extrapolated from the US Census 1920 McDuffie Co. GA, Enumeration District 66, Sheet 3A, on which she's stated to be nineteen; absent on US Census 1930, McDuffie Co. GA, Enumeration District 958, Sheet 4A. No death filed at McDuffie Probate Court (checked 17 Jan 2007) so it probably occurred before 27 Sep 1927 (date records began there).

**Clarence McGahee, a farm laborer . . .** linked to Ola by David Evans, source unstated, booklet op.cit. . (Evans spells it "McGahey" throughout.) US Censuses: 1920 and 1930, ibid. Draft Registration Card Form 1 921 no.33, Registrar's Report 10–3–241, dated 15 Jun 1933. Gravestone seen 5 Feb 2004.

**"wild, wild, wild" . . .** 'Statesboro Blues'; discographical details see Appendix: Career Discography.

**Ethel Floyd . . .** see Chapter 9.

**Willie told Library of Congress folklorist John A. Lomax . . .** Interview recorded Atlanta, 5 Nov 1940; release details Appendix: Career Discography.

**Walt Strickland** . . . interviewed at his antiques/junk shop, Statesboro GA, 31 Jan 2004.

**Lannie Simmons** . . . birth date US Census 1900, Bulloch Co. GA, Briar Patch District, Enumeration District 92, Sheet 11B, enumerated 12 Jun 1900; death date Georgia Deaths Index 1919–98, certificate no. 32088; advertisements *Bulloch Times*, 4 Apr 1922 and 18 Aug 1927, seen in *Statesboro: A Century of Progress*; quotations and other detail from phone interview with great-niece Alice Budack, Statesboro, 30 Jul 2004.

**Naomi Johnson** . . . interviewed at her home, 205 Elm Street, Statesboro, Georgia, 2 Mar 2003.

**Rayford Simmons** . . . US Census 1870 Bulloch Co. GA, "the town of Statesboro", Page 1, enumerated 8 Jul.

**Brooks Simmons** . . . US Census 1920 Bulloch Co. GA, City of Statesboro, Enumeration District 14–15, Sheet no. unreadable, enumerated 21 Jul; 1930 ditto, Enumeration District 16–8, Sheet 14A, enumerated 8 Apr; and Georgia Deaths Index. Clothing store location detail and profile re his liberal views from Delma E. Presley (e-mails, 7 and 8 Jan 2007).

**he's the only one to be specific** . . . You could say all this was straightforward until David Evans wrongly attributed the clothes-store ownership to Lannie Simmons (and on the same page called him Lannie Smith); David Evans, op.cit., p.9.

**Lillie Mae Brown** . . . interviewed at her daughter's home in Statesboro, 2 Mar 2003.

**Doty Litchenstein** . . . details filled in by Delma E. Presley (e-mail, 12 Feb 2007).

**the school year started in January** . . . all detail, except as otherwise stated, from Sister Fleeta Mitchell, interviewed at her home outside Athens GA, 14 Apr and 1 Aug 2001.

**the boll weevil had arrived . . . dramatic slump in cotton production** . . . data from Bruce Bastin, 'Atlanta Blues', booklet to the LP *Atlanta Blues 1933*, JEMF-106, LA, 1979, p.1. (Cotton bale production 1920: 1,415,000; in 1921: 787,000.)

**Marjorie Miller was succeeded by John Allen Williams** . . . Miller appears as music teacher, 1920 US Census Bibb Co. GA, Macon City, Enumeration District 35, Sheet 12A, enumerated 12 Jan.; testimony re Williams from Fleeta Mitchell to Art Rosenbaum, quoted in his notes to the cassette *There's A Bright Side Somewhere*, Nathaniel and Fleeta Mitchell, with Lucy Barnes and Brandy "Doc" Barnes, Ruth Bowden and Rosa Johnson, recorded Athens GA, 29 Sep 1979, 20 Mar 1980, 8 May 1991 and 12 May 1991; Global Village Music C223, NY NY 10025, 1991; notes by Rosenbaum and Michael Schlesinger, 1991. All quotes from Mitchell to Rosenbaum taken from these notes.

**Willie, Fleeta . . . also taught clay modeling and practical craftwork** . . . sources here are my interviews with Fleeta Mitchell; Anne M. Evans and David H. Evans Sr interview with Robert Owens, Statesboro GA, 22 Aug 1975 and David Evans, booklet, ibid, p.9.

**Willie Battie Smith told David Evans** . . . ibid.

**The matron was Alice, the principal's wife** . . . 1920 US Census Bibb Co. GA, Macon City, Enumeration District 35, Sheet 12A, enumerated 12 Jan.

**Miss Essie Mae Hubbard Carlisle** . . . Her father, Frank Hubbard, owned the undertaking business at which her husband, John Carlisle, worked. She was twenty-nine in 1920. Source: US Census 1920, Bibb Co. GA, Macon City, Enumeration District 35, Sheet 11 A, enumerated 12 Jan.

**the cassette Art Rosenbaum had produced** . . . *There's A Bright Side Somewhere,* op.cit.

**In the early August evening** . . . 8 Aug 2001.

**Little Richard** . . . J.R. Johnson, in 2001 Curator of the Macon-based Georgia Music Hall of Fame, interviewed 8 Aug 2001; said Little Richard had talked re Uncle Ned onstage at Macon Coliseum Mar 2001, and that June told Johnson he and the group had gigged together.

**On one of the original handwritten sheets of the 1920 US Census for Macon City . . .** US Census 1920 Bibb County GA, Macon City, District 25, p.24.

**Folklorist Peter B. Lowry discovered that Willie . . . sung tenor in the Glee Club . . .** phone interview with Lowry at his home in Austinmer, NSW, Australia, 14 Sep 2004; David Evans reports the Glee Club information in his booklet, op.cit., p.20 without acknowledgment to Lowry.

**Willie makes his first documented appearance . . .** US Census 1910 Jefferson Co. GA, Militia District 460, Enumeration District 35, enumerated 16 Apr; discussed in Ch. 6.

**Robert, telling his 1970s interviewers . . .** transcript of interview of Robert and Catherine Owens by David Evans and Cheryl Thurber (then Evans), Statesboro GA, 15 Jan 1976.

**"Eyeballs were very small . . ."** For details see this book's penultimate chapter.

**Hazel McTear's sister Annie . . .** interview with Annie Jackson, recorded at her home in Thomson, GA, 4 Feb 2004.

**He teased Kate about it . . .** Kate McTell Seabrooks, interviewed by Anne M. Evans and David H. Evans Sr, *Blues Unlimited* no.125, UK, Jul–Aug 1977, p.6. ('There's A Hand Writing On The Wall' was recorded and popularised by Blind Joe Taggart and Joshua White, Chicago, c.Oct 1928; Paramount 12717, US, 1928.)

**Sometimes we had money . . .** ibid, p.9.

**Evans summarises Willie's prowess . . . Horace . . . Gold Harris . . .** Evans, booklet to *Atlanta Blues 1933*, op.cit., p.9.

**Blind Joe Reynolds . . .** quote from Wardlow, p.178.

**Rev. Gary Davis . . .** pistol anecdote told by Arlo Guthrie, Elijah Wald reported to the *pre-war-blues@yahoogroups.com* e-mail discussion group, date unnoted; car-driving stated by Davis to Mary Katherine Aldin, e-mail ditto, 25 Jun 2003.

**he's said to have had two [cars] . . . Gertrude Parrish) . . .** In transcript of interviews by David Evans & Cheryl Thurber (then Evans) at Blind Lloyd's home, Savannah GA, 17 Jan and 14 Sep 1976, Lloyd states that McTell had two cars and wanted to sell him one. Evans, booklet to *Atlanta Blues 1933*, op.cit., only identifies the girlfriend as Gertrude, but I belive it must be Gertrude Parrish. There are only two plausible Gertrudes in Statesboro area on the 1920 Census; Lloyd says the mother of McTell's was named Willie Mae; Ms Parrish lives with her aunt, so her mother is unidentified; but Gertrude Roberson's mother's name is Rosa, which would seem to eliminate her. (US Census 1920 Bulloch Co. GA, enumeration district unstated, Sheet 12B, and enumerations district 12, Sheet 6A, respectively.

**Blind Lemon Jefferson . . .** portrayed thus in *Leadbelly*, dir. Gordon Parks, written Ernest Kinoy, US, 1976.

**Peter B. Lowry and . . . Bruce Bastin interviewed Moss . . .** 'Tricks ain't workin' no more: Blues From The South-East', Bruce Bastin and Peter B. Lowry, *Blues Unlimited* no.67, UK, Nov 1969, p.5, and Bastin, p.129.

**James Holman's life was revisited . . .** Roberts; Jenny Diski, *London Review of Books*, 7 Sep 2006, p.23.

**"Baby, I was born to ramble . . . until I die." . . .** Claimed McTell quote from Kate McTell Seabrooks, interviewed by Anne M. Evans and David H. Evans Sr, op.cit.

ELEVEN

**W.E.B. DuBois placed it** . . . quoted from *The Souls of Black People*, 1903.

**"car wrecked, horse fine"** . . . from timeline seen online, 19 Jan 2007, at *www.rootsweb.-com/~gafulton/atlantahistorystuff.html*.

**The pride of Southern Railways** . . . detail from 'Distinctive Equipment For The Crescent Limited', "Southern News Bulletin", Vol.16, no.11, Nov 1929, footnote 4, seen online, 21 Jan 2007, at *www.srmduluth.org/default.htm*. Mileage from Amtrak.

**Eleven coaches long, silver and huge** . . . own observation, journey, 2004; see Michael Gray, 'Rail Good Lesson in the Blues', *Weekend Telegraph*, London, 25 Sep 2004.

**the Hicks Brothers** . . . **"discovered" by** . . . **Dan Hornsby** . . . the suggestion that only Robert Hicks, rather than both brothers, were seen, despite Hornsby's testimony, comes from Bastin, p.107.

**1920s Chicago's 2.7 million citizens** . . . Kennedy, Ch.1.

**the *Atlanta Independent*** . . . timeline seen online, 19 Jan 2007, op.cit.

**over a hundred black-owned businesses** . . . these details taken from the Public Broadcasting Atlanta webpage *www.wabe.org/history/woa1.htm*, seen 12 Dec 2004.

**the great fire of 1917** . . . Kuhn, Joye and West, p.20.

**Ray Stannard Baker** . . . *Following the Color Line*, 1908. This is also the source for the streetcar sign text. For his writing re the Statesboro 1904 riot, see Ch.6.

***Living Atlanta: An Oral History of the City, 1914–1948*** . . . Kuhn, Joye and West, op.cit. First quote pp.9–10, second p.10.

**This "Atlanta Race Riot"** . . . Hoke Smith quote from 'Atlanta in the Civil Rights movement', Atlanta Regional Consortium for Higher Education, online, 19 Feb 2005, at *www.atlantahighered.org/civilrights/essay_detail.asp?phase=1*.

**two dozen black deaths and six white** . . . Figures are disputed; alternative numbers are ten black deaths and two white. There had been an earlier riot (1902) with fewer casualties.

**survey of black schools in the city in 1923** . . . conducted by the Women's Civic and Social Improvement Committee; in J.A. Rouse, 'Atlanta's African-American Women's Attack on Segregation' N. Frankel and N. Dye, eds., *Gender, Class, Race, and Reform in the Progressive Era*; Lexington KY: University Press of Kentucky, 1991, pp.10–23, seen online, 18 Feb 2005, at *www.questia.com*.

**segregated neighborhoods** . . . **close to** . . . **black institutions of higher education** . . . The other main sections were "on the south side, where Clark College (later Clark Atlanta University) was first established; and on the west side, where Atlanta University (later Clark Atlanta University) and later Spelman and Morehouse colleges were located." Source: "Atlanta: History", the online *New Georgia Encyclopedia*, Georgia Humanities Council and University of Georgia Press.

**From the 1850s until the riot** . . . *www.nps.gov/archive/malu/hrs/*, seen 13 Jan 2007.

**By 1930** . . . **almost entirely black** . . . **Jewish immigrants** . . . US Census 1930 Fulton Co. GA, Atlanta Borough, 4th Ward, eg. for Cain St., Sheet 11A (enumerated 5 Apr), to Hilliard St. on Sheet 20A (enumerated 9 Apr).

**the murder of** . . . **Mary Phagan** . . . Most data in this paragraph from Oney, Ch.1, and from Kuhn, Joye and West, p.14.

**'Little Mary Phagan'**, Vernon Dalhart [as by Al Craver], NYC, 27 May 1925, Columbia 15301-D, and 'The Grave Of Little Mary Phagan', Fiddlin' John Carson, NYC, Dec 1925, OKeh 45028; data from Russell, *Country Music Records: A Discography, 1921–1942*.

**Frank Dupree . . .** all detail except the Atlanta street geography (source: see below) from 'A Hangin' Crime: A Balladic Blues And The True Story Behind It" by Chris Smith, *Blues & Rhythm* no.96, UK, Feb 1995, pp.4–7 and no.97, Mar 1995, pp.4–8.

**'Delia' and . . . 'The Dyin' Crapshooter's Blues' . . .** and all other recordings mentioned, see Appendix: Career Discography. For a detailed look at 'The Dyin' Crapshooter's Blues', its antecedents in the traditional "Unfortunate Rake" cycle of songs, and how key ingredients from all this were used in Bob Dylan's own song "Blind Willie McTell", see Gray, *Song & Dance Man III*, Ch.15.

**Black murder . . . was not news . . .** Kuhn, Joye and West, p.12.

**said to have written . . . a song about . . . one Son Moselle . . .** stated, without source or even mention of the decade in which this allegedly happened, in David Evans, booklet to the LP *Atlanta Blues 1933*, JEMF-106, LA, 1979, p.10 (re-cited, as "Mozelle", pages later.)

**We don't know . . . where . . . living when . . . first moved into Atlanta . . .** David Evans (ibid, pp.12 and 15) says McTell's first base was c/o Mattie Johnson, his mother's sister, who lived at 160 Hilliard St, where he says she remained till her death in "about 1936"; but she is not at this address on the 1930 US Census (Fulton Co. GA, Atlanta Borough, 4th Ward, Sheet 21A (enumerated 9 Apr). Nor is any of the seventeen Mattie Johnsons who appear in the 1930 Atlanta City Directory (fifteen of whom are designated "c" for "colored"). Nor is Willie sufficiently established to appear in any of the directories for 1928–34.

**That downtown was not so big: essentially it was . . .** synthesised from a wide range of sources, incl. 1900 map of Atlanta published by George F. Cram, Chicago; 1949 map of downtown Atlanta © the Central Atlanta Improvement Association.

**Martin Luther King Jr . . . 1946 . . .** from Stanford University's 'King and the Black Freedom Struggle Chronology, 1944–1953', seen online, 20 Jan 2007, at *www.stanford.edu/group/King/about_king/king-struggle/1944–1953.htm*.

**old Governor's Mansion . . . Henry Grady Hotel . . .** from notes, sources lost; hotel description from vintage postcard; Westin description from walking past it, Mar 2003.

**In time he would live on Ellis and on Houston . . . North Butler . . . Jackson . . .** some from Evans, op.cit., p.15; also from City Directories data supplied by Todd Harvey at the Library of Congress from earlier notes made there by Joe Dickerson; also drawing on detailed Sanborn Fire Insurance Maps now online at *http://dlg.galileo.usg.edu/sanborn/*.

**he would record on Edgewood Avenue . . .** The Regal session of 1950 was recorded at 439–41 Edgewood Avenue, a two-storey building seen still standing 6 Mar 2003.

**Bruce Bastin writes, "a rough section of town . . ."** Bastin, p.114.

**Martin Luther King Jr was born . . .** on 15 January 1929, to the Rev. and Mrs Martin Luther King Sr, in an upstairs bedroom of a spacious two-storey house at 501, Auburn Avenue. (Source: *www.nps.gov/malu/*, seen 12 Nov 2006.)

**Rosa Parks . . .** She's there aged twenty on the 1930 US Census, Fulton Co. GA, Atlanta Borough, 4th Ward, Sheet 11A, enumerated 5 Apr.

**Hattie Harwell Wilson High . . .** 8 May 1926; from *www.ourgeorgiahistory.com*.

**city forbade the teaching of evolution . . .** 9 Feb 1926; ibid.

**the Ku Klux Klan had re-ignited itself . . .** ibid.

**Atlanta's Hebrew Benevolent Society . . .** 'Atlanta author re-opens 1958 temple bombing case', Lesley Pearl, *Jewish Bulletin of Northern California* [now *Jewish News Weekly*], 14 Jun 1996, seen online 14 May 2005.

the Klan "targeted radicals, Jews, aliens . . ." Kuhn, Joye and West, p.14.

Morehouse College president Benjamin Mays . . . ibid, p.31.

James Baldwin writes . . . in Baldwin, in 'A Letter From The South'.

Mamie Smith, whose first record . . . 'Crazy Blues', NYC, 10 Aug 1920, OKeh Records OK 4169.

Ralph Sylvester Peer . . . sources include Hardy & Laing, pp.618–619; Eugene Chadbourne's 'Polk C. Brockman', All Music Guide, online 9 Jun 2004; Charles Wolfe's liner notes to *The Bristol Sessions*, Country Music Foundation, US, 1987; and Dave Winship's 'In the Summer of 1927', Birthplace of Country Music Alliance, seen online, 16 Dec 2006, at *www.birthplaceofcountrymusic.org/index.cgi?BISKIT=1739005064.*

Vaughan Quartet . . . Henry C. Gilliland and Eck Robertson . . . all discographical data from Tony Russell's omniscient *Country Music Records: A Discography, 1921–1942*, including, from his introduction: "Until now, the recording history of this music has been supposed to begin in June 1922, with . . . A.C. (Eck) Robertson and Henry Gilliland; that date is now pre-empted by . . . the Vaughan Quartet in 1921.", p.7.

Fiddlin' John Carson . . . ibid.

Lucille Bogan . . . 'The Pawn Shop Blues' (c/w 'Grievous Blues' by Fannie May Goosby), Atlanta, c.14 Jun 1923, OKeh 8079; 'Shave 'Em Dry', NYC, 5 Mar 1935; discographical detail Dixon, Godrich and Rye.

Ed Andrews . . . ibid.

Perry Bradford had earned $53,000 . . . Harris, p.65.

Charles L. Elyea . . . Atlanta City Directories, 1928 and 1929. I take the recording location from the Victor recording sheet for one H.E. Barnett (of no blues or hillbilly interest), recorded there by Peer three days later. The alternative possibility is the Henry Grady Hotel, according to Tommy Wheeler's second-hand account of where his father's All-Star Stamps Quartet recorded for Peer two days after McTell. (See *www.american-music.org/ publications/bullarchive/Folsom.html*).

a wooden platform in an empty room . . . assumed from Charles Wolfe's description of the room for the Bristol sessions, op.cit.

Skip James . . . it comes from his brilliant début recording, 'Devil Got My Woman', Grafton WI, c.Feb 1931; Paramount 13088.

Robert Johnson . . . 'Come On In My Kitchen', San Antonio TX, 23 Nov 1936, ARC 7-07-57 and Vocalion 03563.

'Pledging My Time' . . . *Blonde On Blonde*, US, 1966.

"A lone guitar and a point of view" . . . Bob Dylan, liner notes, *Biograph*, US, 1985.

the average working wage in Atlanta . . . extracted from 'The Emergence of a National Economy: 1790 and 1920' seen online, 23 Jan 2007, at *www.uri.edu/artsci/ecn/mead/INTI/ Mic/History/Out.history1.html*.

TWELVE

Jefferson's second release, 'Got The Blues' . . . Chicago, c.Mar 1926, Paramount 12354, US, 1926. This paragraph owes a debt to Tony Russell's entries on Jefferson in both his *The Blues From Robert Johnson to Robert Cray*, pp.46–47 and Russell & Smith, pp.312–313.

**Victor chose first to release 'Stole Rider Blues'** . . . for all McTell discographical detail see the Appendix: Career Discography.

**Gayle Dean Wardlow . . . interviewing H.C. Speir** . . . interview with Wardlow by Patrick Howse and Jimmy Phillips, 1994, collected in Wardlow's great book, *Chasin' That Devil Music*, pp. 143, 145.

**starting at nine o'clock in the morning** . . . "Time: 9:00 to 1:00" is entered on the Victor ledger sheet, transcribed for me from British Sound Archive copy on microfilm by Andy Linehan, National Sound Archive, British Library, London.

**Sippie Wallace** . . . 'Shorty George Blues' c/w 'Up The Country Blues', Chicago, c.26 Oct 1923, OKeh OK8106, US, 1923–4. Snakedancer's maid detail from Harrison, p.68, quoted in Haymes, p.249.

**Bessie Smith** . . . 'Reckless Blues', NYC 14 Jan 1925, Columbia 14064–D, US, 1925.

**Ivy Smith** . . . 'Cincinnati Southern Blues', Chicago, c.Apr 1927, Paramount 12472, US, 1927, quoted in Haymes.

**The no. 80 ran from Tampa** . . . Richard E. Prince, *Atlantic Coast Line Railroad*, Bloomington: Indiana University Press, 2000 reprint p.182, plus phone message from Max Haymes, 27 Jan 2007.

**Peter B. Lowry . . . told me** . . . phone interview to his home in Austinmer, NSW, Australia, 14 Sep 2004.

**'Statesboro Blues' on 4 January, 1929** . . . date from notes made from Victor recording sheets by Tony Russell. Vaguer later dates gleaned from 'When The Wolf Knocked On Victor's Door', Dick Spottswood, *78 Quarterly* Vol.1 no.5, US 1990, pp.63–77.

**The McKee Music Company** . . . *Charleston Daily Mail*, 8 Mar 1929, p.2; *Charleston Gazette*, 4 Apr 1930, p.12.

**Margaret Mitchell . . . hit crossing Peachtree** . . . 11 Aug 1945; she died in Grady Memorial Hospital five days later.

**in the two hours from 11.30am** . . . Victor ledger sheet, op.cit.

**the Carter Family** . . . It is from the very detailed list of recording locations on the Carter Family Discography online at *www.unbroken-circle.com/OCF-discography.php#* that the Victor 1929 McTell and Harris and Harris sessions' location has been deduced.

**Harris and Harris** . . . first session Memphis TN, 21 Jan 1928; their hometown is stated on the Victor recording sheets for this session, transcribed by Tony Russell some years ago; 'Teasing Brown' and 'This Is Not The Stove To Brown Your Bread', Atlanta, 26 and 27 Nov 1929, Victor V38594, US 1930.

**On the Tuesday, starting at nine o'clock in the morning** . . . Victor ledger sheet, op.cit. .

**advertised across the South** . . . *The Port Arthur News*, Port Arthur TX, 2 Jul 1930, p.8.

**where Willie would later borrow Braille books** . . . "South Pryor Street, 'cause that's where I'd go to get Willie's Braille books and Braille records for him from, out on South Pryor, me and him." (Kate McTell Seabrooks, interview by E. Bernard West, 3 Feb 1979, place unstated; see next Chapter for detail and more quotation.)

**Frank Walker, assisted that year by Harry Charles** . . . recalled by McTell in phone interview by Atlanta librarian Alma Jamison, according to Ed Paterson (for whom she had talked to McTell) in 'Atlanta shouts the blues!', *Melody Maker and Rhythm*, London, 26 May 1951.

**Columbia . . . on Pryor Street** . . . Bastin, p.184.

**Fly Summit, New York** . . . born 24 Oct 1889; died 16 Oct 1963. Seen online 4 Aug 2006 at *www.talentondisplay.com/countrycalOCT.html*.

**Johnson City, Tennessee** . . . discographical detail from Russell, *Country Music Records: A Discography, 1921–1942.*

**Charlie Poole** . . . ibid.

**Bessie Smith . . . producer . . . one of the few white people she trusted** . . . Albertson, p.175.

**[Walker] told folksinger-folklorist Mike Seeger in 1960** . . . unpublished interview; quote used in Tony Sherman's "Country", *American Heritage Magazine*, US, Vol.45, no.7, Nov 1994.

**Kennesaw Mountain** . . . twenty-seven miles north-west of downtown Atlanta. The Civil War battle took place 19 Jun to 2 Jul 1864.

**Bruce Bastin . . . calls a "Newton County favorite"** . . . Bastin, p.131. (He reports, p.117, that Atlanta fellow-musician Roy Dunn remembers that as 'Come on Down to My House Baby' it was still popular with local musicians in the late 1930s.)

**Barbecue Bob . . . Curley Weaver** . . . Discographical data from Dixon and Godrich. Curley Weaver: 'No No Blues', Atlanta, 26 Oct 1928, Columbia 14386-D, US, 1929.

**'Travelin' Blues' . . . and then "Atlanta Strut" . . . were released** . . . Release and sales data from David Evans, liner notes to the misnamed 2-CD set *The Definitive Blind Willie McTell* (see Appendix: Career Discography). Evans gives no sources for data, naturally.

**Georgia Tom Dorsey described the pluses and minuses** . . . Harris, p.39.

**Thursday, 24 October, the stock market panicked** . . . summarised from Palmer, pp.346 and 105.

**Cheryl Thurber** . . . interview recorded at her home in Baltimore MD, 11 Nov 2001.

**Blind Lloyd, a South Georgia guitarist** . . . transcript of interview by David Evans and Cheryl Thurber (then Evans) at Blind Lloyd (Randolph Byrd)'s home, 1115 Habersham St., Savannah GA, 17 Jan 1976. Some later quotes from interview, 14 Sep 1976.

**It's been said . . . by Cheryl Thurber and David Evans** . . . booklet to the *Atlanta Blues 1933* LP, p.18, discusses this in the context of McTell's 1940 interview by Lomax; Cheryl Thurber, my interview with her, op.cit.: "Certainly he was aware of the conditions, but an awful lot of times people tended to view the 1930s as a little bit different in the sense that people were in the same boat together, black and white."

**more than four out of five black Americans still lived in the South** . . . Kennedy, Ch.1.

**C. Vann Woodward** . . . quoted ibid.

**Annie L. McPheeters** . . . from 'Mrs. Annie L. McPheeters (1908–1994): Biographical Sketch', seen online 12 Dec 2004 at *www.af.public.lib.ga.us.*

***Atlanta Daily World* . . . launched in 1928** . . . from "African-American Experience", National Park Service Atlanta, seen online 23 Jan 2003 ibid.

***Living Atlanta* reported . . . talked to Buddy Moss** . . . Kuhn, Joye and West, p.306.

**the city's new airport** . . . from essay by Tommy Jones, Architectural Historian with the National Park's Southeast Regional Office, seen online 8 Dec 2006 at *www.cr.nps.gov.*

**"less for his greyish singing . . ."** Russell, *The Blues From Robert Johnson* etc., p.93

**Blind Willie Johnson: "a personal friend of mine,"** . . . to John A. Lomax for the Library of Congress, Atlanta, 5 Nov 1940; details see a later chapter and the Appendix: Career Discography.

**As Michael Corcoran has it** . . . 'The Soul of a Man', Corcoran, p.67.

**Johnson and McTell were in the same temporary studio** . . . Corcoran, p.72., reports

Willie B. Harris' interviewer, Dallas music collector Dan Williams, as saying their sessions had been the same day, April 20, but McTell's had been three days earlier. Dixon, Godrich and Rye corrects the earlier misidentification of Harris as Angeline Johnson (originated by Sam Charters' 1955 interview with this second wife of the musician), but names Harris as Willie B. Richardson.

**Johnson survived another fifteen years** . . . He died in Beaumont Texas, where by 1943 (as indicated by the 1944 Beaumont City Directory) he was known as the Rev. W.J. Johnson and "operated the House of Prayer at 1440 Forest Street . . . the address listed on Blind Willie's death certificate as his last residence." (Corcoran, p.73.)

**Sara Martin's 'Down At The Razor Ball'** . . . NYC, 5 Nov 1925, OKeh 8283, US, 1926.

**"That new way of loving** . . . The " 'new way of lovin' ' often mentioned by blues singers usually refers to oral sex . . . Many Americans associate oral sex with the French, and it's perhaps of some significance that these references start showing up strongly in blues right after American participation in World War One." An e-mail to the Pre-War Blues Discussion Group, 16 Jun 2003.

**the *Chicago Defender*** . . . 1930s, date unknown but widely reproduced.

**Bob Miller acting as Frank Walker's assistant** . . . stated on the Victor recording sheets for this session, transcribed by Tony Russell, op.cit.

**By 1934, one-third of all US rail mileage was in bankruptcy . . . last time most rail companies made a profit** . . . Gray, *Song & Dance Man III*, p.743.

**"field trips"** . . . **into the South were killed off** . . . extrapolated from the invaluable study of 'The Race Labels' and their fieldtrips in Dixon Godrich, pp.16–17, 18–21.

**the Rev. J.M. Gates** . . . Peter B. Lowry, 'Atlanta Black Sound: A Survey of Black Music from Atlanta During the Twentieth Century' *Atlanta Historical Bulletin* Vol.21, No.2, Summer 1977 Special Issue, pp.110–111.

**Curley was . . . in the borough of East Point** . . . "Cirlie Weaver", 1930 US Census GA, Fulton Co. East Point Borough Ward 3, Sheet No.24A, enumerated Apr 15.

**Willie and Ralph S. Peer . . . starting horribly early** . . . 8.30am–12.30; times from the Victor ledger sheets, op.cit. .

**Bruce Bastin argued in the 1970s** . . . Bastin, pp.132–133.

**Peer went on to publish Hoagy Carmichael** . . . entry on Peer by Tony Russell in Hardy and Laing, p.619.


THIRTEEN

**Arthur Edward Satherley** . . . entry in *Encyclopedia of the Blues*, ed. Ed Komara, Vol 2, p.858; "Uncle Art's Logbook Blues", Bruce Bastin and John Cowley, *Blues Unlimited* no.108 (Jun/Jul 1974), pp.12–17; John Edwards Memorial Foundation files (Manuscripts Dept., Library, University of North Carolina at Chapel Hill: Southern Folklife Collection # 20001, the JEMF Records inventory); and 1930 US Census NY Manhattan Borough Vol.353 p.2, enumeration district 31–1012, Sheet 2A. Almost everyone on the page was born outside the US; Satherley, stated occupation Manager, Phonograph Factory, has not become a US citizen.

**Three revisits to 'Broke Down Engine Blues'** . . . 'Broke Down Engine', 'Broke Down Engine Blues No.2' and 'Broke Down Engine Blues No.2' again.

**you can tell he's a wonderful mimic** . . . Re this: Kate McTell (interview by E. Bernard

West, 3 Feb 1979, place unstated; further details follow): "He could change his voice so if you didn't really see him you wouldn't know whether he was black or white."

**Judie died in McDuffie** . . . details Ch. 5 Notes.

**in January 1933, Elbert . . . died** . . . details Ch. 5 Notes.

**Rev. Andrew W. Williams** . . . Gravestone, Spread Chapel A.M.E. Cemetery inscription says born 16 Feb 1885 (died 12 Dec 1968); other data from 1900 US Census Jefferson Co. GA Militia District 81, enumeration district 26, Sheet 1, and 1910 US Census ditto, GM District 1460, enumeration district 35, Sheet 13B.

**If they were Andrew's children, Sarah bore both** . . . 1910 US Census, Jefferson Co. GA, Spread, enumeration district 35, Sheet 2A.

**Sarah Gilmore was one of a large number of children** . . . information from interview with niece Annie Vaughner, Wrens GA, 4 Nov 2001, gravestone at Spread Chapel, ibid (born 8 Nov 1886, died 17 Apr 1971), and 1910 US Census ibid.

**Pleas Gilmore Senior, born in slavery . . . Alice Whigham . . . becomes the wife . . .** 1900 US Census Jefferson Co., GM District 1460, enumeration district 21, Sheet 18B; 1910 US Census ibid; Alice Gilmore's gravestone dates are 29 May 1867 to 13 Jun 1970.

**Ruth Kate is born next . . . Kate's younger siblings** . . . 1920 US Census, Jefferson Co. GA, Militia District 81, enumeration district 46, Sheet 2A.

**The interview was conducted by E. Bernard West** . . . Typed partial transcript Atlanta History Center Archives, File no. 1989.305, Folder 12, Box 38. Tapes held Atlanta History Center library.

**playing through the master tapes and transcribing their contents** . . . 6 and 7 Nov 2001.

**"My mother was a school teacher** . . . This was probably true, though the available US Censuses (i.e. up to and including the 1930, by which time she's forty-four) never say so.

**the Paine College archivist** . . . phone calls and e-mails to Peggy Tanksley, Paine College, 14 Sep 2004, 19 and 26 Jan 2007.

**told the Evanses . . . she "went to Morris Brown College"** . . . interview with Kate McTell by Anne M. Evans and David H. Evans Sr, though published under son David Evans' name, *Blues Unlimited* no.125, Jul/Aug 1977, p.4.

**Willie S. McTell and Rutha K. Williams . . . married** . . . these are the names as given on the affidavits signed 10 Jan 1934, Aiken SC and on marriage license no. 24950, North Augusta SC, 11 Jan 1934; copies obtained 5 Nov 2001.

**Kate would say later that . . . Lula Habersham** . . . interview by Anne M. Evans and David H. Evans Sr, op.cit. p.4.

**Aiken County's public schools had integrated . . . 1970** . . . This and other detail re. Aiken is from documents in a huge file of newspaper cuttings and other items held at the Aiken CVB and Chamber of Commerce, noted down 5 Nov 2001.

**"Willie's uncle," Kate told E. Bernard West** . . . this account re selling scrap iron liquor in Atlanta, and Kate's appearance before a judge, is taken from the printed part of the interview, Kuhn, Joye and West pp.177–178. All the rest, incl. re liquor, I quote directly from my own transcript and the typed partial transcript as described. Like Kuhn, Joye and West, I have made cuts in the testimony, and re-organised this by topic, but have not made this clear in the text, solely to avoid a snowstorm of dot-dot-dots everywhere. I'm confident no one checking the full interview would find the editing changes any intended meaning. The same applies to the other two main interviews used in this chapter.

**". . . in Atlanta I hit enough to buy a Model-T car . . ."** Kate tells the Evanses: "We had a car, but we didn't use it on the highways." Cheryl: "Just used it in Atlanta?" Kate: "Right." (*Blues Unlimited* no.126, UK, Sep/Oct 1977, pp.12–13.)

**"We lived at 381 Houston Street . . .** Kate tells Anne M. and David H. Evans Sr (op.cit., p.6) that Curley Weaver's girlfriend Cora Thompson boarded in their apartment.

**81 Theatre on Decatur Street . . .** some detail from a compilation by Monica Burdex, Performing Arts Librarian at California State University Northridge, 2000 of 1920s news items from the *Chicago Defender*, seen online, 29 Jul 2004, *www.csun.edu/~htang/chicago.html*.

**Sally Cramer . . .** see later in this chapter.

**Kate's younger brother Andrew . . .** interviews by David Fulmer, Atlanta, first half of 1992, for *Blind Willie's Blues*, Missing Lenk [sic] Video, Lawrenceville GA, 1996.

**When I met her, she was eighty-one . . .** interviewed at her home, 3 Nov 2001. But in a follow-up phone interview, 1 Feb 2004, she told me she was now eighty-two: so the period she recollects in Atlanta with Willie and Kate McTell cannot be precisely pinned down (even if she could have been exactly right about her age at the time).

**Uncle Bus . . . a truck driver with the Southern Cattle Co . . .** Buster Harris, found newly married to Rosalee on the 1930 US Census Birmingham, Alabama (Jefferson Co.), enumeration district 37–100, Sheet 27A. (Buster is first encountered in 1910, aged two, with older siblings Sallie, Gold and Tom in the household of Tom Sr and Nancy, next door to El McTier and Judie, in McDuffie. Census details see Ch.5 Notes.)


FOURTEEN

***Ma Rainey's Black Bottom* . . . a 1984 play by August Wilson . . .** title of play, record and other Ma Rainey records in Gray, *Song & Dance Man III*, footnotes pp.709–710.

**J. Mayo Williams . . .** profile at *http://dl.lib.brown.edu/pollard/ftbllplayers.html*, online, 12 Dec 2006, and entry by Steve Hoffman, *Encyclopedia of the Blues*, ed. Ed Komara, pp.1079– 1180. Black Patti detail from *www.blackpatti.com*, online 12 Dec 2006.

**Mayo Williams was at the wheel . . .** this account is dated from knowing the session dates and otherwise extrapolated from the account given by Kate McTell, interview by David and Cheryl Evans, 19 Jan 1976, *Blues Unlimited* no.126, UK, Sep/Oct 1977, pp.10–11. Kate is unclear about the woman passenger's identity, and calls her Gladys Knight, though she's doubtful she's right. Georgia White was in Chicago recording ten days earlier, so while it's possible she was in the car, the timing doesn't sit well with the journey.

**Al Capone's heyday . . .** *The Electronic Encyclopedia of Chicago*, Chicago History Society, online, 10 Dec 2006.

**every night at their hotel . . . white musicians . . .** Kate McTell, interview by E. Bernard West, 3 Feb 1979; details see previous chapter's notes.

**Jack Johnson . . . "We was just up the street from him . . ."** Kate McTell, interview by David and Cheryl Evans, op.cit., pp.11–12.

***Chicago Defender* . . . would always give him [Jack Johnson] a plug . . .** stated by phone to me by his biographer Geoffrey C. Ward, following an e-mail exchange 30 Nov 2006.

**the *Defender* ran this small item on page eight . . .** clipping from 20 Apr 1935, seen at the Chicago Historical Society (3rd Floor research center), 1601 N. Clark St., 22 Jan 2004. (NB: This great institution has since re-branded itself as the Chicago History Museum.)

**the *Defender* had given the same address for the Standard Motor Club . . .** in

"Hidden Talents Come Forth When Sorors Welcome Students", *Chicago Defender* (National edn), 17 Nov 1934, p.7.

**Johnson's most recent biographer, Geoffrey C. Ward** . . . e-mail reply to query from me, 30 Nov 2006. (In his biography, "Old Champ" is said to be gin, which he thinks he picked up from a retrospective story in *Time*; but the *Defender* clearly states whiskey.)

**the building itself . . . a Designated Chicago Landmark** . . . this paragraph's detail mainly from the City of Chicago Department of Planning and Development Landmarks Division profile at *www.ci.chi.il.us/Landmarks/S/SouthSideArt.html*, seen online 30 Nov 2006.

**Jack Johnson, the Muhammad Ali of his day, died** . . . 'Jack Johnson Dies in Auto Crash', *Chicago Sun*, 11 Jun 1946, based on Associated Press report from Raleigh NC, 10 Jun 1946; gravestone detail from opinion piece by Joe Rein, unidentified newspaper, 1969; update from Geoffrey C. Ward, phone call, 30 Nov 2006.

**Kokomo Arnold . . . 'Milk Cow Blues' . . . for Decca . . . produced by Mayo Williams** . . . It was his second record, c/w 'Old Original Kokomo Blues', both cut Chicago, 10 Sep 1934, and both sides were big hits.

**Eddie McTier—married Hazel Samuel** . . . McDuffie Co. GA Marriage License no.490; copy obtained from McDuffie Probate Court 2 Feb 2004.

**Annie Jackson, told me** . . . interviewed at her home in Thomson, GA, 4 Feb 2004.

**By 1930 there were already five girls and four boys** . . . 1930 US Census McDuffie Co. GA, Mt Auburn District (Militia District 152), Enumeration District 95–8, Sheet 1A.

**'Married Life's A Pain'** . . . Big Bill [Broonzy], Chicago, 22 Apr 1936; issued on ARC 7–03–68 and Conquest 8777, c/w 'Pneumonia Blues (I Keep On Aching)'.

**William Ronald Calaway** . . . I am grateful to an Amazon review posting by a punter with the splendid moniker "Lawrence of the Radio" for the first two theft details here, online 1 Aug 2006 at *www.amazon.com/That-Silver-Haired-Daddy-Mine/dp/B000E6UKN2*.

**he had also been responsible, in 1934, for springing . . . Charley Patton** . . . Wardlow, pp. 147–148.

**James Brown . . . when he was a shoeshine boy"** . . . Kate McTell, interview by David and Cheryl Evans, op.cit., p.12.

**Bruce Bastin claims . . . "Calaway and Art Satherley's wife owned a motel"** . . . Bastin, p. 134. (He doesn't say how he knows this.)

**Red said later . . . Willie . . . brought him in on the sessions** . . . summarised from interview by Karl Gert zur Heide, Bremen, West Germany, 1 Oct 1977, quoted in Bastin p. 135.

**Bastin writes . . . perhaps Calaway hoped** . . . Bastin p.135.

**Calaway went down to Mississippi** . . . July 1936: Wardlow, p.140.

**Aunt Mattie died . . . Kate reports** . . . interview by Anne M. Evans and David H. Evans Sr, *Blues Unlimited* no.125, UK, Jul/Aug 1977, p.10.

**"Small Paradise"** . . . interview by David and Cheryl Evans, op.cit., p.13.

**The writer Elijah Wald** . . . e-mail response to enquiry from me, 30 Dec 2004.

**"symphonic orchestra" and "full-dress onlookers"** . . . quoted in Wald, ibid, from Wallace Thurman's *Negro Life in New York's Harlem*, Girard KS: Haldeman-Julius Publications, 1928.

**the 600-seater Morton Theatre** . . . details from Georgia researcher Gary Doster; Kate McTell interview by Vinnie Williams, *Augusta Chronicle*, 12 Nov 1980; second Kate McTell interview by Vinnie Williams, with Jill Read (Athens-Clarke Co. Cultural Affairs Director), Dot Jones (also of the McDuffie County Historical Society) and W. Lane Greene, *Athens*

*Observer*, 29 Jan 1981; e-mail exchange with Jill Read 24 Aug 2004; phone call to Vinnie Williams 4 Oct 2004; 'Come To See The Midnite Show' by Elizabeth Cobb, *UGAzine*, Athens, Fall/Winter 1993–4 pp.13–17; 'Show Time at the Morton' by Amy Williams Flurry, *Athens Magazine*, Vol.5 no.6, Feb 1994, pp.13–20; and theatre archives online.

**the Evanses had taken it away . . .** second Kate McTell interview by Vinnie Williams, ibid.

**Douglass Theatre in Macon and . . . Delmont in Augusta . . .** Kate McTell interview by Vinnie Williams, *Augusta Chronicle*, op.cit. .

**Kate McTell "Charlestoned and Black Bottomed" . . .** interview by David and Cheryl Evans, op.cit., p.12.

**Kate told Bernard West . . .** interview by E. Bernard West, 3 Feb 1979; details see previous chapter's notes.

**Sister Fleeta Mitchell . . .** interview at her home outside Athens GA, 14 Apr 2001.

**Wrens . . .** visited 5 Aug 2001 and 8 Feb 2004.

**Keysville: a crossroads . . .** 8 Feb 2004.

**Louisville . . . Leroy Lewis . . .** 4 Mar 2003.

**slaves . . . never . . . auctioned in the way people think . . .** e.g. as relayed unquestioningly by David Evans in his JEMF-106 album notes.

**Bill Love . . . wrote in to the weekly paper *Jazz Information* . . .** reported and quoted in an anonymous column, *Jazz Information*, Vol.1, no. 20, US, 2 Feb 1940; reproduced online at *http://home.att.net/~joeshepherd/jazz/jazz30.html*, seen 11 Dec 2005.

**Minnie Pearl . . .** as it happens, her stage début was in Aiken, South Carolina; she became an Opry star in the 1940s and twenty years later had segments on TV show *Hee Haw* called 'Driving Miss Minnie' (the inspiration for the 1989 movie title *Driving Miss Daisy*). Born Sarah Ophelia Colley, in 1947 she married Nashville businessman and ex-pilot Henry Cannon. She died in 1996 at age eighty-three. Most information by phone from Tony Russell, 9 Jan 2002.

**Buddy Moss killed his wife . . .** Bastin, pp. 126–127.

**Greene County Prison Farm . . .** Bastin says "Greensboro and Warrenton" but the order was the opposite, and "Greensboro" was identified as the prison farm, and dated to May 1941, in the labeling of the FSA photographs by Jack Delano. They can be seen online at *http://memory.loc.gov/cgi-bin/query/b?ammem/fsaall:LC-USF34-044766-E:collection=fsa*. The LP was *East Coast States 1926–35*, Yazoo L 1013, US, 1969.

**Moss . . . in Elon College (the town) . . .** J.B. Long lived in the town called Elon College (after the institution); Moss worked for Long for the decade out of Georgia that was a condition of his release to Long.

**Bo Weevil . . .** Bastin, p.117, though the info seems to be from Tom Pomposello, 'Charles Walker: Blues from the Big Apple', *Living Blues* no.18, Chicago, Autumn 1974, p.14. This includes the information that his real name may have been Freeman Walker. 1920 US Census for Vineville Bibb Co. GA shows Freeman Walker there aged twenty-five in January 1920. (Enumeration District 14, Sheet 5A.) Vineville had by then already long been swallowed up by Macon. (The Academy for the Blind is on Vineville Avenue.)

**"the world's top selling book, next to the Bible" . . .** leaflet from the Margaret Mitchell House and Museum, Atlanta, 2001.

**Hattie McDaniel . . .** most background from the online Movie Database biography. Cheryl Thurber's 'The Development of the Mammy Image and Mythology' is collected in *Southern Women: Histories and Identities*, Columbia: University of Missouri Press, 1992.

FIFTEEN

**seventy-three-year-old John Avery Lomax** . . . born Goodman MS, 23 Sep 1867.

**Ruby Rochelle Terrill Lomax** . . . born Denton TX, 14 Feb 1886. This exact date is shockingly hard to come by—every profile of her merely gives the year; I'm grateful to genealogist "cliffpepper" for the rest, found under "Pepper-Lomax" online, 14 Dec 2006, at *http://wc.rootsweb.com/cgi-bin/igm.cgi.*

**"there is a Negro man with a guitar"** . . . quotes from Ruby and John Lomax and Willie here from Lomax's notes, typed up later by Ruby, on file at the Library of Congress and widely published in record liner notes.

**Uncle Billy Macrea** . . . misspelt "Machree" in the notes; an ancient and frail rural black encountered and photographed with Lomax (by Ruby) on their earlier trip.

**Lomax was enjoying an . . . Indian summer** . . . sources include Wayne Gard's entry on Lomax in the *Handbook of Texas Online*; Porterfield (though this biography does not mention the meeting with McTell at all); Chris Smith's untitled review of same, *Blues & Rhythm* no.116, UK, Feb 1999, p.116; John Cowley's survey 'Library of Congress Archive of Folk Song Recordings' inside Godrich & Dixon, pp.25–27; and the Lomax Papers in the Library of Congress Folklife Center, Washington D.C., seen 26 Feb 2001.

**the Assistant in Charge . . . son Alan** . . . letter from A. Lomax to Division of Music Chief, 2 Apr 1940; expenses estimates ditto; A. Lomax salary stated in 'Miserable But Exciting Songs', *Time*, US, 26 Nov 1945; *Time* quote ditto.

**left home . . . 8 September 1940** . . . detail these paragraphs from Lomax Papers, LoC Folklife Center, op.cit. .

**they had started out from Livingston Alabama . . . arriving . . . [Atlanta] at 6.30pm** . . . details from "small blue notebook in JAL's unmistakeable handwriting", entry for Nov 4–5 1940, found for me by John R. Wheat, Music Archivist, Lomax Papers at the University of Texas, e-mailed 14 Dec 2006, in Lomax Collection Box 3D198.

**a man wrongly claimed to have invented the steamboat** . . . Fulton "locate[d] an efficient new Watt engine in a warehouse . . . [and] installed it in a well-designed boat . . . His patent makes no pretense about inventing the steamboat. It acknowledges thirty years of early steamboat development", begun in France. ('The First Steamboat', by John H. Lienhard, seen online 15 Dec 2006 at *www.uh.edu/engines/epi1084.htm.*)

**'It's A Mean World To Live In'** . . . this is a spiritual recorded for instance by jazz combo The Roy Meriwether Trio on their album *Soul Invader*, Columbia CS 9544, recorded live c.1968; it has also been performed as a singalong by Bernice Reagon Johnson, and listed as 'This World Is A Mean World To Live In' was to be field-recorded from Frank and Sally Titus for the Library of Congress the summer after the Lomaxes met McTell. Bill Gaither cut a secular 'Mean Old World To Live In', NYC, 23 Jun 1938 (Decca 7606).

**'Ain't it hard . . . in Atlanta** . . . sung unaccompanied by Mabel Hillery in interview with Hedy West, 1967, Philadelphia, 1967; issued on *It's So Hard to Be A Nigger*, Mabel Hillery, XTRA 1063, London, 1968. Lomax may have been prompted to ask for it after James "Iron Head" Baker was recorded performing three versions of 'Ain't It Hard To Be A Right Black Nigger" for the Library of Congress in Washington, DC, in May 1936.

**Ruby Lomax . . . died** . . . details seen online, 4 Jan 2004, at *www.deltakappagamma.org / International/whoweare/history/founderbios/ruby_lomax.htm.*

**For the sake of saving $10** . . . letter from Mrs Rae Korson, Head, Archive of Folk Song, to

Larry Cohn, 21 Apr 1960: "This is in answer to your recent inquiry concerning the Archive's recordings of Blind Willie McTell. Because of the extremely fragile condition and short playing life of our original field recordings, we cannot play them except for the purpose of duplication . . . our Recording Laboratory could probably put almost all of them on a single track 7-inch reel of tape costing $10. I am sure that all of the songs could be duplicated if some of the conversation is deleted."

**Cheryl Thurber** . . . interview at her home in Baltimore MD, 11 Nov 2001.

**Blind Lloyd's recollections** . . . from transcript of interviews by David Evans and Cheryl Thurber Evans at his home in Savannah, 17 Jan and 14 Sep 1976.

**Jaeckel Hotel** . . . dates and specifications etc. from City of Statesboro PR leaflet checked against & augmented by Sanborn Maps seen Statesboro Regional Library 3 Mar 2003.

**Naomi Johnson** . . . interviewed at her home in Statesboro, 2 Mar 2003.

**Mildred Bouie Harville, born in 1912** . . . interviewed for me by Delma E. Presley, Statesboro, 16 Nov 2004.

**Annie Jackson** . . . interview at her home in Thomson GA, 4 Feb 2004.

**Broughtons and Hintons** . . . 1880 US Census Newton Co. GA, Hays District, enumeration district 97, p.7; 1900 US Census ditto, enumeration district 88, Sheet 6A. Moses and Amanda's other children were Viney (b. 1854), Henry (1856), Frances [written "Francis"] and Lenny (1859), Moses Jr (1865) and Mary (1869).

**Helen, born . . . Brickstore . . . 1 April 1905. By the time she was fifteen** . . . 1920 US Census Newton Co. GA, Brickstore, enumeration district; exact birthdate from death certificate no. 5626, State File no. 27536, Fulton Co. GA, registered 5 Nov 1958; copy obtained 24 Feb 2003.

**Floyd, was living with . . . Florence and . . . the Franklins** . . . 1920 US Census Newton Co. GA, Hays District, enumeration district 116, Sheet 12A.

**By 1930, Helen's mother Henrietta had moved to Atlanta** . . . 1930 US Census Fulton Co. GA, Atlanta Ward 4, enumeration district 61–63, sheet 8B.

**James Newsome was born in September 1921** . . . We know from the obituary of Helen that Willie placed in the *Atlanta Constitution*, Vol.XCI no.124, 8 Nov 1958, p.18, that this was her son and by then in Detroit; birthdate from Social Security Death Index (no.383–14–7034). Ditto Alice Beasley, Philadelphia, SSDI (no.376–20–0538).

**no extant record of any marriage** . . . Search of marriages c/o Vital Records Office, Atlanta, 13 Oct 2004.

**By late 1944 they were living together** . . . The 1944 Atlanta City Directory lists "McTell, Willie (c) r*248 Houston NE*" (c = colored, r = residence); the 1945 lists, confusingly, both "McTell, Willie (c; Helen) r*262½ Ellis NE*" and "McTell, Willie (c) r*248 Houston NE*". This suggests that (1) their first joint residency listing is in the 1945 directory (which can be assumed to apply to the reality of 1944), but that (2) Willie had the Houston St. address first. Yet David Evans writes: "In 1944 and 1945 they were [both] listed . . . as living at 248 Houston Street and later in 1945 at 262½ Ellis Street." (JEMF-106 booklet pp.18–19). He also adds that "In 1947 . . . Willie was listed as living with a wife named Rachel in the rear of 335 Sams in Decatur": but this refers to the 1946 listing, which is only for "McTell, Rachel (c) h *rear 335 Sams (D)*"—there's no Willie; she has the same entry eleven years later; and in 1958 she is listed as "McTier, Rachel P (wid Wm) r *rear 335 Sams (D)*". They are never listed together: I suggest this is a coincidental name conjunction.

**Barbara Davis remembers** . . . phone interviewed at her home in Statesboro, 13 Aug 2004.

**Millie Jackson . . . Roosevelt . . . Willie Johnson . . .** respectively b. 15 Jul 1944; d. 12 Apr 1945 and d. 18 Sep 1945.

**Paul and Beth Garon . . .** Garon, page no. unnoted.

**Ralph McGill . . .** taken from profile of McGill by Leonard Ray Teel, Georgia State University, *www.georgiaencyclopedia.org/nge/Article.jsp?path=/Media/Journalism/Newspapers/EditorsandOwners&id=h-2769*, seen online, 28 Oct 2004.

**the Reverend Primus King . . .** taken from article seen online 13 Oct 2005 at *http://hpd.dnr.state.ga.us/assets/documents/Reflections/Reflections_Dec_2000.pdf*.

**In and around Atlanta . . . cluster of successful gospel groups** . . . details gleaned from notes by Ray Funk to the Gospel Heritage LP *Atlanta Gospel* seen online 24 Aug 2004 at *http://gospelhighway.50megs.com/GOLDEN/gospelgolden5.htm.*.

**Lillie Mae Brown . . .** interviewed at her daughter's home in Statesboro, 2 Mar 2003.

**Naomi Johnson . . .** op. cit.

**"When The Saints Go Marching In"** . . . Naomi Johnson interview ditto, 31 Jan 2004.

**"Rev" remembers Willie giving church concerts** . . . Rev. Andrew Williams interviewed for David Fulmer's film *Blind Willie's Blues*, Atlanta, first half of 1992.

**he would visit Sister Fleeta Mitchell . . .** These visits were between early 1937 and 1944. Interview with Sister F. Mitchell at her home outside Athens GA, 14 Apr 2001.

**"Tabernacle Church," Robert Owens said . . .** from transcript of interview by Anne M. Evans and David H. Evans Sr, Statesboro, 22 Aug 1975.

***Bulloch Times & Statesboro News* . . .** (The Bethel AME church, established 1886, was on Peachtree Street, Statesboro; Thomas Grove, as we know, was the church round the corner from the black portion of Eastside Cemetery where Willie's mother was buried; and the other church mentioned was the New Hope Baptist Church on Kennedy Bridge Road, about a mile off Highway 46, south of Register.) The cutting, information about it, and placing of the church outside Register, all from Dr Delma E. Presley, phonecall 4 Aug 2004 and e-mail 17 Aug 2004; Bethel AME church details from *Statesboro: A Century of Progress*, p.39.

**Ahmet Ertegun . . .** details next chapter.


SIXTEEN

**Ahmet Ertegun . . .** phone-interviewed at his Atlantic Records office, NYC, 9 Oct 2004.

**the first of two returns to so-called commercial recording** . . . details see Appendix: Career Discography.

**Fred Mendelsohn . . .** several equally unsatisfactory online sources.

**Utah Phillips heard him . . .** phone interviewed at his home, late May 2004.

**Atlanta librarian, Alma Hill Jamison** . . . information by e-mail from Atlanta-Fulton Public Library's Georgia Local and Family History Librarian William A. Montgomery, 28 Oct 2004, based on brief biographical sketch *Atlanta Historical Bulletin* Vol. IV, no.17, Apr 1939, p.141 and clippings in the *Atlanta Public Library Scrapbook 1949–55 & Atlanta Public Library Scrapbook 1955–1959*. Further information from *Journal & Constitution* profile by Alice Richards, Atlanta, 7 Jan 1951.

**This snippet of interview was published** . . . 'Atlanta shouts the blues!', Ed Paterson, *Melody Maker and Rhythm*, 26 May 1951.

**PL3–4717 . . .** This was the new way of writing what was Plaza 34717. (In another part of

Atlanta, eg, JA was short for Jackson.) The numbers could be direct dialed, since each set of three alphabet letters corresponded to a digit. This still applies to phones in the US.

**Helen working as a "domestic"** . . . stated on her death certificate; details below.

**Robert Owen** . . . from transcript of interview by Anne M. Evans and David H. Evans Sr, Statesboro, 22 Aug 1975.

**Barbara Davis** . . . phone interviewed at her home in Statesboro GA, 13 Aug 2004.

**Barbara never saw Helen again. Soon after . . . Willie and Helen moved house . . .** David Evans' account (JEMF-106 LP booklet) dates their move to 1950 but granted Ms Davis' clear description of its position, this must be wrong.

**Peter B. Lowry** . . . phone interviewed at his home in Austinmer, NSW, Australia, 14 Sep 2004.

**David Fulmer** . . . interviewed at the San Francisco Coffee Shop by the Post Office, North Highlands Avenue, Atlanta GA, 5 Mar 2003.

**Hugh Park's 'Around Town'** . . . 'How Blind Willie Came to Write The Dying Gambler's Blues', in 'Around Town' column, *Atlanta Journal*, unidentified date, March 1956; cutting found and photographed for me by local historian Gary Doster, 2004.

**Brown v. Board of Education** . . . 347 U.S. 483, Argued 9 Dec 1952; Reargued 8 Dec 1953; Decided 17 May 1954. Text online at *www.nationalcenter.org/brown.html*.

**future state governor Lester Maddox** . . . his restaurant opened in 1947. He became Governor of Georgia in 1966. All detail seen online, 7 Dec 2004, at *www.georgiaencyclopedia.org/nge/Article.jsp?id=h-1387*.

**Sam Charters** . . . phone-interviewed in Stockholm, 8 Aug 2002.

**George Hamilton IV . . . "Sam Cooke and I . . ."** Leigh, p.136. The interview is undated in the book but Leigh tells me (e-mail 11 Dec 2006) he recorded it on 13 May 1995.

**Cleveland Coot McTier, died** . . . Death certificate State File No. 33379; copy obtained 24 Feb 2003.

**Helen died** . . . cause of death given as "cardiac and resp. arrest" due to "probable cardiac arrhythmia and / or pul. embolus"; State File No. 27536; registered 5 Nov 1958; copy obtained 24 Feb 2003.

**preliminary obituary notice** . . . *Atlanta Constitution* 3 Nov 1958, p.21.

**obituary in the *Atlanta Constitution*** . . . 8 Nov 1958, Vol. XCI, no. 124, p.18.

**I went to Haughabrooks Funeral Home** . . . 6 Mar 2003.

**Geneva M. Haughabrooks** . . . data seen online, 12 Dec 2004, at *www.wabe.org/history/woal.htm*.

**Gary Doster and his wife Faye** . . . description of gravestones when Helen's not seen, e-mail 18 Nov 2004; message re discovery on second visit e-mailed 9 Dec 2004; detailed description of route to cemetery e-mail 27 Jan 2007; sea-level reading supplied 28 Jan 2007, from hand-held global positioning device placed on Helen's tombstone. The co-ordinates are 17S0239964 / 3718772. The device "said" this was accurate within fifteen to eighteen feet. The elevation reading fluctuated from 669 to 685 feet above sea level.


SEVENTEEN

**Robert and family moved to the North** . . . all Robert's testimony this chapter taken from the transcript of his interviews by Anne M. Evans and David Evans Sr, Statesboro GA, 22 Aug 1975 and by David Evans and Cheryl Thurber Evans, Statesboro 15 Jan 1976.

**Emmitt Gates told the Evanses** . . . David Evans, JEMF-106 LP booklet, p.22.

In the early spring of 1959 he suffered a stroke . . . This and Eddie's role taken from Evans, ibid, and Robert's testimony, op.cit.

Ola Ivey, Gold Harris' granddaughter . . . interviewed in the Employees' Room at the Salvation Army Store, Thomson GA, 14 Nov 2001.

Annie Jackson remembers . . . interviewed at her home outside Thomson GA, 4 Feb 2004.

Willie had a second stroke . . . Evans dates this to 11 Aug, but the paperwork at the local hospital consigning him to Milledgeville State Hospital was signed on the afternoon of 11 Aug.

Horace told the Evanses . . . Evans, op.cit., p.22.

"I can't stand up . . ." quoted by Hazel McTear, ibid.

Petition For Commission Of Lunacy . . . all details extrapolated from medical records obtained by Court Order 10 Aug 2001.

he arrived . . . 12 August, without any luggage or money . . . details from admission records, ibid.

And then Milledgeville . . . 8 Aug 2001.

Willie's death certificate . . . Baldwin Co. GA, Militia district 321; State File No. blank; Custodian's No. 5–720; filed 26 Aug 1959.

Bill Williamson . . . interview recorded Milledgeville, 9 Aug 2001.

In 1837 . . . the vast sum of $20,000 for a dormitory . . . history extrapolated from the state historical marker (005–24 Georgia Historical Commission 1961) erected outside the Center Building; own first look at the State Hospital 9 Aug 2001.

two dark gray, discolored-looking medical cards . . . Willie McTier [sic], Admission No. 91198; Hospital No. 109,134.

The Powell Building . . . notes for BAL-25, GA Dept. of Archives and History.

There were many telling statistics . . . Milledgeville State Hospital 117th Annual Report; deaths breakdown p.28, total admissions p.22, no. of operations p.27, electric shock treatments p.82.

Another paper's reporter . . . J.B. Chism Jr. Actually his piece was titled 'Conditions Existing At Milledgeville State Hospital For Mentally Ill', Pelham Journal, Mitchell GA, 5 Nov 1959.

The hospital's more detailed notes . . . Staff Meeting Notes 4 Sep 1959.

Cerebral Vascular Accident . . . For interpretation of the medical information from the notes, I am grateful to Dr M. Blacklee, recently retired General Practitioner, who was kind enough to review it with me in detail, Kirkbymoorside UK, 24 Oct 2001. Any misunderstanding will be mine, not his. I also took advice informally from Prof. Jonathan N. Weber, Clinical Professor, Division of Medicine, Imperial College London and Professor of Biology at St Mary's Hospital London, and drew on extra material seen online 30 Aug 2004 at www.neonatology.org/syllabus/syphilis.html.

Gold Harris . . . on the p.m. train . . . stated on medical card, op.cit. .

taken to Haynes Funeral Home . . . visited 2 and 3 Aug 2001. (Not, as in David Evans' JEMF-106 LP booklet, Haines and Peterson: Haynes and Peterson is the Augusta branch.)

Girard L. Haynes . . . died 10 Apr 1961; details from certificate no. 11186, Georgia Deaths Index.

Kate McTell . . . interviewed by the Evanses, Blues Unlimited nos.125 and 126, Jul/Aug and Sep/Oct 1977, UK.

Vinnie Williams for the Augusta Chronicle . . . 12 Nov 1980.

Sally Cramer . . . interviewed at her home, Happy Valley, McDuffie Co. GA, 3 Nov 2001.

EIGHTEEN

Evans, "Kate had been offered Willie's guitars . . . *Atlanta Blues 1933* JEMF-106 LP booklet, p.22.

Ola Ivey . . . interviewed in the Employees' Room at the Salvation Army Store, Thomson GA, 14 Nov 2001.

**Buddy Moss . . . worked . . . tobacco farm . . . elevator man . . . truck driver . . .** 'Buddy Moss' entry, Once And Future Blues website, seen 21 Oct 2001 online at *www.oafb.net/once243.html*.

Eleanor Walden . . . phone interview at her home Berkeley CA 7 Dec 2006 and e-mail ditto.

Bill Hoffman . . . phone interview at Hoffman Rubin office, Rockville MD, 13 Dec 2006.

Peter B. Lowry . . . Buddy's Atlanta home . . . phone interview Austinmer, NSW, Australia, 14 Sep 2004. Bastin denies Moss' wife braved the gun (email 14 Jan 2009)

According to Curley's daughter . . . "Cora Mae . . . "Cora Mae Bryant" entry, Once And Future Blues website, seen 21 Oct 2001 online at *www.oafb.net/once126.html*.

respected academic David Evans . . . He was, at the time, in the Department of Anthropology at California State University.

the formative official version . . . notes on McTell in booklet issued with *Atlanta Blues 1933*, JEMF-106, op.cit., p.1 and pp.6–24; augmented by the interviews in *Blues Unlimited* no.125, Jul/Aug 1977, pp.4–12, no.126, Sep/Oct 1977, pp.8–16 and no.127, Nov/Dec 1977, pp. 20–22, later notes on McTell in the booklet issued with *The Definitive Blind Willie McTell*, Columbia Roots 'n Blues Series, Columbia/Legacy C2K 53234, NY, 1994, pp.6–20; and soon, perhaps, notes to *The Blind Willie McTell Box Set*, details tba.

Writing of Kate . . . *Blues Unlimited* no.125, Jul/Aug 1977, p.4.

Bo-Rat on March 6, 1973 . . . Eddie McTier [previously spelt McTear], death certificate, no state file no. given, registered McDuffie Co. GA 12 Mar 1973.

Hazel herself died . . . March 21, 1982 . . . Hazel S. McTear [sic] death certificate, State File no. 009163 (or 009183), filed McDuffie Co. GA 5 Apr 1982.

Her sister told me . . . Annie Jackson, interviewed at her home, Thomson GA, 4 Feb 2004.

Robert Owens . . . died . . . on April 5, 1978 . . . Death certificate State File no. 011764, filed 14 Apr 1978; copy obtained 24 Feb 2003.

Robert was survived by . . . obituary, *Statesboro Morning News*, 2 Apr 1978.

Catherine died at seventy-nine in June 1989 . . . obituary, *Statesboro Herald*, 30 Jun 1989. Additional information from Kathleen Edwards, phone conversations from her home in Plainfield NJ, Dec 2006 to Feb 2007.

Gold Harris formally married Margaret Burnett . . . Application for Marriage License Warren Co. GA County No. 83–29, 6 Oct 1983.

Gold . . . died . . . at the age of ninety-eight . . . d. Augusta 15 Jan 1995; Death Certificate State File No. 007440, registered 24 Feb 1995.

Sally Cramer died . . . details from phone call to Valerie Burley, McDuffie County Probate Court Clerk, 22 Feb 2007. Other elderly witnesses have also died in recent years: Mrs. Naomi Johnson in 2005; Mrs. Lillie Mae Brown in 2007; Jack Averitt on 11 Nov 2007; Mrs. Mildred Bouie Harville in late 2008. As of March 2009 Sister Fleeta Mitchell is still alive.

Kate died . . . in hospital in Augusta on 3 August 1991 . . . interview with Ernest Bernard McTell Seabrooks, Phinizy Road Richmond County Detention Center Augusta GA, 5 Nov 2001.

**Bernard and April** . . . Bernard interview ibid (these quotations have been edited down); April Seabrooks interviewed Augusta GA 5 Aug and 8 Nov 2001.

**Great-Aunt Inez** . . . non-interviewed at her home, Augusta GA 8 Nov 2001.

**April's mother Sharon died** . . . e-mail from April Seabrooks, 14 Jul 2007.

**Peer International** . . . e-mails and phone-calls from and to Jonathan Kehl, 1 Apr to 18 May 2004.

**Scott Cameron** . . . e-mails and phone-calls 25 Mar to 31 May 2004 and 19 Jul 2004.

**a lawyer friend of another manager** . . . e-mails 29 Dec 2004 (details held by me).

**The David Evans account of McTell's other supposed wives and children** . . . JEMF-106 booklet, op.cit., as follows: "in Senoia" p.9; "in Florida", p.?; "in Savannah" p.11; "at Midville" p.11; "a daughter named Ethel" p.19; "Alice took the girl" p.21; "daughter . . . about six years old" p.22. Peter B. Lowry doubts Evans' assumption that neighbor Emmitt Gates was Willie's (and Helen's) landlord: e-mail to the present author, 18 Nov 2008.

**Josephine Cook** . . . 'About Josephine Cook', About E49 Staff, Empire 49 ("born from the closing of Megaworks"), seen online 18 Sep 2004 at *www.empire49.8m.com*. Disconnected phone no. tried subsequently (amid much other effort).

**Alice Beasley died in Philadelphia in 1999** . . . Social Security Death Index (SSDI no. 376-20-0538) shows her born 21 Oct 1923, died 29 Sep 1999.

**E. Bernard West** . . . interview in Atlanta History Center Archives (File no. 1989.305, Folder 12, Box 38), recorded unspecified location 3 Feb 1979; my transcription.

**Kate made a will and Bernard was the executor** . . . phone-call with lawyer John Pilcher in Wrens GA, 3 Aug 2004.

**Bernard died in June 2008** . . . 13 June 2008, cause of death unknown as of 24 Jun; funeral 19 Jun; burial alongside Kate at Spread Chapel graveyard. Source: e-mail from April Seabrooks, 24 Jun 2008.

**Frank Edwards** . . . b. Washington GA 20 Mar 1909; d. Greenville SC 22 Mar, 2002. Interviewed Blind Willie's, Atlanta, Nov 2001.

**recently opened a Willie McTell Trail** . . . opened 2006 but markers still not unveiled. I have to declare an interest here (but not a financial one, unfortunately): I was asked to write the text for the plaques; Statesboro made changes that introduced errors; a compromise was reached. The final text may have been changed again, I don't know. They regret there are no funds to pay me for my services.

**Georgia Historical Marker** . . . no.094–10, 1993.

**Dot Jones** . . . driving me round Happy Valley 2 Nov 2001.

**Teddy Jackson** . . . interviewed at his mother's home in Thomson, GA, 4 Feb 2004.

**inducted Willie at the same time as Ronnie Milsap** . . . Georgia Music Festival News press release by Glenn Christian, Atlanta GA, Sep 1990.

**"Georgy Award" was created by Tiffany & Company** . . . induction text from Georgia Music Hall of Fame files.

**Dot Jones** . . . op.cit. As of March 2009, Dot Jones was still alive and well.

**David Fulmer** . . . interviewed N. Highlands Ave, Atlanta GA 5 Mar 2003.

**Joseph R. Johnson** . . . interviewed Georgia Music Hall of Fame, Augusta GA 7 Aug 2001; e-mail 5 Oct 2001.

# BIBLIOGRAPHY

Articles, essays and album liner notes are detailed in the Notes; books are detailed here. These are not always first or best editions/printings: they are those available to me. (ed. = editor, edn = edition)

Albertson, Chris, *Bessie*, New York: Stein & Day, 1972

Arnesen, Eric, *Brotherhood of Color: Black Railroad Workers and the Struggle for Equality*, Harvard: Harvard University Press, 2001

Baker, Ray Stannard, *Following the Color Line*, New York: Doubleday, Page & Co., 1908

Ball, Edward, *Slaves in the Family*, New York: Ballantine, 1999

Baldwin, James, *Nobody Knows My Name: More Notes of a Native Son*, New York: Dial Press, 1961

Bane, Michael, *White Boy Singin' The Blues*, London: Penguin Books, 1982

Bastin, Bruce, *Crying For The Carolines*, London: Studio Vista Blues Paperbacks, 1971

Bastin, Bruce, *Red River Blues: The Blues Tradition in the Southeast*, Urbana: Illini Books edn, 1995

Bennett, L. Jr, *Before the Mayflower: A History of the Negro in America 1619–1962*, Chicago: Thomas Publishing, 1962

Booth, Stanley, *Rythm Oil*, London: Cape, 1991

Breese, Martin, *Breese's Guide To Modern 1st Editions*, London: Breese Books, 1993

Brooks, Tim, *Lost Sounds: Blacks and the Birth of the Recording Industry, 1890–1919*, Urbana: University of Illinois Press, 2004

Broonzy, Big Bill (as told to Yannick Bruynoghe), *Big Bill Blues*, London: Cassell, 1955

Broughton, Viv, *Black Gospel: An Illustrated History Of The Gospel Sound*, London: Blandford Press, 1985

Cantor, Louis, *Wheelin' On Beale*; New York: Pharos Books, 1992

Chambers, H.A., ed., *The Treasury of Negro Spirituals*, London: Blandford Press, 3rd impression, 1964

Charters, Samuel B., *The Country Blues*, New York: Reinhart, 1959; Da Capo Press, revised edn 1975

Charters, Samuel B., *The Poetry Of The Blues*, New York: Oak Publications, 1963

Charters, Samuel B., *Sweet as the Showers of Rain: The Bluesmen*, Volume II, New York: Oak Publications, 1977 and London: Music Sales, 1977

Cohen, Norm, *Long Steel Rail: the Railroad in American Folksong*, Urbana-Champaign: Board of Trustees of the University of Illinois, 1981, 2nd edn 2000.

Cohn, Lawrence, ed. *Nothing But The Blues: The Music & The Musicians*, New York: Abbeville Press Publishers, 1993

*Collins English Dictionary*, Glasgow: HarperCollins, updated 3<sup>rd</sup> edn 1994

Crane, Stephen, *The Red Badge Of Courage*, Ware, Hertfordshire: Wordsworth Editions, 1994 [first published 1895]

Dahl, Linda, *Stormy Weather: The Music & Lives Of A Century Of Jazz Women*, New York: Pantheon Books, 1984

Darden, Robert, *A New History of Black Gospel Music*, New York: Continuum, 2004

Daughtry, J. Carl, *Our World and its Changing Times: My One-Half Century*, Metter GA: self-published, 1982–3

Dixon, Robert M.W. & Godrich, J., *Blues & Gospel Records 1902–1943*, Chigwell UK: Storyville Publications, 1982

Dixon, Robert M.W., Godrich, J. & Rye, Howard W., *Blues & Gospel Records 1890–1943*, Oxford: Oxford University Press, 1997

Dollard, John, *Caste and Class in a Southern Town*, New York: Doubleday Anchor Books 3<sup>rd</sup> edn, 1957

Dunkersley, James, *Americana: The Americas in the World, around 1850*, London: Verso, 2000

*Encyclopedia of the Blues*, ed. Ed Komara, New York: Routledge Press, 2005, 2 vols

Evans, David, *Big Road Blues: Tradition & Creativity in the Folk Blues*, Berkeley: University of California Press, 1982

Flanders, Ralph Betts, *Plantation Slavery in Georgia*, Chapel Hill: University of North Carolina, 1933

Ford, Robert, *A Blues Bibliography: the International Literature of an Afro-American Music Genre*, Bromley, Kent: Paul Pelletier, 1999

Fuller, Thomas O., *Pictorial History of the American Negro*, Memphis: Pictorial History Inc., 1933

Garon, Paul & Beth, *Woman With Guitar: Memphis Minnie's Blues*, New York: Da Capo Press, 1992

*Georgia Atlas & Gazeteer*, Yarmouth, Maine: DeLorme, 2<sup>nd</sup> edn, 2000

Gilmore, Al-Tony, *Bad Nigger! The National Impact of Jack Johnson*, Port Washington NY: Kenniket Press, 1975

Gray, Michael, *Song & Dance Man III: The Art of Bob Dylan*, London: Cassell Academic, 1999

Gray, Michael, *The Bob Dylan Encyclopedia*, New York: Continuum, 2006

Grendysa, Peter A., *Atlantic Master Book #1*, Milwaukee: self-published, 1975

Grossman, Stefan, *Country Blues Guitar* [foreword by Stephen Calt], New York: Oak Press, 1970s

Guralnick, Peter, *Feel Like Going Home*, New York: Outerbridge and Dienstfrey, 1971 [London: Penguin, 1992]

Hardy, Phil & Laing, Dave, *The Faber Companion to 20<sup>th</sup>-Century Popular Music*, London: Faber and Faber, 1990

Harris, Michael W., *The Rise of Gospel Blues: The Music of Thomas Andrew Dorsey in the Urban Church*, New York: Oxford University Press, 1992

Harris, Sheldon, ed., *Blues Who's Who*; New Rochelle, New York: Arlington House, 1979 [New York: Da Capo, revised edn 1991]

Harrison, D.D., *Black Pearls: Blues Queens of the 1920s*, New Brunswick & London: Rutgers University Press, 1990

Hatch, D. & Millward, S., *From Blues To Rock: An Analytical History Of Pop Music*; Manchester: Manchester University Press, 1987

Hayes, Cedric J. & Laughton, Robert, *Gospel Records 1943–1969: A Black Music Discography*, 2 Vols, London: Record Information Services, 1992

Haymes, Max, *Railroadin' Some: Railroads in the Early Blues*, York: Music Mentor Books, 2006

Heat-Moon, William Least, *Blue Highways: a Journey into America*, London: Picador, 1984 [USA 1983]

Hollo, Anselm, ed., *Negro Verse*, London: Vista Books, 1964

Hoskins, Charles Lwanga, *Black Episcopalians in Georgia: Strife, Struggle and Salvation*, Savannah GA: Hoskins/St.Matthew's Episcopal Church, 1980

Johnson, Jack, *Jack Johnson Is A Dandy: An Autobiography*, New York: Chelsea House, 1969

Johnson, Jack, *Jack Johnson—In the Ring and Out*, (ed. Gilbert Odd), London: Proteus, 1977 [1st edn USA, 1927

Jones, Hettie, *Big Star Fallin' Mama: Five Women In Black Music*, New York: Viking Press, 1974

Jones, Hettie, *How I Became Hettie Jones*, New York: E.P. Dutton, 1990

Kennedy, Michael M., *Freedom From Fear: The American People in Depression and War, 1929–1945*, New York: Oxford University Press, 2004

Kerridge, Roy, *In The Deep South*, London: Michael Joseph, 1989

King Jr, Martin Luther: *Stride Towards Freedom: The Montgomery Story*, New York: Harper and Brothes, 1958

Kuhn, Clifford M., Joye, Harlon E. & West, E. Bernard, *Living Atlanta: An Oral History of the City, 1914–1948*, Atlanta & Athens GA: Atlanta Historical Society and UGA Press, 1990

Kurtz, Irma, *Great American Bus Ride*, New York: Simon and Schuster, 1993 and London: Fourth Estate, 1994

Laing, D., Dallas, K., Denselow, R. & Shelton, R., *The Electric Muse: The Story of Folk into Rock*, London: Eyre Methuen, 1975

Leadbitter, M., Fancourt, L. & Pelletier, P., *Blues Records 1943–1970: The Bible of the Blues, Volume Two: L-Z*, London: Record Information Services, 1994

Leadbitter, Mike & Slaven, Neil, *Blues Records 1943–1970, Volume One: A-K*, London: Record Information Services, 1987

Leigh, Spencer, *Baby, That Is Rock and Roll: American Pop 1954–1963*, Folkestone: Finbarr International, 2001

Litwack, Leon F., *Trouble in Mind: Black Southerners in the Age of Jim Crow*, New York: Alfred Knopf, 1998

Lloyd, A.L., *Folk Song In England*, London: Lawrence & Wishart, 1967

Lloyd, A.L., ed., *Folk Songs Of The Americas*, London: Novello and Co., 1965

Lomax, Alan, *The Land Where The Blues Began*; London:Methuen, 1993

Lomax, Alan, *The Penguin Book Of American Folk Songs*, Harmondsworth: Penguin, 1964

Lomax, John A., *Adventures of a Ballad Hunter*, New York: Macmillan, 1947

McTier, Jan, *Kendall McTier Family*, Dearing GA: privately published for the Kendall McTier Family Association, 2nd edn, 2000

Major, Clarence, *Juba To Jive: A Dictionary Of African-American Slang*, London: Penguin Books, 1994

Mitchell, Margaret, *Gone With The Wind*, London: Macmillan, 1936

Morone, James, *Hellfire Nation: The Politics of Sin in American History*, New Haven: Yale University Press, 2003

Naipaul, V.S., *A Turn In The South*, New York: Alfred Knopf [London: Viking], 1989

Nichols, C.H., *Many Thousand Gone*, Holland: E.J. Brill, 1963

Oakley, Giles, *The Devil's Music—A History of the Blues*, London: BBC Publications, 1976

Odum, H.W. & Johnson, G.B., *The Negro & His Songs: A Study Of Typical Negro Songs In The South*, Chapel Hill: University of North Carolina Press, 1925

Oliver, Paul, ed, *The Blackwell Guide To Blues Records*, Oxford: Basil Blackwood, 1989

Oliver, Paul, *Blues Fell This Morning*, London, Cassell, 1960

Oliver, Paul, *Conversation With The Blues*, London: Cassell, 1965

Oliver, Paul, *The Meaning of the Blues*, New York: Collier Books, 1960

Oliver, Paul, *Songsters and Saints: Vocal Traditions On Race Records*, Cambridge: Cambridge University Press, 1984

Oliver, Paul, *Story of the Blues*, London: Barrie & Rockliff, 1969 and Harmondsworth: Penguin, 1972.

Oney, Steve, *And the Dead Shall Rise: The Murder of Mary Phagan and the Lynching of Leo Frank*, New York: Vintage, 2003

Palmer, A.W., *A Dictionary of Modern History*, Harmondsworth: Penguin reprint, 1969

Palmer, Roy, *The Oxford Book of Sea Songs*, Oxford: OUP, 1986 [revised and expanded as *Boxing the Compass: Sea Songs and Shanties*, Todmorden: Herron Publishing, 2001

Porterfield, Nolan, *Last Cavalier: The Life and Times of John A. Lomax*, Urbana & Chicago: University of Illinois Press, 1996

Presley, Delma E. and Banks, Smith C., *Statesboro*, Charleston, SC: Arcadia Publishing, 2003

Ramsey, Frederic, *Been Here and Gone . . .* Athens GA: UGA Press, 2000

*Road Atlas: United States, Canada, Mexico*, Chicago: Rand McNally [54th edn.], 1978

Roberts, Jason, *A Sense of the World: How a Blind Man Became History's Greatest Traveller*, London: Simon and Schuster, 2006

Ruppli, Michel, *Prestige Jazz Records 1949–1969*, Denmark: Knudsen, 1972

Ruppli, Michel, *The Prestige Label: A Discography*, Westport, Connecticut: Greenwood Press, 1980

Richardson, Willis, ed., *Plays and Pageants from the Life of the Negro*, Washington D.C.: Associated Publishers, 1930

Russell, Tony, *Blacks, Whites and Blues*, London: Studio Vista, 1970

Russell, Tony, *The Blues From Robert Johnson to Robert Cray*, London: Aurum Press, 1997

Russell, Tony, *Country Music Records: A Discography, 1921–1942*, New York: Oxford University Press, 2004

Russell, Tony, & Smith, Chris, *The Penguin Guide to Blues Recordings*, London: Penguin, 2006

Sammons, Jeffrey, *Beyond the Ring: The Role of Boxing in American Society*, Chicago: University of Illinois Press, 1990

Santelli, Robert, *The Big Book Of Blues: A Biographical Encyclopedia*, London: Pavilion Books, 1994

Scarborough, Dorothy, *On The Trail Of Negro Folksongs*, Cambridge: Harvard University Press, 1925

Sharp, Cecil & Karpeles, Maud, *English Folk-Songs From The Southern Appalachians*, Oxford: Oxford University Press, 1932

Shaw, Geoffrey, ed., *Twice 44 Sociable Songs*; London: Hawkes & Son, 1927

*Statesboro: A Century of Progress 1866–1966*, ed. Leodel Coleman, Statesboro GA: Bulloch Herald Publishing Co., 1969

Taft, Michael, *Blues Lyric Poetry: An Anthology*, New York: Garland, 1983

Taft, Michael, *Blues Lyric Poetry: A Concordance*, 3 vols, New York: Garland, 1984

Taft, Michael, *Talkin' to Myself: Blues lyrics, 1921–1942*, New York: Taylor and Francis, 2005

Talley, Thomas W., *Negro Folk Rhymes* [ed. Charles K. Wolfe], Knoxville, Tennessee: University of Tennessee Press, 1991 [3rd edition] [1st edn. New York: Macmillan, 1922]

Tilling, Robert, *Oh! What A Beautiful City: A Tribute To Rev. Gary Davis 1896–1972*, Paul Mill, Jersey: Paul Mill Press, 1992

Tilove, Jonathan & Falco, Michael, *Along Martin Luther King: Travels on Black America's Main Street*, New York: Random House, 2004

Ward, Geoffrey C., *Unforgiveable Blackness: The Rise and Fall of Jack Johnson*, London: Pimlico, 2006

Wardlow, Gayle Dean, *Chasin' That Devil Music: Searching for the Blues*, San Francisco: Backbeat Books, 1998

Wells, Rebecca, *Divine Secrets of the Ya-Ya Sisterhood*, New York: HarperCollins, 1996

Wells, Tom Henderson, *The Slave Ship Wanderer*, Athens GA: UGA Press, 1968

Welsh, Douglas, *The American Civil War: A Complete Military History*, London: Bison, 1981

Wexler, Laura, *Fire in a Canebrake: The Last Mass Lynching in America*, New York: Scribner Book Co., 2003

White, Newman I., American Negro Folk-Songs, Harvard: Harvard University Press, 1928 [facsimile reprint, Hatboro PA: Folklore Associates, 1965]

Wilhoit, Virginia H., *The History of Warren County, Georgia 1793–1974*, Washington GA: Wilkes Publishing Co., 1976

# COPYRIGHT ACKNOWLEDGMENTS

T HE AUTHOR and publishers thank the following for permission to quote from or reproduce copyright work:

Barbara Davis (photograph as detailed overleaf); Gary Doster (photographs); Ed Ellis (photograph); David Fulmer (interviews with Ed Rhodes and Rev. Andrew Williams, taken in part from his documentary film *Blind Willie's Blues*, 1996); Duncan Hume (photographs); Library of Congress (photograph), and Jan McTier (the privately published book *Kendall McTier Family*) and Delma E. Presley (photograph). We also thank the following for interview material drawn on within this book: the late David H. Evans Sr., Anne M. Evans, David Evans, Peter B. Lowry, Delma E. Presley, Ed Rhodes, Cheryl Thurber and E. Bernard West. Fair usage has also been made of material from James Baldwin's *Nobody Knows My Name: More Notes of a Native Son*; Bruce Bastin's *Red River Blues: The Blues Tradition in the Southeast*; John Dollard's classic study *Caste and Class in a Southern Town*; David Evans' essay "Blind Willie McTell" in the booklet issued with the record album *Atlanta Blues 1933* (John Edwards Memorial Foundation, 1979); Kuhn, Joye and West's *Living Atlanta*; and less significantly from other works as specified in the Notes and listed in the Bibliography, and from the following songs: 'Writin' Paper Blues', 'Stole Rider Blues', 'Mama Tain't Long Fo' Day', 'Statesboro Blues', 'Dark Night Blues', 'Atlanta Strut', Travelin' Blues', 'Talkin' To Myself' and 'Georgia Rag' by Blind Willie McTell; 'Up The Country Blues' by Sippie Wallace', 'Reckless Blues' by Bessie Smith and 'Cincinnati Southern Blues' by Ivy Smith.

## Photo Credits

McTell studio portrait, probably late 1920s (pviii), courtesy of John Reynolds; Civil War hospital ward with mosquito nets, Washington DC, 1861–65 (p26), courtesy of the Library of Congress Prints and Photographs Division; Jones Grove Baptist Church (p40), and Willie McTell's original gravestone, ("Eddie McTier") (p308), both 1992, courtesy of Duncan Hume; Cato and Reid, Statesboro Riot, 1904 (p92), source unknown; Statesboro railroad lines, 2003 (p114), courtesy of Michael Gray; Nellie and Henry Ellis, c.1930 (p130), courtesy of Ed Ellis; Robert Fulton Hotel, 1950 (p264), courtesy of the Special Collections Dept., Pullen Library, Georgia State University; Helen Edwards McTell's grave, 2004 (p307), courtesy of Gary Doster; the Statesboro Bi-Centenary frank design, 2003 (p336), courtesy of Delma E. Presley; and the author's travelin' shoes (p433), 2004, courtesy of Michael Gray.

# THANKS

## Special Thanks

and much gratitude for invaluable research help to Sarah Beattie, whose work on this book has been utterly crucial throughout; and to Delma E. Presley, for his invaluable Statesboro expertise and researches.

## Many Thanks

also for valuable help to Dr. Jack Averitt; Alan Balfour; Dr. Smith C. Banks; Bruce Bastin; Malcolm Blacklee; Lillie Mae Brown; Mike Brubaker at the Atlanta History Center; Judge Lucy J. Bryant at Warren County Probate Court; Evelyne & Paul Bubernak; Valerie Burley at McDuffie County Probate Court; Samuel B. Charters; the late Sally Cramer; Barbara Davis; Mrs Rhunette Davis; LaShunda D. Dennis at Milledgeville State Hospital; Gary Doster; the late Frank Edwards; Kathleen Edwards: Ed & Johnnie Ellis and Will H. Ellis; the late Ahmet Ertegun; James Chris Floyd; Lavinia Floyd; David Fulmer; Judge Hulane E. George at Baldwin County Superior Court; Carolyn Gilbert at the Thomson GA Chamber of Commerce; Sara Greene at Milledgeville State Hospital; Todd Harvey at the Library of Congress; Mildred Bouie Harville; W. Elizabeth Haynes of G.L. Haynes Funeral Home, Warrenton; the late Mrs Addie Hill; Chester Huffman; Duncan Hume, for permission to use his photographs; Pat Hutcheson and Janice Strickland at the Statesboro Regional Library; Ola Ivey; Annie L. Jackson; Teddy Jackson; Joseph R. Johnson of the Georgia Music Hall of Fame; the late Naomi Johnson; the late Constance Jones; Dot Jones; my editor, Mike

Jones at Bloomsbury; Peter B. Lowry; Ernest Bernard McTell Seabrooks; Ralph McTell; Jan & Lindy McTier; Sister Fleeta Mitchell; William A. Montgomery of the Atlanta-Fulton Central Library; Peter Narváez; Bruce "Utah" Phillips; Herbaline Rich; Tony Russell; April Seabrooks; the late H.W.B. Smith; Walt Strickland; Cheryl Thurber; Annie Vaughner; John R. Wheat and Bill Williamson.

## Thanks Also

to all of the following (with apologies to anyone forgotten): Tom Alderman; Mary Katharine Aldin; Cindy Anderson; John Armstrong at the Historic Statesboro Inn; Chuck Barber; Scott Barretta; Matthew Barton; Miriam Bean; Dylan Beattie; Pamela Beer; Bruce Beggs; Libby Bell; Willie Benefield; Lowell Berenguer; Linda Bitley at Georgia Parks & Historic Sites; Brian K. Blount; the *Blues Access* online bulletin board; *Blues & Rhythm* magazine; Kathy Bonnell; Bonnie at the Curious Book Shop, East Lansing, MI; Stanley Booth; Laura Botts; Pat Bowen; Ralph S. Bown; Beverley Brannan, Carl Fleischhauer and Jan Grenci at the Library of Congress; Kenneth J. Brantley; William Brown; Cora Mae Bryant; Mick Buck; Alice Budack; Brenda Burke at Jenkins County Memorial Library; Randall K. Burkett; Tony Burke; Judge Wanda P. Burke at Jenkins County Probate Court; Deacon Jasper L. Burnett; Maria Elisa Botelho Byington; Ernestine Carter; Nancy Carver; Frances Chantly at Atlantic Records, NYC; Bill Cherepy; the Chicago Historical Society (now the Chicago History Museum); Mr and Mrs Choate in Midville GA; Bryson Clevenger; Andy Cohen; Norm Cohen; Larry Cohn; Wilma Coleman; Michael Corcoran; Nancy Gay Crawford; Virginia Crilley; Dan N. Crumpton; Warren Culpepper; Jeanne Cyriaque of the Historic Preservation Division, Georgia Department of Natural Resources; Denise Dallas; Wayne Daniel; Miki Davis; Oscar Davis Jr.; Shirley Dawkins; Dennis Dees; Irene DeLoach; Dottie Demarest; Faye Doster; Lorna Dorkin at the Chicago Public Library; Wayne Dorough; Donard Duffy; Tim Duffy; Barbara J. Dunn; Bob Eagle; Sam Eason at the *News & Farmer*, Jefferson County GA; Bill Ector; Sharon Esch; Glenn Eskew; David Evans; Lucretia Ferguson; Bob Fisher; Robert Ford; Mrs Mildred Forston; Dave Foster; Frank at CSRA Taxi Delivery Service; Tom Freeland; Paul Garon; John Garst; John Gilks; James Lee Glaze; Mr Goolsby of Covington GA; Robert Gordon; Magdalena Gray; Greg at Once Upon A Time Books, Tontitown, AR; George Groom-White; Adam Gussow; Guy Hall; Wayne Hammock; Robert L. Hammond of Burke County Museum; Greg Hardin; Suzan R. Harris of the Bartram Trail Regional Library / Thomson McDuffie County Library; Nadine Harville; Rodney Harville; Martin Hawkins; Tracy Hayes; Max Haymes; the staff of the Heritage Inn Nursing Home in Statesboro; Joe Hickerson; John Hilgart; James Lee Hobbs; Bill Hoffman; Steve Hoffman; Debra J. Hogan, City of Senoia; Peter Hughes; Rob Hutten; Richard E. Hyer; Ed Jackson; Reuben Jackson at the National Museum of American History Archives Center; Muriel Jackson at Washington Memorial Library, Macon, GA; Greg Jarrell; Greg Johnson; Larry Felton Johnson; the late Inez Jones; Erik Van Keirsbilck; Michael Kerr; Greg Kimball; Bob Koestler; Kelly Kress, Dr. Clifford Kohn; Ms Y. Landman of KLM; Ross Laird; Suzan Laircey; Andy Leach; Earl M. Lee; Ken Lees at the Amadeus Center, University of York; Spencer Leigh; Leroy Lewis; Andrew Linehan, British Library, London; Russell Liner; John Lomax III; Kip Lornell; Eric Lott; Rusty Lovelace; Gary Lucas; Sammy Luckey; Bob Macleod; Elaine Maddox-Weaver of Haugabrooks Funeral Home; Geneva Mallard; Julie A. Malone; Katie Marages at DeKalb History Center; Mark at the Jefferson County Library in Louisville, GA; Dr. John Mason; Helen Matthews; Barry Mazor; Martin McCann; Shawn McCauley; Judy M. McCorkle and her secretary Anita at Statesboro City Hall; Larry McDuffie; Flory Mae McNair; Angela McRobbie; Morris McTier; Will McTier; Leigh McWhite at University of Mississippi Department of Archives and Special Collections; Lorenzo Meachum; Verdora C. Merritt; Jeannie Miller; Gavin Mist; Rev. Robert J. Mixon; Janie C. Morris at Duke University; Karen Mouton; Rev. Charlie Myricks; Liz Nash; Newton County Library; Eric Nitschke; Dawn Oberg; Jas Obrecht; Jim O'Neal; Bill O'Neill at the Virginia War Museum; Cathy Padgett; Leo G. Parrish Jr.; David E. Paterson; Christopher Ann Paton; Paul M. Pearson; Dave Penny; Bob Petrilla; Steve Phillips; Frank Phipps; John J. Pilcher and his assistant Rosella A. Martin; Nolan Porterfield; Dianne Poteet; Don

Powers of Thomson McDuffie County Chamber of Commerce; Samuel Powers; Mary Prendergast at the University of Virginia Music Library; Beverly Presley; the Pre-War Blues Discussion Group; Denise Quick; Jill J. Read; Paul Reddick; Charles Reeves; John Reynolds; Thomas Ridgeway; Thomas Riis; Peter J. Roberts; John Robinson at Sideshow Central; Megan Rocks; Christopher Rollason; Art Rosenbaum; John Rumble; Vivian Price Saffold; Doug Seroff; Amilcar Shabazz; Robert Shackleton; Sue Simons; Neil Slaven; Annie G. Smith; Chris Smith; Mrs H.W.B. Smith; Peter Smith; Cal Stephenson; Barbara Streetman; Michael Taft; Peggy Tanksley at Paine College, Augusta GA; David A. Taylor; Denise DuBois Taylor; Brent W. Tharp of the Georgia Southern Museum; Robert Tilling; Ann Toplovich at the Tennessee Historical Society; Gladys Benefield Turner; Linda Usry; Alex van der Tuuk; Stephen Wade; Elijah Wald; Eleanor Walden; Geoffrey C. Ward; Steven Ward; Helen Washington; Dick Waterman; Jonathan Weber; Steve Weiss; Paul F. Wells; Gaile Welker; Josie A. West at Hardwick Funeral Home, Thomson; Mary West; Rev. Alex Williams; Vinnie Williams; Epp Wilson at the White Columns Inn, Thomson; Stefan Wirz; Jeff Yawn at Archibald's; Alan R. Young and the Young Funeral Home, Covington GA. And to the Authors' Foundation, administered by the Society of Authors in London, for a grant awarded in 2003 to help with research expenses.

# INDEX

Frank, Leo 185–6, 190
Frank Scott State Prison 324–9
Franklin, Virginia Anne 354–6
Fredericksburg 34
Fredericksburg, Battle of 30
Freedman's Bureau 64
Frog Pond (later Thomson) 45
Fuller, Blind Boy 13, 117, 262
Fuller, Jesse 114
Fulmer, David 47, 58–9, 284, 298
  *Blind Willie's Blues* (video) 240, 355

**G**
Gable, Clark 262
Gabler, Lou 289
Garon, Beth 281
Garon, Paul 6, 281
Garrett, John 259–60
Gates, Emmitt Lee 80, 173, 298, 308, 348
Gates, Rev JM 282, 298
Gatewood, Willard B 112
George, Hulane 319–21
Georgia:
  black franchise 282
  blues performers 114–17
  census schedules 70–2
  contemporary 17–20, 40–3, 60–1
  late 19$^{th}$–early 20$^{th}$ centuries 94–6
  lynch law decades 96–113
  lynchings 103–13, 133, 190
  secession 27
  slavery 21–5, 65
  tobacco season 213, 274–8
  Vital Records Office 81–2
  written records 70, 73–8
Georgia Academy for the Blind (Macon)
  42, 115, 137, 148, 163, 166–70, 194,
  268
  *see also* Macon (Georgia)
Georgia Agricultural Census (1860) 69
Georgia Cotton Pickers 222
*Georgia Encyclopaedia* 63–4
*Georgia Historical Quarterly* 112
Georgia Historical Society: library 65–6
Georgia Music Hall of Fame 57, 352
  Blind Willie's induction 354–6
'Georgia Rag' 189, 220
Georgia State Historical Marker 352–4
Gershwin, George 116
Gettysburg, Battle of 30–2
Gibson (Glascock County) 27, 120–1
Gid Tanner and His Skillet Lickers 115, 208
Gilliland, Henry C 196
Gilmore, Pleas and Fannie 227
Gilmore, Pleas Senior 227

Gilmore, Sarah *see* Williams, Sarah *née*
  Gilmore (Kate's mother)
Ginsberg, Allen 16
Glascock County (Georgia) 26–8, 32–3, 39,
  67, 69, 120, 133, 259
  lynchings 105
Glascock Independent Guards (later
  Company B) 28
Glaze, Ruby: identity 223, 229–31
Golden Gospel Singers 282
*Gone With The Wind* (book, 1936) 79, 206,
  262, 263
*Gone With The Wind* (film, 1939) 262–3
gospel music 159, 194, 282–7
Grady, Henry Woodfin 188
Grady Memorial Hospital 235, 297
Grady School of Nursing 296
Grant, General Ulysses S 34–7, 70, 95–6
  and terms of surrender 37–8
Grateful Dead 15
'Grave Of Little Mary Phagan, The' 185, 196
Greene, Sara 318–19, 321–2
Guimarin, Boze 70
Guimarin, Clara 70
Guimarin, George 70
Guimarin, Jonathan 70
Guimarin, Synthian McTyeir[e] (BWM's
  great-aunt) 23, 70
Guiney's/Guinea Station (Virginia) 30, 34
Guthrie, Arlo 178
Guthrie, Woody 13

**H**
Habersham, Lula 232
Hallaway/Holloway, Hattie cabin 134
Hamilton, George IV 301
Hammock, Wayne 316–17, 323
Hammond, Bob 100
Handy, W C 131
  'St Louis Blues' 117
Happy Valley (Georgia) 18–19, 46, 67, 77–
  8, 83, 85–6, 92, 130, 133, 153
Hardy, Jeremy 51
'Harlem Rag' (1892) 88
Harris, Alfoncy and Bethenea 207
Harris, Charlie 104–5, 133
Harris, Golden Jesse "Gold" 20, 42, 53–4,
  86, 124–5, 154, 178–9, 243, 309–12,
  315, 331, 336–7, 341–2
Harris, Joel Chandler 62–3
Harris, Margaret Burnett 42, 53–4, 309,
  341–2
Harris, Nancy see McTear/McTier, Nancy
  Barksdale (Elbert/Albert's wife; later
  Harris

# A NOTE ON THE AUTHOR

Michael Gray is a writer and broadcaster with a special interest in music and travel. He grew up on Merseyside and as a student journalist interviewed, among others, the historian A.J.P. Taylor and the guitarist Jimi Hendrix.

His travel features for *The Times, Daily Telegraph, Guardian, Independent on Sunday* and *Sunday Telegraph* have included taking him to Libya, Guyana, Syria, Finland, Mississippi, the Sudan, France, Egypt and Scotland. He once spent three months in Kenya and another three in Newfoundland. He has traveled by Ferrari through Central America and by balloon over Yorkshire.

He is a *Guardian* obituarist for major figures in rock'n'roll and tennis, and in 1996 he co-authored *The Elvis Atlas: A Journey Through Elvis Presley's America*.

His pioneering book *Song & Dance Man* was the first to study the songs of Bob Dylan, and has long been recognised as a classic work. The massive *Song & Dance Man III*, published in 1999 (2000 in the USA) is still selling, five reprints and eight years later. The even larger *Bob Dylan Encyclopedia*, a 750,000-word hardback, was published in New York and London in 2006.

Michael Gray lives in France, with his wife (food-writer Sarah Beattie) and a wire-haired fox-terrier.

## A NOTE ON THE TYPE

The text of this book is set in Bembo. This type was first used in 1495 by the Venetian printer Aldus Manutius for Cardinal Bembo's *De Aetna*, and was cut for Manutius by Francesco Griffo. It was one of the types used by Claude Garamond (1480–1561) as a model for his Romain de L'Université, and so it was the forerunner of what became standard European type for the following two centuries. Its modern form follows the original types and was designed for Monotype in 1929.